Ex Líbrís

"Unspoiled Heart"

"*Unspoiled Heart*"

THE JOURNAL OF
Charles Mattocks
OF THE 17TH MAINE

Edited by Philip N. Racine

Voices of the Civil War Series
Frank L. Byrne, Series Editor

The University of Tennessee Press • Knoxville

For my mother,
Dot, Edna and David,
Mainiacs all!

Frontispiece: Charles Porter Mattocks, about the time of his graduation from Bowdoin College and his enlistment in the 17th Maine. Courtesy of James M. White, Jr.

The Voices of the Civil War Series makes available a variety of primary source materials that illuminate issues on the battlefield, the homefront, and the western front, as well as other aspects of this historic era. The series contextualizes the personal accounts within the framework of the latest scholarship and expands established knowledge by offering new perspectives, new materials, and new voices.

All original Mattocks material used by permission of Mr. James M. White, Jr.

Copyright © 1994 by The University of Tennessee Press / Knoxville. All Rights Reserved. Manufactured in the United States of America. First Edition.

The paper in this book meets the minimum requirements of the American National Standard for Permanence of Paper for Printed Library Materials. ∞ The binding materials have been chosen for strength and durability.

Library of Congress Cataloging in Publication Data

Mattocks, Charles, b. 1840.
    Unspoiled Heart : the journal of Charles Mattocks of the 17th Maine / edited by Philip N. Racine.—1st ed.
       p. cm.—(Voices of the Civil War)
    Includes bibliographical references and index.
    ISBN 0-87049-834-7 (cloth: alk. paper)
    1. Mattocks, Charles, b. 1840—Diaries. 2. United States—History—Civil War, 1861-1865—Personal Narratives 3. Maine—History—Civil War, 1861-1865—Personal Narratives 4. United States. Army. Maine Infantry Regiment, 17th (1861-1865) 5. Soldiers—Maine—Diaries.
    I. Racine, Philip N. II. Title. III. Series.
E511.5 17th.M38   1994
973.7'81—dc20
[B]   93-21274
                                      CIP

Charley Mattocks is in command in these days,—a man and a soldier, with the unspoiled heart of a boy.

—Joshua Lawrence Chamberlain,
The Passing of the Armies, 1915

Contents

Illustrations

Figures

Maps

Foreword

❧❦

"*Unspoiled Heart*" is the second volume in the Voices of the Civil War Series, which tells in the words of contemporaries the story of that great conflict. The series aims to include men and women of all social levels and races, as well as soldiers who fought on both sides and in the war's several theaters. This book contains the journals of a well-educated Union officer who participated from 1863 to 1865 in the campaigns of the Army of the Potomac. Experiencing imprisonment, he returned to win the Congressional Medal of Honor in the war's last days. This self-disciplined young man meticulously kept diaries, which the editor has prepared with equal care for publication.

The journals tell of the young Bowdoin graduate's service with the 17th Maine during its participation in crucial and exciting parts of the battles of Chancellorsville and Gettysburg. As a major, the diarist commanded successively both that regiment and the famous 1st United States Sharpshooters. Mattocks's account is rich with details of army politicking and aspects of discipline. It concludes with his role in the attack on Lee's Army in its last great fight, the understudied battle of Sayler's Creek.

Especially important is Mattocks's reasonably balanced report of prison conditions while he was held by the Confederates in 1864–65. The editor illuminates Mattocks's version with references to parallel sources and to the most recent scholarship. Besides giving information on officers' prisons in Georgia and the Carolinas, Mattocks provides insights into his attempts to obtain aid from such disparate groups as fellow Masons and Catholic nuns. There is also a suspenseful narrative of his escape, during which he received help from members of the South's anti-Confederate minority, including both slaves and white Unionists. The appealing words of this unusually interesting voice of the war will attract students of military and social history, as well as readers in search of a good story.

Frank L. Byrne
Kent State University

Acknowledgments
❧❧

I wish to thank the staffs of the Cooper and Caroliniana Libraries at the University of South Carolina–Columbia, the Robert C. Woodruff Library of Emory University, and especially Dianne Gutscher and Susan Ravdin, Special Collections Curators of the Bowdoin College Library, and Kay Barry, Oakley Coburn, and Dr. Steve Gowler of the Wofford College Library, and to Michael M. Shetterly and my colleagues in the Wofford History Department. Thanks also to Mr. and Mrs. Howard I. Melton, Jr., and to Michael Musick, Army-Navy Branch, National Archives, who provided shelter and archival help during two hectic trips to the National Archives, and to Meredith Morgan, Stan Ivester, and especially Alexa Selph, each of whom helped make this book possible. Special thanks must be reserved for two men who are responsible for introducing me to Charles P. Mattocks. Arthur Monke, Librarian Emeritus at Bowdoin College first suggested I undertake this project, and it was he who introduced me by mail to James M. White, Jr., the general's great-grandson. Both of these gentlemen gave me the friendship, freedom, and cooperation on this project all authors covet.

Again, thanks to Joyce Blackwell, who works with speed, accuracy, and good cheer, and to President Joab M. Lesesne, Jr., and Dean Dan B. Maultsby, both of Wofford College, who continue generously to support my work. My wife, Frances, and my children, Russell and Ali, have once again been patient.

Introduction

His rival, who had the lieutenant-colonelcy he had been denied, was wounded, and the major took command. The regiment was in trouble. The Confederates may have been retreating along the front in April of 1865, but here at Sayler's Creek a Union brigade, the 17th Maine in particular, was under heavy fire—caught in a maelstrom of minié balls and shells. The young major ran to the color bearers. "Give me the flag," he said, while turning to the men nearby and shouting, "All who will, follow me!" The color-bearers resisted giving up their flags, but go with him they would. He charged over the ridge toward the firing, the smoke, and the roar with "the Regiment, or rather those who could keep up, following with a yell." Over the rifle pits and the breastworks and into the Confederate ranks the men of the 17th Maine stumbled, realizing only in the exhaustion of spent emotion that they had won.

They had overcome greater numbers by a surprising charge—the act of a young officer reversing the natural flow of events through daring and pluck. Major Mattocks had done the unexpected and had garnered the prize—the immediate capture of over one hundred enemy soldiers, twelve officers, two battle flags, and the later reward of the nation's highest military honor. It was a fitting end to what had begun auspiciously, in 1862, at a Bowdoin College graduation on a splendid Maine August day.[1]

Maine and Bowdoin College together produced more than one hero of the Union cause. Among the many was the hero of Sayler's

Creek, Charles Porter Mattocks, a distinguished yet seemingly inflexible leader of men, an optimistic and opportunistic prisoner of war, a determined escapee, a courageous winner of the Congressional Medal of Honor, and a devoted journalist. Throughout the conflict Mattocks fought in and wrote about, he was brave and frank, characteristics that make for a tale well told of a time well lived. This nineteenth-century warrior cheerfully and self-confidently made his way through the Civil War, doing what so many of his fellows did—turning the experience of life in his rugged state and the education from his frontier college into distinguished service to his nation. Mattocks, always self-aware, knew that he was not the least of all the men who were participants in the Civil War and in whose conduct Maine and Bowdoin could be justly proud. Mattocks was a descendant of James Mattocks, who had come to Massachusetts Bay Colony in 1634. The family subsequently moved to the colony of Connecticut, from which many went west into New York and beyond. However, Samuel Mattocks, Charles's great-grandfather, moved his family to Vermont, where he settled in Trimouth in the county of Rutland. Charles's father, Henry Mattocks, was born December 12, 1805, and married Martha D. Porter of Danville, Vermont, in 1839. Before Henry Mattocks died in 1844, he and Martha Mattocks had only one child, Charles Porter Mattocks, born on October 11, 1840, in Danville, Vermont, where his father worked in a bank. In 1850 the widow Mattocks married Isaac Dyer, a prominent and successful Maine lumberman, and she and her young son accompanied her new husband to his home in Baldwin, Maine.

Except for his college preparatory work at Phillips Academy in Andover, Massachusetts, Charles received all of his schooling in Maine. He matriculated at Bowdoin College in 1858 and graduated in 1862. Bowdoin was located in Brunswick, which, in the late 1850s, was a small college town filled with fishermen, shipbuilders, lumbermen, textile workers, and farmers. The college, with nine professors and between 100 and 144 students, had been there for fifty years. The graduates during and around the decade of the

1820s—William Pitt Fessenden, Seba Smith, Nathaniel Hawthorne, Henry Wadsworth Longfellow, Franklin Pierce, and Hannibal Hamlin—had established the reputation of the college throughout the nation.[2]

Although settled in the seventeenth century, Maine had been a state for only thirty-eight years, and the wilderness was still much a part of its existence; the rugged rocky coast was only two miles away, and the immense Maine forest was on its edge. The combination of high academic expectations and a location in the midst of what could still be called a frontier, could create a formidable atmosphere for a serious-minded, highly principled student such as Charles Mattocks. And there are reasons to believe that the atmosphere at Bowdoin during Charles Mattocks's undergraduate years (1858–62) was exciting. It was fortunate for Charles that he was a student at Bowdoin while Joshua Lawrence Chamberlain taught there. Mattocks studied elocution and German under Chamberlain; after Mattocks had lost an academic honor called a "Junior Part," he made the following entry in his diary: "Wednesday. March 20. . . . After declamation I went up to Chamberlain's to have my theme criticized. After we got through with that the Prof. said he was glad to see that I was not *cast down* because I did not get a Junior Part. He then went on to say that I stood within about 5 or 10 marks of [getting the part.] . . . I came here with about the best fit in the class, and stood among the first four or five for the first year and now I find myself the *fifteenth* man out of 44. —rather a poor stand for a *man* of my past reputation. . . . I am determined, and there's no such word as fail now. Chamberlain praised up my themes and *stuffed* me generally."[3]

Bowdoin College played the pivotal roll in the forming of Charles's character, and throughout his life the people he had come to know as a student were his friends and business associates. During the Civil War Mattocks learned that his college experiences provided him with a network of friends throughout the Army of the Potomac, an education he could continue while in service, and a self-confidence that served him well.

Charles became one of the most serious students at the college. His parents had always expected much of him, and until he came to Bowdoin, he had not disappointed them. However, in his early years at the college, Mattocks had decided to enjoy life: "I had been a very exemplary youth, held up as a model of sobriety and studiousness by my teachers, considered a *'dig'* by my school-mates, and myself possessing a high idea of the importance of the most unwavering *'old-manishness'* if I wished to succeed in life—but now! I have become the trial of the Faculty, the *eye-sore* of the Tutors, and the 'Prince of Grinds' among my fellows. What a change!"[4] But the loss of the Junior Part seems to have jolted him out of his playful ways.

After that disappointment Charles determined to resurrect his academic career without sacrificing his popularity. In 1861 he wrote his mother: "Last Wednesday was an important day in my course. I was then elected Peucinian Orator by an almost unanimous vote (only 4 scattering votes). . . . The three highest honors of the college course are the Class, Athenaeau & Peucinian Orations—3 in all— and I now have *one*. To have one of the first three honors in college brings you right up among the 'Deacons.' . . . I think this should console me for the loss of a Junior Part. Hope you will not think I feel *big &c*. I only feel *glad*. . . . Tell father of it, and see if it gratifies him to learn of any success of mine. . . . I want to impress on your mind that I am *not* doing nothing here, even if I dont stand *first* in text-books, as I did at Auburn. Indeed I do just as I think will be of the most benefit to me in life. People will not stop to ask if I got a Junior Part then, you know. I suppose you would be *cruel* enough to say that they would not ask about the Peucinian oratorship."[5]

As a result of the war, some Bowdoin students wanted a measure of elementary military training. In May 1861, with Charles in the lead, these undergraduates formed a military company called the Bowdoin Guards. Furnished guns and ammunition, but not uni- forms, by the government, the military unit consisted of 75 of the student body of 144; Charles Mattocks was their commander. Many students did not take the activities of the group too seriously, as was attested by an article describing the Guards which appeared in the college yearbook in July 1862: "The promptitude with which the most difficult maneuvers are performed, especially the 'march in retreat,' the alacrity and precision with which they 'break ranks,' and their unapproachable style of executing the newly introduced movement of the '*Skeedaddle,*' cannot be too highly praised."[6] In the ensuing war years former "Guards" teased each other about their college exploits. In 1863 Frank Hill wrote Charles: "Dingley in *The Lewiston Journal* pronounces you the best officer in the regiment— all owing, I have no doubt, to the envigorating breezes of Maquoit [Bay], and to your experience as Commander-in-Chief of that Corporal's guard known as the 'Bowdoin Guards.' If you ever are promoted to a Brigadier Generalship, you will be under everlasting obligations to the mudflats of Brunswick."[7]

The arguments over the necessity for war that had stormed over the nation in 1860–61 had created a serious rift between the enthusiastic students and a skeptical faculty led by its pacifist president. Yet, not all of the professors opposed the war. Among them, young Joshua Chamberlain used deception to free himself from his professorial obligations so he could enlist. Chamberlain, newly elected professor of modern languages, was discouraged from enlisting by his fellow teachers. The college gave him a very unusual paid leave of absence for travel to Europe to take his mind off the war, but the young professor and friend to so many students enlisted instead in the 20th Maine Regiment during the same summer of 1862 in which Charles Mattocks enlisted.[8] It is certain that the discussions on campus about the efforts of the faculty and president to prevent Chamberlain's enlistment circulated among the students.

Charles supported the war from its beginnings, and we know that he had an opportunity to enlist with Neal Dow's 13th Maine, but that was before he had graduated, and he chose to pass up the opportunity and wait until after he had earned his degree. He did not like leaving things unfinished.[9] After he graduated from Bowdoin on August 6, 1862, Charles enlisted at the age of twenty-two as a first lieutenant in the 17th Maine Volunteer Regiment. Twenty-five of his classmates also enlisted, three of them joining Charles in the 17th, which was formed during the last week of July and the first two weeks of August and then was mustered into the service at Cape Elizabeth near Portland.[10] The 17th's enlistment officer described Charles on the enlistment roll as being five feet nine inches tall with blue eyes and light hair. He gave no weight, and he listed Charles's occupation as student.

Mattocks's youth, intelligence, education, and enthusiasm marked him immediately for command. Throughout the war his superiors gave him responsibilities not normally placed on one so young. His career as a military man was to be a distinguished one. At twenty-three he commanded, as a major, the 17th Maine Regiment and then the 1st U.S. Sharpshooters. He was always aware of his relative youth; two of the men who would command the 17th Maine, Charles Merrill and William Hobson, were thirty-five years old when they enlisted. As early as January 1863 Martha Dyer, Charles's mother, wrote him: "I should think your men would chafe under the strict rule of their young commander. 'That young Sprig' as they would call you."[11] Throughout the war, his youth in conjunction with his reserved, seemingly haughty, demeanor combined to make him unpopular with some of his soldiers. On the other hand, Charles impressed his superiors and rose in command because of his abilities, of which he was aware. Try as he might to conceal his desire for success, his advancement was also due to his ambition.

We know of his aspirations because on April 18, 1863, eight months after he enlisted in the 17th Maine Volunteer Regiment, Charles Mattocks began a journal that he kept virtually every day until June 14, 1865, just after the 17th was mustered out of service. In his journals Mattocks describes the effort to halt the Confederate attack that disintegrated General Oliver Otis Howard's 11th Corps at Chancellorsville, the fighting of General Daniel Sickles's Corps at Gettysburg (the 17th was in the Wheat Field), as well as several minor engagements. His narrative develops several themes that make for a good story: as a young officer he has to face up to the pressures of training men older and often more experienced than he; he finds himself in the midst of a struggle for power and loyalty among the officers of his regiment; as a young, relatively inexperienced officer he takes command of the 17th Maine and subsequently of a veteran Sharpshooter regiment in order to "shape them up" when they don't want, or think they need, shaping up; he is captured in the Battle of the Wilderness; while a prisoner he describes prison life objectively, and he discusses the problems of exchange freely; he escapes; he is recaptured; he is paroled and exchanged; he returns to the 17th and wins the Congressional Medal of Honor. All in all, an extraordinary story, well told.

Throughout the journals Charles wrote proudly of his accomplishments, but he always took care to guard against anyone, even his parents, believing him to be overly desirous of promotion. But his somewhat overprotective mother knew him. Early in 1863, only four months after his enlistment, and before he began his journal, Charles received the following letter from her: "I hope if you have any wish to step up higher, Nobody will be the wiser for it[,] for a wish might be construed into an expectation of that fact. But you are pretty cunning and are probably strongly entrenched behind your fortifications of modesty & reserve. . . . You need not suppose any thing you have freely said to me has led me to this caution. I only thought of the danger of jealousy in case of the promotion of so young a Sprig in the face of older aspirants."[12] The perceptive Martha Dyer had analyzed her son's desire, his defense, and his problem. But his abilities would not be denied; while other regimental commanders usually held the commission of lieutenant-colonel, Mattocks would command as a major, an unusual level of command for one so young. He was promoted to captain on December 4, 1862, to major on December 22, 1863, to lieutenant-colonel in 1864 while a prisoner of war (the commission was rescinded because of his continued absence), and finally, after the cessation of hostilities, promoted to colonel on May 5, 1865.

The characteristics he exhibited as a college student served him well in the military. Intelligent and serious, he was also diligent and quick. He knew there was a right way to do things, and he was eager to do things right. He seems never to have fraternized with most of his men. Although to some he seemed aloof with a too highly developed sense of propriety, he did make close friends among his fellow officers. It appears that while he was in command, of both his company and then his two regiments, he was more comfortable with educated people, in particular officers from Maine and New England, than others. In his letters home to his mother, Charles goes out of his way to mention the colleges his messmates attended. Perhaps out of necessity, he sought out educated people, for Charles Mattocks was a man of the mind. While in the service he studied German, read newspapers and magazines, and constantly read travel books and fiction.

Charles Mattocks was a straitlaced young man. Yet his shy nature, his devotion to duty, and his hard work did not preclude him from challenging authority when he believed his rights were being infringed upon. While in college, he appears to have rebelled against a heavy-handed administration and faculty—he was frequently reprimanded by the faculty for opposing rules and regulations. After he had entered the army, his mother wrote to him asking: "How is it with a certain youngster, that has been for four years past often at logger heads with his Superiors? Is he more careful? or does his responsibility teach him subserviency to his higher officers? Does the old spirit ever burst out?."[13] Being naturally rebellious was only part of what made up a youthful college student; learning social graces was another important aspect of a college education, and here Mattocks was less successful. His friends believed Charles to be socially reticent: "Most people think the army develops all the *vices* in a young man's character. I hope in your case it will develop more *vices*."[14] Charles must have been shy, for he was teased mostly for his lack of experience with women: "I often wonder some of those Portland ladies do not capture your hitherto not very flexibly heart towards [the] fair sex."[15] In the correspondence between Mattocks and his friends, mention is often made of Charles's lack of experience with ladies—a situation everyone treats as rather unusual for a good-looking, muscular young man.

Throughout his service in the army, it is apparent that Charles

Mattocks was primarily interested in the discipline and performance of his troops, in the mechanics of soldiering, rather than in the camaraderie that is often associated with the military. Among Mattocks's regiment and company were many of his friends. Even though he ended up in command, he kept up his friendship with these people, and command did not seem to place obstacles between them.[16] Indeed, one of his friends—a Bowdoin graduate of the class of 1861—had enlisted as a common soldier.[17] Charles's preference for the company of college-educated officers did not mean that he thought less of his soldiers than he did of his officers, but he kept his distance from most of his men because he was supposed to enforce rules and carry out his duties—to train and mold fighting men. He did not care about popularity, indeed he made a fetish of disdaining it. He was eager to please his superiors and easily chose to act as he believed a proper officer should, rather than choose to be popular with his men. He did nothing to cultivate the goodwill of his soldiers. That they should build a clean and efficient camp, that they should be impressive in review, that they should perform well in drill—these were the elements in Mattocks's mind that made for a good regiment and that would stand his men in good stead during battle. His somewhat Puritanical and high-minded streak and his enthusiasm—what General Chamberlain refers to "as the heart of a boy"—were strong, and they were met with mixed reactions among officers and common soldiers. His friend and college-educated fellow officer, Edwin Houghton, who wrote a history of the 17th Maine shortly after the war, commented on that characteristic in passing, as did a private in not nearly as flattering a manner. In his diary, which was much rewritten after the war, John Haley commented on Mattocks's capture: "I can't think of any officer I'd sooner part with, for he was very pompous and had yards and yards of superfluous red tape about him."[18]

The men in the ranks may not have fully appreciated the training they received from their young major, but the final test of that training and Mattocks's methods was on the battlefield, where he and his units always performed well. In battle Charles never flinched, and there is no mistaking that he was a courageous man. His commanders gave him favorable notice for every battle in which he was engaged, and his immediate superiors, and oftentimes highly placed generals, praised the conduct of his troops. Mattocks and his company or regiment were almost always in the middle of the fighting; it is surprising that he fought from Fredericksburg through Appomattox without being wounded.

When he took over command of the already well-known, battle hardened, and proven 1st United States Sharpshooters—Berdan's Sharpshooters—Mattocks knew that he had been given this command in order to "shape up" the regiment. Unlike the 17th Maine, for whose effectiveness in drill and maneuver Charles had been given credit, these Sharpshooters were already effective fighters, but they lacked discipline in the eyes of their commanders. This was not to be an easy task for a twenty-four year old major. He did things by the book with the 1st U.S. Sharpshooters just as he had with the 17th Maine. He had little choice. He had been given the responsibility to prepare these troops according to the wishes of his commanders, so he required all of his officers to study manuals of drill and skirmish. He administered examinations to the officers on their "homework" just as they in turn put their soldiers and sergeants through the exercises. Perhaps his age, his college training, his reticence, his sense of duty, and his respect for his own lack of experience made it easier for him to do so.

What he did himself, he demanded of others. He was aware of his own abilities but not overly proud; his youth seemed to give him a sense of the importance of what he was being asked to do and of what he was doing. Also there was a sense of daring about his demeanor—a sense of adventure and a sense of satisfaction at being "right," right about those things such as drill and military convention which other men cared little about. The reactions of men in both the 17th Maine and the 1st U.S. Sharpshooters to Mattocks's methods were what might have been expected. As Mattocks's mother had warned, they resented the young man in authority. An indication of the extent of this resentment is found in a history of Berdan's Sharpshooters published in 1892. The author, Captain C. A. Stevens, mentions Mattocks only twice in passing, once as a onetime commander of the Sharpshooters and again when Stevens mentions Mattocks's capture during an engagement in the Battle of the Wilderness. There is nothing more. That reaction to Mattocks's tenure as commander was quite different from what Charles remembered. In 1898, in a letter Mattocks wrote offering his services for the Spanish American war, he described his tenure and experience with the Sharpshooters enthusiastically: "I was for quite a time in command of Berdan's Sharpshooters . . . and while occupying that position I became quite familiar with skirmishing and sharpshooting. These men were used as ordinary skirmishers and for taking off artillery horses and, of course, officers when necessary. A very small number of these men could in a very few moments silence a battery if the horses were in sight. . . . As to my qualifications for this kind of a command, I could produce abundant evidence."[19] That evidence would not have included testimony from the rank and file of the famed Sharpshooters.

Charles's description of his months in command may be compelling, but his telling of the story of his Confederate imprisonment adds an even more important dimension to his journals. The subject of prisons, prisoners, and the complexities of exchange has lain dormant since the work of William B. Hesseltine and Ovid Futch,[20] but it is presently garnering renewed interest. The study of prisons may be, as one historian has described it—a "land mine field,"[21] but despite its pitfalls, scholars are once again investigating the subject. The large number of older published prison narratives has gone largely unread partly because of skepticism about their reliability. The Mattocks journal provides us with a fresh and believable primary source for the renewed study of the themes of prisons and prisoners, the problems of exchange, and the drama of escape.

As a prisoner, Charles maintained the same self-confidence, aggressive demeanor, and optimism that had characterized his command. He was a self-confident and aggressive captive who would not let other people completely control his destiny. The journal entries describe his unrelenting efforts to improve his situation. For instance, he contacted Southerners who lived nearby his prison and who had sons in Northern prison camps and arranged for his relatives and acquaintances to give these Confederate prisoners care packages in return for like treatment from the Southerners. Also he contacted fellow Freemasons to obtain better food and blankets. Freemasonry proved a powerful bond that provided aid from total strangers both Union and Confederate, military and civilian.

Charles remained optimistic throughout almost all of his imprisonment, but his optimism was not naïve; rather it was that of a survivor. When some of his fellow officers, desperate for exchange, read the possibility of a miracle release into vague newspaper stories, Mattocks scoffed at their naïveté. He read his chances for what they were, and his own belief in the possibility of exchange was based on hard fact and realistic probabilities, which made its ultimate failure all the more bitter.

In spite of continuing disappointments in the matter of exchange, Charles never permitted himself to become totally discouraged; he was not satisfied to merely hope, for he was a doer. Self-assured, he lived day to day, took the initiative among his friends, and often did the planning and thinking for his messmates. Bowdoin friends, men from Maine, and other college graduates had sought each other out to form a "mess" in which the men shared their food and other supplies. Although, in his journal, Charles did not give the impression of his having taken the lead among this group, the testimony of his friends, given in their own published reminiscences, clearly established Mattocks's dominance.

In the journal entries Charles was circumspect about his leadership although he made clear, quite matter-of-factly, the extent of his duties. In the daily entries painstakingly written while in flight, he described his group's ordeal. Initially, he escaped with two fellow members of his mess—Charles O. Hunt and Julius B. Litchfield; he described their experiences as equally shared. Yet, from the published remembrance of Lieutenant Hunt, it is clear that Mattocks naturally assumed a commanding role to which his companions acquiesced with ease. For instance, as they swam the Saluda river in the cold of November, shortly after having escaped Camp Sorghum, it was Mattocks who urged his friends on, constantly reassuring them that they could cross the river, that they could make it.

The obstacles to a successful escape were manifest. The authorities in the vicinity of Columbia used dogs to track escaped prisoners. Even if fugitives got away from the Columbia area they had to travel over one hundred miles either to the coast or to the North Carolina and Tennessee mountains, where Union sympathizers were willing to help them get to Federal lines. Forced to travel by night, they sought and received aid from African Americans, for the most part slaves, all along their route. Whether on plantations or small farms, African Americans were eager to provide food and temporary shelter to all escapees, sometimes hiding Yankees for several days. Prison inmates came to know that blacks were willing to help fugitives, so when men did escape they expected black people to help them. Their expectations were not disappointed. However, the situation changed once escaped prisoners entered the mountainous areas of South and North Carolina, where there were very few slaves.[22] All of a sudden, because escaped prisoners could not move along without help, and because there were so few African Americans, it became necessary for fugitives to figure out whether the whites they met were Union or Confederate sympathizers. Being on the run became much more dangerous.

Everyone in the mountains knew that some Union sympathizers gathered up escaped prisoners and guided them from western North Carolina into eastern Tennessee. Everyone also knew there were organized and armed Confederate supporters, indeed a special Confederate regiment, whose task it was to recapture Federal soldiers and punish those Union sympathizers. The punishment often took brutal form. Union officers were in the precarious situation of having to identify themselves to the right people after they somehow determined who the right people were. More than anything, these Yankees hoped that if they were recaptured it would be by people who were under strict authority. The rivalry between pro-Union and pro-Confederate forces in the mountains was bitter, a bitterness that could easily be transposed onto escaped prisoners, often with dire results.

It is here that the journal sheds light on the social history of the Appalachians and of the Confederacy. While in the mountains, Mattocks described the living conditions and the customs of the various people who aided him and the behavior and appearance of the Confederate Indians who ultimately recaptured him. The quaintly immodest gamboling of the mountain girls and the ferocity of his captors caught his attention. However, he was most affected by the rancor, created over the issue of loyalty, that had ripped apart the society of the mountain people.

By entering the mountains, the Union prisoners were walking into another Civil War—that between the Union sympathizers of the western North Carolina mountains and their pro-Confederate antagonists. By the time escapees reached the mountains in large numbers (the latter half of 1864), hateful feelings were running high on both sides. In some ways the nature of Confederate nationalism was at issue here. In the fifteen western North Carolina counties only 10 percent of the farms had over one hundred acres; the average number of slaves per county was just over 10 percent of the total population, but the numbers for individual counties varied widely; one county had a 31 percent slave population, four counties had between 13 and 18 percent, and ten counties had less than 10 percent.

It appears that the political allegiance of most people in the mountains was not driven by the ownership of slaves or large tracts of land since about 90 percent of the population did not fit into either category. Yet, ever since secession most people, including residents of the mountain areas, have believed that the majority of the supporters of the Confederacy in the region were slaveholders and large landowners. For instance, A. J. Loftis, who helped Mattocks and his friends in their escape attempt, in 1866 wrote Charles: "The Rebles and the younion Parties is holding considerable grudges yet at each other[.] The younion Party think the President is to[o] kind to them[.] that tha[they] art[ought] to be maid to Suffer more then tha hav[.]

we want to see the land of the Rebles confiscated and Soled[,] for the Rebles was mostley Slaveholders[,] tharefore tha was Larg Land holders[,] tharefore tha are as well off as tha war [were] with ther Negroes for the Negro has to work for them and find him self and work for what the Rebel sees fit to giv him[.] now Sell his land and we hav got him By the hed and harness and in no way else can we git him."[23]

Recent scholarship indicates that most nonslaveholders appear to have accepted the claims of a Confederacy dedicated to slavery and states' rights, and most were willing to secede because of anger at what they perceived as the North's coercion. At the very least, many mountain people were not opposed to secession strongly enough to buck the swelling tide of pro-Confederate support. The counties that would later be traversed by escaping Yankees had, in February 1861, been divided over the prospect of a secession convention. Yet, after Lincoln had called out troops following Sumter, a majority in all these counties favored secession.[24] Over time, support for the Confederacy would prove thin in these western North Carolina counties, and this ambivalence would cause the Confederacy and the state of North Carolina to send a regiment to these counties to keep the peace and recapture prisoners.[25]

Recapture was only one of an escaped prisoner's possible ordeals, for the mountain air was cold, the mountain streams of western North Carolina treacherous and numbing, the knee-deep mountain snow as frightening and torturous as it was unexpected. The multiplicity of nature's obstacles mocked the escaped prisoner's vulnerability, the scarcity of his resources, and especially his total lack of food. It was a test and adventure worthy the telling, and Charles told it with zest. Fortunately, one of his early companions and several among the larger number of fugitives (Camp Sorghum virtually spewed escapees from its poorly guarded confines) who were gathered to be led to Tennessee in one large group, published reminiscences of their own which, when taken together, corroborate Mattocks's narrative.

Escape was only part of the prison problem, and the prison

problem itself was only part of a much larger series of dilemmas that faced both belligerents. Civil war had never before been fought on such a grand scale, and the scope and complexity of the endeavor required new laws of war. What rules of war existed in the mid-nineteenth century said little about civil war. With the outbreak of hostilities came questions about how the Union should treat captured Confederate soldiers: were these prisoners soldiers, outlaws, or traitors? Confederate officials had no such problem; to them this was a war between two legitimate states.

For most Union officials, treating Confederate prisoners as anything but captured enemy seemed unthinkable; therefore, Confederate prisoners should have been exchanged (trading soldiers on a one-to-one basis thus permitting them to rejoin their fighting units). Yet, President Abraham Lincoln did not wish to legitimize the Confederate government by treating with it as a sovereign authority. This annoyance became a serious problem with the first battles (Forts Henry and Donelson) that generated substantial prisoners; Union officials solved the dilemma by inventing a fiction that maintained that the negotiations about prisoner exchange were between armies and not nations.

Thus an efficacious system of exchange emerged only to be negated in 1863 when the Confederacy refused to treat captured African-American troops as anything but escaped slaves who must be returned to their owners. Northern authorities, under the explicit orders of President Lincoln and Secretary of War Edwin M. Stanton, halted exchanges until the South should trade white and "colored" soldiers equally. Except for "special exchanges," mostly of officers and arranged on an individual basis (even these were severely curtailed after October of 1864), the exchange cartel ceased to function until January 1865. By that time, Southern prisons were horribly overcrowded, and the Confederacy had to face up to its complete inability to cope with captured soldiers. Henceforth, all prisoners were exchanged or paroled (prisoners were freed on their word not to fight until properly exchanged).

Both belligerents had lulled themselves into believing that the war would be short; so naïve had the leadership been that neither side had adequately prepared for prisoners. After the first battles, authorities of both sides continually scrambled to find places where prisoners could be incarcerated. Prison administration both North and South was fraught with abuses; the Confederacy, being short on money and supplies, provided poorly. Pleas to Richmond from prison commandants usually went unheeded, and distance and privation provided ready excuses. Some new research is just beginning to explain the complexities of the issues.

It is time once again for the subject of Civil War prisons and prisoners to be fully researched. Very little work has been done on the subject; W. B. Hesseltine's book, *Civil War Prisons: A Study in War Psychology*, published in 1930, continues to be not only the standard but the only full-scale scholarly study of this topic. Although the issue of prisons has been largely avoided in the study of almost every war, it seems especially so for the American Civil War. The availability of abundant primary source material has informed the study of virtually every other aspect of this conflict, yet when it comes to prisoner narratives, there arises an understandable reluctance to trust the primary source material. Nevertheless, the task of the historian here is not unusual, except perhaps in extent; historians need to distinguish the reliable sources from those that are not. And here is where the journal of Charles P. Mattocks can make a valuable contribution.

Mattocks had an almost clinically rational attitude. His narrative is supported by his reputation: he may have been somewhat "pompous," but he was honest, analytical, rational, and amazingly evenhanded.[26] Those qualities stood him in good stead as a commander of troops and a leader among his friends; they lend credibility to his reporting of events, feelings, and conditions. The clinical way he described the battlefield experiences at Chancellorsville, Gettysburg, and the Wilderness contributes to our willingness to believe his prison and escape story. The last part of the journal is believable as a prison and escape narrative because in the first part Mattocks has already established his character—intelligent, optimistic, and enthusiastic. Joshua Chamberlain said it best in his memorial to Mattocks: "Genuine and generous as a man; faithful and warm-hearted as a friend; broad-minded and judicious as a citizen, frank and fearless for the right as he saw it, he was an example of true manliness. The spirit and enthusiasm of youth held strong to the last, and was manifest even in his manner and bearing. Under trial and discouragement, he was cheerful and brave." Even making allowances for Chamberlain's flowery prose and the special circumstances of a memorial, he does seem to catch here the essence of Mattocks's personality.[27]

In addition, Mattocks's experience as a chronicler may play a role in developing his credibility. Charles had kept journals since he was fifteen years old at Limington Academy. By the time he was a student at Bowdoin he was making long, detailed entries in larger leather-bound volumes—one for each academic year—all carefully written in his precise, compact, and easily legible prose. The importance he had always attached to the keeping of journals is attested by his having preserved them all, from the first three-by-five brown leather pocket diary. Having a lasting record of events, told by himself, was part of Charles's character. Also, since he befriended educated and thoughtful fellow officers who themselves left reminiscences, journals, and diaries, Mattocks's reporting of prison life and of his escape is corroborated by other published sources. In the resurgence of scholarship on the complexities and impact of capture, Mattocks's journal deserves a prominent place.

Notwithstanding his ambition, his desire for promotion, and his difficulties with his troops, Charles always did his duty; in the end, he let his actions speak for him. Not surprisingly, it was his friend, Joshua Chamberlain, who best explained why he, Charles, and others like them, acted as they did. General Chamberlain referred to Mattocks among others when he wrote: "Three of these, college mates of mine. What far dreams drift over the spirit, of the days when we questioned what life should be, and answered for ourselves what we would be!"[28] Character, tradition, good judgment and brave deeds marked each one, and among the foremost of their number was Charles Mattocks.

EDITORIAL POLICIES

Charles Mattocks began his journal shortly before the battle of Chancellorsville. He kept it until his regiment was mustered out in June 1865. During the war he showed a propensity to write, for he published pieces in one of his hometown newspapers, the *Portland Evening Courier*. After the war, he seems to have reread the journals, for there are a few corrections and additions [deleted in this edition], but there are not the signs of an effort to publish other than for the preparation of the paper "In Six Prisons," which he read to the Maine Commandery in 1892. The piece was subsequently published in a book entitled *War Papers Read Before the Commandery of the State of Maine, Military Order of the Loyal Legion of the United States.*[29] Charles did not publish anymore. However, he did prepare numerous papers for reading to organizations of various sorts. Whenever he made speeches to veterans' reunions, at the dedication of monuments, or to civic clubs, he prepared them carefully. There is a collection of a large number of such speeches among the Mattocks Papers still in private hands.

The journals consist of four volumes each roughly 4 by 6.5 inches; they are bound in tan leather; one has pale blue lined paper and the others have pale tan paper. While imprisoned, when Charles believed that it might become difficult to procure new journals, he conserved paper by writing two or three lines where he ordinarily would have written one. After the war, Mattocks had his diary typed and he redrew the maps and illustrations (he had hastily drawn the maps after each engagement); in this edition of the diaries I have chosen to use the original illustrations whenever they are legible. In some cases, the drawings of maps in the original journals are crowded, overwritten, and confusing. Whenever an illustration or map in the original was not suitable for reproduction I have used the redrawn version that accompanied the typed text. All of the text included here is from the original (not the typed) journals and letters. Some of the Mattocks letters are included in the text because they include details that Charles omitted from the journals, and they enhance our understanding of his relationship with his mother and fellow officers.

There are very few words that Mattocks used that are misspelled; where those occur I have let them stand and have silently corrected them in subsequent uses. In cases where a misspelled word is obviously a mistake, the word has silently been corrected. First names and middle initials have been supplied in brackets within the text. Names without brackets or notes could not be identified. Charles had several relatives with the same name; also he was in the habit of referring to people by their nicknames—in both cases it has sometimes been impossible to identify these persons. Ellipses are used to mark where long lists have been removed. Such lists would be of use only to a few scholars, and they would consume an inordinate amount of space. The notes are lengthier and more numerous than perhaps is standard practice in order to provide context for people and events and to corroborate Mattocks's observations. The prison notes are the most extensive because the issues have gained a new interest, are complex and surprisingly rich in literature.

"Unspoiled Heart"

THE JOURNAL OF
Charles Mattocks
OF THE 17TH MAINE

CHAPTER ONE

The First Battle: Chancellorsville

Charles Porter Mattocks
(Portland, Me.)
Capt. Co. A, 17th Me. Vols.

JOURNAL

April 18th Sept. 1863.
Chancellorsville, Gettysburg & Manassas Gap.

In case of death or accident please direct to

Mrs. Isaac Dyer
American House
Portland, Maine
or
Almon Goodwin[1]
Baldwin, Maine

Camp Sickles,[2] *near Potomac Creek, Va.*
17th Maine Regt. April 18th, 1863.
Saturday afternoon.

Rain and mud, the great delights of a Virginia campaign, have for a few days given way to sunshine, and we are now patiently awaiting direct orders to move, having for some days been all prepared for such a thing—so much that the men's knapsacks contain 5 days' rations and their haver-sacks are ready for 3 days' more. The overcoats will be left behind in care of the Quartermaster's Dept. A man fully equipped will have

8 days' rations
60 rounds ammunition
1 wool blanket
1 rubber blanket
1 shirt
1 pr. Drawers
1 " Stockings

All this in addition to gun and equipments will, until the rations begin to disappear, make quite a snug little load for the boys. But no extra clothing will be allowed to weigh them down, and if the mud does not again interfere with our plans we may expect to meet the enemy again, after four months' rest from the Fredericksburg disaster. Four months are none too many to erase the memories and experiences of that unlucky day. I have 57 men now ready for action. I took 71 into F.[3] Quite a number have been detailed since that time, and five, wounded there, have been useless ever since. Where and when this next brush is to be can only be a matter of conjecture to the uninitiated like me. Probably it will be some miles above or below Fredericksburg, though we can easily take, if not hold, the city itself, as our batteries can get very close range, one or two having been planted almost over the place all winter. Maj. [George W.] West is still away on leave of absence, and Lt. [James M.] Brown expects to go soon. Capt. [Milton M.] Young's time is almost out. Col. [Thomas A.] Roberts' will be up in ten or twelve days.

Lt. [William] Roberts of Co. E was to have gone before this, but has concluded to give up his chance and wait until the battle is fought! I am Officer of the Day, this being the first time for 19 days, owing to my cold. We have been policing the camp in good shape with a view to a visit from General [David B.] Birney[4] to-morrow. It is really a splendid camp, and the stockades do great credit to the workmanship of the Regiment.

We have been having a game of football every evening for more than a week. Capt. [Augustus] Golderman[n][5] obtained it while at home. Quite a number of sore shins have already appeared.

. . .

There are now three vacant Captaincies [in the regiment], viz.: [Companies] B, D, and F. Capt. [George W.] Martin[6] has recently resigned to escape a court martial, which would have smashed him. Only 5 of the original Captains, and 1 of the original Lieutenants remain. All the rest have resigned or risen.

Sunday, April 19th.
A splendid day! The Regimental sick have been removed, and all things indicate a move in the course of to-morrow. President [Abraham] Lincoln, Genl. [Joseph] Hooker, and Co., are said to be now in consultation at Acquia [Aquia] Creek.[7] The roads are now in very good condition and if the rain will only hold up we have a good chance at the Rebs.

General Birney[8] and some other General officers rode through our Brigade camp, and seemed especially pleased with the stockades of the 17th Maine. Every one is praising the tents. The place itself is not very good, but the work has made it what it is. General [Hiram G.] Berry visited our camp today, and made a small speech. We gave three times three cheers with a *gusto*. The other Regiments did the same, and he seemed well pleased.[9]

I attended divine service this A.M. in front of Headquarters. Last

Sabbath was the first service for 7 months, and today is the first opportunity I have of going to church for 7 whole months. We now have a chaplain, Mr. [Jeremiah] Hayden, formerly a private of Co. C.[10]

Thursday, April 23d.

Today the 1st New York of our Brigade laid down their arms and refused duty. 8 of the companies were mustered into the service two years ago today, and hence claim that their time is up, but Government claims them till the 7th of May, at which time the other 2 companies were mustered. Our Regiment was called out at 9 o'clock this morning and put them under guard. Our sentinels surround the entire Regt. and allow no passing in and out. One Company laid down their arms yesterday and are now in the hands of the Division Provost Guard. Quite a number of the noisy and unruly ones have been arrested and carried off. None of the officers join in the *bolt.* About one-half of the men are drunk, and seem bound to be as noisy as possible.[11]

Friday, April 24th.

On guard all night! Slept just one hour—got wet as sop—at least our feet, and then at 7 this morning we started on picket. Had not been on the road more than half an hour when down poured the rain. I have had a horrid cold for two weeks and now for 24 hours—yes 36—have been as wet as sop to my knees. We marched about 8 miles this time and are now in bush shelters. The rain has held up this evening. The 40th N.Y. Regt. are now guarding the mutineers of the 1st. We have had some genuine campaigning for the past few days, and begin to think of last Fall's labors in rain and mud.[12]

Saturday, April 25th.

Rain and mud and sunshine, all in one day! Such is Virginia. We have at last managed to get dry. We have a tight rub to keep warm— two of us under one thin blanket. But with a good fire at our feet and a plenty of exercise by day, the night can be spent quite comfortably.

Sunday, April 26th.

I went out beyond our picket line with 25 of my men at 5 o'clock and came back at 8. We deployed as skirmishers where the woods were thick. I had a good drink of milk. We saw but little—no signs of Rebs—except where they had felled trees across one of our roads. We found one field all planted and sowed.

Monday, April 27th.

We were expecting to be relieved today at noon, but it was 5 o'clock before we started. We arrived at our camp at 9 o'clock P.M., where we found Gov. [Abner] Coburn and one or two of his staff.[13] We have had some genuine campaigning for a few days.

Tuesday, April 28th.

We are now ready to march, as usual, but cannot tell when we are to move. Now (10 A.M.) there is really a prospect of going today. This morning Gov. Coburn and a few others made us a speech in front of Headquarters. The Gov. is not much of a speechmaker any way, but seems to be a jolly old soul.[14] Dr. [Henry L. K.] Wiggin[15] was here with the rest and left with them at 9 o'clock to visit the 6th Maine.

Danl. Wilcox of this Co. died at Div. Hospital on Friday of Typhoid Fever. He caught cold by coming over here. This is the first death from sickness I have had. 1 man drowned and 1 died in 9 months seems very fair. Ahead of all so far. The Regt. has lost over 50 men.

Evening.

Started for Dixie about 4 o'clock in heavy marching order. We are now about 6 miles from camp and expect to cross the [Rappahannock] river in the morning. We were marched some of the way at a most terrific rate, and men fell out in great abundance. [Albion C.] Pettengill[16] can hardly go, but he has stuck it out like a hero. I do not think there is another such a man in the Regiment.

Wednesday, April 29th.

Evening; We have marched only one or two miles today and are now in bivouac about half a mile from the river. 4 Corps are already over, and have taken a few prisoners. Everything looks like immediate and thorough success.

Thursday, April 30th. (Written May 2d.)

We have had a terrible march. Did not halt till 9 o'clock, and then we found ourselves about a mile or two from United States Ford. The sun was very hot a part of the day. I started with 60 men and now have 59. Bookin [George W. Booker] fell out at the start. We expect to cross at U.S. Ford in the morning where we now have some force.

The Regiment has marched splendidly, and in fact there has been very little straggling any where among the troops. Everyone is in good spirits and confident of success. I think we shall now bid adieu to mud scrapes and "changes of base." I have had a good load today—a rubber & wool blanket, a shelter tent and an overcoat, and a part of the time a gun for one and another of the boys. Several of them were very nearly "played."

Friday, May 1, 1863.

Today the ball was opened. We started (our Corps) at 7 o'clock in the morning. At 9 we crossed the Rappahannock on pontoons. In front, grinning at our column defiantly, but powerlessly, were innumerable rifle-pits, formerly the property of J[efferson]. D[avis]. but now in our possession. We marched about 2 or 3 miles and drew up in the woods and listened to the firing of infantry and artillery. It was quite sharp at times.

About 5 P.M. we were ordered forward. We came within rifle shot of our Batteries, which were firing with the enemy's. 2 or 3 shells passed over our head—one on the right of my company. There was the usual ducking of heads. We could see the flash of the Rebel Battery, and hear the whiz. We passed our line and took position in

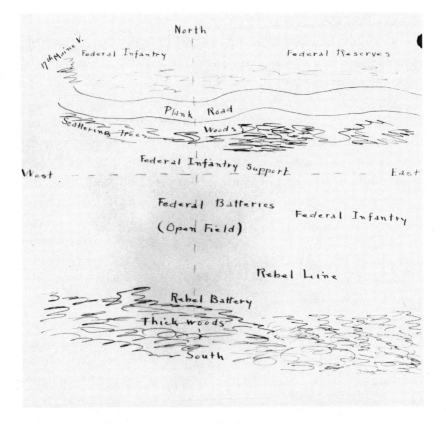

Fig. 1. Chancellorsville, May 1. [Mattocks's map of the action of the 1st Division at Chancellorsville on May 1, 1863. Courtesy of James M. White, Jr.]

the woods on their right flank. I saw a company of "Rebs" which our forces had captured. They were—captain and all—a fine-looking set of chaps. They looked thin and were not so well clothed as our own men.

We are to camp down in the woods on our arms—all loaded and ready for music. The artillery did not hold up until nearly 8 o'clock. There was picket firing nearly all the afternoon, and a part of the time heavy musketry.

Saturday, May 2d. 8 o'clock A.M.

In the same place. "They did say" the Rebs has cleared out, but judging from the way they are firing away now with artillery I should conclude there was some humbug in it.

The best sound we heard yesterday was the cheering and yelling as our forces charged into the woods after the Rebs. I had a chance to see about half a mile of the line of battle. It was like this. [*See fig. 1.*]

Our Batteries are, or were last night, upon the brow of a slope, and the Infantry support between the Batteries and the Plank Road. They were "lying low" when we passed along the road not more than 200 yards from them. Rumor says that the 10th Regulars charged upon and captured a Masked Battery yesterday. We got over 200 prisoners at the point I have marked "Thick woods."

Gen. Hooker just rode along the "plank road" and was greeted with cheer after cheer.

Evening (written May 5)

Midnight rather than evening, but why attempt to write down each day by itself when our "active operations" have forbidden the use of the pen. Then as it was not more than 10 minutes ago that we were listening to a very heavy fire of musketry and artillery, I will commence with the present date.

Tuesday morning, 8 o'clock A.M.

We have had nothing but fighting for the past 5 days—6th day for the army, 5th for our Corps, even 6th for part of it. We have had terrible fighting and terrible loss in our Division. To put it all down I must go back to

Saturday, May 2d.

At about 10 o'clock in the forenoon our Brigade—in fact, the whole Div.—started and marched about a mile beyond the plank road, to the north of it and came into an open field. In front of the field was a piece of thick woods. Through this, with Berdans' sharpshooters

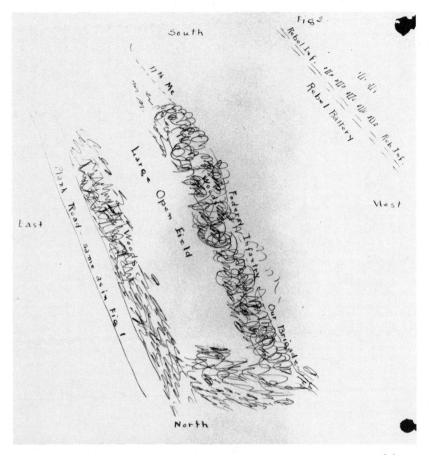

Fig. 2. Chancellorsville, May 2. [Mattocks's map of the morning action of the 1st Division on May 2, 1863. Courtesy of James M. White, Jr.]

deployed in front, our Brigade and Ward's marched, driving the Rebs and taking 365 of them prisoners.[17] But I shall have to resort to a "Fig." [*See fig. 2.*]

We went through to where I have marked "Federal Infantry," and stuck our noses in the ground. We drove them through the woods to this line—or rather the Sharpshooters should have the credit of it, since we did nothing but let the balls whistle by us. While we were lying at the point, the battery opened on us, and our Co. and Co. E were very much exposed till we moved forward a rod or two,

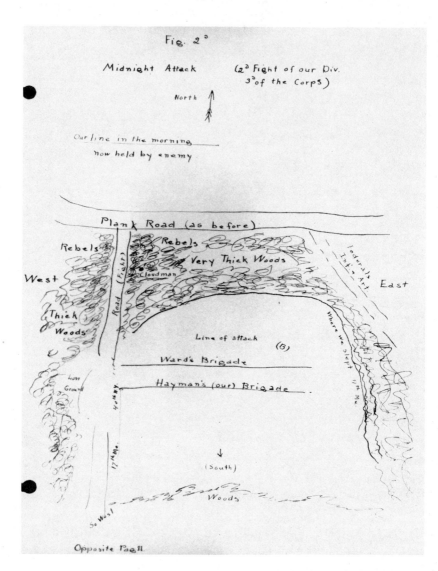

Fig. 3. Midnight Action, Chancellorsville. [Mattocks's map of the midnight action of the 1st Division on May 2, 1863, at Chancellorsville. Courtesy of James M. White, Jr.]

and then I had 1 and Capt. [Ellis M.] Sawyer[,] 2 wounded. J[eremiah]. M. Barker[18] was hit in the hand and shoulder by a piece of shell. Our Battery soon opened on them and they "hushed up." By a flank movement we then advanced to our right and took an open field which we held till dark, 2 or 3 of our Batteries playing all the time. We then fell back to the place which I have marked as "large open field." We then found we had been cut off from the plank road. This was a desperate fix. Our Corps cut off, was determined to try a "Forlorn hope;" so we had to try another fight. We have had so many different doses of it for the few past days that I shall have to number them in order to remember anything. This midnight affair was a bad thing as we fought both Rebs and Federals, and here another figure must come in. [*See fig. 3.*]

When we returned from our afternoon's work we formed the line with fixed bayonets. I have marked out at 10-1/2 o'clock. The night was quite dark and with a sort of hopeless desperation we started on. We had not gone far when bark went terrible volleys of musketry upon both sides of the road. Such a whistling of balls one seldom hears. The 40th N.Y. broke and ran past us or crowded back so that our whole Regt. nearly was in a solid mass. 'Twas then I realized I had a noble company. After everything in front had broken they stood in solid and unmoved ranks. Back they crowded. Almost a Regiment pressed against a Co. I brought the noble fellows to "charge bayonets." They crowded us back, inch by inch. The pressure was awful, but I kept *a line* though reduced to 25 or 30 men at one time. There was Co. A, the 9th company of the 2d Regiment, now in the very front—in an open road. The Rebs had ceased firing, probably for the purpose of inviting us forward once more. The next to the last company in two regiments now became the first of all. At length the other companies succeeded in forming *in our rear*. We then formed a line of the remains of the Regt. on the east side of the road, facing it, with Co. A still on the right. Here we were in a fine fix. The Brigade was we knew not where. Our Regt. had marched up the road in column by companies. On the right of my Co., where I have made in the figure a dot and written "Cloudman," I became aware that there were men. I knew we had been fired upon from that point, but I thought while it was probable they were Rebels I was determined to see if they were not our own men. I sent Corp. [Orin] Bent forward with [John W.] Cloudman to see if there were any troops there.[19] They went about 75 yards and came back saying there were men there, and that they were suspiciously quiet. I then sent again, Cloudman volunteering, and obtained the desired information, though with the loss of a good man. Cloudman went ahead and Bent followed far enough behind to hear but not to see or be seen. Cloudman went about 100 yards in the thick woods along the road and coming upon some men said, "What regiment, boys?" The "boys" replied "Hold on there." "Lay down your arms, &c." He [Bent] heard no more and came back to me. I concluded that Cloudman was a prisoner.[20]

We waited here for about half an hour, when we fell back to the open field from which we started, when we found the rest of the "line of attack" or better now "line of repulse." We then lay down on our arms for the night along the edge of the woods.

This midnight affair ended at 12 o'clock, and although the musketry was horrid at such an hour it was nothing compared with what we experienced the next day. Yet it was more disagreeable. Several men of our Regt. were hit, one in Co. K killed at the first. When the other companies [of the 17th] and the 40th N.Y. were breaking and crowding back, Gen. [John Henry Hobart] Ward rode along to me and said very flatteringly "Captain, your company stands its ground splendidly. I wish the rest would do as well." He rode away and in a few minutes sent back one of his aides to ask my name. I may be supposed to have appreciated such a compliment for my noble Company.[21] Lt. Brown, and Lt. [Edwin B.] Houghton,[22] who had left the staff for the occasion, and my Sergeants,[23] behaved splendidly in keeping the men in their places.

Upon this very field, open as it is, while we were driving Rebels through the woods other Rebs during the afternoon were rushing up and driving our rear and right flank lines into the open field, where one of our batteries gave them grape and canister, and drove them back. They said the musket balls flew thick about our artillerists ears.

We lay down tired and sleepy to awake in the morning to the stern realities of an awful battle.

[*Mattocks pasted the following newspaper clipping under the entry for September 20, 1863. It properly belongs here.*]

Seventeenth Regiment.
Col. Roberts has transmitted to Adjutant General Hodsdon a report of the participations of the 17th Maine Vols. in the battle of Chancellor[s]ville, and the movements of the regiment from May 1st to 6th while on the South side of the Rappahannock. Lieut. Col. Merrill commanded the regiment until May 5th when Col. Roberts rejoined and resumed the command. Of the participation of the regiment in the night attack of the 2d inst., Lieut. Col. Merrill says; 'By orders from superior head-quarters the regiment under my command was placed with a portion of Ward's Brigade in a column under the command of Col. Egan, 40th N. Y. Vols., to take part in a night attack upon the enemy in order to regain the position lost by our forces during the afternoon. The column was formed at 9 o'clock P.M., and marched on the left of the line, supporting the general line advanced at that time by the 3d Army Corps. Our course led us into a narrow road through dense woods. The enemy soon opened upon us a severe musketry fire in front and on both flanks. The regiment in advance, the 40th N. Y., broke and ran upon us throwing the head of our column into confusion. When we were formed into column we had received orders not to fire till a line of battle was formed and the 40th N. Y. wheeled into line; in this position we could do nothing, and were forced back a short distance. The column was re-formed and again advanced, meeting with a fire from the enemy con-

cealed in the woods. No one knew the exact position of the enemy's forces, and we were ordered by Col. Egan to form a line of battle facing to the right; but as it was thought that our own forces were in that direction the line of the 17th was formed facing to the left. The formation was scarcely completed before we received a volley of musketry from our front which we returned with vigor. Soon after, by order of Gen. Ward, the forces with which we acted were withdrawn. [*Remainder of clipping is detached.*]

Sunday, May 3d. The Battle—our 3d Fight.

I number these fights by the places in which they occur. This today is the third time under fire for us since we crossed the river last Thursday, each fight in a different place and at a different time from the other. The first was Saturday afternoon, the second in the night of the same day, and now we find it necessary to do some hard fighting on Sunday.

On Sunday morning at daylight our Corps was drawn up in the same place as our line of attack was formed the night before [*see fig. 3*]. Where I have made a "B" on this figure was planted one of our Batteries. We had no sooner got the Corps formed than the Rebs opened with musketry from the edge of the woods on the west of the road. Our Battery gave them a warm charge of grape and canister. We were soon ordered away amidst a shower of musket-balls. We moved down the road to the East by a flank movement in good order. Our Battery, which I have marked "captured by the Rebs" [*see fig. 4*], played upon the advancing columns fearfully till we got off and then had to leave it for the Rebs.[24] [*See fig. 4.*]

After we had withdrawn to the large open field our Batteries gave them such a peppering as they will not soon forget. They were to be sure mostly out of sight but must have suffered in the woods. Presently our Infantry and theirs became engaged in the woods to the North. Soon a Rebel Battery or rather several opened on us at a good range with shot and shell. Our Brigade supported a Battery after a

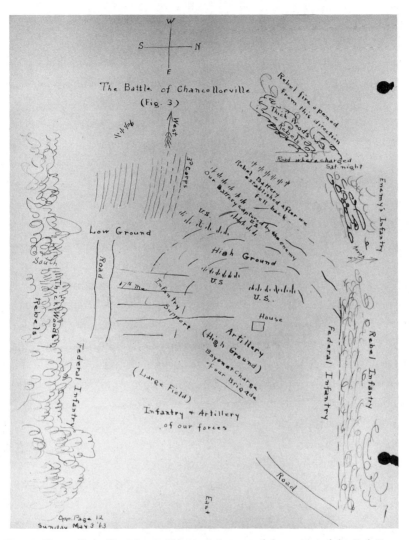

Fig. 4. Chancellorsville, May 3. [Mattocks's map of the action of the 3rd Corps at Chancellorsville on May 3, 1863. Courtesy of James M. White, Jr.]

short time in the very front near the "Road." The left of our Regiment was terribly exposed and our loss was great. One shell exploded in my Co. wounding 5 men, two of them I think fatally.[25] Before we had withdrawn from the upper field Lt. Brown was seriously wounded in the thigh by a rifle shot. Several of my men were hit during this movement. In fact I had some hit during each of these movements, I am trying to describe. Our Artillery did make a most terrific noise. At about 9-1/2 o'clock we began to fall back, and the Rebs to advance. Genl. Birney, concluding they were coming a little too fast, ordered us to advance upon the house (which I have marked at the center of the page) and then for the first time we made a

—Bayonet Charge—

upon the house and the ground around it. We were then east of the house and could not see the ground where the house stood, as we were on low ground. The top of the house was all we could see. So we did not know whether we were advancing against 10 men or 10,000. Then it was I felt something of that which writers describe in speaking of bayonet charges. I lived years in as many minutes. When we reached there, and we went with a yell, we found not more than 20 or 30 Rebs on the hill, but the woods were alive with them and they were in just the place to pour the bullets into us. Upon that small place were several dead and wounded of ours and theirs, but before we left there were more. The street fight of last night and this part of today gave us a chance to see how the air can be alive with bullets. What Rebs were upon the hill found they were in a trap and threw down their arms and surrendered. We immediately left for the cover of the hill by moving to the left and rear on the double quick. We had a great many of our Regt. wounded upon this charge. 'Twas here that Lt. [Dudley H.] Johnson of Co. H was killed. Two or three of the Regt. were killed at the same time and I fear that some of the "missing" have shared the same fate. I only had two men wounded, both slightly. We then moved off at double quick under a perfect shower of balls and shot and shell. General Hooker was riding along as cool as could be under all the fire. All our Generals did nobly, as the list of killed and wounded will show. Genls. Berry and [Brig. Gen. Amiel Weeks] Whipple of our Corps were killed,—Whipple not till Monday though.[26] I see I am anticipating. I had several wounded with rifle shots while we were retiring from the field. We marched off by the road in the Northeast corner of the field on the double quick. Capt. Golderman, acting Major, was walking by my side when he dropped from a shot in the leg.

Worst of all was the shelling; one shell burst in my Co. as we lay on our faces, and made fearful havoc in the ranks. It almost tore the thighs off Corpl. [Charles O.] Blackstone and John [W.] Tucker, wounding [Franklin] Skillings and Goodenow [Charles Goodnow], and tearing, as it then seemed, the entire heel off [Charles R.] Todd's left foot. I was lying behind them, and so bad a set of wounds I have not seen together. Blackstone and Tucker cannot live, so the Doctors say. It was a hard fight and I dare say we shall never see a worse one. There was more desperate work than at Fredericksburg.[27]

They must have taken a great many of our men prisoners. The men behaved nobly. No signs of panic, and hardly a murmur at the hideous wounds our poor fellows received, but I saw some Rebs. wounded as badly and that bore up as cheerfully.

We left many dead and wounded upon the field to be stripped by the enemy, who are sadly in want of clothing. One of my men picked up a nice sword and gave it to me.

By some unaccountable error when the troops began to withdraw, Col. [Charles B.] Merrill marched 3 companies of us to the river, but we were soon ordered to the front once more, where we found our Brigade drawn up in the woods in rear of a goodly number of pieces of artillery. We had not been there long before were opened upon us one or two batteries and a goodly number of screeching muskets. This was at 4 o'clock and was kept up from time to time in the night. A spent bullet struck between my legs on the ground as I lay on my face and I picked it up and still retain it as a trophy. We were tired enough in marching back to the front after we had been to the river, three miles distant. In this march of 6 miles I saw a great many of the wounded and dead as they were lying by the road, or being carried to the rear.

Same date, Sunday, May 3d. 4th Fight

I call this the 4th fight of which I have begun to speak on the last page because it was the 4th position we had assigned us—and when I say position I do not mean the line of battle, as we had more than a dozen different ones—but I mean separate and distinct fights. They are—1st, in the woods Saturday afternoon—2d, the midnight attack—3d, the Battle proper of Sunday, and—4th, the doings here behind our earthworks which we finally abandoned.

In front of us, to the South West, is an open field into which we are trying to entice our wary enemy, but I am thinking they are too sharp for such a game. When our forces first took this position the Rebs undertook to charge on our Battery, but they found it of no use. They rushed forward on the right to flank us but although they could break through the flying Dutchmen of the 11th Corps[28] they found the old 3d firm as a rock even after having borne the brunt of Sunday's struggle.

Towards dark last night I was notified that I had been selected to take my Company and go forward in rear of the sharpshooters as a support to them, but I find it a thing indispensible [indispensable] to make

Battle of Chancellorsville

These earthworks, as I have here sketched them, were not completed till Tuesday. [*See fig. 5.*] Monday night at 8 o'clock when I went forward with my Co. the place in which I have put Ward's Brigade was not occupied, no rifle pits having been thrown up there then. [Samuel Brinkle] Hayman's[29] line was then in front—just in rear of the Batteries. I marched about 60 yards, forward to where I have marked "Co. A," halted and deployed 10 men in charge of Sergt. [Edward H.] Crie at 10 paces from each other and halted them about 20 or 30 paces in front of my Co. I had them all lie flat, and one could not have seen that there was a man on the field. Our orders were to "lie low" and if the sharpshooters, who were skirmishing in

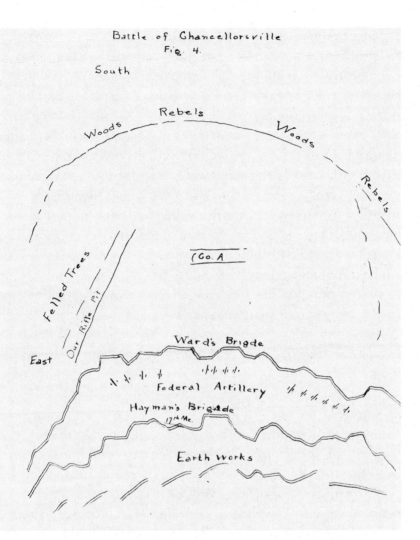

Fig. 5. Ward's Brigade, May 3 [1863], Chancellorsville. [Mattocks's map of the fourth distinct action of Ward's Brigade at Chancellorsville. Courtesy of James M. White, Jr.]

the edge of the wood about 60 or 80 yards in front, were driven in to let them pass, fire and then retreat ourselves if the Rebs advanced in any force, so as to give our Artillery and Infantry a chance to sweep the field. The skirmishers were driven in twice as far as my reserve, but the Rebs did not see fit to follow up, so we continued to lie low and let the thing work. Tired and sleepy as we were after fighting Saturday afternoon, engaging in a midnight affray and then devoting Sunday to slaughter, it was no easy job to keep awake even in the very front of danger. But little sleep before and no sleep after such a battle was enough to tire any one, and many of my men had hard work to keep on the alert. Two or three times the pickets had a small spat, and once quite a large one among themselves, and our whole force in the rear were aroused. The cannoneers stood ready to pour in grape and canister, and infantry to give them the bullets, and Co. A. to fire one sharp volley and skedaddle if the enemy should venture forth from their retreat. But they knew better. We were withdrawn, and had the pleasure of rejoining our Regt. on the morning of

Monday, May 4th
when we found that men had been busy during the night in throwing up breastworks, behind which they could be comparatively safe from Rebel lead. We occupied the second line, and busied ourselves in throwing up a breastwork to save us from the effect of the shot and shell, in which as subsequent events proved, we were successful. We were troubled with nothing during the day save now and then a stray rifle shot, until about 4 o'clock in the afternoon, when upon a sudden the Rebs opened sharply with artillery from the West. They had a splendid range, but their missiles went into our earthworks, or whizzed harmless over our heads. Three struck the breastwork in front of my own Co. but did no harm whatever, a result somewhat different from a shell which struck in my Co. Sunday and wounded 5 at once—two of them mortally. I am strongly in favor of fortifying now.

The day has passed with but little excitement, though, had we not become so accustomed to the sound, we might have counted many a musket shot from the pickets. Gen. Whipple was mortally wounded by one of them.[30] We have come to think musket balls as but a small part of "the show." We had a good time listening to them whistling over our heads as we were hugging the ground all last night. Fortunately we came off all right.

Tuesday, May 5th.

Last night we were routed up by a tremendous musketry on our left. I was inclined to fear the Rebs had surprised us on the flank, but finally concluded that there was some slight ill will between our men and the enemy and they thought to exchange a few shots would calm them. We snatched up our muskets and stood ready but they soon subsided and we again went to sleep. In the latter part of the afternoon we came near getting drowned out with a good rain storm, against which our earthworks were no protection, but served rather to make a wet bed in case we had been ordered to "lie low." But the order did not come, so we went to work and bailed out our holes, in decent shape. At 8 o'clock we were ordered to pack up. After standing an hour or more in wet and cold, we were told to go to bed again. At about 4 o'clock on the morning of

Wednesday, May 6th

we started from our earthworks on an organized skedaddle, and at 7 o'clock in the afternoon I am sorry to record we

Recrossed the Rappahannock

a fact which ought to be draped in mourning. There were only two pontoons but our men were not long in going over. There was not the least sign of panic or demoralization, nothing but a tired look. Regiments returned to their old camps by mere handfuls. I came in with 1 man. Men were allowed to please their own fancy as to speed.

I must confess I was nearly played out. We were all very tired. The enemy did not follow up our retreat at all, for what reason I can not say.[31]

While we were coming home we saw many wounded in sheds and barns along the road. Such bravery and fortitude as our men displayed certainly deserves better success.

Thursday, May 7th After the Battle.

I find myself back in my old tent at Camp Sickles, where I did not expect to tarry again so soon. I suppose I ought to be thankful to have escaped so great danger. So I am, but I am not glad to anchor upon this side of the river again. This is the second time. So be it. They may call it a victory, but I "can't see it," although I do think we killed four to their one.[32] Our Artillery mowed them down like grass. We lost many fine officers. General Berry is dead—brave man, he will never see his old Brigade again. He was picked off by a sharpshooter. During the fight we all saw "fighting Joe" riding about as composedly as could be. He was really handsome.[33] The battleweek has ended and our men are well tired out. I was so myself last night but am feeling finely now. Now that Lt. Brown is wounded I suppose I must plod my weary way alone. Probably he will not be fit for duty for 2 months or more. As soon as convenient I hope that Rebel bullet will allow him to recover. I have never had but one Lt. and now I have none. Houghton was with me but a very short time as a Lt., before he was placed on Hayman's staff. Dr. [William] Westcott & Dr. [Nahum A.] Hersom both lost their horses.[34]

I have made a list of my wounded, &c.

. . .

Total, Killed	1
Mortally wounded	2
Wounded	9
Prisoners	2
[Total]	14 men & 2 officers.

I will soon procure a corrected list of the whole Regt. I think the loss in killed, wounded and missing will not be less than 100.

I learn today that the 3d Corps sustained about one-half of the entire Federal loss, and most of its loss must have been in killed and wounded, while a great many of our Corps were being killed and wounded, the men of the 11th Corps ([Franz] Sigel's formerly, now [Oliver Otis] Howard's)[35] were skedaddling and being captured. Had the 11th behaved as well as the 12th or 3d, events would have taken a different course. The 11th guarded our right flank, and was broken by the desperate dash of the enemy. "They say" these gallant Dutchmen who used "fight mit Sigel" so bravely were caught with their equipments off eating their dinners, of course they changed their base instanter, and left for the *interior.* Col. Hayman, commanding our Brigade, handled us splendidly. He is as brave as a lion.[36] Gen. Birney too distinguished himself and will probably get his two stars now.[37]

The loss of officers in our Regt. was quite heavy. . . .

Total Killed 1
Wounded 5
6 officers.

Lt. Col. Merrill and Lt. Houghton were slightly wounded, but both remained on duty. Lt. [Thomas W.] Lord[38] has borne up like a hero. Dr. Wiggin is here today, and says he fears Capt. [Edward I.] Merrill[39] will not live. Lt. Lord was hit in both legs. As we went on the charge Sunday he lay helpless by the edge of the woods, and raised his sword cheering us on. When we passed him on our return from the charge he still lay there, but now holding up his sword as a signal of distress. He wished to be carried from the field before the enemy got upon him. He was brought off in safety. We had several men killed dead in that, our first real bayonet charge, and I fear many of missing ones shared the same fate. Certain it is that some of the enemy were forced to bite the dust. I saw a Corporal in Co. E, who was by my side, raise his piece and drop a bold rebel, as coolly as one would shoot a partridge. I had almost forgot to mention that as we were watching for Rebels in our rifle pits on Tuesday, we were surprised at the sudden appearance of Col. Roberts, who had just returned from 30 days' sick leave, much improved in health and appearance. So he had a chance to see but a very small part of the elephant. But I may here say that I lost a part of the show myself by marching back to the river under command of Lt. Col. Merrill, while the rest of the Regt., colors and all, under command of Maj. West, were supporting [Capt. George E.] Randolph's Rhode Island Battery[40] as it mowed down the advancing columns. Several of our wounded were killed by this last shelling, as the enemy took range by the hospital—a brick house—near which our Battery was planted. This Battery did splendid work, and gave our forces a good chance to escape. The long fight is at an end. Fighting began on Friday and ended on Tuesday, though there was skirmishing before and after. Our Corps was at first sent to the left but I guess they concluded we were not needed, so we rushed for the right. While we were fighting on the right [Maj. Gen. John] Sedgwick's [Sixth] Corps was doing splendid execution on the left. He did what [Ambrose] Burnside lost 10,000 men in attempting last Fall.[41] He captured the city and surrounded it—taking at the same time the heights before which we lay and were murdered in December. All this was good. By a splendid dash and a brilliant charge he had taken this stronghold, but I am sorry to record it[,] he had to abandon it and cross the river as did we. So here we are. A few days ago we held what (and more) it cost 10,000 men to try to get last Fall. To-day it is gone. I have not yet learned our loss.[42]

CHAPTER TWO

Gettysburg

❦

Friday, May 8th. Camp Sickles
We have been improving the day in resting after our labors of the battle week. We had an inspection this morning, and this was a seedy Regiment compared with the 17th Maine of a month ago. Many of the men had thrown away their knapsacks or blankets, and all of them looked ragged and dirty. But we shall soon pick up I hope.

This evening I have visited the Division Hospital. I find that Corporal [Charles O.] Blackstone cannot live. He has a terrible wound in the thigh, it being nearly carried away, bone and all, by that murderous shell. I very much doubt if he lives forty-eight hours. He bears up under his sufferings like a hero, and seems willing to die. He thinks he has fallen in a good cause, and so he has, but still it seems sad to see so young and ambitious a fellow die here away from friends and home. [John W.] Tucker, whose wound was similar and nearly as dangerous, has been sent to Washington, but I fear neither of them will survive. I saw several of our boys. They are all in good spirits. Poor Todd, the pet of us all, was left behind, and is, I fear, either dead or a prisoner of war. He will, I fear, lose his foot. Skillings and Goodnow have come back to the company. Goodnow is almost well. I saw Capt. Merrill tonight, and I fear he cannot live. The ball that hit his arm grazed his left breast, and he has been today troubled with pains in the breast which the Surgeons consider a bad symptom. Lt. Lord, though minus a foot, is as cheerful as can be and looks at the matter philosophically, concluding that a cork leg is not so bad a thing after all. He will soon get well, I think, but can be of no more service in the *line*.

There is a great deal of suffering among the wounded, many not having had their wounds dressed until today. Corpl. Blackstone is one of the number. He must have suffered greatly, having been more or less exposed to the wet weather, and being jolted about in the ambulance. It seems a wonder that he is yet alive.

We have rumors of a new move immediately—such as crossing the river &c.—a labor to which we are now well accustomed. I should think the 3d Corps might have a breathing spell now. It has done some big fighting. They can never say "skedaddled" to us as they do to the 11th. Col. Hayman called up Captains Sawyer and Young and myself today, to learn why our Companies were marched back to the river instead of remaining in the front with the Brigade. We very briefly informed him that we followed Lt. Col. Merrill's orders, whereupon he dismissed us.

Saturday, May 9th.

Corporal Blackstone died this morning, at 6 o'clock. He suffered very much from his wounds. Lieut. Whittier, of the 5th Maine Battery, called on me today. I learned from him that Lt. [Adelbert B.] Twitchell[1] was quite severely wounded. He lost two or three of his fingers. They suffered greatly, having 6 men killed and 22 wounded and lost nearly all their horses.[2]

We have been doing nothing all day, but to rest from our labors. Received a note from Lt. Brown. He is in hospital at Georgetown, and seems to be doing well. Capt. Golderman is with him. Capt. G. may lose his leg, but Lieut. is all right I guess. The 1st New York went home yesterday.

Dr. Wiggin has been here today. He reports the 6th Maine badly cut up. It seems that General [George] Stoneman has been giving the Rebels fits in the rear, tearing up 21 miles of railroad, going within 2 miles of Richmond, &c.

Sunday, May 10th.

I have just received an extract from the official report of General

Ward, with whom our Regiment served on the night of the charge. It reads thus:

Extract of Official Report of the battle
of Chancellorsville of 2d Brig. 1st Div. 3d Corps.

To Lt. Col. Chas. B. Merrill of the 17th Maine and Lt. Col. [William S.] Kirkwood[3] of the 63d Pa. and the officers and men of their commands, temporarily assigned to me, my grateful acknowledgments are tendered for their valuable assistance and gallant conduct on the night of the 2d of May, and to Captains Ellis M. Sawyer and Charles P. Mattocks of the 17th Me. and the companies under their command my especial thanks are due.

(Signed) J.H.H. WARD
Brig. Genl.
(sd.) Official
I. W. Cooney
Capt. & A. A. G.[4]

Corporal Blackstone's funeral took place today at Division Hospital. Mr. Hayden, our new chaplain, officiated. I fear John Tucker will soon follow Blackstone. If he does survive I shall think there is really hope in a straw, for his wound seemed almost as bad as Blackstone's. We hear nothing from poor "Toddy," but conclude he is still in the hands of the enemy, if indeed he is still alive. He was left near the brick house which was burned.

It has been a splendid day. The quiet contrasts strangely with the heated encounter of a week ago. We are having a genuine rest from our toils. Mr. Hayden preached at 5 o'clock this afternoon. He has an estimable quality in a chaplain, and that is brevity and common sense. He is also a brave man as was proven by his conduct during the battle. He was in the front attending to the wounded, where many of our bold Surgeons should have been.

Lieut. Roberts of Co. E, is very, perhaps dangerously sick with lung-fever—a bad thing in the army. Capt. Merrill grows worse, and probably will not recover. I believe they find our killed to amount to 6 now. The Regt. lost 106.

I cannot help admitting that Genl. Ward's notice of me and my Co., two pages back, somewhat flatters my vanity. He complimented me in person during the Midnight Attack, but that he should mention me in an official report seems quite a "big think." If he did not injure his conscience by the operation it is all right.

We had divine service at 5 this afternoon, but I see I have already mentioned this. I am trying to get a chance to send Lt. Brown's valise to him, but fear I shall not have an opportunity immediately. He must wait patiently.

Sabbath Afternoon, May 10, 1863
Camp Sickles, Near Potomac Creek, Va.
My Dear Mother:

A week ago today was as pleasant as this, but that Sabbath afternoon was devoted to butchery[,] this to rest. Since that time there has been much suffering in this region. The wounded have in many cases been sadly neglected—not purposely but in many cases necessarily, in some alas! from the cowardice of Surgeons. This doctrine of Surgeons remaining in the rear so far out of danger while poor fellows are suffering for immediate aid, is about exploded in the minds of those who have seen the thing *in the front.* I saw one young lady in the very front of battle dressing wounds and aiding the suffering where few Surgeons dared show themselves. That girl is Anna Etheridge, a second—a more than—Florence Nightingale. You may have read of her. She is always to be seen riding her pony at the head of our Brigade on the march or in the fight. Genl. Berry used to say she had been under as heavy fire as himself.[5] Many of the wounded of last Sunday's fight have been and still are lingering along in the hospital near our camp. One of my Corporals—a splendid young man—who had his life torn away by a shell, died after much but patient suffering yesterday morning. He was a genuine martyr, and felt that he was really dying for his country. Another must soon follow him, and a third was shot dead upon the field. My noble company—and it is a noble one—which I have successfully protected against disease I find I can not shield against such carnage as this. Their conduct, and theirs alone, saved a disgraceful panic on the night of the 2d of this month. So says Brig. Genl. Ward. I told you he complimented me at the time. He has since done so in his *official report.* Can you wonder that I feel a little exalted? Colonels and staff officers may expect to be mentioned in the official reports of their commanding Generals, but it is rare that a mere Captain of the Line is selected for such a favor—that too without any personal knowledge of the individual. You are well aware that it is the legitimate ambition of a soldier to obtain notice for services upon the field of battle. I shall never feel guilty for what I may gain in that manner. Political intrigue and personal influence may bring you the *straps,* but give me a chance like that of sunday and the other 4 days. But not to me alone, to my men rather be the praise. When two Regts. were panic-stricken they stood by me like heroes, and from the 19th they became the 1st company of an advancing column. Would I resign now? Would I leave them now? Would I abandon men who showed themselves willing to give their own lives to save mine? No, not for anything would I leave them and by them I mean the service generally. Almost the last words that wounded fellow said to me yesterday were "Well, I am glad you got out of it safe, Capt."—that too upon his death bed, suffering terribly with a hideous wound which he received while lying exactly in front of me, and from which perhaps his own person saved mine. Co. A is now *more* ahead than it ever was. Our field officers felt that its conduct saved the good name of the Regt. and so it did. But I dare say I have said enough upon this subject. I can never describe this battle to you upon paper. It was so different from Fredericksburg. There we fought with invisible foes, but here "we came we saw" and whether we conquered or not is another thing. We killed more than they did as their own reports will show. Stoneman's raid has not been barren of results, and does much to inspirit the whole army. Strange to say, there is nothing of last Fall's despondency and insubordination. Everyone thinks we gained even if they "can't see it." Tell me what you think of it at home.

You will probably have a chance to see Lt. B. now, as he can not get well in less than two months, and will probably be allowed to go to Portland. One of our Captains is not expected to live. A ball grazed his breast and shattered his arm. This battle will be a good capital to organize the Invalid Corps upon. Cripples will soon overrun the country at this rate. Our Regiment was very fortunate compared with others in the Brigade. We now number but 400 muskets of the 950 that left the State of Maine. Such is war, but much of it is sickness. There are few companies where as in mine the loss in battle is greater than the loss by sickness. As yet I have had but 1 man die by sickness, and all the men are remarkable healthy. Warren Flint has had typhoid fever but is gaining now. Brown is well and escaped all right except his breeches which received a bullet hole. In fact my men's clothes seem to be riddled with balls. A knapsack saved one fellow, as Houghton was saved by his at Fredericksburg. By the way Lieut. H. had a very narrow escape this time. His horse was shot under him. On saturday Lt. Brown had a ball put into his canteen where it remained—snug shooting that. . . .

Dr. Wiggin was on hand during the fight, caring for the wounded. I am glad Itie has taken to making putty-heads, as they will be just the things to replace the heads that the Rebels shoot off his 9 months men. Bloodless heroes! How I wish they could have had a taste of this last fight. When they return please don't recognize them as soldiers. One out of ten of them has not seen a live Rebel, and none of them a dead one. . . .[6]

Monday, May 11th.

Today we had a Corps review under Genl. [Daniel Edgar] Sickles.[7] It was noticeable that the ranks were thinned out somewhat by the recent fight. Generals Berry and Whipple can no longer appear at our reviews. They have fallen and nobly too.[8]

Now that we are safely across the river we learn that Stoneman has been making havoc in the rear of the Rebels. He has torn up ever so much of their railroad, advanced within two miles of Richmond, and then reached Yorktown, in safety. So he got all the glory, while we did the fighting. The Rebels are quite willing to acknowledge a fearful loss in *this* fight, and I do not see how they could do otherwise. The New York Herald has again been *tabooed* from the army on account of disloyal sentiments. It comes down on the "Committee on the Conduct of the War," and now it is out against Hooker, and proposes to supersede him by Sickles or Stoneman.[9]

Tuesday, May 12th.

I have appointed [Joseph F.] Hobbs Corpl. for bravery during the battle.[10] He takes the place of Blackstone who was mortally wounded and died a day or two ago. Lt. Houghton has been recommended for 1st Lt. of Co. H, and 1st Sergt. [Grenville F.] Sparrow as 2d Lt. in Houghton's place. Sparrow left Maine as 3d Sergt., and Houghton as 1st Sergt. That is doing very well indeed. There will be a good number of promotions now in the Regiment. Houghton will still remain on the staff of Col. Hayman.

This has been the hottest day we have had since last September—when we were in the forts, doing the arduous duties of garrison.[11] Our ambulances have been busy in getting the wounded from the other side of the river. 1200 are there now, they say, *to* be taken over tomorrow. A great many dead and wounded were burned when the woods were fired by the shells.

Wednesday, May 13th. Camp Sickles

Still we have the hot weather. It has been warmer than yesterday even. We have been doing nothing except to try to keep cool. I had an excellent skirmish drill with my company this morning from 5 till 7 o'clock, and I find that a very good time in this hot weather. I shall very soon commence the drill in bayonet exercise. I have thus deferred in order to learn the simplest things first.

I sent Lieut. Brown's valise to him today, which I hope he will get in due season. I am very much at a loss which of my four Sergeants to appoint 1st Sergt. in case of Sparrow's promotion. There is a scarcity of good writers in the Co. now, and I am in a sad fix. Corpl. Hobbs and [David M.] Spaulding have returned to the Co. Their wounds will keep them off duty for some time yet.[12] Hobbs will probably get a 30 days' furlough.

Saturday, May 16.
We have had no drills of any kind today, and it seems much like Sunday—or like what Sunday ought to be. They have at last got Todd. He was taken prisoner and paroled by the enemy. I saw him yesterday at Division Hospital. He will not lose his foot, I think. [Edwin P.] Hatch is in danger of losing his arm, but I hope he will save it yet. Two of his fingers were amputated, and now the whole arm is terribly swollen.[13]

My cold, now two months of age, still continues, or the cough, I should say. It is better, to be sure, than it was, but it does hold on well. Col. Roberts is off duty again. His cure does not last so long as the remedy. I think he cannot stand it long at the present rate. Lt. Col. Merrill has resigned, but the resignation has been returned disapproved. He will perhaps get it through by trying again.

Saturday, May 22d.
A very injudicious, but flattering, communication in the Portland Press about this Regiment in the midnight attack, has caused quite a breeze in the family. The article referred to praised Companies A and E, and all the rest are mad.[14] They have managed to engineer a paper through Col. Roberts tending to do away with

Ward's official report (see under May 10th) and show that Co. A and E did not deserve the credit which they got. I bolted and I guess he will not publish it. Some of the *line* have shown a very mean spirit in the matter. My first impulse was to write and publish a word to the effect that in praising 2 companies, the rest should not be censured, but now that they have shown such a spirit they must blow their own horn. Some of them did not do their duty and they know it. Those very ones are the most indignant now. Those are the ones who are now crying "I fought well," and some are just fools enough to believe them. Gen. Ward saw the whole thing and spoke of it at the time. So did Capt. Golderman, to whom I have written. He will write such a letter to the Col. as will take some of these fellows down.

Here is the article which has divided a house against itself.

The 17th Maine at Chancellor[s]ville.
To the Editor of the Press:

Honor to whom honor is due. The following particulars come to me through private and entirely reliable sources.

In the night attack made upon the rebels under Jackson, the 40th New York and the 17th Maine were drawn up in column by companies and marched along a road upon Gen. Ward's left flank. The New York troops were in advance. They had not proceeded far, when a murderous volley was poured upon the head of the column by the rebels whom they had approached in the darkness. For a moment it staggered, and then pressed on. Another volley was too much for them. They broke and fled to the rear. In the darkness and confusion the Maine troops were thrown into disorder, and the backward movement continued until it came to Co. A., commanded by Capt. C. P. Mattocks, of this city. This company, animated by the spirit of its gallant leader, stood fast, as also did Co. E, Capt. E. M. Sawyer, the next in the column. Order was soon restored, and the regiment rallied. Co. A from being the 19th in the column became the first, which position it held during that perilous night.

The subjoining extract from Gen. Ward's official report will show in what manner the men whom Portland has sent to the field, and of whose names she may justly be proud, bear themselves in the presence of the enemy. [*See entry for May 10th.*]

Wednesday, May 27th.

We returned from a three days' picket excursion today. We had a splendid time and excellent weather.

This afternoon we had a big time. Our Division was drawn up and witnessed the presentation of the long promised "Kearney Badge" or "Cross of Valor."[15] Four men from each Co. of the Div. received one, upon the recommendation of the Captains. In my Co. they were

Sergt. [Fayette M.] Paine
Crie
Corpl. [Joseph F.] Lake
Priv. Brown, J[acob]. C.

Sparrow would have had one, but I thought his commission would do for him. They are of bronze and are quite pretty. It was a notic[e]able fact that almost every color Sergt. in the Division was among the no. of recipients. Corpl. Lake was acting as color Sergt. during the battle and did himself credit.[16]

Saturday, May 30.

Today Capt. [William] Hobson[17] and I rode over to the 16th Me. We had a fine time, called upon Capt. Mayhew and the 5th Battery. We got home before dark, having made a very good day's work of it.

The prospect now is that Col. Hayman will have to go home as Col. of the 37th New York. The star seems loth to mount his shoulder. We are all sorry, as he is a brave officer, and a most excellent instructor in Brigade drill. If he does not get the appointment, Col. [Thomas W.] Egan of the 40th New York will have command of the

Brigade. I suppose Houghton will remain on the staff at any rate. He has got an excellent place and is a fool if he don't keep it. Capt. Smith, now A. Inspector Genl. will be A. A. Genl.

Wednesday, June 3d.

We have been paid off today up to the 1st of May, and I have given Col. Roberts $175.00 to take to mother. This makes $600.00 I have sent in all, and that too from the last two payments. We have a new Paymaster now, and he is a gentleman, which Maj. Mann was not.

Last Sunday I awarded a prize of $5.00 to Corpl. Bent for the best gun in the Company. It was in splendid order, as indeed were several of them. Col. Hayman inspected 10 competitors for the prize and said he could see no difference sufficient to warrant a decision. Maj. West then tried them, and selected Corpl. Bent and [Corpl. Ivory] Pray, between whom the $5 should lay. They drew lots and Bent won. They are all at work very hard upon their pieces, and they look finely.

Thursday, June 4th.

The 37th New York Vols. went home today. Our Division turned out and cheered them.[18]

Mr. [Royal B.] Todd of Portland arrived here today, having come on to see his son, Charles, who was wounded at Chancellorsville. He expects to take him home with him. He can not go for a week or so.

I killed a lizard in my tent today. He was a beauty, and has lived with me for two or three weeks. I have a new pet, a young bird that one of the boys caught and gave me. We had a Brigade Inspection by Col. [P. Regis] De Troubriand [Trobriand], who now commands our Brigade. Col. Hayman has gone home with his Regiment—the 37th New York.

The 38th N.Y. went home with the 37th. Col. Roberts went today too. In fact every one seems to be leaving. We now have no Col. George Tucker[19] started this morning on a 5 days' furlough to Washington.

Thursday, June 11th.

Mr. Todd went home today with his son. He has been with me just a week and has been very agreeable company. Hatch, Roberts and [John W.] Flint[20] all go today on 30 days leave. Their time will be out the 12th of July. The Brigade was inspected yesterday and again today. They seem determined to keep us in good order.

Saturday, June 13th. Bealton [Bealeton] *Station.*[21]

At 2 o'clock Thursday afternoon quite unexpectedly our Corps started for this place. We marched about 15 miles that day, not halting for the night till 10 o'clock. It was very warm but the men held out very well. I started with 40 men in all, Sparrow acting as Lieut.

Yesterday we started in the morning and marched all day, arriving here at sunset. We are now in a fine white oak grove, and expect to stay a few days at least. We marched about 22 miles yesterday, and a hard march it was. A great many men fell out by the way. It was a hot day, and many feet were blistered. We carried 3 days' rations. I got in with 30 men, 10 having "played out" on the way.

I hope we may stay here long enough to enjoy this splendid camping ground. The cars are now running to this point with supplies. We are only a stone's throw from the railroad. This is upon the whole the prettiest place we have ever had.

This morning one of the men caught a young quail and gave it to me. I have caged the young fellow, and propose to send him home. The Regiment is now reduced to 370 muskets. When we were here last Fall we had nearly 800. So it goes.

Sunday, June 14th.

Bealeton Station was left behind at sunset. We marched till 12 o'clock and made 10 miles. At Catlett's Station[22] we halted, and bivouacked till 4 o'clock when the bugle started us again. We did not start till 6 o'clock on

Monday, June 15th.

We had a most horrible march. 8000 men fell out from this Corps from sheer exhaustion. I stacked arms at night with 7 men. I had no great difficulty in keeping along although I now have quite a heavy knapsack of my own, and have had a sick man's gun to carry most of the time. We have passed several of the 9 months' Regiments along the railroad. They say we have marched 12 miles in the hot sun. This is the most of a scorcher we have had yet. Sparrow is acting Lt. and kept up like a hero. We first stacked arms at about 2 miles from Bull Run Creek. We had "turned in" and I was having a nice sleep, when whew! went the bugle at 9 o'clock. We then marched to near Blackburn's Ford, and were established as a picket. Each man slept but one hour out of three. I went to bed at 2 o'clock.[23]

Tuesday, June 16th. Near Bull Run

A day of undisturbed rest a few rods from our picket posts of last night. We are now where the first Bull Run fight began.

Wednesday, June 17th.

Started at 3 o'clock, and arrived near Centreville at 5—only 3 miles. A great number of the 25th Maine have been over to see us. They seem to think us heroes, and we make no serious objections. We tied up for the night in an open field.

Thursday, June 18th. Near Centreville.

7 A.M. Same place. The 25th and 27th Maine are still visiting us. We have had a day of unalloyed rest. The heat has been very much like what we experienced Monday, but we have not been marching as then.

Friday, June 19th.

We started for Gum Springs, 10 miles from Centreville, at 2 o'clock P.M. At 9 we halted, and soon bivouacked for the night in a most delicious rainstorm. It commenced to rain at sunset, and we had to march in mud and water ankle-deep. We were wet to the skin, but slept nicely. I still carry my knapsack and think I march quite as easy as I ever did without it. It serves the purpose of both mule and shoulder-braces to carry it myself.

Saturday, June 20th. Near Gum Springs, Va.

We are now on picket very near the small village of Gum Springs. Strange reports of guerrillas are among the men.[24] They say, and I guess there is good grounds for it too, that one wagoner of our Brigade was shot, four men of the Corps killed, and three officers either killed or captured by guerrillas on the march of yesterday afternoon. Two of these wolverines were captured, and I hope they will be made an example of. This region was always noted for these prowling bands, and the quicker the captured ones are hung the better.[25] One good will result from their depredations, and that will be a decrease of stragglers. This will cure a great many of their habit of falling out upon every trivial pretext. There seemed no disposition on the part of the men to fall out as an order was issued about guerrillas. Many pretended to think it was a bugbear to keep the men from straggling, yet not many cared to test the truth of the report. Today they have come to the conclusion that it will be risky business to drop out every now and then. Sick and tired men will now be quite a rare commodity on the march. On the retreat from Chancellorsville hardly a man complained of the rapid march and muddy road until we reached the north side of the Rappahannock, and then quite a number were taken suddenly ill. Many men have no higher rule of conduct in such cases than personal ease. If one thinks he can go along more comfortable after a short rest he will take it—not if he belongs to Co. A however.

Sunday, June 21st.

We were relieved from picket at 4 o'clock, and retired to an open field where the rest of the Corps now lies. There has been fighting nearly all day. We could hear the cannonade very distinctly. The ball was opened by [Maj. Gen. J. E. B.] Stuart's Cavalry upon the advance of the 1st ([Maj. Gen. John Fulton] Reynold's [Reynolds's]) Corps near Middleburgh. "They say" the enemy was driven 6 miles.[26]

The 1st Maine Cavalry were engaged at Aldie, near this place, with heavy loss a few days ago.[27] Col. Doughty [Lt. Calvin S. Douty] was killed.

Each Regiment of our Brigade is now encamped by "divisions doubled on the centre at company distance," which arrangement brings Cos. A and K upon the same street. We expect to stay here two or three days, and perhaps longer.

Monday, June 22d.

Nothing new, with the exception of a battalion drill this afternoon by Maj. West. We were out from 5 till half past 6. We succeeded in getting a little fresh meat from our Division Commissary today. We have had no mail since a week from Friday, and are almost out of the world as for news. We now and then see a newspaper from Washington which tells us of "wars and rumors of wars."

Tuesday, June 23d.

We had a battalion, or rather, brigade, drill this afternoon under Col. de Trobriand, and it was all that the men could do to stand up for the want of suitable rations. We have had nothing but hard bread without half enough even of salt pork.

Wednesday, June 24th.

We had no drill this afternoon and spent the time in doing nothing. I had an excellent breakfast this morning at the house of one Lewis, near here. This is my

First meal in a house for 8 months

and it certainly tasted good. I had some nice milk, which is to us quite a rarity.

Every one thinks we shall move in the direction of Goose Creek in the morning, but I do not know what ground there is for such a conclusion. I have had four men return from the hospital within two days. I now have 46 men *present* for duty, including [Frederick W.] Bosworth and Sparrow. If we ever get a mail it will either bring Sparrow's commission or a notification to that effect, I think. I have all the men I started from Potomac Creek with.

Thursday, June 25th.

This morning at 6-1/2 o'clock our Corps started from Gum Springs, and night found us wet and tired at the Monocacy Aqueduct, only 25 miles from where we started from. We came by the way of Edwards' Ferry.[28] We halted about 1-1/2 miles the other side of E. F. for dinner. From this reckoning we made 15 miles in the afternoon, though it took us till 10 o'clock at night to do it. It rained all the time after 5 in the afternoon and we were many of us wet to the skin. Some companies came in with a very few men. One had but 4 muskets. I had 29 men out of the 46 I started with. None of mine fell out until we reached White's Ford. This Monocacy Aqueduct is a fine piece of mason work. We passed directly under it. We had a fine day for marching—no dust—or we could not have done so well.

Friday, June 26th. Point of Rocks, Md.

We arrived at this place today at 11 o'clock. It is only 5 miles from Monocacy Riv. where we camped last night. It has been raining nearly all day, and judging from the wet bed in which we found ourselves this morning I should conclude it rained a *little* all night. We "slept out" with *nary* a shelter tent pitched. It was too dark, and we had no stakes or pins. We had fairly waked up and pitched our habitation this morning when we got orders to move. At 6 o'clock we were on the road once more, and picked our slippery way along as usual in the mud. But yesterday, it must be remembered, we

Recrossed the Potomac

and have Virginia mud to deal with no longer. We have made a sojourn on the "sacred soil" about 8 months this time. The first time we only visited the good people two weeks. We have crossed the

Potomac into Va. three times and the Rappahannock three times, yes, five, counting our short and bloodless passage at Warrenton last Fall, and now we are away up to Harper's Ferry. Whether we shall see the ghost of John Brown I cannot say.

Our road yesterday afternoon was the tow-path of the canal[29] and we moved along *"right smart."* We never marched 25 miles in one day before, except the two days last Fall when we made 52 miles in chasing Stuart's Cavalry. But the march of yesterday was simply nothing compared with that of a week from Monday. This makes two weeks we have been without a mail. That beats the Peninsula.

I have visited the village of Point of Rocks. It is quite a place. The Rebs destroyed a train of cars here last week. They were disguised as Union Cavalry, and took the place after the manner of the Greeks. They did but little damage however. Several of us indulged in a breakfast at a house near our camp this morning for a rarity. We had a plenty of fresh milk and were well pleased on the whole.

Saturday, June 27th.

We marched from Point of Rocks to Middle Town, or near it, today, making it all 15 miles. It was a good day for marching, and I did not have a man fall out. I have every man I started with from Potomac Creek, and five or six more. We are now once more the largest company for duty. The men have stood the marches admirably.

Near Middle Town, Md.

We passed through the fine little village of Jefferson. Here for the first time for 9 months our entrance was greeted with the "red, white and blue" from doors and windows. Here too for the first time for 9 months our eyes were feasted upon pretty girls and well dressed citizens! One beautiful damsel threw me a nice bo[u]quet, but sad to say! she neglected to attach her name. As good luck would have it, I took supper at a house near our camping-ground and, by describing the house where I saw the fair one, learned her name, which is Miss Floyd of Ohio, visiting with Dr. Culler of Jefferson. I of course sent my regret and regards to (her by) a young Miss who lived at the house where I *supped.* A wonderful house! Since I began campaigning I have paid fabulous prices at times—now and then have paid no more than the value—but until today have failed to find the man who would give me a meal "without money and without price." This man—I have forgotten his name—actually refused any pay from six of us, although he had been feeding the hungry at this ruinous rate for two days.

Still no mail, but they do say it is now on the move with us. Since we crossed the Potomac our route has been through a very fertile and beautiful tract of country. I have never seen such fields of grain. I fear some of the loyal citizens will have heavy bills against "Uncle Sam" for fence rails and grain. We can not help destroying some property, but our troops have done very well.

We are now near the thriving village of Middle Town, through which we expect to pass in the morning.

Sunday, June 28th. Near Walkersville, Md.

A day's work of 15 miles, a splendid day and easy march, fine country, pretty girls, loyal citizens, and now and then something to eat—for example, a good bowl of bread and milk tonight for my supper. We came through Middle Town and Frederick City today. The latter is a thriving and pretty place abounding in side walks and pretty girls—rarities to us who have been roughing it on the banks of the Rappahannock. Through Jefferson, Middle Town and Frederick City we marched in "column by companies" and the Regiment, I fancy, made a very fair display.

We crossed Catoctin Mountain today, and are now in a new valley, quite as beautiful and fertile as the one we have left. We are now about 6 miles from Frederick City. One thing is noticeable since our entrance into Maryland, and that is the loyalty of the people. At any rate they seem by their good deeds to be for us. There is not that sourness in the countenance of every passer-by which greeted us in our wanderings over the "sacred soil" of the "Old Dominion."

Our marches too have been, for the most part, very easy. The roads are excellent and the weather has been fine. I still carry my good knapsack, and have come to the conclusion that it is quite a good institution.

We have had an abundance of black cherries. They are nearly as large as the "tame" cherries of New England. *Perhaps* I ate a few too many last night. I know not to what else I can attribute my loss of appetite this morning. [Peter P.] Bodkin returned from hospital to-day.[30] I have now 47 men for duty present.

Monday, June 29th. Near Tenneytown [Taneytown], Md.

We started from near Walkersville this morning, and are now 20 miles from that place. We passed through Woodsboro, Ladiesville and Taneytown. We had quite a nice little halt at Woodsboro, where a fair damsel treated us to home-made Blackberry wine and custard pie. To my unpractised [unpracticed] eyes this little brunette was a beauty. Her name is Miss Phipps, address care A.E.J. Phipps, Woodsboro, Frederick Co., Md. If our wanderings ever carry us to Woodsboro again I hope to be assigned to provost duty. The country about here is really beautiful, and the inhabitants pay us every atten-tion. This evening, men, women and children, young and old—have been wandering through our camp. We are in a very pretty grove, where we pitched our shelters at 6 o'clock. We have now marched almost through Maryland, and perhaps tomorrow night will find us in the Quaker State. We are now only 3 miles from the nearest point. I had forgotten to mention our reception in Taneytown. We marched through "in column by platoon." The young damsels sang union songs and waved handkerchiefs to us as we passed along. The boys have got up a new game. They take a newspaper, and write on the margin, "Regards of———, Co.—— 17th Me. Vols.," or "Please address &c.," and then throw this tender missive to the first pretty girl that takes their eyes. When we got the blackberry wine we took pains to leave our card.

Today we hear that Hooker's head is off, and that Meade is

assigned to the command of the army.[31] So the thing goes. We may yet have a regular system of changing commanders every month. We also hear that Vicksburg has fallen with 16,000 prisoners.[32] Good, if true.

Tuesday, June 30th. Near Emmetsburg.

Only 9 miles today, which brings us 1-1/2 miles from the Penn. line. We did not start from Taneytown until 1 o'clock. The march was a very agreeable one with the exception of a smart shower toward night. We halted at 6 o'clock, and I am now enjoying myself upon a nice bed of straw in my *shelter*. A good citizen opened his yard to us, although a guard had been posted, and bade us help ourselves.

This has been a month of active campaigning. We have marched since June 11th (when we left Camp Sickles) the snug little distance of 165 miles, and I have toted my load every inch.

I should not be surprised if we begin the month of July with a fight. We are now close upon the enemy, and I somewhat think there will be a few guns fired July 1st.

Sergt. Sparrow's commission as 2d Lt. in this Co. and 2d Lt. Houghton's as 1st Lt. in Co. H came today. The Regiment was mustered today for pay. [John F.] Totman joined us on the march. He has been in hospital some weeks. We now have 2 officers and 47 men present in the Regt., *all* for duty. I am five muskets short, but dare say they will be issued soon.

We are suffering for shoes in the Regt. Some men are actually barefoot. A supply has been expected for the past week.

Houghton still remains on the Brigade Staff.[33] I shall appoint a new 1st Sergt. and one Sergt. as soon as blanks can be obtained, which I hope will be in a day or two at most. We hear various rumors of more daring Rebel raids in Pennsylvania and Maryland.

Wednesday, July 1st. (Written July 3d).

Toward night we moved to the Catholic Institution of St. Joseph near Emmetsburg. My Co. and Co. C were detailed to guard the grounds and buildings, which are really beautiful.[34]

Thursday, July 2d. (Written on the field, Friday morning, the 3d.)
Yesterday morning we started from Emmetsburg at 3 o'clock A.M. to the battlefield near Gettysburg.[35] We were put under a heavy but ineffective shelling at 4 o'clock. At 5 we went in with our muskets and in just an hour had 17 men killed and 84 wounded—all with musket balls. The Regiment behaved finely. I shall attempt no description of the fight here. My letter to the Courier will answer for that.[36] In the afternoon the Rebs made a grand charge on our line, which is only a mile and a half long. They were repulsed at every point.[37]

❧❧

Battlefield near Gettysburg Pa
Friday morning, July 3d
4 o'clock A.M.
My dear Mother:-
Another terrible fight and yet I am safe. Our Regt was in the thickest of the fight—close musketry—and lost over 100 men in one hour. This morning cannonading has commenced and while I am writing a *few* shells are bursting over my head. The Regt has quite a number killed. No correct statistics can be given now. I had two men killed[,] Jacob C. Brown and J. A. Hodsdon, and probably 10 wounded with 6 or 8 missing. Some of these may come in. Webster Brown is all right. Our loss in officers is heavy. Adj. Roberts, leg. Capt. Jogg, probably mortal in stomach. . . . My 1st Sergt [Alvin F.] Blake was shot by my side. He is wounded in the leg. My two men were killed close by my side—next to me. One of my Sergeants was shot through both thighs. Lt. Col. M. & Maj. West are both safe. The Color Sergt. was killed instantly. It was not a protracted fight, but being at close range the work was deadly. I had three men load-

ing for me, and I blazed away at the Rebs. The Regt. behaved most splendidly. We shall have a heavy loss. We can make out 101 now that we know who are killed or wounded. Many of the missing must be wounded too. You may judge something of these affairs by my telling you that after taking out the wounded and those who carried them away, I could stack but 18 muskets. At one time I had but 12. I went in with about 40 muskets. We have received a new supply of ammunition and expect to *go in* again today. Perhaps however fresh troops will do the duty for us.

Our Brigade was left behind (9 miles) at Emmetsburg as rear guard. We started from there at 3 o'clock yesterday morning, and came within half an hour of being cut off from the main army. We arrived early enough for all *practical* purposes.

Gen'l. Sickles lost a leg. It is feared that Adjt. Roberts will lose his leg. The "pack up" is ordered and I will close. Shall try to write a little more before this goes. Hoping that I may be as well favored of Providence today as yesterday. . . . Love to father & the Co. A did nobly.

Same Place. 1/2 mile advanced.
10 A.M. the 3d.
The fight is going on easily in front. We are now the rear line and I can write a little more definitely. My loss is 2 killed, 7 wounded, & 1 missing—10 in all. . . .

Genl. Sickles died this morning.[38] We are now expecting heavy reinforcements and expect a complete victory.

I enclose a list of our Co. which I hope you will send Lieut. Brown. All these wounds were from musket balls. It was a genuine musketry fight, such as we had never seen before. The loss of each side must be heavy and it may be more so before this day is ended. Give my love to all the folks. You see how lucky I am. We have but 4 Captains for duty now. Within two months to a day we have lost in battle 4 Capts. 2 Lts. killed, 6 Lts wounded—in all 12 officers. Chas Sawyer is safe.

In haste Charles

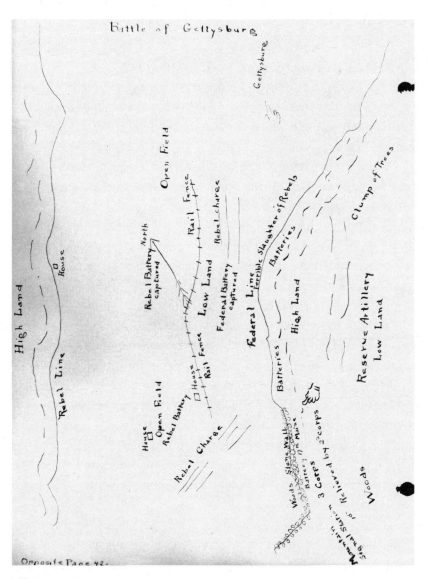

Fig. 6. Gettysburg, July 3. [Mattocks's map of the late morning action of the 17th Maine on July 3rd, 1863. Courtesy of James M. White, Jr.]

Battle of Gettysburg, Penn.[39] *(Written July 6th.)*

Our Division (Birney's) held the extreme left. Ward's Brigade being upon our left. The enemy made a desperate attempt to take the apex of the triangle where I have marked "terrible slaughter of Rebels." [*See fig. 6.*]

Being driven back with terrible slaughter after having fairly reached the muzzles of our guns, they then came on with other troops furiously upon our left where they were well received by the 3d Corps. This however, took place upon July 3d. They actually drove us back perhaps 20 rods, although we charged twice after fairly repulsing them opposite our Brigade. We were formed behind a formidable stonewall and they had to advance upon it through the woods. Our Battery played over our heads and did good execution. The Rebs finding they could not well gain the stonewall, rushed on partly beyond our fire by the flank and tried hard to take the troublesome battery. We remained behind the wall until they had almost flanked us. We then retired under a very heavy enfilading fire through a wheat field over a ridge, which gave us a few moments' rest. We then charged forward to the ridge where we were exposed to a murderous fire. Our Battery was got off in a few moments, and we fell back still further, our ammunition being exhausted. We were now relieved by the 2d Corps, who drove them two miles (they say!) before dark.

I have two or three men loading for me, and blazed away myself while we were behind the stonewall. [Joseph A.] Hodsdon and Brown, of my Co., were shot dead by my side here. Sergt. Paine was severely wounded in both legs on the ridge. 1st Sergt. [Alvin F.] Blake was hit soon after the last charge. Corpl. Lake, acting Color Sergt., did bravely.[40] I gave him a pair of Sergeant's chevrons on the spot. Blake was made 1st Sergt. in the same manner. I had 2 men killed and 7 wounded. Tucker was probably captured, having straggled on the march. The loss of officers of the Regt. stands now (July 6th) thus—

all but Lt. Whidden and [William H.] Green being hit on Thursday by musket balls.

. . .

Total, Killed, 2. Wounded, 6— In all, 8.

We went in with 23. Capt. [Almon L.] Fogg lived about 30 hours. Lieut. [Hiram R.] Dyer, commanding Co. G, died instantly. Capt. [Milton M.] Young was almost the first man hit in the Regiment. It is a wonder that more were not killed. Capt. F. was hit on the ridge when we were firing lying down. One man was killed and two wounded *out of the three* who ran to his aid.

Loss of Co. A.

. . .

Killed, 2. Wounded, 7. Missing, 1. Total, 10.

Our Co. did not lose any under the shelling of Friday [July 3rd], though 3 were killed and 7 or 8 wounded in the Regt., but I am anticipating. Many of my men had narrow escapes. The bullet holes in clothing are numerous. Marston had a ball put through his coat and vest on the breast, cutting his suspender off. The Surgeon thinks Blake will save his leg.[41] [Sergt. F. M.] Paine will, I think, get well, but it will be a long time before he can use his legs. [Private Charles] Milliken's arm may have to be amputated, but I hope they will all escape without the loss of any limbs. [Private F.] Skillings and [Private D. M.] Spaulding were both wounded at Chancellorsville. Both were slightly wounded, then and are not much worse this time. They are in just good condition for sick leaves.[42] Some of the companies in the Regt. have lost as many as 6 in killed alone—including those who have died since. I have almost forgotten my date. I am writing this on the 6th, so I anticipate now and then. This dating back has its disadvantages, but on the whole is the best way.

Friday's Battle.[43]

Friday, July 3d, 1863, was a sad day for Lee's army. Having been baffled in their slight attack upon our centre and desperate assault upon the left, they determined to try us upon the centre once more. A most desperate charge was made, of which I have spoken under date of yesterday. We were rushed at double quick to support the centre. Here we lay under a horrid, but not very effective shelling. 3 men were killed and 8 or 9 wounded from our Regiment. A great many prisoners were brought in while we lay here. The shelling lasting from 4 till nearly dark, and was vigorous on both sides. We did nothing but stick our *noses* in the ground. I did not lose any one this time, though we came near it; one piece of shell came very near my leg.

Saturday, July 4th.

Last night our Company was on picket in front of the Brigade. We had to listen to the groans of the wounded, and our bed was close to dead men—mostly Rebs. I almost got lost walking ground trying to care for the wounded. I gave them water and assisted the stretcher-bearers who came to take them off. Many were between the hostile lines and could receive assistance from neither side. I had long talks with some of them about various matters. They are all sick of the war, but are by no means discouraged. I have mentioned one or two incidents of this night's experiences in my letter to the Courier.

This morning at daylight the skirmishers were advanced to feel the position of the enemy. They report them fallen back a little—say 2 miles. We are now masters of the field, and the day has been spent in burying the dead and bringing in the wounded. It has been more or less rainy all day. Only a very few shots have been sent by the Artillery, and that by the Rebs. We heard heavy guns at the distance in the evening. There was skirmishing all day.

Sunday, July 5th.

We are now in undisputed possession of the field; the enemy being reported 5 miles away in the direction of Cumberland Valley.

Parties have been all day busy in burying the dead and caring for the wounded. The Rebel list of casualties must be enormous. It seems 4 to 1. Our loss is already estimated at 18,000.[44] Bobby Lee will go home with his tail feathers out.

Monday, July 6th.
We are in the same place as yesterday, except having moved out of our wet and muddy rifle pits. We are in the woods and have been expecting to go away in pursuit of the enemy at any moment, but I think we shall stay here all night.

I have walked over a part of the field. The dead are not buried yet and the stench is become awful. I should hate to live here. Yesterday I was at one of our hospitals and witnessed the amputation of the limbs of the wounded, the sickening details of which I will not relate. Photographic artists have been busy in taking views upon the battlefield. Groups of the dead, graves, dead horses, and in fact almost everything forms the "base of their operations."

The following promotions have been made in the Regt. for bravery. . . . Promotions like the above, if made sparingly and honestly, can but have a good effect. Of course there is a chance for abuse, as in all good things. The whole affair rests with company commanders.

Tuesday, July 7th.
This morning we were routed up at 2 o'clock, but did not get off until 5. We halted for the night near Mechanic[s]town—about 18 miles from the battlefield.

Wednesday, July 8th.
We marched about 15 miles this time. Night found us near Middletown. Nothing for variety except a drizzling rain all day.

Thursday, July 9th.
Today we have not marched much more than 10 miles. At noon we crossed South Mountain—the very battlefield of last Fall.[45] Since we left the banks of the Rappahannock we have passed over quite

a number of the old battlegrounds. Manassas, Catletts' Station, Bull Run, Chantilly, South Mountain, are among the number. We are on really historic ground.

Friday, July 10th. Antietam.
Tonight finds [us] on the battlefield of Antietam after a march of about 9 miles. How long we shall stay here remains to be seen. The Rebs are supposed to be near this place.

Saturday, July 11th.
Last night just as we were getting ready to retire we had to rout up and march four miles, making a day's work of 13 miles. Tonight finds us 4 miles further to the front. We are in rear of the 5th Corps and expect to engage the enemy tomorrow. I learn that the 1st, 2d, 5th and 6th Corps form the first line of battle and that the 11th, 12th and 3d are their supports. We (the 3d) are nearly in the centre. No one can explain why the ball does not open.

Sunday, July 12th.
The same inaction. We have changed our position to perhaps 1/2 a mile forward. No fighting and no excitement of any kind. The usual number of rumors, the usual amount of premature success— more than the usual number of reinforcements, but thus far not a gun have we heard.

Monday, July 13th. Same place.
The same and more so! Same place, same rain, no fight, [Maj. Gen. Darius Nash] Couch, [Maj. Gen. John Gray] Foster, [Maj. Gen. John Adams] Dix,[46] &c., *ad inf.* coming to a focus here to bag *Mr. Lee,* but we "don't see it" yet. Cavalry everywhere, militia arriving and such things without end. Nothing of the kind perceptible here. Nothing real, but rain. Narrowly escaped being drowned out this forenoon. Hungry although I have enough pork and hard bread to eat. Lazy, sleepy, &c., all the time. Got a mail today.

Tuesday, July 14th. Near Williamsport.

We moved upon the Rebel earthworks near the river! and found them deserted. The enemy are safely across the river. They had fortified strongly and we should have had our hands full to dislodge them. We are now in the enemy's work or a little beyond them, where we propose to lie down to pleasant dreams. I suppose we shall take up the trail in the morning, and perhaps a few days will find us once more upon the banks of the Rappahannock. So be it.[47] We got more out of the Rebs this time than [Maj. Gen. George B.] McClellan[48] did at Antietam—and that too without being two or three times at Bull Run and Chantilly and then running to Washington for protection. The capture of Vicksburg comes at the right time.[49] Things generally look well.

Wednesday, July 15th. Near Sharpsburg.

We started this morning very early and halted today noon after a march of about 10 miles. We are now near Sharpsburg, which is a very small mean-looking village anyway. We passed over a part of the Antietam battlefield, saw the marks of the conflict—saw many of the graves—crossed the bridge where Burnside distinguished himself—in fact we have made quite a business of visiting battlefields of late. We have now marched 250 miles since leaving the Rappahannock about one month ago, and those of us that are left are good for another 250 this month. I never felt better in my life. This style of campaign agrees with me excellently. The general health of the Regiment is very good. I now have 36 men present for duty. The Regt. has but 232 muskets for duty.

Thursday, July 16th. Near Harpers [Harper's] Ferry.

Here we are bivouacked in a fine grass field only 3 miles from Harper's Ferry, where John Brown frightened the good people out of their wits some time since. We have marched about 10 miles today. This forenoon we passed through Krampton's [Crampton's] Gap, where the enemy were routed last year after a few minutes contest.[50] It is a snug place any way and there is but small chance for any flanking games.

We hear now that Lee left Winchester this morning. It does not seem to me that we are following him up very fast, else why only 10 miles a day. He will either go home, or make a stand in the vicinity of Bull Run and Manassas. We may have still another fight before the thing is wound up.

Friday, July 17th.

We were started very suddenly this afternoon, and after a very rapid march of a couple of hours

Crossed the Potomac for the fifth time
since taking the field last
September!

We halted about 2 miles from the bank. Harper's Ferry, though once a beautiful village, is much dilapidated now. We passed through Sandy Hook which must be a grandchild of Harper's Ferry. We are once more in Virginia. Jonas [Reynolds][51] went out to forage a little hay to sleep on and came back with the following articles of merchandise.

1	Sheep skin
1	Calf skin
1	Pot Milk
1	Pot Butter
3	Beets
4	Cucumbers
2	Onions

We at once *confiscated* them.

Saturday, July 18th. Near Keyes' Gap, Va.

We started early this morning and marched about 8 miles, when we halted and pitched tents. This half day's work suits me very well, especially when blackberries are so abundant. This afternoon I visited the Division Picket Line in company with Col. Merrill. We had a good supper at a house, and when I got back I found that Jonas had a supply of Blackberry sauce, milk, &c. I then had to have supper No. 2, which satisfied me for once.

This is a very beautiful valley, if a circle hemmed in by mountains can be called a valley. This section is said to be infested by guerrillas, and I think it may be so, as the woods and mountains would offer a good chance for that kind of warfare. Even these stories do not wholly prevent straggling.

Sunday, July 19th.

Noon. We are now pulled up in a hay field—perhaps for dinner—perhaps for the night—and enjoying a beautiful day. Jonas still maintains his reputation for foraging. We have had a good supply of milk all day, and now he has just come in with some splendid blackberries. These berries are the nicest and largest I ever saw, and in places the ground is almost black with them. We eat them raw when there is no time to make sauce, but generally there is time to prepare them in the most approved style. We bought a bag of flour at a mill the other day and fritters have since been a staple with us. Our pack mule skedadled two days ago, and I have taken to my knapsack once more. I carried it every mile until we got to the battlefield. Think I can still carry it.

Monday, July 20.

We had quite a hard march today through the heat. There are many defiles in the road which retard our progress and make us more tired than rapid marching. We have made about 14 miles today, and are now near Ashby's Gap. The present movements of the army puzzle us all. The 2d, 3d and 12th Corps are on this road, but no one seems to know where the rest of our forces are.

We are continually feasting on blackberries. Genl. Ward, now in command of the Division, has issued very strict orders against straggling. I hope he will break up the habit as it is a disgrace to the Army. Men are beginning to be on the look out as they get *tied up* at

Division Headquarters. There are too many unarmed men for the good of the service.

Tuesday, July 21. Near Ashby's Gap, Va.

We have remained *in statu quo* today. Company inspections were held this forenoon which were *supposed* to be thorough. What we are waiting here for seems a great mystery to the uninitiated. We have been recently fitted up in very good shape with clothing, &c.

An order was read today, saying that 3 officers and 6 enlisted men would be detailed from all the *old* Regiments in the Corps to go home and attend to the Conscripts—that they would be selected strictly with reference to soldierly qualities, &c., &c., & so on. Quite a number of our officers have expressed a desire to go. Some will have to be disappointed, of course, but not I, as I am willing to stay away from home for the 3 full years if need be. There is a good prospect that 3 years of service will be needed from all of us.

Wednesday, July 22d.

We started at 2 o'clock and marched till 10 at night—a hard job—and crossed the same stream some five or six times, in water almost to our knees. Our pilgrimage ended in Manassas Gap—on the road to Front Royal. We must have marched 10 or 12 miles.

The "Conscript Delegates" were announced this morning, and to my surprise my name heads the list. . . .

Thursday, July 23d. (Written on the 25th). Linden—Manassas Gap.

Early in the morning our Regt. was selected to support a battery on a high hill near the village of Linden, about 5 miles from Front Royal. We remained there doing nothing until 2 or 3 o'clock, when we found ourselves with the rest of the Brigade advancing in line of battle to support our line of skirmishers, who were doing a brisk business with the Rebs. Our line pressed them about half-a-mile, when bang! went their artillery. They shelled us, now and then with only three or four pieces, but with splendid range. This was kept up till about 7 o'clock. Although the range was good and the shells exploded all about us only one man in the Regiment was hit.

Acting Sergt. Maj. Bosworth, of my Co., was wounded by an unexploded six pounder shell in the thigh. The wound is severe and they are afraid it will prove fatal. He was about a rod from me, on the right of the Regt.[52] I had almost forgotten to note that Co. A took its new place—2d in line—this morning. Cos. C & K and D & H are temporarily consolidated, thus giving us only 8 companies. We have but about 10 officers on duty, beside the Field. The two last fights used up our officers very rapidly.

For some strange reason our batteries did not reply—so we had to lie low and not even have the satisfaction of hearing a good Union response. But we were lucky. We were not called upon to fire though the skirmishers kept up a very brisk firing. It was a splendid sight. The ground is rolling and in places hilly—but little woodland—and we could all the while see both lines of fire, and a part of the time, the skirmishers themselves. Toward dark the bright flash and the wreaths of smoke were really beautiful. I wished that all battles could be fought with as little bloodshed as this. The casualties must be great for the number engaged, but then the fight is the merest skirmish compared with our previous battles. Perhaps this one is not ended.

Friday, July 24th. 10 A.M.

Last night I was detailed with 3 men from A Co. to go on picket. We covered the Regiment and fell back at daylight.

Early this morning the skirmishers discovered that the enemy had *skedaddled* and left us in possession of the field. Our forces advanced toward Front Royal about a mile and a half (our Division—other troops ahead) & are now resting in a field by the roadside. We have heard a few guns toward the front. The valley of the Shenandoah is in full view and a splendid sight it is. We may or may not have more fighting today. The prisoners say they belonged to the rear guard, &c., &c., & so on. They left their dead (only a few any way) on the field. A good number of our skirmishers were wounded and a few killed. Our men brought in quite a number of the enemy's wounded this morning.

Our rations are up and the boys are getting hungry. We get enough of fresh meat but no bread. Jonas has *foraged* some flour and potatoes & I guess we shall not starve. We have about 3 hard bread left, but as long as the flour holds out we can feast on fritters, which answer my purpose very well—even better than hard bread.[53]

Monday, July 27th. Near Warrenton.

I have omitted to write for some days. After the fight at Manassas Gap, we marched to Warrenton, or through it rather and encamped in an open field, where we now are.

We have just heard that the Conscript delegates will leave to-morrow morning. We are getting ready for the great event. The idea that after so long a period in active service and with 350 miles of marching, we are once more to see the civilized world is indeed not a little gratifying.

Six men & 3 officers will go from every Regt. How long they will stay I can not say. Perhaps it will be a six weeks' job—or longer even. Poor Bosworth is very severely wounded but I entertain hopes of his recovery.

CHAPTER THREE

Home Again

❧❧

Wednesday, July 29th. Washington, D.C.

We arrived here last evening and stopped at the "National," which by the way is a fine house.[1] We go on tonight for N. York.

Friday, July 31st.

We arrived safely in the good city of Portland today noon, and at 2 o'clock reported to Maj. [Russell B.] Shepherd,[2] of the 1st Maine Heavy Artillery comdg. at Camp Abe Lincoln. We shall not have a great deal to do at present.

Sunday, Aug. 2d.

I am Officer of the Day at this Camp, being the first they have had. Things are a little loose as yet. The men of the old Regiments are used as a guard. There are about 150 Conscripts here now.[3]

Saturday, Aug. 8th. Portland, Me.

I have had a very good time this week. Not having anything to do after Monday, I obtained a leave of two or three days and attended Commencement at Bowdoin, where I have had a very good time.[4] Fourteen of our Class were there. We had a good time at Class Breakfast. But we could not help thinking of those who have fallen in this war. [Thomas H.] Green, [Willard M.] Jenkins and [George W.] Edwards were not there.[5] Then some are now suffering from wounds. [Frederic H.] Beecher, wounded severely at Fredericksburg and then again dangerously at Gettysburg, is now a sufferer at the hospital.[6] Bowdoin Sons have won glory but it has not been bloodless. They have suffered nobly and fought nobly for the cause, and now to see some of their number among the Copperheads is really disgusting. The Commencement was a slim affair anyway. Perhaps I am prejudiced in favor of the past.

The Conscript Camp is now on Mackies' [Mackie's] Island,[7] and the Conscripts will have hard work to escape.

Saturday, Aug. 22d.

I have not written in my Diary of late because there is nothing to write. Two days of duty and five of loafing tell the story of a week with me. Last week I spent two days in Baldwin, and this morning I returned from a two days' stay in Brunswick. Goodwin[8] went with me and we had a very good time on the whole. Things are quiet there during vacation. The term commences next week and perhaps I shall go down again.

Mackie's Island.

I am this afternoon in my good wall tent on the island to do a little writing. Shall go back to the city at 6. The steamer runs three trips a day—at 9, 3 and 6 o'clock.

Monday, Aug. 24.

Once more on the island. Goodwin and I went to Brunswick last week and had a very good time for a day or so there. Everything looks natural. I shall have to perform the very arduous *duties* of Officer of the Day here tomorrow, and then Wednesday will bring me on as Officer of the Boat. 100 men will start for the 19th Regt. tonight. The 16th & 19th will then have had 200 men each. Now the 3d & 4th must have their 200 before the 17th can come in for a share. We shall remain here nearly all the Fall, I guess.

Tuesday, Sept. 8th. Mackie's Island, Portland Harbor.

I have sadly neglected my Diary and all similar cares, not because my military service calls upon my time, but rather on account of laziness, which I find is developing itself finely under this home influence.

The prospect now is that the 17th will get its 200 men soon as they are accumulating very rapidly. They are a better lot than the average, being from the Eastern part of the State in a great degree. Many are from Aro[o]stook County.[9] I am glad that they are strangers, because I think it better for the Regt. We shall send 100 at a time to Long Island, Boston Harbor. From there they will go by transport to Alexandria, and then ho for the U.S. Military R.R. to Warrenton.

Thursday, Sept. 10th. Long Island, Boston Harbor.

Capt. [Joseph] Perry[10] and myself arrived at Long Island, Boston Harbor, at 4 o'clock this morning with 103 conscripts for the 17th. We started with 103 & got every man here—a thing which has not been done before. I had a guard of 6 non-commissioned officers, and we all had to keep well on the alert. I brought up New York bounty-jumpers in irons—locked together in pairs. They are the six who offered the old drummer at Camp Berry $600 for a pass over the guard line. They are *sharkers*, and would leave if they could get an opportunity. One of them did get his hand out of the irons, and succeeded in getting on the deck of the steamer before he was discovered. None of the guard got much sleep, but the fact that we got the scamps all here will console us for loss of sleep.

Saturday, Sept. 12th. Long Island, Boston Harbor.

We are getting the Conscripts under discipline. I have had mine out upon drill twice a day, an hour and a half each time. They are not armed yet, so we are confined to company drill, which they are beginning to do up in good shape.

Capt. Ilsley and Lieut. [William H.] Greene arrived this morning with 90 more men for our Regt. They started with 92 men, and lost 2 on the way. We are now encamped altogether. The men have A tents—5 in each, and are very comfortable.

We officers board at the hotel on the island, kept by Mr. Stearns, formerly of Portland. This island is a wilderness compared with Mackie's. Hardly any visitors are allowed here and we see nothing but soldiers from one day's end to another. However, our stay will be short.

Sunday, Sept. 13th.

This has been a long and dreary day, no religious service, no Sunday morning inspection, no anything, save a drizzling rain all the time. Capt. Ilsley and Capt. Perry have both had a trip to Boston and back. All four of us are living in one wall tent, together with a young conscript, whom we have made our "fidus Achates." Upon the whole we have a very fair sort of time.

Wednesday, Sept. 16th.

We were expecting to be off long before this, but here we are with no prospect of going until Friday. The steamer, *Forest City,* our transport, is now cleaning at Boston and will not be got ready as soon as was expected. We are losing some fine weather by the delay. I hope we shall not have to encounter the line storm. Lt. Greene has gone to Boston, to return in the morning. Capt. Ilsley is relieved from duty and ordered back to Portland. Lieut. Reed, 30th Mass., is assigned to duty with the Detachment.

We have got the conscripts well in hand now—have a guard-mounting—boots blacked—equipment ditto &c. &c. & so on ad infinitum. The first Detachment is called Co. A, and the second, Co. B.

We have 6 non-comd officers from Mass. Regiments besides the 6 we brought with us. The guard that came with the second Detachment was sent back.

The conscripts make quite a show in Company drill now. I have put Co. A through nearly all the movements and they improve very rapidly. There are some old soldiers among them, and these serve as guides to their movements.

Thursday, Sept. 17th.

Today I had the pleasure of going to the city and paying Capt. [William H.] Savage a short visit.[11] He returned to the island with me, and we are now celebrating together.

Saturday, Sept. 19th.
On board Transport Steamer Forest City—off Cape Cod.

There is a good swell on and writing is not so easy as might be expected. We started from Long Island this morning at 5 o'clock, though the men were all embarked last night. This is a fine steamer and we shall probably have a fine passage to Fortress Monroe and Alexandria unless we have the bad luck to encounter the "line gale." The men are just beginning to be sea sick and we shall have a fine time of it before we get to our stopping-place. The N.H. Detachment will be left at Portsmouth, Va., for the Department of the South. The Maine, Vermont and Mass. Detachment go to Alexandria for the Army of the Potomac. It will take about 60 or 70 hours to reach Portsmouth in good weather. We shall probably turn over our men to a guard in Alexandria and then return in this steamer to Boston again.

I am beginning to feel a little sea sick—just enough to convince me that all my Bay of Fundy experience did not make an "old tar" of me.[12]

Sunday, Sept. 20th. 6 P.M.

This is the first time I have felt much like writing in my Diary. I have only eaten once today. The most of the time I have felt just sea sick enough to keep my bed. Many of the men have been "throwing up Jonah" today, as it has been quite rough. We are now off Cape May, and are going about 11 knots an hour. We expect to make Fortress Monroe by 10 o'clock tomorrow forenoon. We have a little freight to leave there, and then we leave the New Hampshire men at Portsmouth. Then we shall be off for Alexandria. If we are favored with good weather I suppose we may reach our destination sometime Tuesday. If we have to go to the Regts. with our conscripts we may not see the State of Maine until the very last of this month.

Yesterday I was Officer of the Day, and in the afternoon we came near having a riot. A drunken scoundrel belonging to the N.H. Detachment had a quarrel with a sentinel, and got a severe kick over the eye. He was then taken by the guard, and as he was too free with his tongue, I ordered him strung up in the rigging. He was taken on deck and the guard made a "spread-eagle" of him—gagging him with a bayonet, &c. Some of the N.H. roughs undertook to make a rush and cut him down, but they did not like the looks of so many bayonets and loaded guns. We were all ready to give them a warm reception, but they did not give us the opportunity. When I went below at the first of the trouble one of the "roughs" made a pass at me behind my back, but was brought up very suddenly by one of my own men. Capt. Perry was quite conspicuous in tying up the man, and consequently they threaten vengeance to him. We had the fellow in the rigging, tied by hands and feet, for about two hours, and then took him down and kept him under guard with his hands in irons behind him. He is still under guard. The day we came on board I found, on going below, a ring formed and a couple of conscripts having a "turn" with their fists. I slipped in and gave them both a good choking. A few minutes after Capt. Perry found two more at the same game. He "went in" to separate them and about half-a-dozen pitched on to him. He, with the assistance of a 1st Sergt., succeeded in quieting them by giving them a few clips and drawing their revolvers. They got handled roughly by the ex-Policeman. The other day in Camp one of our men got disabled for life by a rupture which he himself made by purposely tipping over a barrel on which he had been made to stand, for punishment. That was the same man I made "stand at attention" five hours in Camp Berry for re-lighting his candle after "taps." His name was Bates—formerly of Co. B at Mackie's Island.

On board Forest City.

. . . We are all enjoying ourselves this evening as well as could be expected. I had almost forgotten that it was Sunday until a short time ago. Some of our officers under the same delusion, had a fine game of cards this morning. It reminded me of a similar mistake I had made on Picket in Virginia. Such accidents will sometimes happen in the Army. It seems a sad thing that we cannot tell the Sabbath by instinct.

Capt. Perry and Lieut. Green have both been about as willing to cling to their berths as myself. We cannot help making fun of each other, although there is not a "tar" among us. Lieut. Reed is on the semi-sick list. The officers have been *quiet* all day, as it was quite rough this morning and their bile got a little stirred up.

We heard from the election in Maine the day before we left Long Island. [Samuel] Cony, the Union-Republican candidate for Governor has 15,000 majority.[13] Bion Bradney was the Democratic candidate.

Monday, Sept. 21st.

We made Fortress Monroe at noon today. Stopping there a few minutes, we steamed down to Portsmouth, Va., and landed our New Hampshire Detachment—200 men—the merest trash—hardly worthy to be called men. We then put back to Fortress Monroe, and remained at the wharf for an hour, as we had some freight to discharge. I availed myself of the opportunity to visit the fortress. Had a very pleasant stroll through the grounds and over the parapet. It is a splendid fortification. The grounds inside seem a paradise compared with the dreary shore without. We left this place at dark, and started once more on our way to Alexandria, where we shall probably turn our men over to a guard to be by them forwarded to the Regiments. We shall at once return by this steamer to Boston. It seems too bad that with all our travels we have to be denied the pleasure of going to the Regiments ourselves.

Tuesday, Sept. 22d. A.M.

We are approaching the city of Alexandria, where we shall probably remain a few hours, before we return—or start to return.

We are sailing—or rather steaming along the old Potomac at a fine rate. For two days we have been in historic ground. Several wrecks were to be seen yesterday at the old Norfolk Navy Yard, the remnants of the conflagration. We passed quite near the Rip Raps, where so many worthless soldiers are condemned to serve their time. Craney Island, now used for a hospital, was in full view. We had a splendid view of Norfolk, when we touched at Portsmouth. It is really a fine city, presenting a striking contrast to the country around, which viewed from the water is anything but delightful. We passed many oystermen toiling in the famous oyster-beds of the Old Dominion. There are plenty of soldiers and more than a plenty of contrabands around Portsmouth, which by the way is not a very delightful city, if city it must be called.

Col. [John H.] Jackson,[14] 3d N.H., left us at Portsmouth. We are now under command of Lt. Col. [Charles F.] Morse of the 2d Mass.[15]

I have entirely recovered from sea-sickness. Today & yesterday I have been all right. Shall enjoy the trip back hugely. Thus far we have had good weather, a good voyage, and a good time. They give us very good fare on the boat—much better than what we had at the miserable hotel on Long Island.

Last night one of the boat hands was caught selling liquor to one of the soldiers. So this morning he was tied up in the rigging— "spread eagle"—for about an hour. He could hardly stand when taken down. We have long been trying to catch them at this trick. Whiskey has been sold for $5 & $7 a half-pint by these scamps, to the soldiers, and now this fellow has met his deserts. He ought to be court-martialed and sent to the Rip Raps.

Wednesday, Sept. 23d. Alexandria, Va.

We arrived at Alexandria last evening. I turned over my men and got a receipt. Have not lost a man, but the officer to whom I delivered them has lost five already. We remained on shore last night at the "City Hotel."[16]

We started on our homeward trip at five o'clock this afternoon. I shall hardly reach Portland by Saturday night, as we had hoped, unless we take the cars instead of the steamer at Boston. We have delightful weather still. At Alexandria Depot today I met Mr. Lord, my old Preceptor at Limington. Our Conscript (17th Maine) started at 9 o'clock this morning. [Edwin] Emery and [Josiah A.] Temple went off in good spirits.[17] They have had some rough customers to herd with on the passage. They will soon be with the 17th.

Sunday, Sept. 27th. Boston, Mass.

We arrived here this morning after a pleasant trip. I cannot deny that I was a little sea-sick, though the confession is somewhat humiliating to my pride. I heard upon arriving at Long Island this morning that I am detailed on a Court Martial now convened at Portland. That will be nice, as it will hold its sittings in the city, and I shall not have to go near Mackie's Island.

This morning I met Day of our Andover class, and in the afternoon accompanied him to Cambridge where he is now attending the Law School. We also paid a visit to Mount Auburn, where we of course had a splendid view. I returned to the city this evening, and then made a call at Savage's, where I had a very pleasant time. Savage has gone to Portland to stay.

Tuesday, Sept. 29th.

We arrived in Portland by boat this morning, after an absence of three weeks. I am glad enough to get back. I find myself a member of the Genl. Court Martial as I anticipated.

End, Sept. 29th, 1863.[18]

Saturday, Oct. 3d, 1863. Portland, Maine

Much to my surprise I am still in the "Natural Seaport" of the Canadas. My detached service has proved much longer than I had any reason to expect. I have now been away from the Regt. two months, and the prospect is that another month will hardly finish my duties. I am at length beginning to get not a little impatient to get back to the 17th once more. Since I returned with my conscripts on Tuesday I have had a very easy and pleasant time. The Court Martial never takes up more than three hours a day, and often not so much. The most of the cases are for desertion. Some of the scamps will get shot, I think. We have about two cases a day. Nearly all of them plead "Guilty," and they then say they are ignorant of the law, &c., &c., & so on. We have some very fine officers on the Court Martial. Thus far we have had a very pleasant intercourse. We have a good room in the City Buildings.

This morning's paper announces the appointment of Maj. West as Col. of our Regt. Lt. Col. Merrill is thereby superseded. He must feel like death. I have my doubts if he resigns after all. His friends are mad enough, and, of course the Major's friends are exultant over this victory.[19] The vacancy occurred on the 9th of May.

Spent the evening at Miss Holyoke's[20] with Frank Carter. We had a very pleasant time, and I propose to "continer."

I met Capt. Golderman, formerly of our Regt., whom I had not seen since he was wounded at Chancellorsville. He was, I think, expecting to be Major of the Regt., but he says he has given up the plan.[21] I suppose we shall now have a contest between Capts. Sawyer and Hobson for the vacancy occasioned by the promotion of Major West. Sawyer is now the Senior Capt., but Hobson has strong influence on his side. I hope it will soon be decided, and then things can take their course as of old. There are many vacancies in the "Line." Lieut. [James O.] Thompson has resigned.[22]

Sunday, Oct. 4th.

Attended church at the 2d Parish all day. Dr. [John] Carruthers gave, as usual, a very good discourse. We have been having dull weather of late to make up for the pleasant spell of the first of this week. It has been raining a very little this evening. The funeral of Mrs. Dr. Dwight[23] took place at the house, today, and was largely attended.

I have not had many letters of late from the Regt., but expect some soon full of gossip about the appointment of Maj. West. I am anxious to hear how the thing goes. Some say that Lt. Col. Merrill will not resign, but stick it out to the last. I have no means of knowing what the prospect is.[24]

Monday, Oct. 5th. 9 A.M.

Here we are this morning about to try some deserters and others of that ilk. The members of the Court Martial are . . .

Pres. Col. [Hiram] Burnham.
Lt. Col. [Seldon] Connor
Capt. [John H.] Roberts
Capt. Mattocks.
Lt. [T. D.] Chamberlain
Capt. [Auburn P.] Harris.
Capt. [S. T.] Keene
Lt. [J. A.] Perry
Lt. [F. B.] Ginn.
Judge Advocate Lt. [William T.] Parker
Prisoner.

Friday, Oct. 9th. Court Martial, City Building.

We still hold our Courts for the trial of "those who owe their greatness to their country's ruin"—e.g., the Sergeant who sold exemptions to Drafted men for $50 each. Many are cases of Desertion, in which the miserable scamps all plead ignorance of the law and innocence of the crime, or at any rate so far as intention is concerned. Some of them are really pitiable cases. Many have been advised not to report to the Provost Marshal after being drafted, and are now before us on the grave charge of Desertion. I only wish we could have the privilege of trying their evil counsellors. They would not have so easy a chance at our hands as they would desire. Ignorant men are often led into this crime, which law has made desertion, by heeding the advice of their abler but not more honest neighbors. The officers of this Court-Martial are as a whole a very good set of men, and thus far things have been conducted in a very creditable manner. Col. Burnham, of the 6th, makes a very good President, and Lieut. Parker, of the 1st Artillery, is a most excellent Judge Advocate, although this is his first experience.

For future reference, as well as present recreation, I will here note down the proceedings of a session. Of course this will not apply to all our meetings but still it is nearly the thing to go by. I should remark that, as a general rule, the prisoners plead guilty, and then make a written statement through the Judge Advocate tending to mitigate the crime, or show no evil intention.

Court Martial.

The meeting convenes at 9 o'clock in the forenoon. The roll is then called by the Judge Advocate. Each member appears with sword, sash and belt. The order of seats I have noted down under date of Oct. 5th. The Judge Adv. then states to the court what cases he has on hand to be tried during the day. In fine we have

1. Roll Call.
2. Reading Records last meeting.
3. Business stated by Judge Adv.
4. Court Sworn.
5. Order convening court & charges read to Pris.
6. Plea of Prisoner.
7. Examination of witnesses or the statement of Prisoner in case of pleading "Guilty."
8. Finding or Verdict.
9. Sentence.
10. Adjournment.

Tuesday, Oct. 13th.

The Court Martial still continues. I went to Baldwin Saturday and returned on Monday. Had a very fair time. Albert brought me down to the 6 o'clock train in the morning. My (23d)

Birthday occurred
October 11th, 1863. Sunday,

upon which eventful occasion the subscriber was 23 years old. My last birthday occurred in old Virginia while we were marching "on to Richmond."

Last evening Lizzie C[arter]. and I took a walk to Miss Hersey's and getting caught in a shower *of course* had to stay to tea, which I did not very much regret upon the whole. We had a very pleasant time upon the whole.

Wednesday, Oct. 14th.

Our G.C.M. still flourishes. Our cases present a charming variety. Yesterday we tried a fellow for stealing and selling a pair of breeches and today the case was "Desertion" of two years' standing, the verdict "Guilty" and the sentence "Death."

Yesterday afternoon Miss Hersey and Miss Carter and the subscriber had a very pleasant walk of *five* miles to Cape Elizabeth, where we visited the cemetery, &c. We took tea at Mr. Carter's and played euchre[25] all the evening. I am upon the whole having a very nice time. About one hour's duty and then the whole day to myself. Tomorrow we adjourn.

Saturday, Oct. 17th.

Today Lizzie and I went to Baldwin, where we found mother established in housekeeping. We had a very good stage ride from Gorham. Father went up by private conveyance.

Sunday, Oct. 18th.

We have been having a very lazy day. No church or anything of the kind.

Monday, Oct. 19th.

This forenoon I had the longed for pleasure of going on a short gunning tramp, the results of which were one fat partridge and two squirrels. We returned by stage and cars to Portland in the afternoon, where we find everything as we left it.

Tuesday, Oct. 20th.

The Court Martial held a session this morning for the first time since Saturday. We adjourned over to Thursday, so I jumped on to the Kenn[ebbec]. Train and tonight finds me in Brunswick, where I am enjoying myself with Tutor [Edward N.] Packard.[26] It seems very odd to see one of my own classmates elevated to the *high* position of *Tutor,* for which I always entertained so *wholesome* a respect![27]

Wednesday, Oct. 21.

Had a very pleasant ride to Yarmouth and back with Miss [Nancy P.] Swett. We visited the "Philomathean" in the evening, where we saw several old acquaintances.[28] Took tea at Mrs. Allen's.

Thursday, Oct. 22d.

I returned from B. this morning in season to take my seat on Court Martial. There being no case for trial, we adjourned to Saturday. Have been doing nothing all day.

Friday, Oct. 23d.

This afternoon I went up to the Courier office and indulged in writing a *leader* for tomorrow's paper. I held forth upon "New Regiments; How are they to be officered." It will make just a column.[29]

Saturday, Oct. 24th.

We disposed of one case at Court Martial today, and then adjourned, to Monday. Took a ride to Westbrook this afternoon.

Tuesday, Oct. 27th.

I have made application to be sent back to my Regt. Whether it will be granted is very doubtful indeed, though I shall try hard before I despair. I am heartily tired of Home Guard duty, not because I am "spilin" for a fight, but just for the sake of being with my Company once more.

Thursday, Oct. 29th.

I hear nothing very sure about getting away, but I guess that everything is safe. Shall probably get away by the first of next week. The Court Martial will probably continue all winter, as the new Draft will make new cases.

Saturday, Oct. 31st.

Today we have found out that Capt. C.P. Mattocks is ordered back! Good news after three months of loafing in the good state of Maine. I shall try to be off by Monday morning and it will be a long time before I get detailed again for the purpose of getting conscripts "or any other man."

Monday night, Nov. 2d, 1863.
On board Steamer from Fall River to New York.

I am now on my way, rejoicing, and shall soon join my Regt. "Pussey" goes back again as Servant. Lt. [John] Morrill of Co. G accompanies me. We are having a very pleasant trip upon a most excellent steamboat.

Tuesday, Nov. 3, 1863. Washington.

We arrived here this evening after a very pleasant journey from Portland. Lieut. [Putnam S.] Boothby joined us at New York and we now have quite a delegation for the 17th. We are now at the "National," and propose to take our departure as soon as possible tomorrow.

Thursday, Nov. 5th.
Near Warrenton Junction, Va. Camp, 17th Maine Regt.

We reached our Regiment "post varios casus" at 9 o'clock last evening, having taken the cars from Alexandria at 2 o'clock. By some very mysterious plan of Providence I have got cold. I am glad to be back in the "bosom of my family" once more. Today we have had a battalion drill twice. I acted as Lt. Col. in the absence of Capt. Sawyer and owing to Lt. Col. Merrill's being in arrest. Col. West is now fully established and will soon bring things to a head.[30] The Regt. numbers 500 men for duty. When I went away 200 men constituted the fighting strength of the 17th Maine. So much for my Conscripts.

Friday, Nov. 6th.

Today Col West and I visited the 20th Maine, Gen. [Samuel W.] Crawford,[31] the Regulars, and Col. [Joshua Lawrence] Chamberlain,[32] and of course we had a very fine time. I saw [William E.] Donnell,[33] who is now A.A.A.G. for Col. Chamberlain. We saw the Regulars on "Dress Parade, Guard Mounting, &c.," but they did rather poorly for Regulars.

The whole Division is now encamped here (near Warrenton Junction) in line of battle, every Regiment being doubled on the centre so as to deploy at a moment's warning. How soon we shall move is only a matter of conjecture, but we all expect to be off very soon.

P.S. Evening.

We have just received orders to move by daylight in the morning, and some think we are soon to engage the enemy. The Army is in good fighting trim and will give Lee a hard fight, if engaged.[34]

I have about 50 muskets ready for the campaign, and hope to soon get some more men from Hospital.

Sunday (Evening), Nov. 8th.

As we had been ordered we started yesterday morning at daylight. We marched very rapidly about 15 miles to Kelly's Ford on the Rappahannock, where was found a force of the enemy. Our Regiment was assigned to Ward's Brigade with a view to a charge in column with the 3d and 4th Maine. The 20th Ind. was assigned to our Brigade and Col. De. Trobriand led on the 20th and Berdan's Sharpshooters as skirmishers. The advance reached Kelly's Ford at about 1 o'clock in the afternoon of yesterday, and at once charged across the river in a skirmish line, having taken the enemy by surprise. We followed close behind but without any of our help the fearless Sharpshooters had taken a rifle pit on the other side of the stream which they forded, and at the same time bagged about 300 Rebels who were in the rifle pit and the neighboring houses, some of them being found asleep and others playing cards, &c., & so on, little dreaming that we were so close upon them. This was a most brilliant affair. The plan upon the next page will show how the thing was managed. Two companies of Berdan's Sharpshooters were drawn up in an extended line along the bank opposite the Rifle-pit. A Company of Sharpshooters then plunged into the stream right in the face of a rifle-pit filled with Rebels. Now the Rebs thought their time for work had come. They raised their heads above the embankment to pick off the bold Sharpshooters now hardly half a dozen rods from them, and advancing to cross the stream, which was nearly waist deep and running with a strong current. But as soon as a head was raised several muskets, or rather, Sharpe's rifles, were levelled and a Sharpe's rifle in the hands of Berdan's men means death or wounds. This part of the shooting was done by Berdan's two companies which had been drawn up to cover the advance upon the rifle-pit. In this manner the whole rifle-pit full was bagged and what few tried to run away were shot down in the act. The Sharpshooters and the 20th Indiana then dashed on to the house on the right (see diagram) where they found a sleepy reserve who at once surrendered. [*See fig. 7.*]

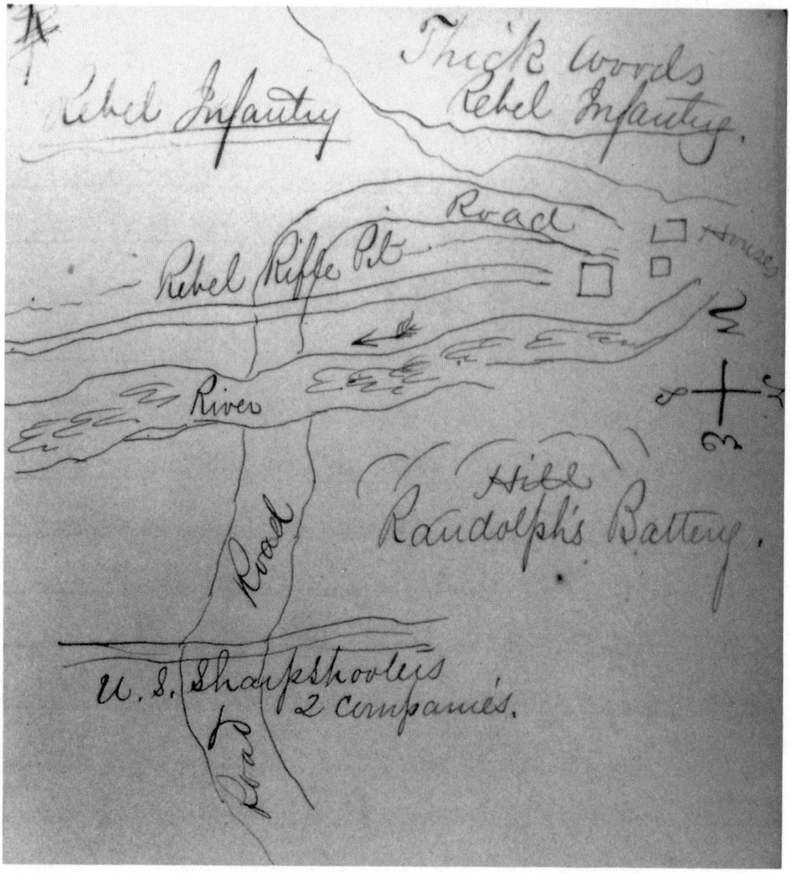

Fig. 7. Kelly's Ford, November 8. [Mattocks's map of the action of the 17th Maine at Kelly's Ford on November 8, 1863. Courtesy of James M. White, Jr.]

300 men were thus captured, belonging to the 2d and 30th North Carolina Regts. At this moment Randolph's Battery[35] opened from a high hill on the right of the road, assisted by a 32 pounder Parrott or two far to the left, but both converging their fire upon the woods directly in front, or rather to the right and front.

We then (Ward's Brigade) at once crossed ready for a charge in column if need be. Our Regt. was halted just to the left of the road after fording the stream, which by the way is very narrow at this point, hardly worthy to be called a river. There was some firing from the front upon our skirmishers and at us at long range, but no

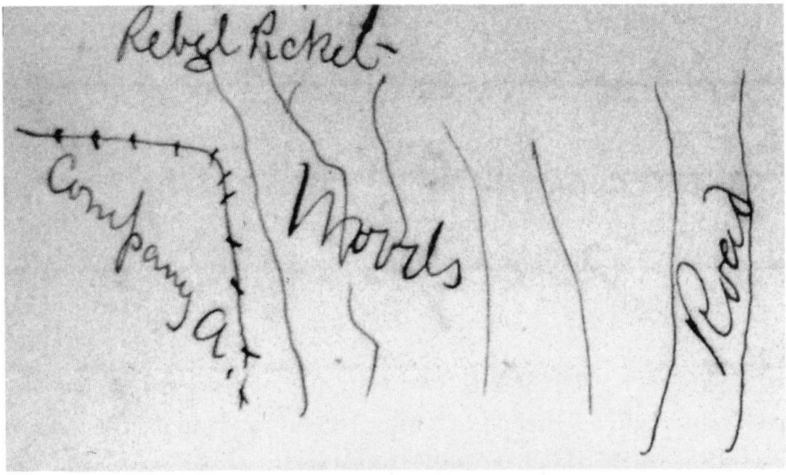

Fig. 8. Picket Duty. [Mattocks's drawing of the disposition of Company A on Picket Duty on November 8, 1863. Courtesy of James M. White, Jr.]

artillery on the enemy's side opened. Some musket balls passed over our heads as we lay down, but no one was hit; one ball struck between the 2d and 3d Division (mine) of our Regt. as we were "doubled on the centre." The Rebs say we took them entirely by surprise. Even their artillery horses were out grazing.

Our Brigade (Ward's) lay in position till about 7 o'clock, when as usual Co. A was detailed to go on picket. We packed up and started with 10 men from Co. H. We were posted in front of the woods with the Rebel pickets not more than 75 yards from us. One post was not more than 50 yards from one of mine.

The nearest post was at the corner of the line, as I have marked. [*See fig. 8.*]

The Rebels had their pickets in considerable force in the woods on our right and front. We could hear them all night. During the night we could distinctly hear them, and at one post far in the distance we saw a column of infantry pass a camp fire. Whether this force passed off or was massed in the woods on our right we did not know. About an hour before daylight I was ordered to throw forward the left of my company onto a line with the woods. The 3d

Maine pickets on my left did the same. We then advanced as skirmishers through the woods about a quarter of a mile to the road I have marked out. It was dark in the woods and we every moment expected to receive a volley after the manner of Chancellorsville in the midnight attack. Old Company A, however, advanced with a splendid line, deployed at skirmish inte[r]vals, and came out to the road safely. We ran on to three or four Rebs who threw down their muskets and got away from us before we knew that they were not our own men.

At about 8 o'clock this A.M. (Sunday) we started for Brandy Station, which we reached this afternoon after remaining for some time in line of battle about three miles back.

We are now in bivouac with the rest of the Corps near Brandy Station. The whole Army convoyed near this point this afternoon, and it was the most splendid sight I ever saw. We saw at one and the same time the colors of Meade,[36] of the Cavalry, of the Reserve Artillery, and of every Corps in the Army. This was all in an open plateau and soon the whole force began to ascend the high ground which we now occupy. This was done in six different columns abreast each other, and was less grand only than the sight of the open plain.[37]

Our Skirmishers have been driving the enemy's ahead of us all day. I had forgotten to say that I joined the Regiment as it passed after we had searched through the woods. There was real suffering among the "Regulars" last night on picket. Our feet and legs were set as sap and we had no fires, but had to lie on our faces and speak in a whisper, no fires, no sleep for any body. Our knapsacks were not even unpacked, and we are all sleepy enough tonight.

Monday, Nov. 9th. Brandy Station.

We are now in bivouac in a piece of woods near Brandy Station, where we have received several calls from acquaintances in the other Maine Regt. Lt. Chas. Hunt of the 5th Battery has just made us a call and took dinner which was poor in the extreme.

The 5th and 6th Maine Infantry distinguished themselves at Rappahannock Station last Saturday. Out of 23 officers engaged

three were killed and 13 wounded. They charged the enemy's earthworks in a skirmish line, which perhaps accounts for their loss in
officers. They went in with about 313 and came out with 178. At
Gettysburg our Regt. went in with 330 and came out with 200. But
our proportion of killed was not so great. We had but 16 killed. The
6th also lost quite heavily at the Second Fredericksburg. These are
the only two fights in which the 6th ever met with much loss. The 5th
Maine took a great many prisoners last Saturday. Col. [Clark S.]
Edwards himself received about 30 swords from the hands of the
Rebel officers.[38]

Tuesday, Nov. 10th.
We moved this morning to an old Rebel Camping ground only
a few rods from our yesterday's halting place. I am now occupying
an old Rebel stockade over which we have spread our shelter tents.
The enemy abandoned this place last Saturday in a great hurry.

Wednesday, Nov. 11th.
I have got the "Regulars" well at work at building stockades
after the Camp Sickles plan. The following is the size of each hut—
all measurements being from the outside.
Plan. [*See fig. 9.*]

Fig. 9. Officers' Quarters. [Mattocks's drawing of the Officers' Quarters.
Courtesy of James M. White, Jr.]

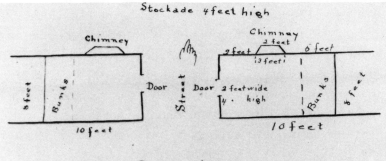

81

In the Rebel hut which we occupy there is a most excellent fireplace, all finished off in fine shape for our use. It had not been used more than one or two days. Our Company streets are about 35 feet wide, and the houses are two feet apart. There are six houses on each side. Col. West is getting up a very fine house.

Thursday, Nov. 12th.

Several days ago I announced a new batch of Non-Commissioned officers. I have had a goodly number of them since I first began. . . .

Friday, Nov. 13th.

This morning I was detailed to go to Warrenton Junction with a detachment of 50 men to escort the Paymaster from that place back to the Regt. We started at 9 o'clock in the morning and arrived at the Junction about 5 in the afternoon after quite a hard march of 16 miles.

Saturday, Nov. 14th.

No signs of the Paymaster until 3 o'clock this afternoon, when he arrived with two (or three rather) friends, clerks & *sich.* We at once started but had not gone far when a tremendous shower came up. We felt our way along to Bealeton Station—5 miles—where we were forced to halt for the night on account of mud and darkness.

Sunday, Nov. 15th.

We arrived in Camp with our Paymaster at 11 o'clock. We started at 7-1/2, thus marching 10 miles & more in 3-1/2 hours, and that too in a rain storm. It cleared off just before we got here. We had a high old time last night. Eight of us slept in one small ambulance. It rained very hard all night, and the men did not get much sleep, I am inclined to think. I am quite sure that I did not sleep a great deal night before last, owing to the porosity of my old blanket and the low temperature of a November night.

We had a good time in the ambulance telling stories. I got pretty well wet before we halted for the night. Maj. McFarland took his new experiences well.

Tuesday, Nov. 17th.

Movements have been brought to a head in regard to organizing a Regimental Brass Band. I am appointed Treasurer of the institution and shall thus have the trouble of a good deal of extra money. I do not at all fancy the job but may as well make the best of it. We are now quite comfortably in camp but expect to be off very soon. Last night quite a number of new commissions had come. Houghton is now Captain of Co. H. He started as orderly Sergeant in this Company. [Edward] Moore, Captain Company C, Thompson, Captain Company K, both started as 2d Lts. Their commissions came among the rest.

Thursday, Nov. 19th.

The prospect of a move at once is good but I can not say when or whither we shall go. Some say we are to occupy Culpepper.

Friday, Nov. 20th.

We had a Brigade Inspection today. Capt. Strait, the Inspector General of our Brigade, told me that I have the best Co. in the Brigade, a remark which he has often made. I suppose some of my neighbors will go into figits as they did when Gen. Ward's order was issued after the battle of Chancellorsville.

Brown and I have been busy at work on the Quarterly Return of Clothing. We are through with the 1st Quarter of this year. Temple is copying the papers.

Sunday, Nov. 22d.

We have had a lazy day of it. The non-arrival of our new Chaplain has prevented any religious service. Lieut. Brown still retains command of Co. E.

Wednesday, Nov. 25th.
We are under orders to be ready to march, but bad weather has delayed operations.

Thursday, Nov. 26th.
Broke camp this morning, and crossed the Rapidan in the afternoon. We are in bivouac near the river now.

Nov. 27th. Friday morning. Same place.
We expect to engage the enemy before long.

Saturday, Nov. 28th.
We engaged the enemy at about 4 o'clock in the afternoon of yesterday in a thick growth of hard wood and pine. We were under fire about an hour, in which the Regt. lost 52 men out of 400. Poor Brown, my 1st Lieut., was killed instantly. The fatal bullet entered on the right side of the mouth and came out just back of his left ear. He was in command of Co. E and fell with his face to the foe. Capt. Sawyer was mortally wounded before the action had fairly begun, and I am now acting Major in his place. He was hit in the bowels.[39] The three right companies, E, B, and A, suffered very heavily from a flank movement on the part of the enemy. The "Regulars" behaved splendidly. The Regiment as a whole did finely. The three right companies lost about 38 men of the whole 52. The loss of Co. A was . . .

Total killed	2
" wounded	<u>9</u>
Loss	11

Some of the men had very narrow escapes. [Corporal Josiah A.] Temple was the first man wounded. While we were engaged, we saw no other Regiment, except the 86th New York, which came to our relief just as we were being outflanked on the right. When we became fully aware of the flanking movement the three right companies were swung around at a right angle with the Regimental line.

Fig. 10. On the Rapidan, November 27, 1863. [Mattocks's drawing of the dire situation of the 17th Maine in the fighting on November 27. Courtesy of James M. White, Jr.]

Plan. [*See fig. 10.*]

This plan shows all we knew of the fight, and shows as well to what a fire the right of the Regt. was exposed. The Rebs used only musketry, while we had the help of Randolph's Battery. They had the brow of a hill & we had a hollow, but still we held the ground, and so it has been ever since the army left Warrenton Junction. We have had nothing but a series of running fights. We have been advancing all day by a mile at a time. Have heard fighting, but have not been engaged. We are now in line of battle opposite the enemy's breast-works, which they have thrown up in a hurry. They are in plain sight, across an open field, through which runs Mine Creek.

This morning I rode back and found Lt. [James M.] Brown's body, and had it buried. I had not even time to see it covered with earth. He is buried in an open field about half a mile from where he fell. I had a piece of smooth board, upon which I cut his name, rank,

&c., together with the square and compass. His sword, belt, watch, and a few other articles are in my possession, but his pocketbook and its contents are not to be found. When we fell back his body could not be carried away, but was taken out by the 4th Maine in the night.

1st Lieut. James M. Brown
Co. A, 17th Maine Regt.

Sergeant Lake was wounded at the very last of the action. [40] He had been doing his duty very bravely. He was by my side nearly all the time. We both fired now and then.

Sunday, Nov. 29th.
We are still in bivouac opposite the enemy. Have just heard of the death of Capt. Sawyer. He died in 24 hours.

Capt. Ellis M. Sawyer
Co. E, 17th Maine Regt.

Lieut. Fred. Sawyer, of Co. E, was slightly wounded in the leg. The Regt. had 7 killed at the time. Capt. Sawyer's is the only death since.

Monday, Nov. 30th.
We expected to have made a charge upon the enemy's works last night or this morning, but I guess it has blown over. We still face each other. Our Regt. has moved a little way out of the woods and is now supporting the 4th Maine Battery. I have taken up my abode at Head Quarters. Lt. Col. Merrill went to the rear *sick* this afternoon. So I am now 2d in command by seniority. We are virtually cut off from all communication with home. Do not expect a mail for a long time.

This Battery opened this morning for a short time, but the Rebs. only got one shell over to us, and that was unexploded. It struck two men, but did not hurt them. I have had a line ready to send home for a number of days, but have no chance. There is a good prospect of short rations soon. We are making *up the bed* in this open field behind the Battery.

Tuesday, Dec. 1st, 1863.

Monday was spent in cooking coffee and looking at the enemy's entrenchments, but at about dark we started upon the only genuine night march we ever had. It was a long time ere we got started, but from 10 o'clock until 7 in the morning we were steady at it. Morning found us across the Rapidan at Culpepper Ford. We made 16 miles, much of the time we had to go in "double quick." Nothing but cold and being sleepy troubled me. I came near getting asleep on my horse.

Wednesday, Dec. 2d. Camp de Trobriand

We are back in camp once more, which we left only a week ago. Capt. Sawyer and Lieut. Brown, poor fellows! are left in the enemy's lines. They were both decently buried. We marched last night again and arrived here at daylight this morning. Three hours' sleep last night is the only chance to close our eyes we have had for two nights and two days.

. . .

Officers,	Killed	2	Wounded	1
Enlisted men,	"	6	"	42
" "	Missing	1		
	Total loss	52.		

December 3d, 1863.

We are getting fixed up in our old camp once more.

Dec. 5th.

So far along, and we are ordered a quarter of a mile away to build up again. Some Regts. of the 1st Brigade have stolen all our tent wood.

Dec. 6th.

I have been recommended by Col. West to the Gov. for the vacant Majority in this Regt. Col. Egan, commanding Brigade,[41] endorses it, and so does Maj. Gen. Birney. Visited the 20th Maine today, where I learned that Col. Chamberlain had gone to Washington sick.[42] [Lieut. Howard L.] Prince was on hand.[43]

Tuesday, Dec. 15th.

I am once more at Regimental Head Quarters. Lt. Col. Merrill started for Maine this morning, where he is to be assigned to the arduous duty of recruiting soldiers for this Army. The order came from the War Depart. I have at last completed and forwarded my Clothing Returns for the month of November.

I am now acting as Major and Capt. Hobson, as Lt. Col. My Co. has the left of the Regt. as I am now second in lineal rank. The Captains are all busy at work making the men stockade the tents after the old model, 8 x 10. Leaves of absence are to be resumed. Capts. Houghton and Moore will go home first. I have had my share of home guard duty and do not *pine* for a leave just now.

The Captains now rank thus

1.	Capt. Hobson,	Company	I.
2.	" Mattocks,	"	A.
3.	" Jno. Perry,	"	D.
4.	" [Benjamin C.] Pennell,	"	B.
5.	" Thompson	"	K.[44]
6.	" Moore,	"	C.
7.	" Houghton,	"	H.
8.	" Green,	"	G. (announced Dec. 19)[45]

Wednesday, Dec. 16th.

Our Sanitary Commission boxes arrived here today. Among them was one that mother sent on the 26th of May. It was all right though so long on the way.

I have just written to poor Brown's brother in Edinburgh. The poor fellow had no relative in this country, and only what few acquaintances he had gained in the course of two or three years. I have felt his sudden death more than any other we have ever had. Living together in the same tent so long, it seemed like losing a part of myself. I could not realize that he was dead until I found the body the next morning. His countenance was as natural as life except where the fatal bullet pierced his face. It is quite probable in view of all the circumstances that he fell a victim to some Rebel Sharpshooter. He was killed just as he was giving some order to his men. But he was always brave, never more so than when he fell. With his inferiors he was never popular until after a long acquaintance. He had no hesitation in picking out *shirks* and making them do their duty, which accounts for his unpopularity. In time, my men learned his true value.

He seemed to have had a realizing sense, if not an actual presentiment, of his danger. In looking over his valise I have found every thing in most excellent order, and far down under everything, so as not to attract attention, was a small package directed to a friend in Me. upon which was written "Not to be opened unless you hear of my death." What was in this very mysterious package I am as yet wholly ignorant. I sent it as directed.

Thursday, Dec. 17th.

We have kept in doors all day to escape the rain and mud. I have sent recommendations for furloughs to the Surgeon in charge of the hospitals where Corpl. Temple[46] and Priv. Goodnow are. Shall try to get all the wounded ones home as soon as possible. I hear that Lake is expected to live. I sincerely hope so, for a braver fellow never lived. Sergt. [Jesse A.] Stone will have to be discharged on account of a trouble in his head, which has already rendered him partially deaf.

We have rumors of a prospective move back across the Rappahannock, but I guess the mud will prevent. Received notice tonight of Priv. John Tucker's discharge. He was pronounced mortally wounded at Chancellorsville. It seems a miracle that he should live.

Friday, Dec. 18th.

I find myself a Court Martial by order of Col. West. I am appointed to try all petty cases that occur in the Regt., and shall have my hands full. Have dispatched three of these victims today. One fellow who skedaddled from a fatigue party plead as an excuse that he should not have run away from work, except that he thought there would not be anything done about it. He finally concluded that such a Defence could not help him much in which opinion the *Court concurred*. This was one of the six who were tried before me on Mackie's Island last October. He does not seem to learn wisdom very fast.

Saturday, Dec. 19th.

Have had up some more victims today before the Court Martial. All of them are skulks, and will get but scanty justice.

The mail has arrived (A.M.) and from a letter from mother I learned that the Portland Press of Tuesday announced my appointment as Major of this Regt. Since writing this I have seen the paper containing a full list as recommended by Col. W. after the battle of the 27th of last month. Sparrow is 1st Lt. of Co. B, and Sergt. [Benjamin] Doe, 2d Lt. of Co. K. All the promotions are *into* new Companies—a grand idea, which will free the promoted Sergeants from the bonds of old intimacies and friendship. I was always in favor of the plan, but now we'll try it.

Tuesday, Dec. 22d.

The commissions have at last arrived, and now I suppose we are all safe for being mustered without further delay. The 2d Lts. I suppose will find some trouble as but 2 Companies, (C & K) have enough men to muster 2d Lts. Doe, 2d Lt. in "K", promoted from Sergt. in "A", will be mustered. He is at home now òn furlough.

The men are busy in building up their huts. My business as Field Officer's Court Martial still continues lively. Col. W. is determined to bring shirks and skedaddlers up with a round turn.[47] The Regimental Band Fund is coming on finely, and we hope to make a *go* of it at last. No leader is yet engaged, but I shall try to get [John Harrison] Woods of the Class of '64 at Bowdoin.[48]

Wednesday, Dec. 23d.
We had a Corps review under Genl. Meade today, which was respectably brief but *cold*. I was mustered today as Major with rank from Dec. 22d.

Dec. 22d, 1863. Major
The Lieutenants will probably be mustered tomorrow. I was mustered by Lieut. [William P. Shreve] Shrieve, 2d U.S.S.S. Asst. Commissary of Musters for this Div.

Friday, Dec. 25th.
"A Merry Christmas" for us all. We had a very nice dinner. The Col. has been away as Officer of the Day, and I held my first "Dress Parade." The Col. returned at dark, quite chilled with the cold.

Sunday, December 27th.
The Col. is placed in arrest by Col. Egan, Comdg. Brigade, for protesting against a guard detail, and for refusing to obey an order as Egan is inclined to think. The order in question was not received. This leaves me in command of the Regiment once more. I think however that the Col. will be released from arrest very soon. Egan has had the Adjt. up to enquire about the matter.

We had a most excellent dinner on turkey and similar luxuries today. It has been raining all day which prevented an inspection or religious services.

Col. W. has recommended Capt. [Isaac S.] Faunce, formerly of Co. D, to take my old Company. The Gov. will probably commission him.[49]

Friday, Jany. 1, 1864.

We have been duly celebrating New Year's with a good dinner of turkey and similar articles. The weather is quite mild, but we have an abundance of mud. I have commenced to build a very nice stockade for my own benefit, having been fairly frozen out of my "A" tent.

We wished to secure $200 for Capt. Sawyer's family for his horse. Finding that it could not be sold for even $150, we concluded the end would perhaps justify the means if we had a lottery. So we got up 20 tickets at $10 each. I took 2 1/2 and one of them drew the prize, saddle, bridle, &c. I then traded with Dr. Hersom for the old Col. Roberts horse, giving $60 *to boot,* which leaves me with a very good and very cheap nag. I have bought a new saddle of the Quartermaster, and am now all right.

Sunday, Jan. 3d.

Capts. Houghton and Moore returned last night. Houghton has been assigned to the Brigade to act as Asst. Insp. Genl. Col. W. is Corps officer of the Day, and I held parade and inspection.

CHAPTER FOUR

In Command

Monday, Jan. 4.
Col. West has been assigned to the command of the Brigade, which leaves me
In command of the Regt.
I entered upon my new duties this morning.

Near Brandy Station, Va.
Jan. 4th, 1864
My dear Mother:
Your letter with the "dummy corner" advice was read with great interest, and I will attempt to heed the warnings.

I have but a moment to spare. Already I find myself sole commandant of the *17th Me.* Col. West has been assigned to the command of the Brigade, which he will probably keep for two or three months, and perhaps longer. So your "young hopeful" has the honor to command one of the *largest* and best Regiments in the Army of the Potomac. I shall continue the *regime* I have always adhered to, and can then tell you whether the management of a company will apply to a Regt. Capt. Houghton has returned and brought your things and my new clothes. He is detached as Asst. Inspector Genl. of Brigade with Col. W. The Brigade is quite small at present, owing to the reenlistment and furloughing of the *veterans*. Everything is going along finely, and I have no fears of the result even if I am a *youngster*.

Now I wish father would come out and see *my* (!) Regt. about this time. Tell him he ought to do so. I hope J. S. [Porter][1] will come. I shall write him a line about the matter. I hardly think I shall be able to comply with your invitation to come home under the present circumstances. *The* commandants can not well leave at present. Col. W. was thinking of going home this winter, but his new position will hardly allow of anything of the kind. I do not seem to get many papers lately, and what of the "Atlantic"?

Business is pressing and I must close. Regards to everybody. Many thanks to "Moses" [Porter][2] for his kind wishes. . . . Red ink is abundant, as well as red tape.

❦

Wednesday, Jan. 6th.

Col. West has a very good prospect of retaining the command of the Brigade for a considerable time. He is fixing up his Head Quarters in fine style, and will no doubt remain in the enjoyment of them some time. I have completed my *office,* but the bed room will require a day or two more. The office is 10 feet by 8, and the *bed room* a wall tent opening from the "Off." I have a most excellent glass door, upon which I propose to paint some fine devices. As yet I have no floor for my sleeping room. Shall have to hew one from logs, as boards are "played out" in this vicinity. I have a very nice table, and book case, &c.[3]

Saturday, Jany. 9th.

The order to move has come at last, and we are off at 7 in the morning. The new camp will be about two miles to the front in a good growth of wood, where we can once more fix up. This will make the third attempt at Winter Quarters, and I hope the last. However, it will be much more convenient to wood, and I think we can get up much better and more healthy quarters, though the Regt. has most excellent houses already. We have to haul all our wood, and of course can not get teams enough to supply 450 men.

Col. W. still remains in command of the Brigade, and will for some weeks probably. I have just received a commission for Capt. Faunce, as Capt., Co. A. Faunce was originally Capt. of Co. D, but resigned about a year ago on account of ill health. He is ordered to the Regt. without delay. I was, I suppose, the means of his getting the place, and I have no doubt of his being successful.

Sunday, Jany. 10th.
We broke camp this morning and are now hard at work on new quarters, which by another Sabbath will be all finished in good shape. I have no doubt that this camp will be second only to "Camp Sickles." I have had my stockade hauled and shall put it up in good shape once more.

Monday, Jany. 11th.
My house is up! We are making excellent progress. Gen. Birney has issued an order calling this camp after the donor of the *mittens* to the Division. It is to be called

Camp Bullock

in honor of Mr. B. of Philadelphia, who has proposed to give a pair of mittens to every man in this Division.

Col. West has established his Head Quarters in a nice Brick house near this camp, occupied by a Mr. Bennett, who is h'an "H'Inglishman." An anti-rail order has been issued, and we are supposed to respect private property.

Camp Bullock. 4 Miles from Brandy Station
Jany. 12th, 1864
My dear Mother:
I received a letter from you with one of Col. Merrill's enclosed. I perceive that you still abide at that miserable hotel. I did hope father would get him a house this winter.
I would beg leave to inform you that I have been commissioned

and mustered as Major, so that the so-called Capt. C.P.M. no longer exists. It seems a little overstrained to use the old title too long.

Col. West remains in command of the Brigade, and I am alone in my glory. Capt. Hobson acts as Lt. Col. and of course shows proper respect to his *superior officers*. Hobson seems to take the thing with remarkable grace and has shown more of the soldier in this thing than ever before. West has his Head Quarters about a quarter of a mile away, where [he] has taken possession of a nice two-storied brick house; very kindly allowing the family to occupy the back rooms. But I had forgotten to tell you that we have moved and are now building our third winter quarters for this season. We are about two miles further to the front, and in a nice growth of hard wood. The Regiment will have some very fine huts—all of a size eight by ten, mud and stone for chimneys, shelter-tents for roofs, and everything in good shape.

As soon as Col. West is relieved from command of the Brigade, he will probably go home on furlough. So you see I shall have the honor to command the 17th for quite a long time. I am one of the kind that never objects to any of these things you know, as it offers a most excellent opportunity for "putting them through." I have a very fine tent, and perhaps you will wonder how I came by a nice door with a large square of glass. It was once the property of a storekeeper of *Culpepper*. Upon the glass I have painted "Commanding Officer 17th Me. Regt." &c. All done in most excellent style by a regular signpainter. We shall have our camp all finished in good shape by the end of the week. Then we shall try to resume drills, where I shall have to try myself at handling a Regt. instead of a company, which of course is more difficult and complex.

I have a large double house all to myself, now that the Senior partner is away, for you must know that the Col. and I were proposing to tent together. You would be surprised to see how familiar we have grown. It is one round of fooling from morning till night. I tented with Col. Merrill a short time, and it was the same there. So you see that by attending to my own business during the quarrel, I have distanced the wire-pullers of both sides, and have no favors to ask of either. I am now more than ever convinced that I took the only sensible and honorable course. I am as I always desire to be in this business, entirely free from obligations to any clique. Having never asked for anything I am at liberty to give when and where I think proper.

This new Capt. of Co. "A" was my recommendation. He was formerly Capt. of Co. D. but resigned a year ago. I used to be a Lieutenant when he was a Capt. high in lineal rank, and now he is glad to come back and take rank below us all. Those who used to be Sergeants when he was a Capt. will now outrank him at Captains. Company "A" was offered to Savage, but he declined on account of ill-health and business. I guess he did not care to try the thing again.

Your sympathies for "poor soldiers" are groundless. We are and have been comfortable all the time. We have just received 10 Recruits (8 arrived & 2 left in New York) from Col. Merrill's lot. The Col. only came to Alexandria. But the mail is off.

Wednesday, Jany. 13th.

This evening, by special invitation, the officers of the Division made Genl. Birney a visit to see Mr. Bullock of Philadelphia, the donor of a pair of mittens to every officer and man of this Division.[4] Col. White[5] of P[ennsylvania]. made the presentation speech, and Genl. Birney responded. Several ladies were present, among them the daughter of Hon. John Minor Botts,[6] who resides near this place. Botts himself was present and (they say) made a strong Union speech.

Our men have nearly all the houses completed, and before the week ends we shall have a splendid camp. The houses are made upon the old plan (8 x 10) with chimney upon the upper side, the houses of each Co. in one line, all facing to the centre, where we have a double street.

Thursday, Jany. 14th.

My house is now finished, and it is certainly the finest little thing I have ever seen. The house itself is 8 feet by 10, and in rear of this, connecting by a door, is a wall tent. I have a floor of hewn plank on both, and a fire-place in the house and small 10 lb. stove in the tent. Everything is decidedly cozy, and our table is well supplied through the exertions of [Cornelius] Boyle and Larrabee,[7] our cooks. We have nicer buckwheat cakes for breakfast every day than I ever ate any where before. The only trial I have in changing from "Line" to "Field" is in giving up "Jonas," my old cook and steward, who has always been close to my heels, everywhere, battlefield not excepted. We already have two cooks at Hd. Qrs., and of course I would not wish to introduce a third.

Capt. Faunce, formerly of Co. "D", has been commissioned Capt. of my old Company upon Col. West's recommendation, made at my suggestion. The Company is fortunate in getting so good a man. He is an excellent drill-master, and will make the "Regulars" come up to the old standard, I trust.

It is to be hoped that we shall not be compelled to build another camp this Winter. This is the fourth time we have established ourselves. John Minor Botts will cease to trouble us, now that we are using another man's wood. He is, no doubt, a patriotic man, but his ardor cools when he fancies his pocket is to be touched. He is paid for all his wood, but I presume he was like the man who received an allowance for a rail-road track cutting up his fields—He "didn't want to sell."[8]

I presume that Col. West will be in command of the Brigade for some time. Col. de Trobriand expects to be made a Brigadier.

Sunday, Jany. 17th.

Today Col. West and Staff inspected the Regiment. Capt. Houghton, A.A.I.G., called for a list of deficiencies in arms and clothing. Adjt. Boothby gave Capt. Thompson a verbal order to furnish to him, the list required. He replied that he should do no business (or "no unnecessary business") on the Sabbath. I then had the Adjutant write him an order in my name to hand in the list before three o'clock, to which he sent a note in reply to the Adjt., stating that "In accordance with orders from the President and the Genl. commanding the Army, he should refuse to do any unnecessary work on the Sabbath." At four o'clock, he not having complied with the order, I at once placed him in arrest, and assigned him the limits of the Regimental camp. I am, of course, sorry to see anyone throw himself away with any such groundless authority. The order which Capt. T. relies upon applies only to the business of Army Head Quarters. I think a great deal of Thompson, but he has disobeyed an order—one, too, from Brigade Headquarters through me, and I shall of course be in duty bound to give him the privilege of a *G.C.M.*

The Inspection today passed off very well, considering the length of time since the last. We have now been in this camp just one week, and have in that time done a great amount of work.

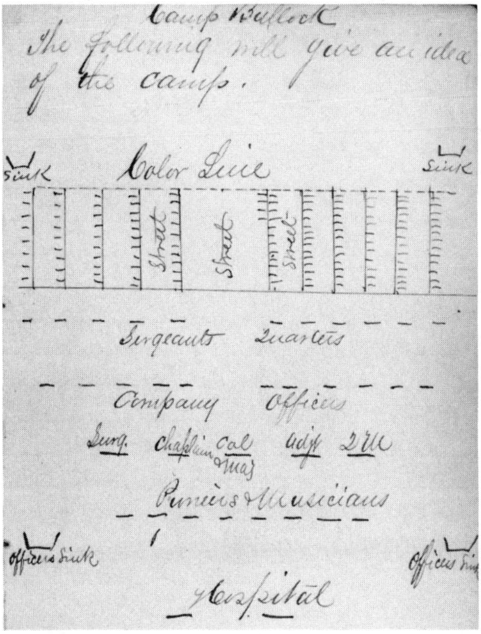

Fig. 11. Camp Bullock. [Mattocks's drawing of Camp Bullock. Courtesy of James M. White, Jr.]

Monday, Jany. 18th.

I have made out strong charges against Thompson, and he will be tried this week, I suppose. The first charge is "Disobedience of Orders," and the second "Conduct prejudicial to good order and military discipline." He had somewhat to say about the authority of a Brigade Commander's ordering an Inspection on the Sabbath. I do not see how he can escape conviction, and if he is convicted he must be of course dismissed the service.

We are still at work on our houses and the Regt. will have a splendid camp in every respect. The line officers have got their houses upon one and the same line for the first time since we began our soldiering.

The following will give you an idea of the camp. [*See fig. 11.*]

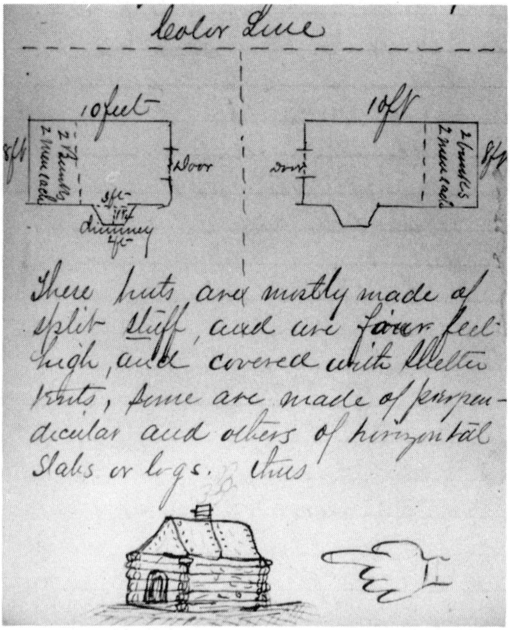

Fig. 12. Camp Quarters. [Mattocks's drawings of the layout of the camp houses and of one log hut. Courtesy of James M. White, Jr.]

By this arrangement the colors can be escorted to the color line from the Colonel's tent through the double street. The streets are 30 paces wide, the houses facing toward the centre. They all are, or will be floored with split lumber. The following will give the idea of a house of the right and left wing respectively. [*See fig. 12.*]

These huts are mostly made of split stuff, and are four feet high, and are covered with shelter tents, some are made of perpendicular and others of horizontal slabs or logs. . . .

Tuesday, Jany. 19th.

Several of our Non-Com'd Officers came near being very summarily reduced today. They were on guard at Brigade Head Quarters last night and all came home, even the one whose post was with his relief then on duty. Sergeant [Aldridge R.] Abbott of Co. B has already been reduced. A Corporal of Co. G. was reduced the other day, or rather today, for neglect of duty the other day. There will be a general cleaning out of inefficient officers and Non-Commissioned Officers.

Lieut. Sawyer of Co. E tendered his resignation the other day, and I endorsed it "Approved, and earnestly recommended for the good of the service." It still came back, disapproved. I have now sent in a request to have him brought before the examining board, and then—off goes his head! He is charged with incompetency, and neglect of duty in providing for his men, as to quarters, &c.

Wednesday, Jany. 20th.

Capt. Thompson was before the Court Martial today, and has obtained a postponement of one day. He is intending to plead temporary insanity. He says he does not know what he did last Sunday! How he will succeed in such a plea I do not know. It is certainly a curious kind of insanity, which will leave a poor man so suddenly, and yet stand him in good *play* on occasion. He will probably have to try a medical examination.

We had the best Dress Parade I ever saw in the Regiment this evening. This afternoon I inspected every Company (but C) in arms and ammunition. Co. C has a funeral, and were excused. We are expecting Captain Faunce every day. Capt. Joseph Perry arrived last evening, after an absence of six months on detached service.

Head Quarters 17th Maine Regt.
Jany. 22d, 1864
My dear Mother:

I have but a few moments amid the many cares of the "supreme command." You made a remark that I always had the luck of getting the work. It is about so. I was no sooner a Lieut. than I had command of a Company. Now I have had command of the Regt. quite a while as a Major. It was only twelve days from the date of my commission as Major to the taking command of the Regt. You may wish to know how unlimited my authority is. Col. West does not meddle at all with me, but trusts everything to my poor judgment. I am having just such a time with the Regt. as I used to with my Company. Non-commissioned officers (which means Sergeants and Privates) get reduced, officers severely reprimanded, and innumerable Privates have to face the horrors of a Court Martial. They are getting polished of[f] in fine shape. Every body, including Inspectors say we have the best camp in the Army. The tents of both men and *officers* are made upon one uniform plan. I take more pleasure in "hazing" these shoulder-straps than in putting poor privates through, who are never so much to be blamed as their immediate officers. I have ordered one Lieutenant before a Board of Examination, and have court-martialed one Capt. who will probably be dismissed the service.

Now you may think all this adverse to personal popularity. It may or may not be. Them who wish to do their duty as a universal rule prefer my system. The Capt. (Thompson) against whom I have preferred charges has been and is now one of my best friends. He refused to furnish a certain list of clothing &c. called for by the Inspector Genl. through me on Sunday, on the ground that he could not be compelled to do unnecessary work on the Sabbath. Strange to say I am getting along finely with officers and men. I have a school twice a week, at which I hear recitations from the Co. commanders. How long the Col. will remain away is uncertain. But the mail is off . . . .

Saturday, Jany. 23d.

Today I was surprised, as well as delighted by the arrival of my classmate, [George G.] Kimball, all the way from Washington.[9] He will remain one or two days, and perhaps longer. Capt. Faunce arrived this evening with Dr. Wescott, who comes back to settle up his affairs.[10]

Sunday, Jany. 24th.

Today, Kimball, Houghton, and I went to the 20th Maine to see Prince, Donnell and others. This morning Genl. Birney inspected the Regts. and Camps of the Brigade, by riding through. The men were drawn up at open order. Tonight he comes out with a report, in which he says that our

Camp is the best in the Division,

and actually orders one Regt. to rebuild, taking the 17th Me. for a pattern. Of course we feel highly gratified at the puff. Our Brigade as a whole stands first as to camps.

Tuesday, Jany. 26th.

Last night we all (or five of us) attended the

3d Corps Ball

at the Head Quarters of the 3d Division. It was a most wretched time, and we were all disgusted.[11] Capt. Hobson left for Maine this morning where he will endeavor to get a good number of recruits. Boothby is assigned to the same duty, and I trust they will both do well. I met Lt. Col. [Thomas W.] Hyde[12] at the Ball and was quite glad to see him. I have never met him before since 1862 at Commencement. He says we have the best camp in the Army, and he has so reported at Army Head Quarters.

Wednesday, Jany. 27th.

Today we have been gladdened by the unexpected appearance of 11 Recruits, all the way from the State of Maine. I have assigned them to Company I. They are armed with the Enfield Rifle Muskets, which we shall soon exchange for "Springfields," I hope. These recruits are all volunteers, and are fine looking men. They are, as a general thing, young, and will make fine soldiers. One of the Recruits assigned to Company A a few days ago died of Small Pox at Division Hospital. He was a genuine Penobscot Indian. I think the other seven will escape without any attack whatever. They, or three of them rather, are still in "quarantine."

Thursday, Jany. 28th.

Today I had my first attempt at battalion drill. In the forenoon I put them through by myself, but in the afternoon Col. West gave us a Brigade drill. 180 of our Regt. are on picket, so that the Companies are very small even after consolidating into but six companies. The Brigade drill was very good, and the Col. has proved it to be true that he who can drill a Regiment well will find no difficulty in handling a Brigade. The Regiments of the Brigade are quite small, but it makes the drill all the more lively. If our Regt. was as large as when it left the State, we should have to make two battalions.

Friday, Jany. 29th.

We have devoted the entire day to policing the camp, in order that we may get once in proper shape, and then devote our attention to drill. It has been a very long time since the Regiment has had a Battalion drill (till yesterday), and both officers and men have got sadly behindhand. However, we hope to be in a better state very soon. Genl. Birney will inspect the camps and troops every week.

Capt. Thompson's case is still unfinished, and bids fair to remain so for a week to come. It is hard to say what will be the result of the trial. I do not see how he can escape conviction.

Wednesday, February 3d.

Our Camp is now in very fine order, and I am, I think, justly proud of the Regiment as a whole. I have four lessons a week in the 2d vol. of "Casey," two for Captains and two for Lieutenants. They seem to be very well interested, and I think the study will be productive of great good to all concerned. Regimental Commanders will have to recite to the Brigade Commander hereafter in compliance with an order from Genl. Birney, in which he complains of the gross ignorance of guard duty manifested by officers and enlisted men of this Division.[13]

I saw Col. Hyde this afternoon at Brigade Head Quarters. They all went to Gen. Birney's party last evening.

Head Quarters 17th Maine Regt.
Near Brandy Station, Va.
February 14, 1864
My dear Mother:

As you perceive, I have been a wretched correspondent of late. The fact is I have work for nearly all my time, not that I have to do so much, but while I am in command of the Regt. I am determined it shall not deteriorate, and I am even enough presumptuous to think I can see a slight improvement daily. They are all *"Regulars"* now you know. Houghton is still on the Staff and Col. West has started for home on a leave of absence of 15 days. He has promised to call upon you, and I hope he will not fail to do so.

I find some of your letters are not fully answered. One of Jany. 11th describes your expedition to Baldwin, when you got snow bound. Fernald's[14] pants do very well. I do not need a nice overcoat out here. My new clothes fit fairly, but are all too large although I am as fat as a pig. I have a gymnasium and exercise daily. I am putting the Regt. through on drill in fine style, and the way things have to take up is a caution. You ask if my new dignity renders me impervious to bullets. "I couldn't state."

Yours of Febry. 3d is quite long and interesting. Am sorry that Adjt. Boothby did not call. You speak of a report that Lt. Brown was shot by one of his own men.[15] I never heard of such a rumor before, and do not believe anything of the kind. I wish you would get Albert to find out from whom George Rounds heard this story. We have heard nothing of the 3d Corps being ordered to Tennes[s]ee.[16] I received the Express box in due season, and it was a very acceptable one. The preserves are delicious. Hope you will not send anything by the San[itary]. Comm[ission]. as it is too slow. My expenses are a little more than when I *footed it.* One of our Captains is acting as Field Officer but I am on a steady pull all the time. I do not dislike it.

Will you please send my photograph album (cartes de visite') by Col. W. I know it seems too good to have here, but then I guess I shall not hurt it much. I have heard nothing from Lizzie or Sarah, though I wrote long if not interesting epistles to both about a month ago. I hear from Savage occasionally, & he seems as patriotic as ever, although his health will prevent him from taking a very active part in military affairs.

Give my love to *everybody.* Sergt. Emery is doing finely, and will soon be promoted I think. Temple is still in hospital at Alexandria. Write soon. Tell father that I hope he will make money enough to buy a house. Even I have a house of *my own,* though it is made of split logs, and covered with cotton cloth. Tell Lizzie and Sarah that I am convinced they have forgotten the soldiers.

❧❧

Friday, February 19th.

I have issued an order for a written examination of the Sergeants of this Regt., on the 1st of March. The five best in the examination will be recommended for 2d Lieutenancies. I shall get up 100 questions and a few will be examples in spelling. All the rest are to be simple military questions, such as every Sergeant ought to be able to answer. The Board to conduct the examination is

> Capt. Faunce, Co. "A".
> Lieut. [George A.] Whidden, Co. "I".
> " Verrill, Co. "C".

This Board will decide the excellence in examination, and forward the whole to me to be reviewed. The Sergeants are quite hard at work, and will improve the next fifteen days. The Line Officers' School continues in full vigor, and is productive of great good. Sergeants have the usual recitations to their Capts.

Monday, February 22d.
We have had a great time this afternoon and evening. Mrs. George H. Wilson and daughter (Annie) from Portland have been here all the afternoon and evening. They now live in Washington at Armory Square Hospital, and are on a visit to the Army.

Head Quarters 17 Me. Regt
Brandy Va Feby 27 1864
My dear Mother:
    I write to tell you that we are off on a five days' expedition in the morning at daylight. The probability is that we shall cross the Rapidan, and perhaps—there is no telling what. Love to all. Col. W. writes that he saw you in P. How did you like him?

March 6th, 1864.
I have rec'd a leave of absence, for 15 days, and am off this day for the State of Maine, where I propose to have a fine time.

March 21, 1864. (Monday).
I have just returned to the Regt. from my leave of absence of 15

days, in which time I have enjoyed myself very well. I was in Portland eight days, and found but little time to devote to writing in my Diary. I shall now resume my seat on the Court Martial.

Head Quarters 17th Me. Regt.
Brandy Va. March 22d 1864
My dear Mother:

I send by Mr. Larrabee, our cook, a bundle or two. The writing-desk and lamp belong to Col. Roberts. Please send them to him at Congress Place on Congress St. The undershirt you will please lay aside for me. *Ditto* the sword, which by the way is the one that one of my men picked up on the bayonet charge at Chancellorsville.

I got here all right yesterday, and am once more settled to my business. The Col. said he had been lonesome during my illustrious absence. I was exceedingly sorry that Lizzie was not at hand when I came away. Tell her that I shall soon answer her letter, which I find at my elbow.

Wednesday, March 23d.

I have resumed my seat on the Court Martial, and we are busy on the cases. We have just tried a Corpl. upon the charge of engaging in a sort of mob against a guard. The graceless scamp pleads guilty, and will offer nothing in mitigation of the offence. He displays a most unlimited amount of "cheek," but a good sentence will bring him to his senses.

17th Maine Regt. Brandy, Va.
Mar. 25th, 1864
My dear Mother:

Please send that military overcoat at once to Mrs. Jos. A. Perry, No. 104 (Rear) Brackett Street. Tell father the notes were three in number—one of Sept. 4, '63 for $300. One of Nov. 2d, 1864 for $200 & one of Nov 2d 1864 for 264, in all $764. I enclose a receipt for the notes which you may give him if he will give a new note embracing the interest and all as in the receipt. Please [have] three new notes made, thus—one for $300, one for $200 & one of $274—all to date Jany 1, 1864. I had almost forgotten the $100 father paid Col. West. So one of the notes can be $174. But father must give up my order for the $100 and the receipt sent by Col. W. This will make the thing all safe I believe. Have it attended to at once. I sent home a small package the other day by one of our men, a part of which is for Col. Roberts.

I am in a great hurry. They have broken up our corps. Hereafter our Division will be known as *"Birney's."* Remember 17 Me.— Brig. Birney's Div. 2d Corps. We are feel[in]g quite sorry. But they say it is only a temporary affair.

***

Sunday, March 27th. 1st U.S.S.S.

This morning much to my surprise as well as disgust, I received the following document.

Head Qrs. Birney's Div. 2d Corps.
March 26th, 1864.
Special Orders
No. 77
(Extract)

Major Chas. P. Mattocks, 17th Me. Vols, is hereby assigned to the command of the 1st U.S. Sharp Shooters during the absence of its Field Officers.

He will assume command at once.

By command of Maj. Genl. Birney.
(sd.) F[itzhugh]. Birney
Maj. & A.A. Genl.

Now here is a job. This Regt. (S.S.) has been severely censured by Inspectors and it is expected that "little I" will make a radical change. How I shall succeed remains to be seen, but one thing is sure, I shall not be easily discouraged. It will be anything but palatable to them to be commanded by an outsider. The Regt. has been in service two years and a half, while I first put on the "blue" about 21 months ago.

The Col. (Berdan) is out of the service, the Lt. Col.[17] was killed last November, and the Major is now Judge Adv. Genl. of the Army.[18] The War Dept. has refused to commission, or rather to muster, any more Field Officers. So the prospect of my remaining some time is good. I have been over this evening, and issued my order assuming command, though Capt. [Frank E.] Marble (late commanding) held the parade. He seems to take it as well as could be expected.[19]

❧❧

Head Quarters 17th Me. Regt.
Brandy, Va. March 27th, 1864
My dear Mother:

My honors as well as labors accumulate. I have this day been assigned by Maj. Genl. Birney to the command of the 1st Regt. U.S. Sharp-Shooters, known as Berdan's Sharpshooters. I was not a little surprised, and not less disgusted at first at the idea of leaving the 17th. The Sharp-Shooters are in a low state of discipline, having no Field officers present, and but one any way. He is a Major, and now on duty in Washington, and will not return. There is no prospect of their having any Field officers at present. I shall be lucky if I get away from them in a month or three months. I suppose it must be looked upon as a "big thing," but from choice I should have remained with the 17th. I move to-morrow. They are in the same Brigade, so that I can see the *folks* often. I shall have a job, as I am expected to put the "scallywags" in good order—"like the 17th Maine."[20] It has been my fortune to have work. I was no sooner a 1st Lt. than my Capt. was sick—no sooner a Major than the Col. was detached, and now when we are both back I am detached myself. I shall of course put them through to the fullest extent.

Your knowledge of military matters perhaps does not tell you that the Sharp Shooters have a very peculiar duty in action. They are the skirmishers, go ahead and "kick up the muss" as they say. In fact it is almost a new branch of service. This Regt. has been in service ever since the early part of the war, and the men come from all parts of the loyal North. I have visited their camp to-day, and received as welcome a reception as could be expected. Of course the officers do not very much like the idea of having an outsider put in to command them. But then they are soldiers enough to submit with good grace. They have been commanded by a Captain who will now become my *Lt. Col.*, so to speak!

So you see I am established with an undisciplined and poorly drilled command of 300 men, and am expected to bring order out of *chaos*. Do not think these men are *roughs*. The rank and file have no superiors in regard to character and intelligence. They have run down of late and need a little seeing to. I presume Col. West will seize upon the occasion to get Col. Merrill ordered back. I do not think he will succeed.[21]

Your letter of March 20th is before me, and I think I see in it a better state of feeling about my being in the army than ever before. I wish the war would end to-morrow but until it does end I suppose I shall remain in the service, provided I am as fortunate in life and limb as heretofore. My new position neither increases nor diminishes the danger in action as I am aware. The Lt. Col. commanding the Sharp Shooters was killed in the last action.

You speak of my visit. It was to me very agreeable, although quite brief. I hope you enjoyed the trip to Boston. I am sure I did, though I regretted that Lizzie was not to be found when I left. Tell her I am planning a long and elaborate epistle for her when I get established in *my* regiment.

I hope Mr. Weston's Northern Monthly will prove a little more interesting as the new numbers come out—otherwise I pity the contributors as well as the subscribers. It seems that Neal Dow had a *big* reception.[22] I suppose father did have a great time over him. Ask him if he remembers the time he presented me as an aspirant to Neal's favorable consideration. I am glad I did not enter the army until the last lesson of the Brunswick course was recited.[23]

Your long letter written just before I started from camp has I think been carried home. So I have to answer it from memory, but I can, I think, remember nearly all you said in it, for it contained a goodly amount of good advice, which I never forget if I do not always follow. Your solicitous questions in regard to how I feel in the matter of personal religion are perhaps too hard to be answered. I can say honestly that the war has made me no worse morally than I was when I entered it. In fact I trust I am firmer in my opinions. I, of course, do not deny any of your statements in regard to the great benefits of religion, but I do not feel the *desire* perhaps which one must before meeting with a change. I try to do my duty in my present capacity, and live a life I shall not have to look back upon with remorse. You see, I am in a sort of lifeless condition anyway, as I have been for a long time. I can give you no clearer idea of how I stand. It is not your fault that I am no better than I am, I can assure you.

Tell father not to *swell* too much upon any new position, for I may not keep it long. By this new arrangement our Brigade are very large. In ours we have 11 Regiments. Each of the two brigades of our Divisions has a Regiment of sharp-Shooters, who are really the principal skirmishers for the Brig. My new status is "1st United States Sharp Shooters, 2d Brigade, 3d Division, 2d Corps." Hereafter you will direct my letters to me at 1st U.S. Sharp Shooters. Let the very next one come to the 17th.

Monday, March 28th.

This forenoon we had a Brig. drill under Maj. Genl. Birney. I took out the invincible Sharp Shooters for the first time. We did fairly. They are clothed in every shape (some of them), and present anything but a martial appearance. By *stupendous* and untiring efforts I propose to soon get them to *look* better.

I have forgotten to note that the 3d Corps has been broken up. Our 3d Division goes to the 6th Corps. The 1st (ours) and 2d Divisions to the 2d Corps. We are now the 3d Division of the 2d Corps. The 3 Brigades of our Division are consolidated into two. The 1st Brig. is broken up, and its Regts. distributed in the other two. We are now called the 2d Brig. The old 2d (Ward's) has become the 1st. Brig. Genl. Alexander Hays is assigned to our Brig. We have 10 Regts, the 4th Maine among the rest. The 2d Sharp Shooters remains in the (now) 1st Brig. under Genl. Ward. This (1st) Regt. numbers less than 300 effective men, but the 2d is quite large. Only 40 of this have re-enlisted, while a great number of the 2d have.

Tuesday, March 29th.

This morning on a very short notice we started for a Review of the Corps, under Genl. [Ulysses] Grant,[24] but the rain sent us all back to our camps.

Things are going smoothly, I think. The officers are much more cordial than I could have expected. I tent with Capt. Marble, the Senior Capt., Acting Field Officer. He has been in command of the Regt. more or less all winter, and although he feels a little sore to have me sent here, yet we get along very well. Major [Edward T.] Rowell, of the 2d Sharp Shooters, was here this evening. He and *our* Quarter Master are graduates of Dartmouth in the class of '61.

Head Quarters 1st U.S. Sharp Shooters
Near Culpepper, Va. Apr. 7, 1864
My dear Mother:

As you percieve [perceive], I am still with my Sharp Shooters. Things are going along much more pleasantly than I ever expected. I have already made several radical changes in their manner of doing business, and think I have reason to congratulate myself upon

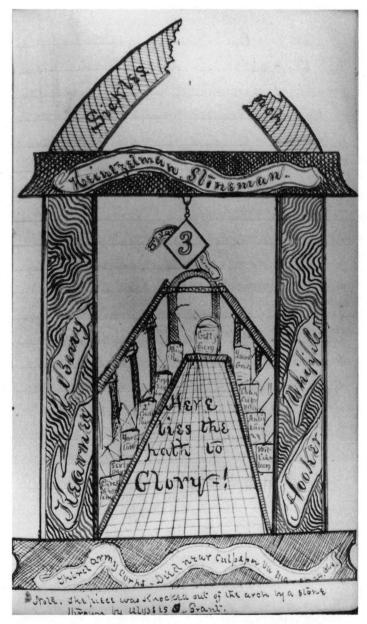

Fig. 13. The Tomb. [Mattocks's drawing of a tomb for the defunct Third Corps. Mattocks's note refers to the breakup of the 3rd Corps and the reassignment of its divisions to other corps. Mattocks apparently believed the reorganization was ordered by General Grant. Courtesy of James M. White, Jr.]

any success thus far. These fellows have been used in a most wretched manner, having been commanded by everybody. Their Field officers have quarreled among themselves and with the Line continually. Courts martial, arrests, protests, and insubordination have been always on the program. But I am, *as usual,* modest but self-confident at once, and have not the least fear of unfavorable results. You need not be surprised if, now and then, one of the officers of this same celebrated Sharp Shooter Regt gets court-martialed, &c.

We have just heard that Lt. Col. M[errill]. is ordered to his Regt., and we are expecting him to-day. Col. West feels as well as if our army had obtained a famous victory. He has been figuring for Merrill's return, in hopes that he may then compel him to resign. I suppose Merrill will get some new detached service, so as to get out of Col. W's clutches. It is upon the whole a rich quarrel, and tends to sharpen the wits of each of the combatants.

The 17th is in splendid condition, and has attracted a great deal of attention during the winter. We have recently changed our camps. The entire Division had to exchange camps with another Division owing to this consolidation of Corps. We have had a few days of very rainy and disagreeable weather, but the sun has at last made his appearance and we are having a very nice time.

I have instituted thorough and systematic schools of officers and non-commissioned officers. I am a self appointed Pedagogue of the officers, and the way I put them over the road is a caution to delinquents. There is much that is ludicrous in military as well as other affairs. For instance, these officers have been in service nearly a year longer than I. I am younger than the youngest 2d Lieut. The Captain, whom I relieved as commandant, was a captain before I was even a 1st Lieut. Yet by immense assurance I manage to wade through with it all. Then again these fellows are popularly supposed to be proficient in the skirmish drill. There too I have to make them believe I know more than all of them. Such things can be successfully done by studying our text-books, which by the way I do incessantly.

We are all in excitement to see what Col. Merrill will do upon his arrival. The Col. will be sorry he got him back unless it results in his resignation.

I have no time to write any more just at present. . . . P.S. The box of leather has arrived. The syrup is not *extra*.

Saturday, April 9th, 1864.

I am still laboring with my Sharp Shooters, and am doing as well as could be expected under the circumstances, as the saying is. Have got them into the *idea* of scouring brasses and rolling overcoats for inspection. Capt. Marble, their former commander, is going to New York on recruiting service. Although it must have been disagreeable to him to have an outsider assigned to duty over him, our relations thus far have been very pleasant. He is too old a soldier to kick in the harness under any circumstances. Lt. Col. Merrill of the 17th is ordered back after four months of recruiting service in Portland. Col. West feels very much pleased to have him back as he hopes soon to get rid of him. Their relations are anything but friendly. It has been said that Merrill has used his influence to prevent men from enlisting for the 17th. Adjt. Boothby professes to be able to substantiate these charges. How the whole thing will end is yet to be seen. The Col. thinks that Merrill will resign in Washington, but it seems more probable to me that he will manage to become a shining light in some General Court Martial.

Gen. Hays has been assigned to the command of our new Brig. as our old one is consolidated.

Head Quarters 1st U.S. Sharp Shooters
Near Culpepper, Va. Apr. 12th 1864
My dear Mother:

Your letter of March 26th has not yet been answered, and that of Apr. 6th has thus far shared a similar fate. This rainy weather is favorable for letter writing, and I propose to give you the benefit of an hour or two.

As you perceive I am still in my tyranny over these unfortunate and ill disciplined Sharp Shooters. I have now got a position where a small amount of change or improvement will show even to the least critical of military men. As is usual in such cases the Captain, whose nose was put out of joint by my assignment, is to be sent on recruiting service. He has used me very gentlemanly indeed although it was a hard case for him, as he had been for a long time in command of the Regt. and was a Captain before I entered the service. Promotions cut up strange freaks at times. I suppose Capt. Hobson will be back soon. I hear he has not tried to get us any recruits. If he is not very careful, he will get punished again, to say nothing of that Lieut. Colonelcy which he once considered "Hobson's choice." Lieut. Col. Merrill has not arrived yet, and Col. W. is on tip toe, thinking he is in Washington pushing his resignation. The Col. thinks he will soon be rid of him but I fear he may find that "The best laid schemes of men and mice" &c. However he will continue to harass the poor unfortunate to the bitter end.

You are perhaps not aware of the responsibility of my present position. The Sharp Shooters always go ahead in a fight and kick up a muss. Though they are a lawless set in camp, yet in action they are highly prized by the Infantry, for whom they "cast up the highway and gather up the stones." Then again the Generals look to the skirmishers to give them information of the position, number and movements of the enemy. Now the most of the Regiments are of course commanded by Colonels or Lt. Colonels. This is the only Regt. in this Brig. (10 Regts.) commanded by so low and so humble an institution as a Major. Then again I must be by far the youngest Field officer in the Brigade. So, take the thing as a whole, I think I can not accuse myself of modesty in thus putting these fellows through.

The 17th is really in splendid condition this winter, and are daily attracting the favorable attention of everybody, although there is not a little jealousy toward "The Regulars," as they are now sometimes called. It will, I fear, be some time before the Sharp Shooters can be properly called "Regulars," but they have got to come to it, and that too in the course of a month. I fancy I am beginning to get the seedy look off, although it was at first seemingly a hopeless task, and so considered by many, but you know I do not stop for slight obstacles. The responsibility of the arms of this Regt. is no small affair. These rifles cost $42, and it would not be prudent to make a mistake in my accounts or to lose one, as I could not pick up another on the road, as they sometimes do in the *common* Infantry, as *we* say.[25]

I have scribbled all this—enough for any reasonable person's letter, without saying one word in regard to your two letters. I suppose Albert will be in California before I return again. Has Erastus [Rowe][26] concluded to remain in P. this summer, or does he propose to branch out once more? Tell him I shall be ready for the maple syrup at any time, although I hope for his sake that the Paymaster will arrive before the syrup does. We are all dead broke, but as our business is always on the credit system, things go along very well. Capt. Houghton is now on the staff of the 1st Brigade. Ours is the 2d. He will probably remain on some staff during his term of service. These officers who once get away from their Regiments are apt to remain away. I am half afraid the same remark may yet apply to myself. However if I never get in a position any less suited to any peculiar fancy than the present I shall have no reason to complain.

I have not yet received the April number of the new Maine magazine, which you say Mr. Weston has done me the kindness to send. Gov. Cony has not yet made his appearance, as far as I have ascertained, but we are looking for him every day. I am glad your landlord has advanced the price of board, if it will only open father's eyes in regard to the comforts of house keeping. I do hope I shall have a home to spend my next week in Maine at; if I am fortunate enough to get to Maine once more. We hear the usual Spring braggadocio about going to Richmond. Every new commander is going to do up the business in a hurry. I only hope they will give Grant the men to do the business with. I am very well satisfied with your allowance of newspapers. I think I shall re-open a correspondence with "Mrs. Aug. Ray." Tell Itie[27] that if he comes out and wins twenty two *fights*, he may be Lt. Gen., as Grant is now. That's the only sound military course for him to take. Tell Erastus if he will come out now, he can soon have a chance to see the Elephant, for I presume we shall stir him up in the course of a month. Meanwhile I shall be very busy drilling any skirmishers. I shall of course feel not a little proud to have such a command in case "we are called upon to meet the enemy once more," as they used to say in the fighting orders.

I find some congenial spirits here. There is one graduate of Dartmouth, and an other who was a short time in Yale. The latter is the Adjutant, who has just returned from a leave of absence. You know that an adjutant is the right hand man to *us Colonels*(!) We are just inscribing the battles on *our* flag. The Regt. runs up 25 engagements, while the 17th can only squeeze out nine at the best. So you see what veterans I have the honor to command. They were at Williamsburg, Fair Oaks, 7 Days before Richmond, Yorktown, 2d Bull Run, Antietam, Fredericksburg, Chancellorsville, Gettysburg, and last Fall's series of *affairs,* besides a great many smaller fights. I had forgotten to mention Malvern Hill. We have companies from Vermont, New York, Michigan & Wisconsin. There is one Vermonter here by the illustrious name of [Henry] Mattocks,[28] from Rutland. Were any of our family from that place? Be sure to answer this very important question, as I wish to know more of such matters. Have you heard any new developments in Col. Merrill's case? Many of our officers think he will resign at once. Yet he may push through and try to outlive everything. The quarrel between West and him is interesting, and, at times, very amusing. It is a constant war of wits. Who will conquer, remains to be seen. I am still on good terms with both *horns of the dilemma.*

To-morrow we shall have a review under General [Winfield Scott]

Hancock,[29] our new Corps commander. We feel keenly the breaking up of the old Third Corps. It seems but a poor recognition of our services as a corps. But we might as well undergo the trial as any other Corps. I presume, however, that it is all for the good of the country. I am one who never gets demoralized (to use a much abused term) although I am not so hopeful of speedy success as some.

April 15th 1864

By the pressure of business my very interesting reflections have been suspended and your letter has been waiting with commendable patience.

We now have Brigade Dress Parades every night. Last night *my* Adjutant [Roswell Weston] had the misfortune to be gloriously drunk, and fell off his horse in the presence of the whole Regt. This morning, which is the first time since that he has been in a condition to comprehend speech or writing, I put him in arrest. I have preferred charges against him, and he will be at once court martialed and perhaps dismissed. This is the first case of drunkenness among the officers since I have been here and I am bound to make an example of the poor fellow. I wish the lot had fallen upon some other officer, for this young man is of excellent family, well educated, and a most excellent Adjutant, but he will steam it. I am death on a man who will get drunk on duty. They may be drunk in battle. I have seen such cases.

Col. Merrill has not yet arrived. It puzzles us to know where he can be. I presume he will soon once more astonish us with some great work of strategy. The 17th has now a very fine Brass Band, and they are all feeling large enough. Quite a number of soldiers are going into the Navy. You know a recent [regulation] allows it, if they pass the required examination. I have received that most delicious can of strawberries, chocolate &c. I found no note in the box as it was broken open when it arrived. The thing got split by some sad accident, but the can of preserves was all right.

Write soon. Hope father will at once fix up that note business.

❧❦

Thursday, April 14th.

The Adjutant of the Regt., Roswell Weston, has returned from a leave of absence, and tonight at Brigade Dress Parade was slightly overcome by what appeared to be a too great indulgence in whiskey. He not only neglected to properly form the Regt., and equalize the Companies preparatory to Dress Parade, but after we had started, and I had by chance discovered that we had 10 Companies of various sizes, while we ought to have 8 of equal sizes, the poor fellow was unable to remedy the matter. So I did it myself. He succeeded in going through the reporting to the Asst. Adjt. Genl., but when we were on the way back he actually fell off his horse and had to be helped to remount. He succeeded to ride the camp with his feet dangling out of the stirrups. He was of course an object of ridicule as well as contempt to every man in the Regt. He is now apparently in a state of beastly insensibility, and can not attend to the duties of the Adjutant's office. My course is plain. I shall have to let the law take its own course, although I exceedingly regret the necessity I am thus placed under. This poor fellow is a young man of fine education and abilities, and is a loss, or will be rather, socially as well as in a military point of view. He is thoroughly acquainted with the duties of the Adjutant's office, and is almost a cyclopaedia of General Orders, and things of that kind. I suppose his brother officers as well as brother drinkers will be his zealous apologists, but it will all be of no avail. There is not influence enough in this Army to prevail upon me in this case.

Friday, April 15th.

The deed is done! I have made out sweeping charges and specifications against the Adjt., and furnished him a copy. The other copy will go forward to Brigade Head Quarters in the morning. I put the Adjutant in arrest this morning, and assigned him the limits of the Regimental Camp.

This evening in less than half an hour after sending the Adjt. a copy of the charges, I received the following communication: — (Verbatim)

> Camp 1st U.S.S.S.
> April 15th, 1864.
> Major:-
> We, the undersigned, having learned this Evening of the Charges & Specifications preferred against 1st Lieut. R. Weston, Adjt. of the Regt., having long known and been associated with him, and appreciate his feelings as an officer, would most earnestly ask that said charges and Specifications be withdrawn, and Lieut. R. Weston restored to duty, provided that he will give his assurance to the Major not to commit himself again.
>
> (sd)
>
> Captain R[udolph]. Aschman
> Lieut. Theo. Wilson
> 1st Lt. Jean Louis Rilliet
> 1st Lt. H[enry]. E. Kinsman
> Lieut. E[liakim]. R. Blakeslee
> Capt. W[illiam]. G. Andrews
> Lieut. E[dwin] A. Wilson
> M[ichael]. McGeough, 2d Lt. Co. H.
> Lieut. C[harles]. W. Thorp
> Captain G[ardner]. B. Clark
> Lieut. Isaac Davis

This paper is of no particular value to me except that there is a half sheet of it without writing on it. This I can use to write a pass or order on when my own supply of stationery fails! No great loss without some small gain! I shall *probably* forward the charges in the morning.

Saturday, April 16th.

Glorious news today. The Paymaster has been visiting the 17th. Of course I happened around and was

Paid off to March 1.

much to my gratification as I could find but thirty-five cents in my pocketbook. The two months' pay amounts to $295.

I forwarded the charges against the Adjutant this morning, although I "slept on" the strong request, &c, of the officers. If I had decided to put the matter to vote, I would have sent a circular to them. They will soon get used to my way of doing up business. Last night, at the school, I informed a Lieut., who had not got his lesson, that Genl. Birney's order would be carried out, and any officer unwilling to learn would be sent before the Board of Examination, where he would have an opportunity to demonstrate if there was or was not any necessity of studying a *mere text book.* I also very politely whipped all the officers over this fellow's shoulders.

I have schools of officers three times a week and Lieut. Rilliet, Act. Adjt., has the Sergeants over the coals as many times also. I fancy I can already see a great improvement in my lawless command. I am bound to improve "especially the appearance of evil" in these fellows, and I think that by the time the appearance of evil is destroyed, the evil itself will be *"non est."* To the privates I say not a word, but I am *hazing* the officers most unmercifully, and of course, but very few of them fancy the operation. There are a few who see and approve the drift of all this. I don't care a fig (so long as I accomplish the end for which I am striving) viz: to make a good and well disciplined Regt. out of a mob of three hundred men. It is one of the easiest things in the world, if a man only is *lavish* of the immense power which is by the military code granted to a Regimental commander.

In reply to the communication which I have copied under date of April 15th I sent back the following very ungracious endorsement.

Head Qrs. 1st U.S. Sharp Shooters
April 16th, 1864.
Respectfully returned. The within request can not be granted consistently with military discipline. The request, though perhaps prompted by good motives, is certainly very unmilitary in all its bearings. It is to be hoped that, for the good of the service, no company commander would exercise the same leniency toward his First Sergeant, that he recommends the Regimental Commander to use toward his Adjutant.

No one more than the Major commanding regrets the necessity of this case, but there seems to be but one course to take.

Hereafter similar petitions, requests, remonstrances and advice, when unsolicited, will not be taken notice of.

> I am, Gentlemen
> Your Obedient Servant,
> Charles P. Mattocks
> Maj. Comm'd'g 1st U.S.S.S.

This endorsement will perhaps be not a little distasteful to the poor fellows who so far forgot themselves as to sign the petition. If there is any one thing I detest in military matters, it is a town-meeting system of managing affairs. I think I have killed it here for the present.

Tuesday, April 19th.
This forenoon we were inspected by Capt. [John A.] Darling the new Brigade Inspector, who found less fault with us than could have been expected. The inspection was quite thorough. Yesterday we were inspected by Lieut. MacMichael [William McMichael] of Genl. Birney's Staff. I suppose we shall get a "raking down," but then it will not be so severe as formerly. I will at last get form and comliness [comeliness] out of the crowd, but it all takes time. It is worse than any of the "Twelve Labors of Hercules." This morning we had a sort of review drill under General Birney, preparatory to the long expected review of the Corps under Lt. Gen. Grant.

One of our men fired a rifle in camp tonight as Genl. Hays was riding past. The Genl. saw it and rushed for him. The man darted in among the tents of Co. B, whereupon the Genl. waxed wroth, and told me to hold the company commander responsible. I have done so, and Lieut. Wilson has found out that the piece was fired by a man of Co. C, Capt. Clark.

The Adjutant and myself are having a very extensive correspondence upon military Law. He demands a list of the witnesses I am to summon against him. His counsel, upon hearing that I refuse to give the list, tries to *wool* me by saying that I am obliged to furnish the list, or rather, that, if I refuse, the Judge Advocate can be compelled to furnish a true copy of the list. Upon this I refer his learned counsel to De Hart and Benet upon this point.[30] I have also instructed the Judge Advocate not to furnish the list, as I have not notified the witnesses and do not wish to have things "cut and dried."

Wednesday, April 20th.

This afternoon we had a very good skirmish drill. General Birney was riding by and paid us the compliment to stop and look on. He seemed very much pleased. These fellows are very proficient in the skirmish drill, but that is all they are good for. They are poor at marching in step, and it is not to be wondered at. They have had no music to march by, and, as soldiers, have been very much in the condition of "Topsy" in "Uncle Tom's Cabin." They are not "brought up" but *"growed."* They are however gaining every day, and I shall expect to see soldiers in a month where I saw rowdies a month ago.

The 17th is improving every day and the Band is really splendid. We have a Brigade Dress Parade every afternoon. The Sharp Shooters have the right of the Brigade.

Thursday, April 21st.

I am in hot water about our Cartridge Boxes. The Division Inspector has recommended that we turn in our Sharp's Boxes and draw the common Infantry Box (cal. 58)[31] but I have sent up a petition of the officers for the Sharp's Boxes. I hope to yet beat the over-wise Inspector. Some of these Inspectors know much "more than the Law allows," and I wish some one would give them a little good advice in regard to the value of good common sense. The millennium in the Army will never come until a more sensible and intelligent set of staff officers is obtained. But I suppose we should not look for perfection in this "show," and certainly it would be folly to look around any of our General's Head Quarters for any of the commodity. I suppose I may yet get out of the fix.

Lieut. Rilliet, Acting Adjutant, has commenced to drill the officers in the bayonet exercises. He is progressing finely, and I will soon have the fellows so that they can make a splendid show in this drill. Every company can soon drill finely, and then we can call ourselves a well drilled skirmish battalion.

We have some fancy movements in skirmish drill. Everything is done by the bugle calls. One *Faking* thing is to sound "lie down" and then "forward." The "green breeches" creep along as close to the ground as so many mice. Sometimes we sound "commence firing," when they still keep up the creeping, or more properly dragging. General Hays looked on today, and seemed much amused, as indeed does every one who sees us. I always was very fond of skirmish drill, but never more so than at the present time. I fancy that with a little practice and discipline this Regt. can make a most splendid show in skirmish drill. They understand the skirmish calls on the bugle so well that it is rare sport to drill the battalion. We are excused from all Brigade drills, and do not ourselves drill in battalion movements. Target practice and skirmish drill constitute the sum and substance of our daily military existence.[32]

We hear that there is to be a match drill one of these days by several picked regiments. Of course we expect to be *called in* on the skirmish contest. The 17th Me. propose to beat anything on the manual of arms. Meanwhile I shall be putting these fellows through. We should feel cheaply to be beaten at our own hobby by one of the "common Infantry" Regiments.[33]

Friday, April 22d.

Today our Corps was reviewed by Lieut. Genl. Grant. It was a very fine affair. This is the first time we have had a chance to see the hero and conqueror of twenty-two battles. He is a very plain, unassuming man, but we hope that he is the man who has so long been needed in the brave but ill-starred Army of the Potomac. My Sharp Shooters really looked very well, and it is getting to be [a] matter of pride for me to take these fellows out. The white gloves were all clean, and the men carried themselves very well past the "conquering hero."[34]

I still keep up the recitations in Tactics. The officers recite Mondays, Wednesdays and Fridays to me. The Sergeants are put through by Capt. Aschmann on Tuesdays, Thursdays and Saturdays. Lieut. Rilliet, Acting Adjutant, drills the officers in Bayonet Exercise each day from 11 to 12. So among us all, officers, Sergeants and Privates get but little rest. The other day, as I approached the guard house with the Inspector, the *numheads* did not turn out the guard. I of course *chucked* the Sergeant of the guard in arrest, but think I shall release him in a day or two. This is the first time I ever placed an officer in arrest without preferring charges. I forget however. I did place two in my old company in arrest a little while once just for punishment.

The Adjutant is still in arrest, and will probably be tried by Court Martial next week. He may get clear, but it is a hard road for him to travel. I hardly think it will result in his dismissal. He has employed very good counsel, and will make a desperate attempt. He tendered his resignation the other day, but it can not get by Brigade Head Quarters because he has not got the required certificate of non-indebtedness to the Ordnance Dept. I really pity the poor fellow, but in justice to myself could not have done any differently had he been my own brother. He has had many drunks before, but none of them were so public. Yet with all his sprees, he was never put in arrest.

Capt. Marble expects every day to go to New York on recruiting service, but the order does not seem to come to us yet. I think he will get away however during the next week.

Lieut. Col. Merrill of the 17th has not yet arrived, but we expect him. He was ordered back some time ago.

I am in almost daily correspondence with Kimball of our class. He is my business agent, and is very active in getting up some chevrons and stripes for our non-comm'd officers. I have an idea of polishing these fellows off. I have got the Cartridge boxes inspected, and shall be allowed to turn in the odds and ends, and draw a new supply to replace them. We shall start on the campaign with quite a stock of green pants, as well as enough extra shoes and stockings to make the men comfortable.

Today I met [Isaac W.] Starbird of our Class. He is still a Captain in the 19th Me. His promotions have been like "angels' visits"—only more so! for the poor fellow came out as a Captain. However he may some day take a sudden start, though I very much doubt even that. He is not one of the starting kind—never was born for a Napoleon![35]

Sunday, April 24th.

The Adjutant's trial came off today, although we shall not hear the result for some time. Some of the officers twisted the truth in the Adjutant's favor, but I do not think their efforts can save him. I was called as a witness as I expected. He summoned several of his fellow drinkers, among whom was Lieut. Rilliet, who—unmercifully, saying that the Adjutant's horse *did stumble,* &c.

The Adjutant tried to make an opium defence, but unfortunately for him, no one had seen the youth take opium. He will undoubtedly be convicted of something, but what the sentence will be is a matter of conjecture. I am inclined to think he will find it hard work to escape dismissal. I pity him and I pity myself, for in the office he has no equal in the whole Regiment. However I do not feel at all guilty of having overdone my duty. Putting him through and thus establishing a precedent, I at once "define my position," and prevent a repition [repetition] of his offence by other officers.[36] The Acting Adjutant, Lieut. Rilliet, seems to have much trouble with the officers in their official relations with him.

Things, generally, are going very *placidly,* and I have every reason to felicitate myself upon my progress thus far. Lieut. Rilliet is drilling the officers in the bayonet exercises, and I propose to have the whole battalion at it before many more days.

We expect to move from our huts into an open field in a day or two—a good change for us all.

Sunday, May 1st.

We are now very pleasantly encamped in an open field. By "we" I mean Birney's entire Division. The weather has been very agreeable, though a trifle too cool for the mode of life. The different Regiments of the Division have been having ambrotypes taken by an artist who has placed his establishment in the field near the troops. Such work as this seems to flourish on the Sabbath as well, or perhaps better than on any other day of the week. It seems a pity that those even who have no respect for the Sabbath would not be content to use it as a day of rest. No day like Sunday for visiting among our Generals, and I fear there is no day in the Army equal to it for carousing and riding about the country. I presume the Army will move this week, and then we shall have "music."

❧

Head Quarters 1st U.S. Sharp Shooters
Camp near Brandy, Va. May 1st, 1864
My dear Mother:

I find three of your letters in one of the pigeon-holes of my desk, none of which has "ans." written on one corner, from which significant fact I conclude that I have never answered them *by detail,* although I have scratched off one or two sheets since the receipt of the first one. It is a very pleasant Sabbath evening and, as I am sitting alone in my tent, perhaps there can be no better or pleasanter employment than to favor you with a few lines descriptive of the trials, labors and sufferings, as well as the delights and pleasures of a Sharp Shooter—an amateur rather than a professional. Before proceeding to this rich literary and military treat, I will first look over your letters, and at least answer all the questions there asked.

In that of April 16th you describe a very pathetic visit of Dr. Carruthers, in which it seemed he soft-soaped a certain young Major—formerly of common Infantry but now of the highest order of Rifles!

A similar effusion in the *Northern Monthly* did not escape my notice, although I saw it in a borrowed copy. The article in the *Advertiser* about a nice camp referred to the 17th. I am glad to learn that the firm of "I[saac] Dyer[37] and 42 others" owns a box in the P.O. and shall be still more rejoiced when I hear that the same enterprising and famous firm has so far ventured in worldly speculation as to become the owner of a house to live in. I think sometimes that it is "roughing it" to live in a shelter tent six feet square, but then I am conscious of being "monarch of all I survey." I do hope that father will soon come to a realizing sense of the wretchedness of boarding. It certainly will be a most wretched way to bring up a child—boarding on Fore Street. Such things tell in years after. I have not yet received that Maple Syrup, for which my mouth continues to *water*. One can of strawberries thus far, but that a nice one. These things take time as well as patience.

We have no Chaplain in this Regt., and that's "what sort of a man he is." You say Capt. Hobson wishes to get out of the service. It is not to be wondered at. I hear that he has not tried to get many recruits for the 17th. Col. Merrill has not returned yet, although a copy of the order has been sent to the Regt. As might have been expected, he was mustered yesterday as "absent without leave," because, as West says, he was not there to answer to his name when the roll was called. How this great war of wits will end, it is hard to say. I am a thousand times rejoiced that I never mixed up in it, but busied myself with my own affairs. I am sure now that I took the only proper and honorable course, and many others have since wished that they had had even the little foresight which I used. If they were blind they ought to have seen better. If Merrill had been openly attacked in Court Martial, they would have had a chance to come forward and say before him what they secretly wrote on paper. Merrill has always used me finely and I take no delight in his downfall, but I fear he will have a disagreeable position, if he serves under West. Then again there is a settled feeling against M. in the Regt., which cannot conceal itself, especially if he is not in full power. Even when he was, the officers did not hesitate to almost publicly discuss him, and I am not certain that some of them did not leave the "dis-" off.[38]

Your letter of the 23d speaks in very sympathizing terms of our Adjutant. I have never had a case of *discipline* that was so much contrary to my personal inclinations. This fellow is a perfect little gentleman, one of the best Adjutants in the Brigade, and in every way a person one would like to have about him. The result of his trial has not been made known, from which we infer that the sentence can not fall short of dismissal. To see the poor fellow suffer under the uncertainty and suspense does almost make me regret the severity of my course, but still when I think of the hundreds of men in this Army who suffer under drunken officers, I feel more than justified in my course.[39] It was the first case, and offered a very practical method of "defining my position" on the whiskey question. I think I can see that the officers are well aware that it will not be safe to get drunk under the new administration.

You speak of breaking up the 3d Corps. We wear the old badges, and any Corps cross is still in full sweep. My *photos* were taken at Hasseltin's, 130 Middle Street. I am now a subscriber to the *Portland Press,* to an occasional copy of the *Advertiser* and the *Recorder* will do me very well. The *Mirror* partakes of the nature of "small potatoes" too much.

I enclose "Gnus" two deniers for the purpose of increasing his cart fund. They are fresh from "Secretary [Salmon P.] Chase's paper mill."[40] I suppose Itie is driven to death with business. Hope he will prevail upon his father to buy a house.

Perhaps you wish to know how I am getting along with my Shooters. We are really flourishing. The detailed officers are being ordered back, and I now have eight captains in duty here. Some of these were Captains before I was a 1st Lieut. Everything is going along very finely. When I came here the men never thought of using blacking or cleaning their brasses, but now they begin to do it as in the 17th. The first of my *reign* there would perhaps be two or three men on one of our Inspections with blacked boots. This morning there were but two who did not have their boots blacked. This you know is to be considered as a great military triumph!! Such things tell on discipline, if not in battles. I feel immensely delighted with progress thus far. I had a most remarkable capital. I should be much at fault if I had not made a month tell in their appearance. There is not any prospect of my soon returning to the 17th, and I do not know as I wish to, for as I have "got my hand in," Maj. Genl. Birney or Maj. Gen. Some one else might detail me to take some other set of "ragamuffins." My language might be construed as conceited, but it is upon the general principal that a tradesman is better than an apprentice. An officer who is once detailed seldom escapes a second call. I hope however that such may not be my fate, although I am not very much abused by being put in command of these fellows. You would laugh to see me put them over the road. Before we took up this field camp, I used to make the officers recite to me three nights a week—and other things in proportion. I drill them with a vengeance, and for a marvel, they really seem to have awakened from their slumbers, and are now much more attentive and soldierly on drill than many of our neighbors. But the 17th takes the palm from anything in this Division. It is really in splendid condition, and has been improving all winter. I visit them very often. It seems like going home to go up to their camp. We are about a hundred rods apart, and visit with each other considerably. We hear rumors of [Ambrose E.] Burnside's Corps,[41] but do not yet know whether he is to join us here or attempt a flank movement in connection with our movement. Perhaps—yes probably—before I write again, we shall be on the move. In all human probability the Sharp Shooters will fire the first gun discharged by the old Kearney Division in the Summer campaign of 1864, and I pity the unwary Rebel that gets within range of these chaps. We have ten telescopic rifles on the way from Washington. Some of them weigh 30 or 40 pounds, and are to be carried in the Ammunition train. The Army is, as it always is in the Spring, in excellent spirits, and we all hope that another Chancellorsville may not dampen our ardor. Time will tell if the Army must once more be sacrificed to drunkenness and incompetency. Everybody has faith in Grant, as they have previously had in [Irvin] McDowell, [George B.] McClellan, Burnside, or Hooker[42] and as *we now* have in Meade. Faith in a man is but a small part of surety of success. It is not high treason to say that Genl. Lee is a hard man to compete with for the honors of war.

But I think I must close and return to my bed of government hay, intended for my horses, but appropriated for my own use just at present. We expect somewhat to move this very week. I will write a line before that event transpires. . . .

P.S. Tell Lizzie I propose soon to devote a couple of sheets of "Comm. Note" to her own edification. A year ago to-day the first gun of Chancellorsville was fired.

❧❧

Tuesday, May 3d.

Everything indicates that we shall move at midnight. We are all ready, and men and officers carry eight days' rations.

CHAPTER FIVE

Capture and Macon Prison

In prison at Lynchburg, Va., May 10th, 1864.

Since writing the above the unlucky subscriber has started from camp at midnight as proposed, has met the enemy, has been unceremoniously "gobbled," and is now a prisoner of war at Lynchburg, Va. To *portray* this interesting little episode in his military career the writer will go back and treat the past as present.

Wednesday, May 4th.

Having started at midnight of yesterday we have not halted but to eat or rest a little until sundown tonight. The men have done splendidly and seem determined to put the thing through, and it is to be hoped that defeat will not dampen their ardor. We are now encamped upon the battlefield of Chancellorsville, where one year ago a splendid army was sacrificed, by the drunkenness of its commander.[1] Our march today has taken us over much of the old ground. We passed (next day, however) through "The Cedars" where the Sharp Shooters last year captured so many of the 23d Georgia. We shall have to be used as flankers I presume as we approach nearer to the enemy.

We halted just before sunset at the very place where our old Brigade made a charge (last year) up the hill to rescue the wounded and prisoners.[2] It was here that we had our first officer killed. Lieut. Johnson, of Co. H, fell here. I have picked a few flowers from the spot as a souvenir of the sad event. We are near the wood through which we made the famous but useless bayonet charge under Genl.

Ward. It was here that I chanced to attract the attention of Genl. W. and was afterward mentioned in his official report.

Adjutant Weston (still in arrest) accompanies us on this move, and marches in the rear of the Regt. with the Surgeon.

Thursday, May 5th.

We started once more this morning, and *of course* the Sharp Shooters were detailed as flankers. We marched until about 12 o'clock when, hearing firing in the direction of [Maj. Gen. Gouverneur K.] Warren's[3] column (on our right), we immediately marched back, left in front, our Brigade now leading the Division. We had not far to march, but at 2 or 3 o'clock joined the line of battle, being on the left of the left of the 2d Corps. My Sharp Shooters were now double-quicked to the front and ordered to deploy as skirmishers to cover the Brigade. General Hays rode up to me and gave me the choice of a support. I chose the 3d or 5th Michigan. Col. [Byron R.] Pierce soon came up with the 3d, at which I was much pleased. I had already deployed Companies F, H, I, G, K, and B, holding the other three in reserve. This line exactly covered the Brigade. I connected with [Brig. Gen. Gershom] Mott's[4] skirmishers on the right and Ward's (2d U.S.S.S.)[5] on the left. We were in a very good growth of wood, but were soon ordered to march in retreat and then by the flank, so as to close up Mott's interval, who had gone on a reconnaissance to the right and front. After making the connection on the right we were ordered to advance once more. This last movement brought us across a brook which ought to have been kept between us and the enemy. The covering for the men was not so good here. Presently the firing commenced, and instead of the (our) line of battle following up our advance, the 3d Mich., our support, was suddenly withdrawn, without any notice to me. We were hotly engaged. I then, upon my own responsibility, and according to a general instruction to conform to the movement of the line on my right, moved in retreat firing. We found the (our) line of battle behind a nice breastwork alongside the road. We had had a very sharp skirmish and had fairly held a line of battle with our skirmish line of Sharp's Rifles. The moment the skirmishers had formed with the other troops, our line of battle began to blaze away, as is usual with many, although they could not see a single "Reb." Yet the fact of hearing a ball whistle overhead is often a sufficient incentive for some of our Infantry Regiments to commence firing. Hearing occasionally the peculiar report of a Sharp's rifle in the woods in front I concluded that some of my Sharp Shooters had become a little too much interested in their sport, and might remain long enough to get between two fires, and thus be sacrificed. Accordingly I succeeded in quieting the fire of our line by telling them that the skirmishers had not all been withdrawn. I then jumped my horse over the breastwork and "went in" in search of my "green breeches." I found here and there one who was amusing himself behind a tree with a pop at the enemy, who by the way were pouring in a heavy but wild and ill directed fire. What few Sharp Shooters I found I sent back in double quick. I yet heard the occasional crack of a Sharp's rifle across the brook. So across I rushed my horse and just as I emerged from the low bushes growing around the stream, the firing in front of me ceased, and where the air was almost thick with balls, there was now "nary a whistle," but instead, directly in front of me about forty or fifty yards, was a Regiment of "Johnies" yelling "Come in, come in," and at the same time levelling their muskets at me to convince me that it was of no avail to "skedaddle" then. I hesitated a moment, and was upon the point of turning my horse and trying a run for life. But then there was the fact that the thick bushes and the brook would impede my course more than that of two or three hundred bullets. It was but a short moment, but I had time to weigh all the chances. It was simply death or capture, and I very ungallantly chose the latter. I raised my hat and started toward them. They at once flocked around me, and of course claimed my pistols and sword, which I gave them as a sort of "Hobson's choice." I was at once conducted to Capt. Brown, Asst. Inspector General on Brig. Gen. [Henry H.] Walker's[6] Staff, who exchanged horses with me, as he has a special

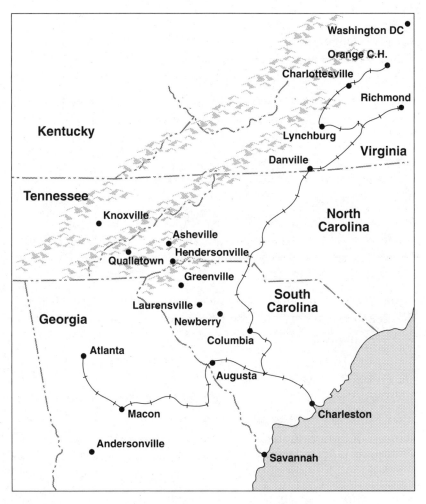

Map 1. Mattocks as Prisoner of War.
[Locations where Charles Porter Mattocks was imprisoned.]

fancy for mine with her sleek sides and nice trappings. I was then sent to the rear and delivered to the Provost Guard. I had been here but a moment before Capt. [Simon] Brennan of the 3d Mich. came in. Capt. B. had supported the Sharp Shooters and was captured while hunting up stragglers, just as I was. Presently Capt. Nash and Lieut. Lee [T. J. Leigh][7] of Gen. Ward's Staff came in. So Birney's Division is very well represented. The fight is still raging quite furiously, and a charge by our Brigade (as we have since learned) has just caused not a little commotion among the "Johnies." As yet here has been but very little artillery used on either side, owing to the nature of the field, which is nothing more nor less than one waste of woodland fitly called "The Wilderness."[8]

At night we were moved about a mile and a half to Parker's Store, where there has been something of a cavalry skirmish. We now number about 10 officers and 150 men. But they say that a large squad of prisoners have already been sent to Orange Court House, 20 miles away. I suppose we shall soon follow in their illustrious footsteps. However, we now make up our beds and lie down to think of the varying fortunes of a soldier. We hear that Gen. Hays, our Brigade Commander, is killed.[9] Lt. Kinsman, of the Sharp Shooters, is reported killed.

Friday, May 6th.

This morning we were started for Orange Court House, a destination we had hoped to have reached under different circumstances. We were conducted closely watched, by a detachment of Lee's Body Guard, who were certainly very nice chaps. They showed us every favor possible and even allowed us to ride their horses when we were tired. The sun poured down hot, and the march and heat told on us. I took it all very well except my feet, which became a little tired, in heavy riding boots. We arrived at Orange Court House at dark, and are now ready to repose upon the steps of this same Hall of Justice. Among the *gentlemen* we have met is Maj. Payden [W. G. Paxton],[10] of Lee's Staff, who came along this morning and "raked down" the officer of the guard back of Parker's Store for allowing petty stealings from the prisoners. Capt. Pipfer [Capt. L. M. Pipkin],[11] of Lee's Body Guard, who *escorted* us to Orange Court House, is a very fine gentleman. 2d Lt. [John M.] Hopper,[12] of the Pro. Guard, Maj. [R. M.] Bridgford[13] commdg., at Orange Court House, had the lowness to take our rubber blankets. I had a nice new poncho, but, before the wise youth got his clutches upon this same article the former, and only genuine proprietor, had easily managed unobserved to make a few damaging incisions with his pocket knife, the better to impress upon the youth the fact that stolen blankets *will* leak. I do not wish to be revengeful, but should he chance to lie down with this same blanket for a protection in a rain storm, I would not wish to interfere with the course of nature, which perhaps might cause a few refreshing drops of water to pass through the holes I made.

❦

In a Tobbaco [Tobacco] Warehouse at Gordonsville, Va.
En route for Hotel de Libby or elsewhere.
May 7th 1864.
My dear Mother:

By the kindness of a Confederate officer I have an opportunity to drop you a line. Perhaps you have heard I was killed, as I was alone when I was gobbled. . . . In my anxiety to save my men I lost myself, for a time at least. It is not so glorious or convenient a thing to be taken prisoner. They took my horse, sword, pistols, &c. and finally I am left happy over a sound body, a "soiled" suit of clothing and one blanket. Yesterday we were marched 20 miles under a scorching sun to Orange Court House. We were pretty lame and even I will acknowledge myself *tired* for once. This morning we came by cars to this place, 9 miles. To-morrow we start for *some* place. They talk of sending us to Georgia, but I am inclined to think we shall pull in in Richmond. We go to Lynchburg to-morrow. Write to Col. West. Write to S. Brennan, Georgetown [Michigan], that his son, the Capt. is with me. This is all they allow to be written. Will write again. Do not know my future address. Love to all. I am in good spirits. Tell Lizzie I can't write her this week! Your Maj. saw the havoc the S.S. made among the enemy. They did finely.

❧❧

Saturday, May 7th. Orange Court House.

This morning we were escorted to a large open field, where the Provost Marshal or some other dignitary searched our men, and the most of the officers. There seemed to be no system except with some of the Provost's *subs,* who seemed determined to take everything but our eyeteeth, and I think they would have taken them if there had been any filling in them. Fortunately however nature does not often allow eyeteeth to decay—consequently dentists do not fill them—consequently the Provosts of Orange Court House left us our eyeteeth, for which all thanks.[14]

Three men from the 17th Me. have just arrived. From them I hear that Lieuts. Doe,[15] [Wellington] Hobbs,[16] and Sawyer were wounded. Some or many others may have been ere this. *Night.* We are now in a shed (!!) at Gordonsville, at which place we arrived on the cars from Orange Court House. I have made an error. The search of which I have been speaking took place at Gordonsville, instead of Orange Court House. The matter of place and even time is unimportant now. The matter of meanness or decency is the all important item to prisoners.

Sunday, May 8th.

At 2 o'clock this afternoon we started by cars for Lynchburg, which is to be our stopping place for some time. They talk of sending us to Georgia subsequently. We prefer that to the "Hotel de Libby" at Richmond.[17] We have had a great time on the cars today. The young ladies at the Seminary at Charlottesville, seeing us coming on the cars, took us for Confederate soldiers, and began to rush down across the fields toward us, scaling fences with more celerity and vigor than feminine modesty would dictate or allow perhaps under ordinary circumstances. On they came, a perfect avalanche of petticoats and crinoline, waving handkerchiefs and screeching like mad, when suddenly they discovered that they were making all this ado about a few "Yankee prisoners," ugh!! Such screeches and such skaling [scaling] of fences I never saw, and such skedaddling back. They surpassed the Rocky Mountain Sheep. It was now our turn to cheer and yell, which we did as much to their disgust as it was to our own delight. All along the road we were looked upon by the citizens and soldiers with mingled contempt and surprise. Perhaps though I ought to except the soldiers, by whom we have been very well treated.

Monday, May 9th.

This morning at daylight we arrived at Lynchburg, and are now established at the military prison at this place. The men who came with us about 600, are confined in a grove near this building.[18]

Our ride yesterday was really delightful. We amused ourselves with jokes and Union songs. At three miles this side of Charlottesville our engine partially gave out, and we were obliged to leave half the train. At this juncture two or three of us thought we would make our escape. One of the number got into a culvert near the engine, but was seen by the guard, and thus the whole scheme failed. When we arrived at Lynchburg two of us came very near getting away, owing to the smallness of the guard, but a reinforcement soon arrived and prevented us.

Thursday, May 12th.

We are still at Lynchburg Prison. Nothing very definite is heard as to the success or defeat of Grant. I should judge that both parties will claim the victory. The fighting around Richmond seems to be very unsatisfactory. [Brig. Gen. William W.] Averill's cavalry seems to be doing some damage to the enemy by their raid.[19]

We had an accession to our squad of officers today. An officer of the 3d Mich. Cavalry, who has been confined in "Libby" since

October, jumped from the cars while on the way from Richmond to Danville the other day. He was too weak to make any progress at escape, and was recaptured in two or three days. He looks very much emaciated by his long confinement. We now have 111 officers here, including Brig. Genls. Shailer [Alexander Shaler][20] and [Truman] Seymour.

In Prison at Lynchburg, Va.

May 12th, 1864

My dear Mother:

I write to inform you that I am still in good health and spirits. I wrote on the 6th [7th] giving the details of my capture on the 5th. I am unlucky to be a prisoner, but perhaps should be duly thankful for my narrow escapes. Love to all.

Since Brevity is the soul of wit I am happy to subscribe myself.[21]

Sunday, May 15th.

Our prison life wears along as well as could be expected. Of course we do not feel sensible of the highest possible felicity, but in the forlorn situation of prisoners of war, living upon a small piece of pork and a small loaf of bread each day, breathing a small amount of genuine fresh air, seeing but few new faces, and enjoying not a few other varieties similar in many respects, it is not to be wondered at that we are willing to be exchanged or paroled at any day. Still we may remain prisoners for six months to come. We trust however that such may not be our fate. Our officers amuse themselves by playing cards, reading and talking. If we could write long letters it would be a gratification. As it is, one side of half a sheet of note paper must convey our regrets and regards to friends at home. Even these few lines must contain nothing in the slightest degree disrespectful to this great confederacy or any of its officers. As for reading matter it is a thing of the past. A book is snatched at with wonderful eagerness. Now and then we manage to get a paper smuggled in, and then we all assemble to hear the news, which of course we interpret in the *Union* "patois." At present Grant seems to be at or near Spottsylvania Court House, some twelve miles this side of where we were "gobbled." The "Rebs" claim a victory, but General Lee's official dispatches are certainly very dubious. Fighting seems to have been continuous since we left the field. How it will all terminate is hard to say, but we all have confidence in Grant. Two mighty geniuses are contending for the possession of Virginia. I have learned from unmistakable sources that the Capt. Brown, of Walker's Staff, who became the possessor of my horse, when I was captured, has since been killed. We hear of great losses on our side. Gen. Hays, our Brigade commander, is certainly killed. Among those reported killed are Maj. Genls. Sedgwick and Warren.[22] The Rebel General Stuart, the famous cavalry leader, he recently died of wounds.[23] We are kept in a state of pleasing excitement by these daily rumors. We hear today that Averell's Cavalry is now within 60 miles of this place.[24] The guard tell us that our cavalry has been cutting railroads at a most fearful rate, so much so that all the trains from this place today had to return. Such are the rumors that serve to relieve the monotony of our prison life. Brig. Genls. Shailer and Seymour (of Florida fame)[25] are confined in a room adjacent to *us* of the "common herd." Lt. Col. [Clark B.] Baldwin of the 1st Mass., late of "our Mess," is with them.

Monday, May 16th. "Hotel de Yanks."
We are still living along in primitive style—*barring* the high fence that shuts us up from the outer world. I must here speak of our Commissary Department. We have 10 messes and each member of our Mess takes a turn (like the man at the grindstone) in the office of Commissary. Each one acts one week. It is now my week and I must here insert a list of "ours."

Mess No. 4. "Hotel de Y."

Maj. Mattocks, 17th Me., *late* comdg. 1st U.S.S.S.
Capt. Brennan, 3d Mich.
Capt. Nash —Brig. Genl. Ward's Staff.

1st Lt. Leigh —Brig. Genl. Ward's Staff.
2d Lt. [Hannibal A.] Johnson,[26] 3d Me. late Act. Adjt.

Capt. Brennan and I share the voluptuous ease and comfort of an old rubber cape and a wool blanket. We all have exchanged our "greenbacks" for confederate scrip. They give us $5 for 1. The following is a list of prices of articles we buy "on the sly." Everything except a loaf of stale bread and a small bit of ham daily is contraband to us prisoners.

Playing cards -poor-	$11. pr. pack.
Wool Blankets - " -	$25 each.
Eggs	$ 5 pr. doz.
Coffee	$15 pr. lb.
Meal	$ 1 pr. lb.

And other things in proportion. These prices are all in confederate scrip. One fifth of the price in greenbacks will buy the same. To say that we are all hungry *all the time* would give but a faint idea of our condition. I have serious thoughts of splintering my knees. They are getting so weak that going up and down stairs is quite an effort. However we keep up excellent spirits, and there is hardly a blue face among us. "Blue Devils"[27] are decidedly contraband according to our system of tariff. We are all devoted converts to the "ad valorem" system of duties. But the confinement, want of exercise and short rations begin to tell upon us. When we came here we were well bronzed by the weather, but pale faces are beginning to be the order of the day.

Card playing is by far the most popular amusement, and I am sorry to say that gambling seems the only real amusement for some of our officers. Even Sunday did not interrupt the gaming mania in the case of a few.

I scribble away thus at length in my Diary as much for my own amusement as for any better purpose, for perhaps I may not be allowed to retain these same ruminations. If any one does me the favor to deprive me of this little book I trust he may be well repaid for his trouble. I trust that so mean a man may not meet me.

Our prison is really a wonderful specimen of architecture, and I often wish I could sketch these rare sights in the Confederacy. The following is no work of art but does full justice to the original. [*See fig. 14.*]

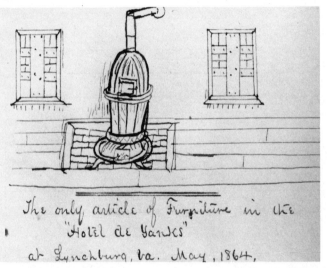

Fig. 14. "Hotel de Yanks." [Mattocks's sketch of the stove in the "Hotel de Yanks." Courtesy of James M. White, Jr.]

The only article of Furniture in the "Hotel de Yanks" at Lynchburg, Va., May, 1864.

However, the stove is ornamental rather than useful at this season, and so we do not mind its slight faults as a *heater*. We shall soon be sent farther South.

Tuesday, May 17th.

We "Yanks" are busy discussing the prospects of our future travels. Some think we shall go only to Danville in this State, and others prophesy Americus,[28] Georgia. We are really indifferent as to the *place* of confinement so that the time be short. But I dare say that neither will be very much to our liking. Some of the officers in charge of us say that we shall be exchanged very promptly, while others are not so confident. So, judging from the past, I see but a very dim prospect of exchange.[29] The Gettysburg and Chickmauga [Chickamauga] prisoners are still in "durance vile" at the "Hotel de Libby" in Richmond. Ten or twelve months of imprisonment may not prove a very palatable dish; but whatever may be our luck, common sense will drive away the "blues." We are sorely puzzled for anything to read. As yet we have no books at all, but are hoping to accumulate a little Library one of these days. Until then we must amuse our unlucky selves with sleeping and playing cards. Our eating is purely an imaginary enjoyment—intellectual rather than physical.[30]

Fig. 15. Lynchburg Prison. [Mattocks's sketch of his boots and ration bag at Lynchburg Prison. Courtesy of James M. White, Jr.]

Lynchburg Prison
Yanks & Co. Proprietors

My Pillow
and My Bed

How lucky that I wore big boots!!![31]

May 25th, Wednesday.Yankee Prison, Macon, Georgia.[32]

Since my last scrawl in this wonderful volume we have travelled through Va., No. Carolina, So. Carolina, and now find ourselves in Georgia. Dates of these little events are of small value to the "future historian," so that I get in all the facts and incidents of our pilgrimage. Then suffice it to say that between the 17th and 24th of May we "Yanks," 110 in number, were transported in cattle cars, box cars, passenger cars, corpse cars and various other varieties of these steam driven vehicles, to Danville, Va., where we remained two days—well treated as a whole.[33] In fact, Danville is the only place where *outside* Confederate officers came in to visit us. In this manner I made the acquaintance of Maj. Seibles of S.C. He called on us twice, and seemed every inch a gentleman. At Danville we had an abundance to eat. Corn bread was the leading article on our bill of fare, but then it was of most excellent quality. Danville is quite a name for me. I was born in Danville, Vt., attended the Academy at Danville, Me., and now pull up as a prisoner of war at Danville, Va!

From Danville we went to Augusta, Ga., where we halted for a few hours. Augusta is a beautiful town of about 15,000 inhabitants. While passing through South Carolina we had a very narrow escape from a railroad accident of a serious character. We were lumbering along in our dilapidated old cars, when very unexpectedly the one I was in commenced a most delectable exercise by running on the sleepers instead of the track. It was a terrible jar for a few minutes and we thought the thing would go over. So out went Guard and prisoners promiscuously, all anxious to save their own individual "bacons." None of us were injured, but our ideas were shook up a little. We dumped two of the cars over and a few of us rode on the tops of the cars, where we had rare sport viewing the country and yelling at the astonished negroes. So many "Yanks" are a source of great wonder to the natives, and they congregate at the stations to get a view of the captured invaders. Of course they ask us many foolish questions, and perhaps we give as foolish answers.

Some of the scenery in North and South Carolina was very pretty, but Georgia, from Augusta to Macon, is really a rich country and seems to be in good condition. The (our) men (some 400 to 500 in number), who came on our train, have been sent to Andersonville in this State. At Macon we were put into the prison yard, where we found about 1,000 officers ready to receive the new members to their ancient and honorable fraternity. Like all such associations, they have a sort of initiation for the new comers, which consists of howling at them, and yelling "Fresh Fish! Fresh Fish!!!"[34] An indignity this is, but one which we are willing to hear, and wish they were all as fresh as we.

This is a much better place than any we have had, because we are now out of doors, with sheds built by our own hands to lie under nights.[35] The days are quite warm and the nights cool. But thus far the climate has agreed with me very well. I have lost some flesh, but am still well, though not so strong as *of yore*. But the climate and the long confinement has told fearfully on some of the officers. They say our men are dying off at a terrible rate at Andersonville, Ga., where there are 15,000 poor fellows, longing for parole or exchange. I trust they may have a chance to go home before many more of them sicken and die. They are, I presume, very much crowded for room, and, being 100 or more miles further South than we, are more injured by their confinement than we can be.[36]

Our rations here consist of corn bread, meal, a little ham, very little beans and rice, and now and then a spoonful of salt. We have two roll calls a day. One of Capt. [W. Kemp] Tabb's orders compel a man to fall in on time or be shot down!![37] Vermin are abundant, but constant washing of clothing and persons prevents any real suffering from "creepers."

On our way we succeeded in buying Chamber's Information for the People[38] in 12 vols., and have established a sort of Library. Capt. Mattison is Librarian, and we are running the thing in shape. Things are going along very well, although there is some monotony in living on a four acre lot. I find quite a delegation from Maine. I have made a list.

Maine Officers. Length of Imprisonment.
arranged according to rank, &c.

Major C. P. Mattocks, 17th Me. 3 weeks.
Geo. H. Pendleton, Master, U.S.N. 5 months.
J. R. Day, Capt. 3d Me. 11 months.
M. A. Cochran, Capt., 16 U.S., 8 months.
S[amuel]. H. Pil[l]sbury, Capt., 5th Me. 10 months.
W. H. Larrabee, 1st Lt., 7th Me. 3 weeks.
M[arshall]. S. Smith, 1st Lt. 16th Me., 3 weeks.[39]
L[ewis]. C. Bisbee, 1st Lt. 16th Me. 11 months.
J[ohn]. H. Stevens, 1st Lt., 5th me. 5 months.
G[eorge]. A. Deering, 1st Lt., 16th Maine. 11 months.
S[amuel]. E. Cary, Lt., 13th Mass.
J. C. Norcross, Lt. 2d Mass. Cav.
G[eorge]. D. Bisbee, 2d Lt., 16th Maine, 11 months
M. C. Wadsworth, 2d Lt., 16th Maine 11 months
J. W. [James U.] Childs, 2d Lt., 16th Maine 11 months
G. A. Chandler, 2d Lt., 5th Maine 10 months
N. A. Robins, 2d Lt. 4th Maine, 11 months
J. N. Whitney, 2d Lt., 2d R.I. Cav.[40]
H. M. Anderson, Lt., 3d Maine
W. C. Manning, Lt. 2d Mass Cav. (held as hostage at Saulsbury [Salisbury], N. C.)[41]
W. H. Fogg, Master's Mate is here with us. 10 months

The above list was made out May 28th. There are perhaps other officers here who originally came from Maine, but these are all the ones that register themselves as Maine men. 1st Lt. Wm. H. Smyth, son of the "Prof.",[42] is here. He belongs to the l6th U.S. Inf. [Melville A.] Cochran[43] of my class and I often talk over the old times we had in college. He has been in "durance vile" ever since Chickamauga.

❦

In Prison at Macon, Georgia.

May 29th, 1864

My dear Mother:

No pen, no ink, but little paper but an abundance of good spirits. We have been here about one week, and I hope you will write me a long letter. Direct to me as Prisoner Of War, Macon, Ga. You are allowed to write all you please.[44] I see no prospect of exchange or parole[45] for some time yet. There are some here who have been in the hands of the enemy 10 months. I suppose a special exchange would benefit me greatly just at present, but I shall not ask it. I presume father could get [Sen. William Pitt] Fessenden[46] to interest himself. I hear that Col. West is wounded.[47] I am willing to bear my part but feel that I ought to be elsewhere just now. My health is still good, though the climate is telling on some of the officers. The men are at Andersonville in this State. Please publish in the Press the following names as being here, Geo. H. Pendleton, Master U.S.N. (Yarmouth) Captured off Georgetown, S.C. Jan. 7, 1864. (Write his wife, Yarmouth), 2d Lt. Johnson, 3d Maine, 1st Lt. Larrabee, 7th Maine.

But I must close. Love to all. Do not be alarmed about me. I shall not be sick.

Pendleton messes with me. He is well.

❦

Sunday, June 5th, 1864. Prison. Macon, Georgia.

One month ago today I bid farewell to liberty. One month ago we were 800 miles away, battling with the enemy near the Rapidan. One month hence I trust our forces will be in the doomed city of Richmond, although we can not be there to share the dangers and the glory. In prison life "drags its weary length along." It is a rare place for character to discover itself. I firmly believe that there are officers here who daily felicitate themselves upon their present immunity from bullets, and hope that exchange will not come until the end of this season's campaign. Their plump cheeks and jolly faces seem to indicate a natural talent for prison life. All privations and trials are to them but the trifling price of personal safety. It is too true, and was never plainer, that many men and officers do not object to being captured at the beginning of a hard campaign. Twelve months of hard fare and close confinement seem not to have cured some of their taste for this manner of life.

I have written four letters home, the last one today, besides one to the "Portland Press" containing names of Maine men, &c. How many of these will ever reach their destination it is hard to imagine, but I presume that out of the four one at least may go through. We still eat our corn bread, all of which we now bake ourselves. When we have saleratus[48] we get up quite a respectable meal, but we have not had any saleratus until two days ago. So if the reverse of my proposition is true, one can imagine how many respectable sit-downs we have had.[49]

For the past week I have been more dead than alive, with an attack of "Prison Fever," very similar to the illness a recruit in the army has to go through. But I am now, I think, fully recovered. I have lost a great deal of flesh—perhaps 15 or 20 pounds—no great loss probably in this sultry climate. The weather thus far has been tolerable, and as far as heat is concerned, far better than I had expected. The nights are as cool as in New England. I feel now fully acclimated and *inured* to the rigors of this prison diet. Our four acres of ground are improved by baseball and cricket daily, although I have not felt "sprawl" enough to take a share yet. In college such sports were great favorites with me. I shall soon get into it.

Our knowledge of the outside world is decidedly limited. One day we hear that Grant is pitching shells into the fated city of Richmond, and that [Maj. Gen. William Tecumseh] Sherman has taken

Atlanta. The next day we hear that such is not the case.[50] Capt. Tabb, the commandant, of this camp, has been relieved, they say, and is now in Richmond.[51]

I am still zealous in studying my German, and hope to be able to converse intelligibly in the "Muttertongue" before my imprisonment ends. I would not however have any term extended on account of my love for German. One of our Colonels is busying himself with ringing the changes of the Greek. Perhaps he is preparing to open a school here, for I am not certain that our fate may not be like the Swedish prisoners that Peter the Great banished to Siberia, where they became artisans, farmers and schoolmasters.[52] If such is our fate I shall start either a newspaper or a *corn bread restaurant*. The latter would be by far the most lucrative as well as the most intellectual occupation, for the Confederacy will soon have to publish its papers on corn husks.

We still continue to see no prospect of exchange or parole. I think we may as well fold our arms for the season.

❧❦❧

Military Prison, Macon, Ga.

June 5, 1864

My dear Mother:

I take this fine Sabbath morning to inform you of my continued existence, if not of continued prosperity. One month ago to-day I had the misfortune to fall into the hands of the enemy, and I presume that one month hence will find me yet a prisoner of war at this place. The change of diet and the confinement made me refuse my rations for a day or two last week, but now I am wholly recovered and am fully able to do my share in the "mess." This is the fourth letter I have written you and I trust one or more of my productions may reach you. At any rate do not give yourself any uneasiness about me. This confinement and separation from friends is terribly galling to me, but then it is the fortune of war, and I try to bear it patiently. I am longing to hear from home, and I trust you will not discontinue writing. If at any time they allow "boxes" to be sent to us, be sure to send me a flannel shirt, two pr. socks, soap, towels, saleratus, sugar, coffee, tea and some papers and magazines.[53] You may wish to know how we spend the day, for me, I eat, read and sleep. I am however busy in learning to speak German. A Testament and German Grammar constitute my library. There are several Germans here and I am studying under their instruction. Some of the prisoners, Yankee fashion, amuse themselves with their pocket knives. Hope you will write to Almon now and then. I would write to him but I have no envelopes or money to buy them. Do not attempt to send me any money, as it is *"contraband."*[54] Remember to direct to me (without Regt.) as "Prisoner of War, Macon, Ga. By Flag of Truce." I presume they will not allow newspapers to be sent by the mail, but you can put them in a box. The prospect of exchange seems slim to us. Could we be exchanged or paroled without delay, or even after a moderate delay, there would seem to be something to live for. As it is many are giving away to despondence and seem to be more dead than alive. Some are ill calculated for a prison-life, while others seem to grow fat and rejoice in their present security from bullets. I really believe that the safety from battle alone is the great prop to some of these fellows. We hear but little from Grant, and only know that he is somewhere on the peninsula. I hear that Col. West was wounded, but am inclined to discredit the rumor. Please write to him for me. Tell me if they are raising any more Regiments in Maine. Hope they will fill up the old ones first. Tell Col. W. to take charge of my horse, for I suppose I have *one left*. Remember me to Mr. C's family, to Albert & Erastus and all friends. Do you hear anything about exchange? I do not at all relish the idea of confining my travels to four acres of land for the next six, eight or perhaps twelve months. There are "convicts" here of 12 and 15th months' standing. *They* call *us* "Fresh Fish." I trust we may continue *fresh*. Our living consists of Johnny cake and ham or bacon, with a few beans, peas, rice &c. We are getting to be great cooks. Of course, like all prisoners, we have more or less sport in the course of a day. The guard is around, not among us, so we are "Lord of all we survey" (4 acres), and we exercise our authority to the extent of playing jokes on each other, playing ball and cricket, cards, chess, checkers, quoits,[55]—but all are marred and monotonized by the galling thought that we are and must continue to be prisoners of war. A Mr. Pendleton, Master in the Navy, of Yarmouth, Me. is in my Mess. He has been a prisoner five months, but has never heard from his wife, although he has written frequently. Write to her. He was captured at Georgetown, S.C. and was confined at Charleston for some time. When you write don't fail to tell me what is said about the prospect of *exchange*. Mention it in every letter. I was afraid I might be reported "killed" instead of simply "missing," but I trust for your sake, that such was not the case. I do not yet know much of the loss of either of the Regiments in which I am most interested. I have heard that the loss of each was heavy.

I have written an exceedingly long letter for a "Yankee Prisoner," and perhaps have trespassed on the good nature of the examining officer. If it is allowed to reach you I trust that it may serve to allay your and father's anxiety, if not to amuse you. Tell Itie to be a good boy, and practice drawing for it would be of great advantage to him if he should ever be a prisoner of war. Tell him I shall surely bring him something this time—*when* or what I cannot say. Tell father that the prisoner of war appeals to him for a home—not a hotel—to go to, when he is released from durance. I do hope that father will pause in his business long enough to settle down in a house at last. I should think he would for Itie's sake if not for his own. Be of good cheer, and believe me. Your aff. but unfortunate son

Monday, June 6th.

About 60 officers arrived this morning who were captured about Richmond. They report Grant within a mile and a half of the city.[56] Things look cheeringly just now. There were no victims from our Division. I am anxious to hear of the losses of the old Brigade, but as yet not a new arrival from among my old friends. Even my desire for news does not make me wish them to be so unlucky as to be gobbled as I was. Still, if any of them do come, it will be a very great pleasure to have a talk with them.

I sent a letter to mother today, which I wrote yesterday. It was really a long one for a "Yank," covering one half a sheet of Com. note, and written closely, two lines on one. I spread out the sheet so as to make but *"one page"*—an old and much practiced "Libby Prison" evasion of the "one page" order. Hope it will go through.

Friday, June 10th.

Great excitement in camp today. Our five Brigadier Generals, all our Cols, and Lt. Cols. and 9 of our Majors were taken away. It is supposed by some that they are going to Savannah to be exchanged. Others, especially the old "Libbyites," will not credit anything of the kind, but think they are going to some other place for confinement.[57] Upon the whole it has created a sort of hope among the rest of us. The Majors were taken alphabetically. One more would have included me. The Brigadiers were [Henry Walton] Wessels, [Eliakim Parker] Scammon, Seymour, Shaler and [Charles Adam] Heckman.[58] They went off in excellent spirits, and I hope they will not be disappointed in their expectations. These Brigadiers are no loss to us as they have acted like a set of old women throughout. There were 50 in all to go away. There are about 1150 of us left. I am now quite comfortably situated in the large building.

Sunday, June 12th.

Last night at about 8 o'clock we had a cool-blooded murder in the prison yard. One of our officers was at the spring, or brook rather, washing, and was on the point of returning to his quarters, when the sentinel outside the palisade deliberately shot him. A ball and three buckshot entered at the right shoulder, the ball, passing through both lungs, breaking two ribs, and lodging in the left shoulder. The poor fellow was brought up by some of the officers, and taken to the hospital outside, where he died at 2 o'clock this morning. It seems almost impossible that the sentinel could have thought him trying to escape, as he deliberately fired upon him without any challenge or warning whatever. Our knowledge of the matter is no hearsay as a friend of the unfortunate was by his side when he was hit, and says that they had already turned to come back. This is the second man we have had fired at in this camp. In the other case the aim was not so accurate, and the officer was not hit. But it shows the disposition of the cowardly bloodhounds. Capt. [George C.] Gibbs, commdg. the Prison, says the matter shall be investigated, and the soldier, if at fault brought to justice. That a sentinel should fire upon a prisoner, without a word passing between them, and that too before 9 o'clock (the hour for retiring to quarters), is an outrage and a disgrace even to the *"chivalrous"* (!) Confederacy. If we are ever allowed to breathe the free air of the North once more the thing shall be laid before our Government. The rest of the Sentinels seem to be very much unconcerned. I suppose the shooter—the murderer rather—is now a hero among his fellow soldiers. They are no soldiers though, but a lot of boys who have never been to the front.[59]

Friday, June 17th.

The soldier who murdered one of our officers has received a sort of Confederate justice. He has been promoted to Sergeant and furloughed for 30 days.[60] He must be quite a hero at home when it becomes known that he has killed one Yankee. It matters not with many of these people whether a life is taken in manly open fight upon the battlefield or within the limits of a closely guarded prison. The poor victim was not attempting to escape, nor do I believe the murderer thought so. It was simply one of those cases where a solider can commit a crime and still justify or even render himself famous under the specious screen of "obeying orders." That the scamp desired the opportunity can not be doubted. But that he should be justified, and even rewarded by his officers seems worse than all. They thereby become participants in one of the most rascally murders I have known of. If these scamps would go to the front a while they would find that even in the heat of battle it is considered disgraceful and cowardly to bayonet the wounded or to endanger the life of a prisoner even by keeping him exposed to the same fire which his captor must continue to face. Whenever we have been guarded by old soldiers we have been well used as far as was in their power, but these Home Guards and Militia are the most bloodthirsty men I ever knew. Yet even among these Militia and frequently among the old soldiers we find many who have no heart in their work. They are homesick and disheartened, and care nothing for the issue—only that it may be immediate.

I am now very much buried in [Paul Belloni] Du Chaillu's Travels in Africa. Have just finished Bayard Taylor's novel "Hannah Thurston."[61] This is Taylor's first attempt at Novel writing. It is a very agreeable work, though the traveller rather than the novelist, appears upon almost every page.

I have written as long a letter as is allowed to Mother today. I have endeavored to drop a line from time to time to prevent them from undue anxiety in behalf of their "young hopeful." I am still busy with my German, and can speak a little\mit\some of the Germans here. My German Grammar and a Testament I picked up on the battlefield have often been my only companions. The bible which my mother gave me when we left the State of Maine was captured with my horse. I very much regret the loss. The authorities are cutting down our meat (fat pork) to almost nothing. They issue a very little molasses instead. One day's ration is about this

> 1 1/4 Pint Meal — coarse, about 1 1/4 lb.
> 1/4 Gill Molasses
> 1/4 " Beans ("Nigger")
> 3 oz. Bacon (including "skippers")
> 1 teaspoonful Salt
> 1/6 Gill Rice (including bugs)
> 0 much Soap (soft)
> Water ad libitum.

Our coffee is made of water and burnt meal, bread or rice. No sugar, no milk, no anything. Yet we do not really suffer on our fare. The only thing which we find it very hard to do without is a partial vegetable diet. Many have already been attacked by the scurvy owing [to] the want of vegetables. I did buy raw onions for a while, but my money is gone now. We had some in our mess yesterday, and were glad to eat them, stems, tops and *all*. A few onions will make a bean or rice soup very palatable. If we could have such a ration as is issued to our own troops, we should think ourselves happy. Their sugar and coffee, and the many little extras of which a Rebel never dreams, would be a great luxury to us unfortunates. Since I was captured I have not seen a piece of fresh meat of any kind. Of course we feel hungry all the time. This corn bread, which, by the way, we cook for ourselves, fills us up very quickly, but in an hour we question our memory to ascertain if we have eaten during the day.[62] But poor rations, snug quarters, hard beds, are almost no privations compared with the present and prospective loss of our liberty. When our fifty ranking officers left us we all had a hope—though many dared not *expect anything*—that they were to be exchanged at once. We now read in a rebel paper that they have been put in Charleston and exposed to the bombarding fire of our forces. We can hardly force ourselves to believe it, but still we have to know of worse things next time. *Verily* the Rebellion is on its last legs.

Today we have the gratifying but questionable intelligence of the fall of Atlanta. We further hear that the wealthy people are "migrating" from Macon, through fear of a raid. If Sherman has taken Atlanta it is a great blow to the enemy. We have a camp rumor that we "Yanks" are to be taken to Savannah for safe keeping. The authorities do not allow us to have the newspaper as usual today. So we infer that there is something in the wind. Grant's progress around Richmond seems to be almost too slow. Yet we have faith in him. Hope he will have it by the 4th of July.

Sunday, June 19th.

I have finished my letter to Mother, but there is no way of telling how soon the mail will go. In the letter I have given directions about sending boxes of clothing and eatables to me if the authorities allow anything of the kind one of these days. We are in sad need of a few luxuries from home. Anything but cornmeal is a luxury to us now. I never knew how good raw potatoes were until I was a prisoner. At Lynchburg I ate sliced raw potatoes with salt and they were very nice. Many of our officers are now being afflicted with scurvy, on account of having no vegetables. A great many brought this trouble-some complaint from "Libby." We now hear that the 50 officers who left here ostensibly for parole have been sent to Charleston Jail. This has as yet had no effect on [Maj. Gen. Quincy Adams] Gil[l]more's target practice.[63] Sometimes I think we never shall be exchanged.

[*Beginning here CPM wrote two or three lines where he other-wise ordinarily wrote one in order to conserve his paper.*]

A Dream in Prison—&c.

The matter of exchange looks dim enough. I must here record a dream that one of our officers had the other night. He fancied that, about 20 years after the close of the war, he was in an eating saloon in New York City, when Lincoln, [Maj. Gen. Benjamin F.] Butler,[64] and [Edwin M.] Stanton[65] entered and took a seat. The conversation was quite interesting to the dreamer. Butler asked Lincoln if he knew what had ever become of those officers and men of ours who were confined in Georgia in 1864. Of course "Abe" referred the matter to Stanton, who confessed he had lost track of them. They then concluded it would be judicious to send commissioners South to learn what had been the fate of these forgotten fellows. So "Abe" sent his commissioners to Georgia, who after a dilligent [diligent] search returned with the intelligence that the poor fellows had all died in prison—the last one about two years ago. When we hear that our poor men at Andersonville (Ga.) are dying at the rate of 40 or

50 a day, there is a sort of gloomy humor about this curious dream, which excites some feelings other than those of mere curiosity. I hope the dream may never come to pass, but sometimes it seems among the possibilities of the dubious future. The fellow who tells the story says he actually dreamed it. It is certainly a fine story, and worthy of being remembered. We have many gloomy jokes in prison. We hear that our men at Andersonville amuse themselves by cutting their names, rank and Regiment on head boards for their future graves. These boards they finish up in fine shape, putting on everything but the time of death, which of course they cannot foresee. This they leave for some more fortunate companion to do. We suffer but little compared with what our poor privates endure.[66] As prisoners of war in what claims to be a civilized country, we suffer enough to disgrace all the military glory the Southern Confederacy can acquire in 50 years. Our long confinement and our treatment will not have a tendency to make us love our deluded Southern brothers. "When this cruel war is over" even I think we shall remember some of them. Such fellows as wantonly shoot a prisoner of war without pretext will I think not be easily forgotten. I once heard a preacher say "Love your enemies, but not their bad actions." That is exactly our own case just at present.

Wednesday, June 22d.
Today we have had a very great excitement in the prison yard. By some arrangement between some of our officers and the prison keeper it was thought best to send 3 or 4 of our officers to Andersonville, and then on parole to Washington to "urge upon our Govt. the necessity of exchange." Accordingly two delegates from each 100 men met and elected four of their number to go. They drew up a set of resolutions, which they proposed to send to the Rebel Secy. of War without even consulting the "outsiders." Of course there was quite a stir. A meeting was held and spread-eagle speeches made. The Resolutions were trotted out and read, but no action was really taken on them. Fiery speeches were made on each side. The Resolu-

tions were sent out to the Rebel authorities during the hubbub. The whole thing partook very much of a town meeting of the roughest kind. After we were tired with yelling as well as now and then listening to the speakers, Lieut. Lee of our Mess ascended the "rostrum" and gave us a very laughable pantomine [pantomime] speech, in which his persistent silence received much more applause than the windy sentences of his predecessors. Upon the whole we had a great deal of sport out of the affair, and, although there was a little show of feeling among some, there was on the whole a disposition to fairly discuss the matter.[67] Perhaps one cause of the dissatisfaction is the "cut-and-dried" appearance of the whole affair. It seems to many of us that we are being made "cat's paws" of, both by the Rebels and the officers who have got themselves chosen as delegates to go to Washington—which city I fear they will not see in a hurry. I suppose we shall have more meetings and more speeches, but I think it all can not amount to anything. If men were to be chosen to visit the camp at Andersonville to observe the sanitary condition of the men there, why were not the Surgeons represented on the paper? The resolutions speak of the "hopelessness of release," which certainly is a reflection upon our Govt. I for one believe that our Govt. is ready and most willing to exchange at any time man for man, but the Rebs intend to compel us to the exchange they propose—man for man as far as it goes and then parole what we have left, for them to put into the field again as at Vicksburg.[68]

[*Here are one and a half pages in German. Their content is inconsequential.*]

Thursday, June 30, 1864. Macon Prison, Ga.

I will lay aside my *Dutch* long enough to put in a word or two of English. It is now nearly two months since I had the mishap to fall into the hands of the enemy. It is needless to record that these two months have not been the shortest or the happiest of my life. Charley Hunt,[69] of the class of '61 was brought in the other day. He told me that I was at first reported killed—then wounded & prisoner, and finally left in doubt. The only serious regret at all this[,] is the great anxiety such rumors must cause my dear Mother. Of course she must have heard all the rumors. As yet I have heard nothing from home. Hunt brings a little more news from the 17th. Color Sergt. Emery[70] is wounded and at home. [Capt. William W.] Morrell[71] of the 20th Regt. was killed on a charge, and Prince, of my class, was wounded. Hunt seems to have the impression that Col. West is wounded, but does not know for a certainty. I wish I could get all the news.[72] I am now in daily hope of a letter from home. But I may yet wait two months more ere I hear a word from those who perhaps are now worrying about poor me. Meanwhile I will console myself by studying "Dutch." If I succeed in making any headway in speaking the "muttersprache" it will be a pleasing and profitable momento [memento] of my first attempt at prison life. One thing is certain, I am studying quite hard, and fancy I can see some progress already.

Today I can say I have almost suffered with hunger. Our appetites are good, and on the last day of the four our rations are decidedly short. We never leave a crumb in our plates. I do long for something good to eat. Two months of corn bread and no meat— no vegetables of any consequence—have left their mark. I have lost not a little flesh, but my health is still excellent and if I were confident of release in two months I could better content myself. But here we are, and here we may have to remain for a year to come. It is that uncertainty of the future that most of all things galls us. We tried to get up steam enough to have a sort of celebration on the coming 4th of July, but there was not life enough in the prison to do anything. Yesterday a Confederate officer came in and bought up "greenbacks" at the rate 4 1/2 Confederate for $1 U.S. This buying or any trading [is] in violation of orders. So this case must have been sanctioned by the authorities as it was done openly. I have bargained an old pair of buck gauntlets for $30 in Confederate money. For the same gloves I paid $5 in U.S. money 6 months ago. This shows the high price of things in the Confederacy.

We hear nothing new from Grant or Sherman, but are hoping to hear of the continued success of both. We have a great interest in

Sherman as we cherish vain hopes of raiding parties, which shall open the prison gates to us poor fellows. We hear nothing as yet of our proposed embassy to Washington. God grant that the exchange of prisoners may soon commence. Yet we cannot blame our Government. The U.S. only ask an exchange of all soldiers—man for man and officer for officer. To this the enemy do not agree. The negro business too will make new complications. Really the prospect is anything but flattering just now.

Sunday, July 3d, 1864.

"One year ago today I remember well." Just a year ago today at this very hour almost[,] our Brigade was put in "double quick" on the center of our line of battle at Gettysburg, at the time when the enemy opened with 120 pieces of artillery and attempted to break our line by their brave but fatal charge. A year ago yesterday we were engaged in a close musketry fight, at some points only 25 yards. Our Regt. lost 140 killed and wounded in less than an hour, many of them being hit by buckshot. I hope a year from today will not find me still a citizen of Macon, or any other prison town.

July 4th, 1864. Macon, Ga. Military Prison.

We have had the most genuine and enthusiastic Fourth of July I have ever seen. In the morning we assembled in the large building, and had a prayer by one of the chaplains, and then a succession of patriotic and somewhat spready speeches. The cheering and clapping of hands were earnest and loud. After we had been at it about two hours the Rebel authorities put an end to our celebration and forbade any future demonstrations. But there was more or less hilarity during the entire day. Early in the morning while the guard were in and were busy in putting us through "roll call" or rather "counting noses," some one held up a nice little American flag and we gathered around it, and gave three lusty cheers, and sang "Star Spangled Banner," &c. The Reb. officers looked cross but did not disturb us then or attempt to take the flag.[73] In the evening we had an exhibition of "the Elephant," which was of course manufactured for the occasion from two men, a blanket, and a couple of sticks for tusks. Lieut. Lee of our Mess exhibited the wonderful h'animal and walked him around the prison yard while we took the part of the small lads of a country town on the arrival of a circus. It has indeed been to all of us a most earnest and apparently patriotic "Fourth." The speeches all touched upon the grave subject of exchange but there was not the least desire to censure our government for this long and tedious confinement. Many here are suffering terribly with scurvy; and yet but few of them complain of their lot. Some of them have contracted the rheumatism by special confinement in damp cells infested by vermin of all kinds, all the way from lice to rats of fabulous size and ferocity. I trust and believe that our Government is not in any proper sense responsible for the trials of prison life which have been forced upon a thousand of our officers and 15,000 of our men for one year without the least interruption. True, our authorities might have prevented, or at least abbreviated this suffering by acceding to the unjust demands of the Rebels, but there is a great question at stake, and we only claim an even exchange of man for man. The prospect for us is still dim enough. If I were sure of seeing my regiment by November I should feel as though each day here were some gain toward that end, but when we are told that we are likely to winter here, each day seems but a small part of the not cheerful future. Yet it is no place for "the blues" here, and the casual visitor might think we were having a good time. I will admit that with a pocket full of money a man could render himself physically comfortable, but with an empty purse and ravenous appetite like my own there is but little practical delight in this style of life. Even if they would allow us to get boxes from home we could make our corn meal go down better. As for that, however, I do not so much complain of the quality as the quality [quantity]. In our mess we are all great eaters, and today even I am celebrating the "glorious Fourth" upon a stomach half filled with corn bread. We now get up very good corn bread in the ovens which some of our ingenious ones have prudently constructed. By cheating ourselves of bean soup, we can now and then have a mess of baked beans, which are to us really delicious. Those who have money can send out and buy vegetables of all kinds. Blackberries at $1.25 a quart are too dear a luxury for many of us and we have to punish ourselves by looking at those who are able to buy them. To show the high price of everything here I must note down a thing or two. When I was "gobbled up" I had a pair of buck gauntlets, which I have kept along. They cost me when new just $5. I had worn them 3 months. The other day I sold them to a Reb. speculator for $25 in Confederate money, the rate of exchange being 4 1/2 Confed. for 1 U.S. so I got more than the original cost. But the highest thing is a pair of top boots. A pair that costs us $10 or $12 in "green backs" will sell here for $150 or more in Confederate scrip. Yet with all their poverty they will not look at a silver watch but will give fabulous prices for gold ones. Their money is as plenty as it is worthless. The people at the North think it will be terrible when our currency depreciates to half value, but what would they do to see gold quoted at $20 and none in the *market* at that. I must put down a few current prices of articles they bring into the yard and sell daily. They are thus

Blackberries, qt.,	$1.25
Rice, qt.	2.00
Tomatoes, qt.	1.75
Eggs, doz.	4.00
Soda, lb.	6.00
Molasses, qt.	6.00
Butter, lb.	6.50
Potatoes, peck	5.00
Knife & Fork	8.50
Tin Plate	5.00
" Dipper	5.00
6 qt. Tin Pail	37.00
Writing Paper (qr.)	12.00
Flour (lb.)	1.00
Tobacco (lb.)	4.50

and other things in proportion!! Such prices seem enormous but we must remember that a Rebel dollar is worth about 5 cents in *metal*.

Of late the authorities have got into a big scare about their beloved prisoners and have brought three more pieces of artillery to bear upon us. They now have 6 field pieces ready to pour in the grape and canister. Men sleep by the cannon every night, and the sentinels, although overworked, are most always wide awake enough to fire at, if not to hit, an escaping prisoner. Two of our officers however, got out the other night by crawling under the fence where the drain runs through. The sentinels fired at but missed the second one.

I have not yet heard a word from home. I am all the time worrying lest they have heard the rumor of my being killed, and are still laboring under that delusion, while I am here in the State of Georgia, well and hungry. I have written 7 letters and intend to keep it up although I have some doubts of the letters ever reaching their destination. As yet I have no really good information from the 17th or my adopted Regt, the Sharp Shooters. All the Maine officers who come in seem to have the impression that Col. West is wounded, but as yet I am not wholly certain of it, although I think he must have come in contact with a Rebel musket ball. I hope he is all right, but presume that he as well as myself has at last had a streak of bad luck.

Tuesday, July 5th New Mess—Rumors.

I have now joined a new mess. There are four of us and all from the good State of Maine. Capt. [Julius B.] Litchfield and Lt. [Nathaniel A.] Robbins[74] of the 4th Maine and Lt. Whitney of the 2d R.I. Cav. are my fellows in corn bread and bean soup. Robbins is a graduate of Bowdoin, and Whitney was in the class of '64 when I was ruminating beneath the classical shades (!) of that honored Seminary. I am very much pleased with the mess, and think I shall much prefer living in these shanties to being cooped up in the house where the nights generally were too warm at first. By the way, though we have very hot days, yet I never saw so cool nights in the month of July at home.

Wednesday, July 6th.

Today we have an unusual and cheering variety of prison rumors. They say that [Gen. Joseph E.] Johns[t]on is still falling back, and that Sherman has thrown three of his Corps into Johnston's rear. Even the Rebel paper admits that their idol, Johnston, is continually falling back, but claims that he does it to draw Sherman into his meshes.[75] Yet there are today curious indications even open to our own limited observation. Four of the pieces of Artillery which have hitherto menaced us have today been withdrawn, and taken we know not whither. A Regiment of Cavalry has passed by outside at a point visibile [visible] to us. Negroes and others say that the Rebs. are fortifying near here. In fine, everything looks as though they were afraid of a cavalry raid from Johnston's rear by some of Sherman's Cavalry. Of course we look on with no little of interest, but yet entertain small hopes of any release by an armed force. The Enemy had to take the prisoners out of Richmond. If they move us from here I cannot say where they could safely convey us. I presume they have a place looked out and we need not trouble ourselves with conjectures. Some of our officers manage to amuse themselves hugely with cricket, base ball, fencing, &c., although there is but little room in this little four-acre yard for 1400 men to live and play ball in the bargain. Yet they keep at it. Some, however, are continually gambling—even on the Sabbath. The want of all authority and discipline is daily becoming more apparent. No one acknowledges any superiors, and angry disputes and even fisticuffs are getting quite common. It is indeed degrading for two officers to settle their troubles by pounding each other, yet it cannot be denied by the gravest philosophers that it is a more natural than refined method of proceeding. Then, too, there is a sort of demoralizing influence in this manner of life that makes a man feel more like fighting than doing anything more useful or dignified. When an officer is, or thinks he is insulted, the only question he asks himself is whether he is physically superior to his opponent. Sometimes one is so far gone as to neglect this important precaution. In such a case, he wades in, relying upon the crowd to rush in and end the fight before the weakling gets hurt.

We have as yet had but little sickness. The camp is not in the neatest possible condition, but is daily improving. We should be very thankful for one thing—we have an abundance of good water, although the soap is a trifle in quantity and less than a trifle in quality being poorer than any soft soap I ever saw at the North.

Sunday, July 10th. Fresh Fish !!!

Today we have received a new installment of victims from the Army of the Potomac. Among them was Lt. Col. [Homer R.] Stoughton of the 2d Sharp Shooters. There were two officers from our Brigade. From them I learn a little of the 17th, the first really reliable information I have had since my capture. Col. Stoughton tells me that Col. West was shot through the thigh by a musket ball, but was doing well while in hospital with him. I hear also that Lt. [James G.] Sturgis[76] of Co. G was killed by a solid shot while building breastworks. He speaks of several others, officers, as killed and wounded but knows none of them by name. I am informed that Capt. [Charles D. Merriman] Merryman and Act. Adjt. Rilliet of my adopted Regiment—the 1st Sharp Shooters—were both killed.[77] From all sources we have most pitiful tales of deaths and wounds. We often look upon ourselves as unlucky, but perhaps our capture alone has saved the lives of very many of us.

"A new broom sweeps cleanly," and my new mess suits me to a charm. We have enough to eat, now that I am the only voracious member of the ones, while under the old arrangement I was half starved all the time. We have been exercising ourselves with getting new dishes to tickle the palate—poor palate perceives I fear that everything savors of corn meal. I think I must put down a few of my recipes for cooking, &c., (e.g.)

Boiled Pudding. Take 2 qts. corn meal, mix with heaping teaspoonful salt, same of soda, four times as much vinegar or 8 times yeast, 1 gill of pork fat, and water to the consistency of batter. Put same in a small cloth bag, and set it in boiling water for two hours.

Sauce for same. Pour 1/2 gill molasses, 1/2 spoonful salt, 3 spoonfuls flour, (well mixed) into 1 pint of boiling water. Let it remain, well stirred, for 10 minutes.

Vinegar. Mix 1 pint water, 1/2 gill molasses, same of meal, and let it stand in the sun for 4 days.

Yeast of Emptings. Mix meal and water to the consistency of batter, put in a very little salt and let it stand for 3 days. Use 3 spoonfuls of this with 1 teaspoonful of soda for a loaf of bread.

Baked Apple Dumplings—(Danville Dec. 20, 1864)

Thursday, July 14th, 1864.

I am still vigorously at work with my German. I have now commenced to keep a Diary in German, a task which affords instruction as well as good amusement and serves to while away the hours of confinement. Still no word from home. My finances are reduced to the small sum of one Confederate dollar—which will buy a quart of blackberries, two sheets of paper or a pint of peanuts! My stockings are very much worn and I have come down to the prison level of bare feet and do not think of putting on my boots at all. This week I have been exercising myself in needlework on Whitney's shirt. I have almost remade it, and it really looks quite well. Every week improves my cooking, and I can now get up a very decent meal considering the means and material we are blessed with. The best thing we have is boiled pudding. This is made of nothing to be sure, but corn meal, pork fat, etc, but then it is to us, a variety, and that is a great thing for us. Even our corn meal or crust coffee has quite a decent taste. There is much to learn in a place like this. In a sanitary point of view there is much of interest here. 1500 of us are living on a small allowance of corn meal and just enough of fat meat to well grease the pan, and yet, with exception of the scurvy, contracted in Libby Prison, there is less sickness than among 1500 men in one of our best regulated camps. We lead an idle life, have no anti-scorbutic food of any consequence and certainly our minds can not be in a very healthy state, and yet, we are healthy beyond expectation, although many are faily [failing] slowly but not less surely. I say the prisoners are healthy. Perhaps I use the wrong term. They are simply not sick. The long confinement and dim prospect of release has made many of them wilt away. Now I account for our unexpected health in this way,—our food is easily digested, and perhaps much better, if less palatable, than such things as we used to eat. The simplicity of our diet alone is our protection. Yet with all this philosophy I am willing any time to return to my former condition of plenty and good living. We all look forward to the day when we can once more have our liberty and everytime we sit down to our corn bread we vow future punishment to anything good to eat, if we ever do get home again there will be some tall eating done.

Today we have rumors of exchange, removal and the fighting around Atlanta. The Macon paper admits that Atlanta will have to be given up by Johnston. They have already brought many women and children to Macon for safety. We are unofficially, and perhaps unreliably informed, that we shall be moved from here tomorrow. I presume the authorities are afraid that Sherman may send a raiding party to Macon.[78] Of course we would be most happy to be liberated without the form of parole or exchange, but unfortunately, we do not expect anything of the kind. I presume our next journey will take us to Alabama. There is a rumor that the Rebel Govt. has made new and more liberal proposals for exchange.

Saturday, July 23d, 1864.

This week I have been at swords' points with my digestive organs. It seems to be a very general rule here that one must be sick once in a while. The healthiest of us have taken our turns. This diet does not allow much regularity, although in itself it is anything but variety. I am now better but feel as if I had had a hard week's work. One night I was very sick, being attacked with a chill and fever, which however, yielded to a double dose of quinine which fortunately for me, Whitney had stored up long ago.

Today we have conflicting rumors about the fight going on at

Atlanta. Yesterday's papers said that Sherman was shelling Atlanta.[79] Today, they claim that Sherman has been whipped. During the past week General Johnston has been superseded by the appointment of Genl. [John B.] Hood of Texas. Why the Rebel Govt. should remove such a man as Johnston seems hard to understand. It shows they did not consider him a match for Sherman. Of course we do not believe that Sherman has yet been whipped. The rumor further says that [Maj. Gen. James B.] McPherson is killed.[80] If Atlanta is taken we are told that we shall be moved from here to some other point for safekeeping—Rumor designates Columbia as the probable place. From the Army of the Potomac we hear nothing particularly encouraging. Lee's Army does not seem to be so much surrounded, cut off, &c.(!) as it was. We do hope that Grant may effect something.

This summer has witnessed the third Rebel invasion of the North. [Maj. Gen. Jubal A.] Early, commanding the old Stonewall Jackson corps, managed to dash up past Harper's Ferry & after levying taxes in money, cattle, &c. burning and destroying railroads and public property generally—started on his way back with a rich supply, but was overhauled at Snicker's Gap and made to disgorge all his trains, plunder, and part of his artillery. So say the Rebel papers as well as the published extracts from Northern ones.[81]

We have a new, and apparently, a very good prison commandant,—Lt. [Samuel Boyer] Davis. He was taken prisoner at Gettysburg, and perhaps has learned by experience how to treat prisoners.[82] "Fresh Fish" arrive weekly. We now have about 1900 "victims" here. The other day one of our officers blacked up with coal, and picking up a spade, tried to play nigger past the guard. He got by the sentinel, but the officer of the guard detected the cheat and brought him to bay with a cocked revolver.[83] He was kept out one night, and then brought back to us. The prison authorities are on a very sharp lookout for tunnels, and the other day succeeded in discovering one nearly completed. I have had no share in any since the one I first invested in was discovered.[84]

The mails do not go from here with any regularity. Hereafter I shall write only when a prison mail is made up. I have wasted precious paper in writing every week. I hope soon to have a word from home and ascertain whether my anxious parents consider me alive or dead.

My great daily trouble now is corn bread. The very sight of it disgusts and sickens me. Hitherto I have relished it when hungry, but now I am become, like the old Libbyites, sick of corn bread. It is fun to hear these old fellows mourn for the old days of even Libby prison, where they were allowed to get boxes and letters from home. They really lived high there compared with the fare of this wretched and abominable place. Yet, if one had money here he could live well. I have spent my last Confederate dollar (greenbacks went long ago) for some little things to eat. Whitney sold a gold dollar for $15 in Confederate money.

Wednesday, July 27th.

Finally it is decided that we are to leave Macon. We go to Charleston it is said. Tomorrow morning is the time appointed for us to leave this famous place and 600 of us are selected for the distinguished honor. This includes *my* mess. All the Field officers are on the list. There is a stupendous plan on foot to capture the guard and run the train to Pocataligo and there take to the woods, and attempt to make our escape in a body to our own lines, only 12 miles distant. Of course, the arms of the guard would be in our hands. The unarmed members of the party would be supposed to give a strong moral support. I have been solicited to join the organization but declined as I am of opinion that it would be impracticable, and then again, it would be causing bloodshed which we have virtually promised to desist from when delivering up our swords and accepting quarter. I believe it the duty of every prisoner to escape when opportunity offers—either individually or with associates, but such party has no right to shed blood or take up arms until they reach their own lines. [Francis] Lieber, in his work on Military Law, says that when more than two prisoners escape or attempt to escape together and are caught in the act, they are liable to death.[85] Now, I am fully determined to make my own individual escape before we reach the city of Charleston. If I do not succeed until the train is captured I suppose I shall have to join my fortunes with the crowd. My desire of escape is great enough to risk a little in making an attempt for the North Star.

CHAPTER SIX

Charleston and Columbia Prisons

ю́s͡о̄Ꙩs

Thursday, July 28th.
Started from Macon at daylight. (See under Aug. 31.)

Friday, July 29th.
Arrived at Charleston, S.C.

ю́s͡о̄Ꙩs

Charleston, S.C. Aug 2d, 1864.
My dear Mother:

The mail goes to-day and I avail myself of the opportunity to inform you that I am for the present in very good condition. Charles Hunt of Gorham is one of my messmates and we are having as good a time as could be expected. The prospect of exchange brightens. There are 600 of us here hoping to see home ere long. But still the thing was interrupted once more. I wrote a letter two or three days ago, announcing my arrival, in which I requested you to send $2 1/2 in gold. You need not send it unless you hear from me again. I am in most excellent condition as to health, although I feel somewhat weak and am not so fleshy as I was once. One should be thankful for good health while he is a prisoner of war. How long we shall remain in Charleston I do not know. They feed us better here than in any other place yet. Yesterday I ate my first piece of fresh meat for 3 months. Not a word from you yet. Direct Maj. Chas. P Mattocks, Prisoner of War at Charleston Aug 1, 1864.

Wednesday, Aug. 3d.

The 50 officers who have been confined here before us were exchanged & sent North today.[1]

Monday, Aug. 8th.

Consolidated our Mess with Pendleton and [Edward H.] Sears.[2] They have sent to the Fleet for boxes of eatables and money and we have a prospect of renewed life. We are really almost dead, or rather have been, until within a few days. Hunt has joined our Mess, and has made himself still more welcome by selling his gold watch and appropriating the proceeds to the benefit of the Mess. The watch was a very good hunter and sold for $750 in Confederate scrip, which reduced to Green Backs, amounts to 150, or in gold 37.50. This money will not buy much here, yet, it will greatly alleviate our trials and *gastronomical* sufferings, which are more real than imaginary.

Military Prison. Charleston, S.C. August 14th, 1864.

My dear Mother:

I continue to drop a line occasionally, although I have not had anything in the shape of a letter from you since I was captured. I trust however you are all well. My health is still good and my appetite indicates no future malady. We are now settled in the city of Charleston, and I presume you can get a box to me. Please send one immediately containing 1 pr. of my old pants (Brunswick), two pr. socks, 1 pr. coarse shoes, No. 9, Soap, & Towel, Writing paper, Envelopes, blank book about 6 inches by 4, *not ruled,* for money account, leather covers, stiff, almost anything to read, cheap pocket knife, 2 pr. old Drawers of any kind, 1 pr. slippers, any home newspapers, 1 old pocket-hankerchief [handkerchief], 31 boxes Baking Powder, Few Nutmeg, Pepper, Soda.

Eatables are not allowed, but clothing and medicine can come. Put in a very little chocolate and coffee. If the box comes my men are greatly in need of Tobacco. Tell Erastus to put in 3 Briar root pipes and 5 lbs. smoking Tobacco and a few matches. The address must be Maj. Chas. P. Mattocks, Prisoner of War by Adams Express to Hilton Head, care Capt. Wm. S. Gayer [Wm. J. Gayer], Provost Marshall, Charleston S.C. By Flag of Truce. By this same address please send by express in an envelope $10 in gold. For the present that will be money enough to make me at least a little better off. We are all anxious to learn more about the exchange prospect but all seems doubtful, although fifty of our officers have been specially exchanged. Charlie Hunt is in my mess. Six of us discuss our rations together. We are all from Maine but one. I am now daily expecting a letter from you. More than three months now since I have heard a word from any of you and you may suppose I am impatient. Remember me to all friends. Wish I had Matilda Rhodes' address. Write me full particulars of the casualties &c. in the 17th. Your letters can be as long as you are willing to make them. Seal the letter and then the contents need not be seen until broken open for examination by the proper officials here. . . . Love to Itie. Have you got that house yet.

❧ ❧

[*Here CPM once again wrote in larger script, perhaps feeling more confident of obtaining writing supplies.*]

August 15th, 1864. Roper Hospital, Broad St., Charleston, S.C.
The light dawns again! The troubles of moving from place to place, the cares of housekeeping, and a most thorough physical lassitude and *ennui* to speak in the manner of novelists, have prevented me from continuing my lucubrations in this erratic Diary.

But "ye writer must go back." When we first arrived in Charleston the limited but secure hospitality of the jail yard was most freely extended to us. Here we remained about 10 days, sleeping in one of the cells by night and wasting ourselves in the jail yard by day. Some of the officers had the good luck to get tents, but there were not enough for all hands. From the jail the Field Officers and their Messes, were very unexpectedly promoted to the Work House, a building adjoining the jail. Many of our officers were too high spirited to choose to move from a jail to a work house. Alas for human pride! Refusing even a Corporal's warrant has been the bane of many a soldier, and lost to the Army many a General perhaps. The rest of us, more philosophic than our neighbors, snatched at the bait, and considering a work house a more honorable boarding house than a jail, moved our Lares and Penates to the Work House where we soon settled down upon the principle that "contentment is better than wealth."[3] There was a peculiarity in the architecture of both buildings; the windows in particular are more substantially constructed than in any hotel I ever sojourned in at the North.

The windows of the work house were made evidently with a view to beauty, while at the same time, the cunning artificer did not intend them to be any less strong than those of the jail. [*See fig. 16.*] In the jail we were locked up at night much after the manner in which we dispose of thieves, cut-throats, and pickpockets at the North. At the Work House we had the liberty of quite a pleasant yard although the view was somewhat obstructed by a wall of 20 feet. Considered in a practical, architectural or culinary point of view the Work House was far superior to the Jail. Architecturally, because the bars in the windows were not perpendicular and horizontal, but ran diagonally to the window sides, thus uniting beauty with strength, which is, I believe, one of the chief points of excellence, according to Ruskin. The practical and culinary superiority consisted in the immense quantity of old rubbish, such as pails, tubs, axes, shovels, hammers, saws, &c., which the "vandal Yankees" were not long in discovering and even wresting from under lock and key. So far along in our new home and we have an order to pack up. Magnanimous Rebs! The jail was too full.—They love us, and of their own accord freely offer us the hospitality of the Work House. Three hundred more arrive from Macon. Too many for the Jail and Work House both. Again our chivalrous keepers become magnanimous and offer us the Roper Hospital—a really fine place. This is really a very fine place for prisoners of war, and had they put us here at the first we should have felt not a little real gratitude. As it is, we know there is no heart in their present kindness. The Jail and Work House ran over with "Yanks" and the next place was Roper Hospital. We have all taken a parole not to pass or try to pass the guard lines, and we have the promise of the use of the entire yard, as well as the whole building, which we enjoy. There are but 200 of us here and there is ample room for all. We have a nice veranda in front of our room where we sit in the shade and deliberate upon the ever doubtful hope of exchange. Many things have, of late, conspired to render our imprisonment more endurable. About the 1st of August 50 of our officers were exchanged—the same 50 who left Macon two months ago.[4] This morning 5 more went away to balance a Maj. Gen. against a Brigadier. Maj. Gen. Ed[ward]. Johnson[5] having been sent down by our Govt. for one of the Brigadiers held by the "Rebs." General Johnson visited the prisoners in the jail the other day. I had a few words of conversation with him. I was captured by a Regiment of his Division, and he was captured by my Division. In a speech made by Johnson a few days since, he says the Yankees treated him very well,—more I fear than any of us can say of our *chivalrous* enemies.

Fig. 16. Windows. [Mattocks's drawing of the windows in Roper Hospital and the Work House. Courtesy of James M. White, Jr.]

The rations here are enigmatical. One day, all rice, another, all meal and bacon &c.,—no mixture. It is starve one day and feast the next. Just as the 50 officers were about leaving us the authorities fed us finely on fresh beef and flour bread, in order no doubt, to make our Northern friends believe that we were being finely treated. Then, too, we were daily promised that we should be moved "to-morrow"—which was in very truth a prisoner's "to-morrow." This parole with the liberties of this yard and building, which they have offered us, shows also the disposition of the "Chivalry." It is very much like Louis Napoleon's freedom of suffrage.—"Vote as you wish, but if you do not vote to suit me, off goes your head."[6] This parole is simply this—"Sign this paper and remain or refuse and back you go to jail." If we were disposed to be spunky we might accept the harsh alternative. However, after a man has been a prisoner a long time he is less on spunk than a new comer. Any "old convict" will do almost anything that will better his present condition, provided it be consistent with his sense of honor. There certainly is no compromise of honor in this parole, and most assuredly it is an improvement of our condition. The only thing we look at is the spirit of our *magnanimous* keepers.

Exchange is now on everybody's tongue. They say that a proposition has been made to our government to exchange 600 of us, man for man, rank for rank, and leave unsettled the excess and negro questions.[7] Some are sanguine, while others believe nothing, hope nothing. I am neither one nor the other. Perhaps yes, and perhaps no, is my condition. Two weeks more will decide our prospects.

Money is now abundant in the "Maine delegation"—our Mess. Mr. Pendleton succeeded in button holing the French Consul, Mr. de'Sibourg, and to-day he got a box of clothing costing $650 and $1350 in confed. scrip, for which he is to pay in gold at the rate of $1 for $30. This money he (Mr. P.) loans to the Mess, and we are to pay him in "green backs" at the rate of $1 for $5—a most fortunate thing for us, as we are now living very well for prisoners. As yet we have no butter, tea or coffee, but have to content ourselves with ham, flour bread, milk &c., all of which we buy. The only things of our rations we use are some of the rice, bacon, salt, and molasses. The last has only been issued once thus far. Although my first three months have told considerably upon my general health, and I now feel very much debilitated, I yet think I can stand up under a long and almost hopeless imprisonment so long as I have enough to eat. As I was situated at Macon it was hard indeed. I was actually hungry often for even corn bread, but here I do not suffer for the best flour bread the market affords. I am impatient to get back either to my own or my adopted Regiment, but if I am doomed to stay here for months to come I want at least enough to eat as a consolation. Of late, I have amused myself with reading [Edward Lytton] Bulwer's "My Novel,"[8] which is really a masterpiece of "plot work." I am much pleased with it. My German has been somewhat neglected of late owing to my general debility. To tell the truth, I have been almost dead lately, only not down sick, except one day when I had to knock under. My trouble seemed to be a severe short bilious attack. I am now gaining now very rapidly, and eat my regular rations very readily. In fine my appetite is voracious. The other day we bought a barrel of potatoes, which are already half gone.

August 16th, Tuesday.
The prospect still brightens! By prospect brightened we always mean hope of something to eat and to wear. Yesterday Litchfield was informed that a distant relative of his would call in a day or two and loan him a thousand dollars. It seems large to count loans by thousands but we must remember that $1000 means only $200 in United States currency. Upon the whole, I think our Mess can endure for some time to come. I have sent home by mail for a box of clothing and $10 in gold. By underground *mail,* I sent for a 25 lb. box of things to eat. The underground communication is this. Anything we do not wish to trust to the mail we note on a slip of paper, give it to some officer going away, who writes a letter himself to our friends. The scrutiny of Provost Marshals is thus evaded. Everybody is still discussing Exchange. To me the thing remains *"in statu quo."*

I shall have to look out for myself or I shall forget the way the authorities have treated us, and go into ecstacies over the present dispensation of favors. The guard is removed from the yard, which is indeed a very fine one, and under good cultivation. We are stopping at a very fine hotel, *only* we do not go out upon the street nor receive many new guests. There are now about 200 of us here, and we are beginning to have a very lively time for the circumstances. We have gas at night without limit, and without cost. No retiring at Taps and no falling in for roll call for us now. We are emphatically gentlemen of leisure. We do our own cooking, but the clothes are sent out and washed at $5.00 per dozen. We have got tired of rubbing our hands upon each other, with no chance to boil the clothing. $5.00 here is only $1 at home, and $1 per dozen will never fail us unless we have more clothing than at present.

Today we have a large detail of our officers busy cleaning up the rubbish in the yard and the dirt in the building. Col. [Francis T.] Sherman,[9] the Senior officer present, has been requested by the Rebel authorities to manage affairs according to his own views. Everyone seems to take hold of the business with the right spirit, and I think we shall have but very little sickness here at any time. By the way, Sears and Pendleton were both sick last night, but they are convalescent to-day. I am cooking in place of Pendleton to-day.

Friday, August 19th.

Yesterday was the Second Anniversary of our muster into the U.S. Service. The Regiment was mustered for three years at Cape Elizabeth (near Portland), Maine, on the 18th day of August, 1862. So I am now out of my second year and beginning my third under rather unfavorable auspices. This month my health has been quite poorly. Yesterday I fasted in honor of my Anniversary as well as through respect to my digestive organs. I am now dieting on toast and boiled eggs. It is fortunate for me that we have money to buy these little things. Since coming here we have been living very comfortably, & now the only thing we are suffering for is exchange. The prospect is good, but it is a doubtful and most deceitful thing anyway. Some little clothing from the Sanitary Commission has arrived but has not yet been distributed. If there is any one thing of this war more noble and praiseworthy than another, it is the Sanitary Commission.[10] Wherever our officers or soldiers are in distress—even in Southern prisons—without aid from friends—the Commission is sure to send them something to render their stay more endurable. As yet we have been unable to get anything on our own account. The Agent of the S.C. at Hilton Head, hearing that we have arrived here, has probably availed himself of the first chance to send us these supplies. They consist of Shirts, Drawers, Socks, Shoes, &c.

I must record a most worthy instance of kindness on the part of a gentleman of this city. When the French Consul, de'Sibourg, was in negotiating with Pendleton, he chanced to mention that he was acquainted with a Mr. Williams, formerly of Maine, now residing in this city. Litchfield, immediately caught an "idea" which afterward proved to be a very profitable one. He wrote a note to this Williams, telling him he suspected he might be a relative, as his mother (Litchfield's) had a brother by that name who went to Virginia before the war, and had not been heard of since. So "Litch" very logically concluded he might be this same Mr. Williams of Charleston. Upon this very hypothetical relationship he solicited the loan of some money, the same to be cancelled by a check or draft on New York or Boston. Mr. W. received the note and last Wednesday presented himself. It was at once discovered that there was [no] relationship, but still Mr. W. had provided himself with a nice roll of Confederate scrip amounting to $1000. Upon receiving this Litchfield proposed to give a draft, check or something. This was refused, and he was told to forward an equivalent in gold or U.S. currency to a relative of Williams's in Augusta, Me. "Litch" urged him to take a receit [receipt] or some written acknowledgment, but even that was declined. So the money is obtained without any written security, and that too from an entire stranger. In talking with Mr. Williams I found that he used to live in Saco, Me., and is well acquainted in that whole vicinity. I liked him very much, and shall not

soon forget what he has done for us on the strength of our being
Maine men. His full name is

Edward Williams,
Wholesale Grocer,
Charleston, S.C.

In the language of the novelists "I have expectations,"[11] as Mr.
Williams has told me of a Vermonter boarding with him who used
to live at Derby Line, Vt. By good luck I was once acquainted at that
place, and, from being a "native *Varmonter*" am more or less posted
in the State generally. I did not feel sufficiently bold or sufficiently
needy to write him a note, but sent him my name together with the
other Vermont officers, and "hoped he would call," &c. Williams
has promised to call again and I presume will bring his friend with
him.

There is now a belief among many that a general exchange of
officers will begin on Monday next. I am not so sanguine. There is
reason, however, to *hope* that an exchange will soon begin. I trust
that I may be on the "first boat."

Military Prison. Charleston, S. C.
August 19, 1864
My dear Mother:

The mail is going North and I avail myself of the opportunity to
drop a line. I have already written for you to send me $10 in gold and
a box of clothing. I trust that you may get the letter. The list of clothing embraced shirts, drawers, shoes, socks, soap, towels, &c. We
are now confined in Roper Hospital, an elegant place where we have
plenty of room and a good sea breeze. The guard is only nominal as
we are on parole not to attempt to escape. We are much better cared
for now than at any time previous during our imprisonment. I have
not heard a word from any of you yet. Of course I hope you are all
alive and well. Exchange is now the great question with us, and al-

though I am not over sanguine, I can yet say that we have reason to look for a speedy exchange of us all. I sincerely hope I may be a candidate for the "first boat." That however is a thing beyond my control. Charles Hunt of Gorham messes with me. I presume you may see his mother. We enjoy each other's company greatly. I wish I could hear from Col. W. and the Regiment. Even if you hear from me that I do not receive your letters, do not for that reason cease writing. I shall get them all eventually, and there can not be too many of them. I am longing to read them. You are allowed to write as much as you please.[12] Love to all. Have you got that house yet?

My third year of service begins to-day reckoning from the formal muster at Portland. I hope it may end a little nearer the North Star.

❧❧❧

Wednesday, August 24th.

We are now being entertained by General Gillmore's "Swamp Angel" battery which is shelling the city, a range of five or six miles.[13] The missiles strike very near us—some within 100 yards. Two or three have passed over this building. Our forces seem to know just where we are, and evidently avail themselves of their knowledge to the effect of seeing how near they can come to us without hitting. We can endure the trouble as it does us much good to hear Union powder burn even if we are slightly exposed.[14] Since three o'clock yesterday they have kept the thing up without interruption, firing every fifteen minutes. We can hear the report of the gun, and in two or three seconds the shell comes whistling through the air. A few time-fuse shells have been fired to-day, which exploded in plain view just front of this building. There is a great cry and rush to see the explosions.[15]

Exchange stock has gone down wonderfully within a few days. The subject seems more doubtful than at any time recently. How soon that eventful day of departure will come is a matter of the merest conjecture, and those who speculate the least upon the subject are the happiest in the end. I am in a sort of apathy upon the point, and am but little excited by the varying rumors we are cursed with. I will not deny a faint hope, for even

The wretch, condemned with life to part
Still, still on hope relies;
And every pang that rends the heart
Bids expectation rise.

And why should not even a forlorn prisoner of war have the same sweet consolation. To view the matter with the eye of philosophy is indeed the easiest and most practical way of disposing of the subject of exchange, parole and escape. "All things mortal have an end," and I presume our imprisonment will. There are officers here who were captured a year ago last May, and I presume that the fifteen months' residence in the "Sunny South" has convinced them that there is a possibility of their lives ending before the imprisonment. Some of them are really almost worn out. There is nothing mentally, morally or physically invigorating in this mode of life. I am truly thankful that my health has been so good. But, although I have been well generally, I am far from feeling as I did four months ago. I shall know how to sympathize with the bird let loose from a cage in which it has for a long time been confined. I am quite weak but I presume a little good Northern or even Virginia air will make me all right once more. I am ready to try the experiment at any time "the powers that be" may see fit to call upon me.

Our Mess still prospers and we are all well just now. It consists of six of us—all but one from the State of Maine. They are (by rank)

C. P. Mattocks,	Maj.	17th Me.	Portland
J. B. Litchfield,	Capt.	4th Me.	Rockland.
N. A. Robbins,	2d Lt.	4th Me.	Union.
C. O. Hunt,	1st Lt.	5th Me. Battery,	Gorham.
G. H. Pendleton,	Act. Master,	U.S.N.	Yarmouth
Ed. H. Sears,	Paymaster	U.S.N.	Providence, R.I.

Robbins graduated at Bowdoin in '56, Hunt in '61, myself in '62, and Sears at Brown in '62. So we have on the whole, a very pleasant mess. Hunt and I attended school together in the town of

Gorham sixteen years ago. Of course, we are getting to be great friends. I have seen more of him here and become more thoroughly acquainted with him than during the whole three years we were in college together. His brother Harry was in my class.[16] I knew him very well, but Charlie and I were not thrown much into the society of each other. Cochran of my class is in this building, but I do not see him much.

I perceive that I am approaching the end of my luminous Diary. I had commenced to write in a fine hand for the laudable, as well as necessary, purpose of economizing paper, but when Pendleton made the "big strike" of $1000, I concluded not to cramp up my fingers any longer as I saw the way clear to buy another book. I had hoped to finish this book upon good Union soil, but I begin to perceive the futility of such a project. It was commenced in Portland, and I should be happy indeed, if I could end it in the same delightful city. However, I can begin another, hoping to end that there.

One of our officers, Maj. [David] Vickars[17] of New Jersey, was caught stealing wool blankets from a neighboring yard a day or two since, and has been conducted to jail under guard, where I presume he is reaping the fruit of his misdeed.

Military Prison. Charleston, S.C.

August 26th 1864

My dear Father:

I suppose it will seem natural for me to renew a habit I once had of calling on you for money before I had found out how to earn my own. I think I am *earning* enough now, but my Paymaster does not seem to visit me this Summer. Will you please send one hundred dollars ($100) in GreenBacks, or an equivalent in gold if you can get the gold for $3.00 or even $3.50 to Capt. W.L.M. Burger, Assistant Adjutant General, Dept. of the South, Hilton Head, S.C.[18] Send it by Express, prepaid, to him, and he will forward it by Flag of Truce to me. This gentleman has already advanced some money to me and I want to repay as well as to secure some myself with the least possible delay. I ask that you will not delay a single day after receiving this even if you have already sent the $10 in gold I sent to Mother for. Capt. Burger will receipt to you for the money. The package will come safely. In future if anything is sent to me (except letters) let that be addressed to Capt. for me "Prisoner of War" &c.

We are in Roper Hospital on parole. Do not suppose by this that we are sick. The building has not been used as a hospital for some time. I hope mother will send the box of clothing, as I am much in need of it. My health is very good, although I am quite weak for me. There is a faint hope of exchange just now. I presume we shall be ordered to our Regiments when we are released. Remember me to Albert and Erastus and all the family and friends. One of my messmates is a son of Mr. Pendleton of Gorham. You must know him. I have not heard from any of you since April. It seems a long time. Write often. Dont delay the money. I hope mother will still continue to write letters. I shall get them sooner or later. Hope you have bought that house and settled down to housekeeping.

❧❧

Wednesday, Aug. 31st.

For the past week Gen. Foster has given us a double allowance of shells. A few days ago a hundred-pounder exploded just in front of this building, and a fragment weighing 12 or 18 lbs. penetrated the roof of the "Mad House," one of the out-buildings of this hospital, and at present the dwelling place of fifty or sixty "live Yankees." The shell passed down into one of the cells, and was stopped by the floor. It came within two or three feet of an officer. This building is forty yards in the rear of the hospital proper, so it can not be denied that we are in reality under fire. In fact, this square is nearly as much exposed just now as the same number of square feet in any other part of the city. Until within a few days the shells seemed to shun this square, although some went by one end of this building.

More recently, however, Mr. Foster seems determined that we shall see something of the elephant.[19]

Exchange stock is above par to-day on account of a very unmeaning squib in this morning's paper.[20] This is the last day of Summer. I sincerely hope that the last day of Fall will not find me still an unwilling resident of this place.

I must not forget to chronicle a most welcome letter I received the other day. I will give a full account of the affair. When we arrived in Charleston I addressed a short letter "To Any Freemason on Morris Island"[21] and sent it by Flag of Truce. In this I stated briefly my necessities, and requested a box of eatables, such as sugar, tea, coffee, pepper, &c., but said nothing about money. A few days ago I received a letter of which this is a verbatim copy.

> "Hd. Qrs., Department of the South.
> Hilton Head, S.C.,
> August 21st, 1864.
>
> Maj. Chas. P. Mattocks,
> 17th Maine Vols. Prisoner of War,
> Charleston, S. C.
> My dear Brother:
>
> In looking over the last "Flag of Truce Mail" received from the Confederate lines, my attention was particularly attracted to your letter addressed "To Any Freemason on Morris Island, S.C." Being a Mason I took the liberty of opening and reading the same; I found, upon perusal, that it would be much better for me to retain your letter and attend to your request myself at this place, as it could not be done on Morris Island. I have read your earnest appeal for help to several of our beloved fraternity, and must say that if I should accept all the assistance offered, you would be perfectly surprised at the quantity, but I shall merely send you what articles you request, with a few little additional articles, and some money in case you should wish to purchase anything that might not be found in the box. I have received from Col. Charles R. Brayton of the 3d R. I. Artillery, One Hundred and Thirty-three ($133) dollars in Confed-

erate money, for which he, I believe, paid some Ten ($10) in Green-
backs. I also received from Lt. Col. [Stewart Lyndon] Woodford,[22]
Act. Judge Advocate of this Dept. Five ($5) dollars in Greenbacks,
all of which I enclose, together with Ten ($10) dollars in Greenbacks
from your humble servant. I have given a list of the articles you asked
for to Messrs. Dunbars & Franz, Traders at this place, who are also
Masons. They will put the articles up in a box, with some few extras not mentioned in your letter. These gentlemen have insisted
upon sending this as a donation, and positively refuse to allow me
to pay anything for its contents, and will give me no idea as to its
value. I shall send some paper and envelopes over at once to be put
in the box. I have to request that you will not hesitate to let me
know at any time what you may be in need of, either for yourself or
for any of the fraternity or Brother officers, as I shall be most happy
to attend to any requests of the kind for our unfortunate Brother
Masons or Officers. You need not let the return of this money trouble
you in the least. Whenever it is perfectly convenient to you, if it is
years hence, you may return it; besides ask for as much more as you
may want. I would send more now but you did not say anything
about wanting any in your letter, so I only send a little. Hoping that
everything you may wish to alleviate your present suffering may be
found in the box,

    I remain very Respectfully & fraternally your Brother

                           W.L.M. Burger,

                    (Sd) Asst. Adjt. Genl. (Capt)

                     Albion No. 26, N.Y. City

P.S. Since writing the above I have received from Lt. Col. Jas. F. Hall,
1st Regt. N.Y. Vol. Engineers, fifty dollars in Confederate money,
which I enclose.

                     W.L.M.B——."

I consider this about as whole-souled piece of Masonry as one
could wish to see. The letter was directed to Morris Island, and no
one at any intermediate point was under any obligation to notice it.
Yet the very moment the letter has passed the lines and is beneath the

"Stars and Stripes" this Captain Burger opens it and attends to it and more than that sends quite a little sum of money although the letter did not ask for a cent. I have written father to send Capt. B. $100 in Greenbacks, or equivalent in gold, to be forwarded to me after deducting what money he has already advanced. I have also sent home for a box of clothing and a box of eatables to be forwarded by Adams Express to Capt. B.

"Can't take a Train." (July 29th)

Under the date of July 29th I should have recorded the signal failure of the grand project for seizing the train that brought us from Macon to this city. Like all schemes that are prepared with so much display outside and so little brain inside, it ended "Like smoke in air, and in the water foam." When we arrived opposite the point at which it was supposed we could make our way through to "Uncle Sam's" country these brave fellows who were ready to brave every-thing for the sake of liberty, found, as they ought to have anticipated, that there was some danger attached to the carrying out of their project. The Rebel officer in charge had found out that something was on foot, and had put some men on the engine and tender. The plan was to capture the engine carefully and the four guards in each car were to be seized and bound hand and foot, and then their muskets were to be used in taking the guard *on top* of the cars. This was all fine in theory, but to make it a practical success the chief *conspirators* needed more pluck. The least danger any way was the taking the cars, and if they had not the *sand* to do that it was lucky it was never attempted. Had they tried and succeeded it would have been no advantage[,] for men who showed such lack of skill would have been no better off with a train of cars in their possession, for there would still remain the difficult task of going 14 miles through a swampy country, guarded by the enemy's troops and inhabited by a hostile population. Whoever was to attempt to head a plan of this kind needed the nerve. The organization was complete *on paper*. Companies of the *elect* were organized, with captains, lieutenants, and non-commd. officers, all selected without regard to rank, but with reference to their supposed courage and ability. Myself, having no share in the thing for reasons mentioned elsewhere, I watched my chance for my own escape all the way, but seeing no opportunity, I should have gone with the crowd if the train had been seized. We did not know that the plan was abandoned until we arrived within two miles of the depot across the river from Charleston. When the train arrived at the Station and we disembarked, it was found out to our surprise that the cars in front of us had received intimation of the abandonment of the plan, and had availed themselves of the news by jumping out of the cars individually and taking to the woods. About 84 escaped in this manner, and of this number about 76 were recaptured. We have heard of three only who got through. The most of them were hunted down by dogs, and upon the whole suffered considerably. Smith of the 16th Maine, got as far as the bank of the river on the other bank of which he saw a Yankee picket. But he did not attempt to attract his attention through fear of alarming the Rebel pickets. He was too weak from hunger to swim the river, and was at last recaptured. They were sorry looking fellows when brought back to the jail-yard.[23]

There were some laughable instances of Rebelism in the cars. One old militia man, seeing the "Yanks" jumping out, after snapping his musket three times (it took him two snaps to learn that the Yankees had removed the cap) fired his piece in the air, and yelled in agony "Stop the train. All the dammed Yankees are getting out." Another guard, who persisted in not going to sleep, was unceremoniously knocked out the car door. Some of the escaped prisoners met this unfortunate man afterward. He was limping along with his musket on his shoulder, and said, "Go on, gentlemen, I don't want nothin' 't all to do with ye."

August 31st.

The last day of Summer closes upon us. It remains for another book to record whether the last day of Autumn shall find us equally unfortunate.

Friday, Sept. 2d, 1864. Military Prison, Charleston, S.C.

To-day there is an excellent prospect of exchange, and had we not been so often disappointed with this cheering prospect, I should think that, after spending a whole summer in the "Confederacy," no move would be required of us. After the varying prospects and disappointed hopes of the past four months I am forced to the conclusion that there is yet a very good chance of our celebrating "New Years" within the limits of the city of Charleston. In that "dread event" it is expedient to have something to eat, something to wear and something to read or study. The varieties of German Grammar have a peculiar charm, to be sure, but to be fully appreciated the "Muttertongue" should be mixed with a little good Anglo Saxon now and then. [Isaiah C.] Rice[24] and I have been enjoying Bulwer's "My Novel" which I think is charming. As a plot I think it is unequalled by anything I have ever read. But this book only came in my way by unexpected good luck, and now that it is finished, I must go without reading matter for some time. By good fortune, Robbins, of our Mess, has a copy of Shakspeare [Shakespeare], and this is the only book which six of us possess.

Lieut. Milward, of Ohio, will try the exchange business again to-morrow. I hope he may have better success than before. He carries two letters for me—one for mother and one for Capt. Burger at Hilton Head. I modestly mentioned to the friendly Captain that my name would become any exchange list he might happen to be making up. His influence would be valuable. Influence is our only resort here.

❧❦

Military Prison, Charleston, S.C.

Sept. 2d, 1864

My dear Mother:

One of our Surgeons is going North and has offered to take a few letters for us as we shall thus save time by evading some of the red tape process. My health is now very bad and I am consoling myself with the present prospect of exchange. To-day we are especially hopeful from the fact that our Government has sent 600 Confederate prisoners to the Department of the South. My hope is that I may be favored with a ticket for the "first boat." As yet I have not received a letter from you and I can assure you that that is my greatest annoyance just now. Four months seems long enough at best, but this not hearing from one's friends makes the weeks longer yet. My health is now very good and I am gaining strength on a little money very unexpectedly received from a gentleman at Hilton Head. I have written father to send him $100 in Greenbacks, or its equivalent in gold, which he will forward to me. His name is Capt. W.L.M. Burger, Assistant Adjutant General, Hilton Head, S.C. Anything sent to him by express (*for me*) will be promptly forwarded, as I have an understanding with him. I sent for $10 in gold sometime ago, but it does not arrive. I presume however it is all safe. I think there is *no risk* in sending things to me, if they are sent first to Capt. Burger. Sometime ago I sent for a box of clothing. For fear you have not recd the letter I will once more enumerate the articles wanted. . . . Don't fail to send "Kinglake's Crimean War"[25] (only one vol. published yet I think) anything else good to read—old Magazines, Papers or Novels. A book here is one's stock in trade, for after reading it himself he can exchange with his neighbor, but a poor fellow without a book can neither buy nor borrow. I should like "David Copperfield" in pamphlet. Do not, I pray, let exchange rumors deter you from sending these things. Even if I should have the good fortune to be ticketed for the North, I could easily intercept boxes or money at Hilton Head. Should they arrive here safely they would do me a great deal of good, for I am sadly in need of such things. In regard to a box of eatables, I can only say that it would be most acceptable. But do not send any two of these things—money, clothing and eatables—in the same box. If you send anything to eat let it be dried fruit, preserved meats &c., tea, coffee, sugar, condensed milk, nutmegs, baking powders, pepper, mustard, chocolate, dried apples, knife and fork, spoon, anything to cook with. Attend to the money and clothing first.

Please have Fernald make me a vest out of that cloak broadcloth—same as the pants that suited. I have already sent for you to forward me military pants to the same address and if I said any thing about the vest, you need not trouble about this one. If there are any letters for me in your possession I should like to have them sent to the same address.

I trust you will continue to write to me although it has not as yet amounted to much. The thing will get regulated ere long, and we can have a letter once in a while. We are now anxious to hear from the Chicago Convention.[26] For whom does father vote this year? We are as yet in the dark as to the State politics. In your letters you can write as much as you please, but you must remember that I am restricted to one page. I am now writing the second, but presume that under the circumstance the officials will allow this deviation from the rule. Send postage stamps in the box. I wish I could hear from Col. West and the Regt. Remember me to him. How are Mr. Carter's folks? Always remember me to them all. I hope father has attended to my *money letter* ere this. Remember that Capt. Burger's receipt is good for *anything* sent to me. Hoping to hear from you soon and with some faint glimmer for hope of exchange.

Saturday, Sept. 3d

To-day for the second time several of our officers went down [to] the harbor in hopes of obtaining a special exchange, but, much to their chagrin, the U.S. Commissioner of Exchange was not on hand, and had made no plans to receive the unfortunates. So they had to come back a second time, disappointed and disgusted. However, they bring a rumor of a speedy general exchange for which we all pray. I put little faith in Exchange any way. I confess that I am somewhat "demoralized" upon this perplexing subject. The party that went down for exchange to-day are greatly disappointed. So far as they are individually concerned I am sorry, but I hope there will be no more special exchange, although I do not see anything dishonorable in asking for one, but I do believe that special exchanges have a strong tendency to prevent a general exchange. In this case our enlisted men, who from the first have suffered much more than we, will be compelled to remain prisoners during the Winter. If no one could be exchanged until a general exchange were agreed upon between the two governments, the influence which now benefits individuals would benefit the whole, and instead of seeing the 50 ranking officers going and leaving 2000, we should all go together. Undoubtedly the "negro" question is the chief barrier against successful negotiation. The case now stands precisely thus—The South proposes an exchange, man for man, officer for officer and rank for rank, our government retaining the excess which would thus remain. The Rebels apply this to all our enlisted men except such Negroes as can be identified as having once been slaves. Our Government can "go" all this except the "darkey." "Uncle Abraham" will agree to the proposition, as we understand it, if the Rebs will include "Sambo." The North is as determined to claim the Negro as the South not to give him up. So between the two the prospect is dim for about 2000 officers and 3000[0] men now held in Southern prisons, and if we see our homes or Regiments before the 1st of Jany. I shall think we are fortunate. Our private soldiers have already suffered terrible things in Georgia, and I hope that, for the sake of humanity, something ought to be done for them.

In all this trouble many of our officers allow themselves to openly censure our Government, or Administration rather, for not acceding to this last proposal of the enemy. It is certain that the Rebel government will be held responsible by history for the inhumanities of Belle Island and Andersonville. The fact that our Government refuses to accept Rebel terms and conditions of Exchange which ignore a portion of our soldiers, whom we have promised to protect, will afford but a poor excuse for murdering by inches those hundreds of unhappy men whom the chances of war have thrown into the hands of the Confederates. This history of this war is yet to be written by impartial pens, and the writer years hence will not fail to record what Federal soldiers have suffered in Southern prisons. Our authorities have almost invariably, treated prisoners humanely. At any rate, they have not allowed them to suffer from hunger. Rebel prisoners have not been frozen and starved to death as our soldiers have been, in like circumstances, more than once.[27] Such acts as these can not escape the notice of the world. Sooner or later the mask will be pulled away, and if our Gov. is blamed the Rebel Govt. will be detested.

Sunday, Sept. 4th.

We hear that a few boxes arrived by yesterday's flag of truce. In that case I am quite sure of one, it having been put up by Messrs. Dunbars & Frantz at Hilton Head. It is time that I had a letter from home—not a word since April.

The best of anything now is the reported *Capture of Atlanta* by Sherman.[28] We anxiously await further particulars.

Monday, Sept 5th.

Four months ago to-day I bade adieu to liberty. Four months a prisoner and not a word from home. The boxes are not yet distributed. The fall of Atlanta is confirmed. Of course, there is abundant rejoicing in the prison. This event has long been expected and the success must, at this time, have an excellent effect at the North.[29] Gold will go down.

The shelling of this city by Foster continues unabated. Fragments of shells have struck within the limits of [our] yard, without, however, doing any harm to any one. One entered the roof of one of the out-house[s], where some of our prisoners are quartered, and did not stop in its career until it had penetrated to the floor of one of the rooms, tipping over a man's dinner and startling the owner not a little. Another fragment struck in our front yard the other evening, about 12 yards from the portico where we were sitting. The most of the shells explode about half a mile to the East of the East end of this building (Roper Hospital). The danger to life is not very great because the inhabitants have quite generally cleared out, but real estate has to take it at a fearful rate. It is a great annoyance to the good people of Charleston.

Tuesday, Sept. 6th.

I have to-day sold $15 in U.S. money for $90 in Confederate scrip. When we first came here $4 for $1 was all we could get. The fall of Atlanta has made "green backs" and gold advance. Gold is now worth $20 here, while at the North it is $2.75.

Wednesday, Sept. 7th.

The Rebels, thoroughly frightened by the fall of Atlanta, have decided to move the Federal prisoners out of Ga. without delay. Since the first lot of 600 arrived here they have sent 6 or 800 more and now we may expect to see some of our enlisted men coming. I hope it may be so, for they will be more likely to receive help from our Govt. here than at Andersonville.[30] There are now 300 officers in this building (Roper Hospital), 300 in the Work House and as many more in the Jail yard. We (300) have by far the best quarters occupied by any prisoners in the Confederacy. There are some officers on parole in the Marine Hospital, which is the next best building to this.

Generals Foster and [Samuel] Jones[31] have been having a long communication upon the subject of letting us have tea, coffee, sugar, &c., from home. Genl. J. says we may have money and clothing but nothing eatable. I trust that this order will not be enforced.

❧

Military Prison Charleston, S.C.
Sept. 7th, 1864
My dear Mother:

I have a chance to send a letter North by one of our officers who has had the good fortune to get a "special exchange." As this way is much more expeditious and at the same time admits of a longer letter, I am happy to embrace the opportunity. . . .

One thing in particular. Charlie Hunt is my bed fellow, messmate and the most, or rather the only, really intimate friend I have here. I never was much acquainted with him before we were thrown together in Macon. I wish you [to] communicate with his mother, and, when you send a box for me, offer her space for any little package she may wish to send to *her* "young hopeful." Of course when she is putting up a box the compliment would be returned. Be sure not to send clothing and eatables in the same box. You will thus avoid the *possibility* of confiscation. I hope you will not think "boxes" have entirely absorbed my thoughts, and that I do not seem to have any higher ambition than to get a box, or that I am not as anxious as ever to know how you are all getting along. If you could have seen me a month ago, poor, weak and half starved, you would not wonder that I am striving to provide for the future. For the past month I have had a little money, thanks to a friend here and a Masonic brother (the same Capt. Burger) at Hilton Head. But my friend and myself have nearly exhausted our supply. I have opened my eyes to the possibility—perhaps probability—of remaining a prisoner for the coming winter. In that dreaded event I shall rely upon things from home as my only solace and comfort. I have to-day received a box of eatables from this friend of mine, Capt. Burger, a man whom I never saw, but one that I shall never forget. I wish I could tell you all about the whole story about this Capt. B. When I first came here I was compelled to appeal to "Any Free Mason on Island" for *something to eat.* The letter had only reached Hilton Head when the first man seeing it was this Capt. B. He, being a mason, opened it and attended to it in a most liberal manner. Although I said noth-ing about money, he sent me $30, and some traders at the same place sent the box through Capt. B. Now not one of these men ever heard of me, but the men who send the box refuse to state any price, and which [wish] me to consider it as a donation. The value of this most welcome box is about $40 & that a present from strangers. All these things show that there are those "across the lines" who will sympathize with and help us even if we remain here for months and months to come. I am now in my fifth month & many have seen the fifteenth pass. Do not think I am discouraged. I am only prepared for what may come. Whatever it may be my lot to bear in this war, I shall take cheerfully. My resignation however will not hinder me from making myself comfortable when I can. We now can see the way clear for the month of September, but before the end of the month, I shall hope to get something from you. I am not hungry now as I used to be at Macon and I am thankful for it. Yet I am almost entirely destitute of clothing. With the exception of one shirt received from the Sanitary Commission, I wear the same clothes to-day that I did when *I bade farewell to liberty.* I am greatly in need of shirts, drawers, towels, &c., (Put books with clothing *always.*)

You know we are on parole and are not under very severe restrictions as to the contents of our boxes. Yet I would not advise that clothing, eatables and money ever be sent in the same box. Send them all by Express to Capt. B. for me. He understands it all. Still you could drop him a line each time. Still my mind runs on boxes. I presume I shall often send for things which seem to you of no possible use to a prisoner of war. I may have some whims, but now is just the time I should dislike to have them go ungratified. For instance I want a bottle of red ink, a set of Faber's pencils, fine steel pens, drawing paper, India ink, and an *autograph album.* This last is decidedly one of my whims, but you see I wish to collect the autographs of my fellow prisoners.

You may be surprised at my silence upon certain points. If there are somethings I never speak of it is because I am not allowed to mention them. Some day I will tell you all about them. Send me a nice blank book about eight inches by six, and I will write it full for you to read, for I have nothing to do but to read, study and write. Unfortunately however I have had no paper and no books except a German Grammar, which is pretty well thumbed by this time. I should like almost anything in the shape of German poetry. If I am to stay here this winter, it shall not be intellectually a blank in my existence, though perhaps it may be a most dreary blank in all other respects. Worse than want of books or of money—worse than hunger itself,—is the interception of our letters to each other. It has been a habit of so many years for me to hear from you every week, that I regretfully begin the fifth month without a word of news from home.

Yet in this there is hope. We are no longer in Georgia, (and I sincerely thank God for it,) and when we are once regulated here the mail will come promptly. I have no doubt of there being a letter from you now in the city awaiting the official supervision. In your letters you can write all you wish. Tell me all the news and the gossip of the city. Tell Lizzie I would write to her, but this is all I have time for at this opportunity. I doubt not she will manage to see this. I should esteem it a great favor if she would write one of her long and interesting letters. I have never heard from the Regiment except what I have from time to time picked up from captured officers of the same Brigade or Division.

In putting up a box I shall leave it for your taste to select books and reading matter. Let everything be in pamphlet if possible. Any standard work, with a liberal sprinkling of periodicals and magazines, are what we want. *Scraps* are excellent. Paper and envelopes are a great staple. Whenever I write, I hope you will send Mrs. Hunt word. I shall always mention Charlie. By establishing "intimate diplomatic relations" you and Mrs. H. can do up a very good and systematic box business. You wonder why I am so hopeless of an immediate exchange. It is because I do not see any signs of it in extracts from the Northern press, or from any other source. A week ago I saw more hopeful signs. Tell Uncle Luther [Porter][32] that one Thompson of Danville is here with us. He is a Lieut. in the 10th Vt., and knows Uncle L. very well. How are Erastus and Albert? Always give my love to everybody. Has Sarah C[arter]. finished her course at Andover? I have already specified the things I wish to have sent. Two letters beside this are filled with that interesting topic.

I want to hear how the political campaign progresses. *Between us,* what are the prospects of Lt. Col. Merrill's remaining in the service? Do not think I am growing too ambitious. I only wish to keep my eyes open to all *possibilities*. I have already used too much ink, and, perhaps [in] my desire to say so much to you, I have excluded the chance of this letter reaching you. Some official may mark it "Pigeon Hole." Love to father and Itie.

Thursday, Sept. 8th.

My box has arrived and a nice one it is. It weighs about 60 lbs., and contains a choice assortment of groceries, including coffee & sugar. The contents were not disturbed. So it seems that Jones does not intend to enforce his order. The Sutlers who put it up have refused to send a bill or receive any pay. They wish me to consider it as a Masonic gift. The whole affair, as I have recorded it in my other Diary, is a most excellent specimen of the inner workings of Free Masonry. I sent to strangers for a box on credit and have not only received a large one as a present but the unasked loan of $250 (Conf.) in money. Of course, I can not soon forget the kindness nor permit it to go long unrewarded. At present, I can repay them only by thanks but then I may not always be a prisoner of war!

I am now reading for a second time Dumas' "Three Guardsmen," and I hope soon to get the Sequel "20 years After."[33] The Three Guardsmen does not injure by a second reading, but I hope to have some fresh reading from home very soon. In that case I can lend [as] well as borrow. I may however be long disappointed.

Friday, Sept. 9th.

Today, for the first time since I was gobbled (4 1/2 months) I have had a good cup of coffee, or a cup of good coffee, if the grammarians prefer the expression. For this, thanks to the box! We have six cans of nice condensed coffee. Two hams are added to our larder so that, instead of cornmeal gridle [griddle] cakes for our breakfast, we can have ham and sweet potatoes. By using a very little of our rations we (6 of us) live very fairly on $18 (Conf.) per day, which is only 50 cts. each in reality. $8 goes for Sweet potatoes, $7 1/2 for milk at $1 1/2 pr. quart, and the remaining money is expended according to the fancy of the cook.[34]

I have tried the experiment of making biscuit and pies. The pies were good—the biscuit—not. *Dried apple* pies *are now* a *luxury.*

Saturday, Sept. 10th.

Pendleton of our Mess is greatly elated over a prospect of going North on parole to effect the exchange of a Charleston Alderman, now *boarding* at Fort Warren.[35] He *may* be disappointed.

Sunday, Sept. 11th.

Pendleton will have to hang up on his parole. He has already been sadly disappointed several times. He allows himself to "go off on a tangent" altogether too easily. Several of our officers have gone North on parole since we came here. They are paroled for 30 days to effect the exchange of some Rebel prisoner previously designated. Of course, if the paroled officer fails of his object he returns to *captivity*. They will be likely to work against so unfavorable a result. I wish I could have such a chance. I would bring the State of Maine to my aid!

Monday, Sept. 12th.

Pendleton is "dished." He can not get away this time and is not certain of going the next. The truce boat does not go down to-day. A mail from the North has arrived, and will probably be distributed to-morrow. I expect a letter from mother this time.

Tuesday, Sept. 13th.

The mail brings me nothing, but Hunt has a letter from his mother. By a letter which Pendleton has just received from his wife I learn indirectly that my folks are all well. This is the first word for more than four months and a half. In future I hope to get letters regularly, as we shall have a permanent abiding place. Hitherto, letters have hunted us all over the Confederacy. This will now be our home.

Wednesday, Sept. 14th.

For the sake of amusement perhaps as much as for any better purpose I have commenced a narrative of our wanderings and sufferings in the "Confederacy." It will fill about twelve sheets of foolscap. What use I shall make of the valuable production I do not yet myself know. I have written it mostly from my Diary, and, although I do not evince much love for the "Rebs," I have, I think, shown a decent regard for the truth. The Rebels are so inhuman to our prisoners who are unfortunate enough to be private soldiers, that I can never look upon them as I once did. I consider a people sunk fearfully low, when it resorts to such barbarities as the Rebels have in this particular.[36]

Two of the "Sisters of Mercy" (Roman Catholic) called on us today, bringing books, grapes, &c. They have visited our men (6000) now in a prison camp on the "race course" near this city. The "Sisters" represent the condition of these men as truly horrible. Many of them are already idiotic. We took up a contribution for the Sisters to use for the benefit of the poor fellows.[37]

I am far from being a Roman Catholic or from having any tendencies in that direction, but from what I have seen during this war, I am convinced that the Roman Catholics have done more personally for sick and wounded soldiers North and South than any other religious sect. Other denominations and Societies make liberal donations of food, of clothing and of money, but the "Sisters of Mercy" and the "Sisters of Charity" with their black bonnets and white bonnets are everywhere *personally* attending to the trials and sufferings of sick and wounded soldiers. It matters not to which army the soldier belongs. That he needs help is enough for these noble women to know. The "Sisters" have favored us with two visits and would have come before, but failed to obtain permission from the prison officials. One of these was the Lady Superior of the Sisterhood of Charleston. The Society is scattered just now by Foster's shells,—several of their buildings having been smashed in.[38]

I must here record a trick which bears the impress of the genius of the Richmond officials. One of our officers had upon his person at the time of capture, the sum of $550 in U.S. bills. This money was taken from him on entering Libby prison and a receipt given him for the full amount. A month ago he sent the receipt to R[ichmond]. with an order for the money. To-day, he receives an answer with $50 in greenbacks, saying that the "C.S. Govt." has confiscated the remaining $500 as it is probable that so large a sum as $550 could not be private property, but must be public funds. So $50 is the amount that the Confed. Govt. allows a Yankee prisoner to own! This is superior to any Yankee trickery I can conceive of. This same plan prevailed in "Libby." Many valuable boxes were confiscated upon the most trivial pretexts. Extreme poverty has made the Southerners from high to low a set of thieves. There are men among them whom distress can not belittle, but as a whole they have fearfully degenerated from that chivalrous spirit which they once had quite a claim to, and to which many of them still make vain pretensions. Their lying newspapers and not more truthful leaders and politicians teach the people to look upon a Northern soldier as a mercenary invader, and of course when a Yankee is captured he must be treated as a common criminal.

A new proposition has been agreed upon between the North & South. It has for its object to treat all hostages &c. held by either side as other prisoners, by at once releasing them from *special* confinement, &c. This plan savors more of genuine common sense than any project we have heard of late. This will embrace such fellows as the colored soldiers of the 54th Mass. now confined in Charleston jail. We had a very good chance to see these darkies during our miserable stay in the jail yard. They are certainly the most patriotic sufferers I have yet seen in the war. In the jail were some of our white soldiers also, mostly raiders and some of them deserters. These white men are fed on one meal of "mush" (hasty pudding) daily. This villainous mixture of a little corn meal, water, and *they* say no salt, is all the poor fellows get to support life. I tasted of it & it was certainly as unpalatable as anything I ever tried. Now and then, they have wretched boiled rice as a substitute. Meat and vegetables are never seen by the poor fellows. The Negroes are fed on corn bread, each man receiving one small loaf pr. day. The result of all this is the worst form of scurvy. The poor victims look like death. During our stay in the jail yard, these men used to scrape out our dishes, dig out the rind of water melons we had thrown away, and in fact "root" around and eat just such articles as a hog in a farmer's yard.

This leads me to go back and have a general look at what we have had in the shape of rations for the past four months and a half. While we were at Macon (3 months) the authorities never issued a pound of fresh meat or even salted beef,—nothing of meat except a very niggardly allowance of *wormy* bacon—not a vegetable of any kind although scurvy was raging among us. Since coming here we have been better treated in every respect, except during the first two weeks of our stay. We now get poor fresh beef quite often, a little *rice and wheat* flour now and then, and the rest is rice and corn meal with an *occasional* [bit] of lard. They have issued vegetables *once,* and then each man got a piece of cabage [cabbage] leaf half as large as his hand. Even here living strictly on the rations is very hard, and many who do so actually go hungry.

A 2d Lieutenant, who was taken to Andersonville as a 1st Sergeant, has been transferred to this prison, and brings some hard accounts of the state of things at that wretched place. Among other pleasant institutions they had an organized band of fellows who devoted themselves to the lucrative business of robbing the newly arrived prisoners. They employed various plans of operation. They either entered a man's tent while he was asleep, held a knife across his throat, and then awoke him to inform him that he could immediately disgorge any spare "green backs" he might chance to have. If the poor fellow made *any fuss* about the matter his throat was unceremoniously cut, and the body buried. All these things wer[e] done in disguise. It must be remembered that these acts were perpetrated by Federal soldiers upon Federal soldiers, and Federal soldiers found that the time had come for them to act and protect themselves. Accordingly, with the consent of the Rebel General (Wynder [John H. Winder])[39] in charge, they organized a court martial and charged six of the ring leaders with murder, robbery, &c. The culprits were allowed counsel and every form of military law was observed. The proceedings of each day were carefully taken down, and after a few days' sitting, the six were found guilty, and sentenced to be hung. Scaffolds and gallows were built within the prison yard by the soldiers, and a hangman selected for each victim of righteous vengeance. The condemned wretches confessed that they had cut two men's throats and then buried the bodies beneath their own (the murderers' beds) in the tents. They confessed to having buried $7000 in U.S. money, which they had robbed from their fellow soldiers.

Each culprit stood upon a small trap, and his hangman stood near him upon a small platform. When the traps were sprung, the ringleader of the murderers, being a heavy man, broke his rope and came tumbling to the ground. Upon recovering his hangman forced him to reascend the ladder to be swung a second time into eternity. The trial and the execution held in the presence of 20,000 Union soldiers met with general approbation. The time for something to be done had arrived. It was really not safe to step out after dark. [A report of] the trial was sent to Washington. Several of the soldiers have been paroled and sent North to try to prevail upon our Government to accept Rebel terms of exchange. General Winder has recently been removed for alleged incompetency and inhumanity to prisoners. Some of the papers say that the latter charge has never been made against Genl. W.[40] If it has it is curious that it has taken a whole year and a half to find out that Yankee prisoners have been abused. That would be the last cause of removal in the Confederacy.

The fall of Atlanta has frightened the Rebs and they are scattering their prisoners from Ga. Some are at North Carolina, some at Richmond, others at Savannah, and others at Columbia. There is a great scare.

Military Prison, Charleston, S.C.
Sept. 14th 1864.
My dear Mother:

I have an opportunity to send a line. I am still without a word for [from] you. Pendleton has just received a [letter] from his wife in Yarmouth, who mentions a note from you in which you say you are all well. So I have heard from you at last after more than four months. But the information is very meagre and unsatisfactory. I presume I shall get your letter in a day or so as there are still more now in the hands of the Provost Marshal. We are hating ourselves over the exchange question, as it now appears. Remaining here for the winter seems to be one of the evils we may suspect. I have taken due precautions and have told you what I want in the shape of boxes &c. Do not forget to put in the drawing paper, india ink, pencils. I should like one or two of the very smallest camel's hair brushes (for water colors.) You can get them at Larrabee's on Exch[ange]. St.

I shall expect one of your boxes now very soon.[41] Pendleton expects to be exchanged soon in which case he will honor you with a call on his way home. Remember me to Mrs. C's family. How does the draft work? Will Maine send any new Regiments? I am very desirous to hear from the 17th. It is now the fifth month since I have been favored with any communication with the army or with you at home. My health is very good and all I want is an *exchange*. It presents a very good opportunity to cultivate patience. Hunt has received a letter from his mother.

But I must close. I only wrote this to assure you of continued health. My regards to Mr. & Mrs. Perry. Hurry up the boxes.

***

Thursday, Sept. 15th

This day has put an end to the hope which some were sanguine enough to entertain. Many were confident of going home before the middle of September as there are still some who expect to go before the end of the month.

The Naval officers are in high glee at a report that the Federal and Rebel Secretaries of the Navy have taken the Exchange of Naval prisoners into their own hands. This partial exchange may be brought about, but I do not expect a general exchange of prisoners for three months to come.[42]

600 Rebel officers (prisoners) are now in Charleston Harbor under fire in retaliation for our being put under fire in this city.[43] This "under fire" business does not amount to a great deal. To be sure, a shell now and then comes very near us, but the prisoners are all in one square, and Foster's Artillerists seldom trouble that section of the city. Just for the privilege of being so much nearer to our lines and thus having weekly communication by flag of truce, we are quite willing to expose ourselves to this extra danger. For a better prospect of exchange we would expose ourselves to greater danger. Our present parol[e]s allows us many little privileges which we could not otherwise enjoy. We can have all our own money in our own hand instead of having it doled out to us in tit-bits. There is a slim show of a special exchange of us for the 600 Rebs now under fire on Morris Island. This is our only hope. So we hear from an officer recently sent North on parole. Being an "old fish," he resorted to stratagem in writing a letter. This letter apparently contained nothing but remarks upon personal matters, but, upon examination, several phonographic signs were found, which stated that our authorities contemplate exchanging the 600 on Morris Island.

Tonight we have a rumor that Genl. Foster has notified Genl. Jones to remove all the women, children and non-combatant[s] now within the city of C. The[re] has been but little shelling for a day or two and there may or may not be some foundation for this story.[44]

Friday, Sept. 16th.
Another mail was distributed to-day, but it brought me nothing.

To-night we are favored with still another rumor, which is that we are to be moved into the country in order that the Rebel officers now on Morris Island may be taken to a better place.[45] This is the way things work! Six hundred of us are moved to Charleston—the best place in the "Confederacy." Because a few shells come into the city now and then, General Foster feels obliged to send North and get 600 Rebel officers to be placed on Morris Island under fire for the purpose of *retaliation*. To prevent this retaliation the Rebs propose to move us into the interior. Doubtless the first fifty were brought here for the express purpose of putting them under fire, with a view to making Foster *hold up* on his shelling. The 600 and all since then were not brought for the purpose of exposure to fire, but simply because Charleston was a secure and convenient place. The Rebels had got enough of brag and bluster when they put the first 50 under fire and notified Genl. F. that they were so placed. Genl. Foster at once placed 50 Rebel officers of like rank under fire in the harbor. When we were brought here no such notice was sent to Foster. There seemed to be a different spirit throughout the whole affair.

Our Mess is nearly on its "beam end" again. Lately we have lived on three meals a day with $18 (Confed) as our daily allowance. Now we have voted two meals a day on $10, much to the disgust of Robbins and Pendleton, who prefer three poor meals to two good ones. In eight days we shall be reduced to prison fare solely, and then there will be a howl, for our Mess has lived quite decently since coming to C.

We now hear that boxes of edibles will not be allowed to come through. In that case we shall try hard for money. We are looking forward to a winter in the "Confederacy."

Saturday, Sept. 17th.

There has been a fire in the city, and the flames made so good a target for Genl. Foster that he favored us with a piece of shell through the roof of this building. The fire was just across the street from the East end of the building.[46] Lieut. Foote [Morris C. Foot][47] was at dinner when the shell entered the room, and knocked [over] him and the stool upon which he was sitting. No material damage was done, although the blood was started. This is the first fragment that has entered this building although several have struck the out buildings and in the yard front and rear. Foster pitched several shells into the midst of the flames, much to the annoyance of the firemen, who are a set of "beats"—firemen only to escape conscription.

Firing is still kept up in the harbor.

Our Mess (by rank).

Chas. P. Mattocks,	Maj. 17th Me.	Portland.
Julius B. Litchfield,	Capt. 4th "	Rockland.
Geo. H. Pendleton,	Act. Mr. U.S.N.	Yarmouth.
Edwin H. Sears,	A.A.P.M., U.S.N.	Prov. R.I.
Chas. O. Hunt,	1st Lt. 5th Me.Batty.	Gorham.
Nathaniel A. Robbins	2d Lt. 4th Me.	Union.

This highly respectable fraternity has existed for about six weeks, during which time it has been peculiarly fortunate in regard to funds. We have expended upon private and upon mess accounts the modest sum of $3000 in Confed. money, which costs us $150 in gold or $500 "Greenbacks," though at the North $350 "Greenbacks" would buy $150 gold.

Another mail today, and I am still without a line from home. Next Monday will do me something I trust. I can not account for my ill luck.

Sunday, Sept. 18th

The Charleston papers state that over 8000 of our enlisted men died at Andersonville in two months this Summer. This is a fearful mortality, 24,000 men, 1/3 died in 2 months—6 months at the same rate would still them all. Rebel papers attribute all this death and suffering to our Gov't because it refuses Rebel terms of exchange. They claim that this mortality is the result solely of long confinement and not brutality and starvation.

I am now furiously at my German. Have commenced a German Universal History. We hope to get reading matter from home soon.

The Naval officers expect to be exchanged by the "next boat." They may be disappointed, although for their sakes, I hope not. Time enough when we go.

Monday, Sept. 19th.

Army "exchange stock" is below par just now, although some of our officers still have faith in the ever deceptive illusion of going home. Time will cool their ardor. The old Libby prisoners can not be made to believe that exchange will ever come. I myself am, as usual, "demoralized" on the subject.

Tuesday, Sept. 20th.

Lt. Commander [Austin] Pendergrast of the Navy has had official notice that the Naval officers will be at once exchanged.[48] We hope so, even if we of the Army are obliged to remain here until politicians fix up the "Negro question." I do not wonder that our Govt. wishes to have all its negroes recognized as soldiers and exchanged as such. However, when we come to look at the thing as a matter of mere humanity it presents a different phase. There are now in the "Confederacy" 500—perhaps not half that number—of negroes held as prisoners of war or turned over to their former masters. These few slave negroes the South refuses to exchange. During the two months of the past summer 8000 white men have died for these 200 or 300 negroes—that too without in the least benefiting the negroes. The lives of the poor fellows in Georgia might have been saved by our giving up an equal number of Rebel prisoners. We should still have a large excess of prisoners with which to protect "Cuffie." To be sure, these 8000 men have died from the effects of Rebel barbarity, but yet we might have saved them by yielding a comparatively unimportant point. To have done this would have in no wise lessened the dignity of the U.S. Govt. We may not know so much about these *little* things as do the good people at Washington. *Then again* we *may* know quite as well how much human misery has resulted from clinging with such tenacity to the "Negro question." Humanity apart, the Govt. can not be blamed for its course, but when we see 8000 and perhaps twice 8000 white men miserably perish to benefit, or rather to not affect 300 negroes, we can not fall in with the views of some of our patriotic fanatics. Then too this special exchange of a few Generals and Field officers, upon the basis of man for man, and rank for rank, violates the non exchange stand which the Govt. has taken, just as much as a general exchange would. The 35,000 Union officers and soldiers now languishing in Southern prisons will, if exchanged, be of service to Govt., and their exchange is no more a violation of a "Negro whim" than a partial exchange.

"Consistency, thou art a jewel!" If our Govt. refuses to accept Rebel terms of exchange why does it exchange the privileged few on these same rejected terms.

Wednesday, Sept. 21st.

The Naval officers are disappointed. They will have to wait a while.

I have written to Capt. Wilson (now in command of the Sharp Shooters) to fix up my Ordnance accounts. One of our officers just discharged from Hospital describes the sufferings of our sick soldiers as beyond belief. Many are already idiotic, while others are dying of scurvy and nostalgia (home-sickness). The Charlestonians treat the sick much better than the people of Georgia did. There is more kindness and humanity in C. than in any place we have yet visited in Secessiondom.

A year without fresh meat or vegetables and with a sameness of the most wretched food is almost enough to kill ordinary men. Scurvy is the inevitable result of such fare. Many of our officers are trying to drive the scurvy away. If the naval officers go away we shall avail ourselves of the chance to send long letters home. Another mail has been received and I am once more disappointed. "Next time" is my only hope.

❧

Military Prison. Charleston, S.C.

Sept. 21, '64

My dear Mother:

I have no letter of yours yet to answer but will send a line to inform you of continued health, if not prosperity. Hunt has had a letter from his Mother and I hear by one of Pendleton's letters that you are all well—of which I have already written. Pendleton expects to be exchanged and, if he is not disappointed, will call on you when

he goes home. Some of our officers have gone North on special exchanges, but I presume we that are left will remain here for some
time to come. I hope to get some clothing and money soon for I am
terrible destitute, as indeed about 2000 officers and I know not how
many thousand men now held as prisoners. The Charleston officials
have thus far treated us much better than any others. I feel much
better than I did two months ago, thanks to some unknown friends
at Hilton Head who sent me some money and a box. There is
a money lender here, and in case I have to sign an "I.O.U.," I trust
father will cash such a paper promptly. I expect something from
you by this week's flag of truce.[49] I hope Col. West has fully recovered before this. If he is still at home I trust you will remember me
to him.

Keep up *diplomatic relations* with Mrs. Hunt, & exchange favors when you send things to your "young hopefulls." I trust you
will send me something to read. Are they raising any new Regiments in Maine? It was expected that Lt. Col. Merrill would resign
when I was captured. Of course I am very desirous of getting all the
news. We do not yet know who is Governor of Maine.[50] I suppose
Portland is busy over the Presidential election just now.

My regards to Mr. Carter's family, and in fact to *everybody*.
Wish I could see them all, but I am very cheerful over my situation,
although I could find many more agreeable ways of spending six
months or a year than in counting the days in confinement. Tell Itie
to be patient, for I shall surely bring him something this time. Regards to Uncle Luther and Uncle & Aunt Fuller. Write long letters.
The authorities allow it.

❧❧

Thursday, Sept. 22d.

Three officers have been notified to go North for exchange.
These special exchanges still flourish. We would all be glad to have
a "Special," but yet we can not help blaming the authorities for
allowing such a thing. These special exchanges generally take away
those who are smart or lucky enough to get them.

General Butler has just come out with a long and bitter letter in which he refuses to agree upon a cartel of exchange until the "Rebs" "cave" on the negro question.[51]

⚜

Military Prison, Charleston, S.C.
Sept. 22d, 1864.
My dear Mother:

Pendleton expects to go away by to-morrow's flag of truce, and I gladly avail myself of the opportunity to send a longer letter than would be allowed by the ordinary channel. Capt. Pendleton will certainly call on you if he goes home. He has been a prisoner about 9 months, and is, of course, highly pleased at the prospect of going home again. I wish I had a similar prospect, not that I am so home-sick, but because I wish to *get out of this,* even if I were to be at once ordered to the Fiji Islands for duty. My health continues excellent and I do not allow the dim prospect of release to wear upon me. I have become a skeptic upon the subject of exchange. Otherwise I might tell you that there is a prospect of a special exchange of 600 of us. You can not imagine how hard it seems to be five months without a letter from you. That is the greatest trial I have had, although the Macon rations were quite a fill to take. I wrote you a letter yesterday, which was to go by the regular channel but will now be taken together with this by Pendleton.

You may wish to know exactly the routine of a prison day as we are now situated. We are on parole, but you must not understand by the paroles which have sometimes been given in European armies by which the *unfortunate* prisoners are allowed to wander at will through a city, attend balls and parties, borrow money of hospitable citizens, and be favored with various other *small* attentions, which serve to make captivity endurable. Yet our present condition is Paradise when compared with our condition at Macon. There 1800 Union officers slept, ate, walked, and swore vengeance against the Confederacy upon less than four acres of ground. We were closely guarded by ignorant and abusive Sentinels. To approach the line of the enclosure by night or to touch the fence by day subjected one to the fire of our blood-thirsty keepers. Several shots were fired into the yard for real or imaginary violation of the orders. One officer was killed in this manner. Our rations were poor and communication with home one of the *vague uncertainties of Confederate meanness.* Here we have a fine building and a nice flower garden and back yard where we cook. The guard is only a nominal affair as we have given our parole not to escape or to try to do so. Instead of having 1800 men on four acres in a hot sun we have 350 in a large building with about 3 acres of yard room. This building was always used as a hospital until two years ago. It is very much like the Marine Hospital at Portland. We get up in the morning as early or as late as we please, wash, & attend Roll Call at 9 o'clock. Generally our breakfast is later before roll call. Then we read, study, walk, talk of exchange until 3 in the afternoon when we take our dinner which is the last meal of the day. Two meals a day do very well. At present we are economizing our money and spend only $10 dollars a day, which is, in your money (greenbacks), only $1.50. There are six of us in this *"mess,"* so that each man expends the moderate sum of 25 cents, besides eating his rations. This 25 cents is just enough to allow us anti-scorbatic [scorbutic] food (potatoes &c.), and *thus* free our minds from any apprehension of the Scurvy, that pest which has carried away hundreds of our poor soldiers this Summer. Many of the old officers, or rather old prisoners, are now suffering from the disease. Our rations consist of rice, meal, a very little flour and once in a while a little fresh beef. The beef is always roasted by us, for we do all our own cooking. We have built very good ovens with old bricks and manage to bake very good brown bread. Without meat a breakfast consists of sweet potatoes and brown bread, and the dinner, for the sake of variety, of brown bread and sweet potatoes. In the morning lately we have had the luxury of a little swallow of coffee, which was sent to me from Hilton head. With a little money one can live quite comfortably, but if he is compelled to eke out his existence upon prison rations alone he will feel *hungry* all the time, even if he eats all he can hold. A "live Yankee" can not find much nourishment or relish in corn bread and boiled rice day after day. If one indulges in the luxuries of life he needs the wealth of Croesus. Butter is $9 a pound. Eggs $15 a dozen. Sugar $8 a pound. Milk $1/2 a quart. Molasses $10 a quart. Bacon $5 a pound. One sixth of these prices will give the value in "green backs." Some little extras which I received from Hilton Head have helped our larder along amazingly. There being six in the "mess," of course each one performs the function of cook once in six days, and woe to the unlucky cook from whose hands the "mess" receives sour bread or half-baked potatoes. When money was more abundant with us we used to afford ourselves the luxury of bread and milk for supper. Now we have dispensed with that *superfluous* meal entirely. If we do not get some money by to-morrow's flag of truce we shall have to come down to prison rations again. You would be astonished to see what an effect the improvement of diet has had on us since we came to Charleston. I was a fair sample—yes, more than an average one—of the officers when we came here. Although I was not sick, the actual want of proper food and a scanty supply of *improper* food had made me very poor and weak that the least exertion exhausted me. I was hardly strong enough to read or write for an hour at a time. Now I am nearly as fleshy as ever, am quite strong again and feel more like myself than I have since I entered upon my *Summer tour*.[52] Before this change of diet we all had to be sick about once a week, but now not one of our Mess have been sick for a long time. Some, indeed the most, of the officers in this building have not been so fortunate as we. It is an actual fact that you can tell by a man's looks whether he lives on rations or "patches out" with a little money. When we can get hold of anything to read it is eagerly devoured. A good book passes through a great many hands in a month's time. I amuse myself by studying German, writing in an old historical book in lieu of a Diary, and read in whatever I can get hold of. But I think I have said enough of our manner of living. You may wish to know what we think about. Among the various questions which engage our attentions is this vexed matter of exchange as *shaded* by the Negro question. Let me give you one of the results of the non-exchange of prisoners—a statement which you may rely upon as correct. At Andersonville in Georgia during two months 8000 and more of our soldiers died of scurvy, and nostalgia, which is merely the medical term for homesickness. The whole number confined there was about 24000. So one out of three died in two months. At this rate all would have died in 6 months. The only reason that more had not died is that they had not been prisoners long enough. Those that died were mostly prisoners of six and eight and, in some cases, twelve months' standing. You can imagine what become of a man who lives for six months on corn bread and the smallest imaginary amount of bacon, alive perhaps with maggots, while the man himself is not less alive with vermin, the natural and inevitable result of close quarters and only one suit of clothing for *six* or *eight months*. The poor fellows live along in this way for six months or more, and during the whole time do not receive a vegetable, an ounce of fresh meat or an ounce of flour. Until we ourselves came to this city we had not received a pound of fresh meat or a pound of flour. Some of our enlisted men are here (in this city) now, but they are said to be in a horrible condition. Many of them have become deprived of reason—a natural result of the inhuman treatment they have received. Since coming to Charleston however they have been better used both by officials and citizens. The Sisters of Mercy (Catholic) are doing a great deal for us and for the men. A great error exists in regard to Charleston. It is true that it is the "hotbed of Secession," as well as the birth place of the rebellion, but the people of the city, male and female, are more humane and kind to prisoners than those of any one in the Confederacy.[53] They are much superior to the Algerines of Georgia, where they seemed determined to kill us by inches. *Of course* we feel badly when we think that over 8000 lives and the *health* of other thousands might have been saved by an

217

exchange of prisoners, man for man, rank for rank, this including all officers of colored troops, all negro soldiers who were free by birth or the will of their masters, but excluding about 300 darkeys whom the South claims as slaves, and for whom our Govt. still holds out, although after exchanging upon Rebel terms we should have upon our hand an excess of perhaps 20,000 Rebel prisoners to be used as hostages for these same 300 negroes. I do not wish to see Uncle Samuel back down or concede anything, but on the other hand it makes me feel badly to see *8000* white men die *without* in the least *benefitting 300* negroes. From Butler's and others' letters we are preparing to look the coming winter in the face.

Hunt is in excellent health and it is a great pleasure now to have the companionship of an old friend. There is also one of my classmates at Bowdoin here. His name is Capt. Cochran of the 16th (Regular) Infantry. We have three Bowdoin delegates here.

I have written a long epistle to Almon, who is I know not where. I presume he is as happy as ever. Whenever you chance to see any of my *old friends,* tell them to write to me. Tell Lizzie I have been waiting for some decent paper to devote to her. You see that I am reduced to using an old book. We have to make many shifts to get ourselves through a week *comfortably.* I am rejoiced that the Navy officers are going away, as one of them will give me a blanket. You may judge of the luxury I experience upon my "downy couch" which consists of an old overcoat and a hard floor. This I have enjoyed for five long months.

I enclose a line to father upon the all-important subject of my own *individual* exchange which he can easily effect if he goes at it as he would to building a vessel or clearing a field. I do not however doubt his willingness to do anything he can for my benefit.

One thing I wish you to remember. When you write do not be afraid of quantity. Send the letters sealed and stamped with "U.S." and "C.S." stamps if you can get both. The only use of the C.S. stamp is to forward the letters to us in case we are moved to a new place. They are of course not essential. Send the letters to *simply* "Maj. C.P. Mattocks, Prisoner of War, Roper Hospital, Charleston,

S.C. By Flag of Truce." Boxes should be sent by Express either to Capt. Burger, A.A.G., Hilton Head, S.C. or to such other point as may be designated in the newspapers. Just direct the boxes in care of Capt. B. and then he can receipt for them. I have already told you how destitute of clothing I am. I should prefer some of my old white shirts, if the box has not already come. Send a good supply of letter paper large & small and a plain blank book 6 inches by 8.

I enclose the letter which I wrote yesterday, although it does not contain much of anything. I dare not write about the shelling. Capt. Pendleton will tell all about it. *Military* news must always be considered "contraband." Your letters to me are examined here but then you can say just what you please. The more you write, the less thorough is the examination. Money, photographs, postage stamps, &c. are safe in letters. If you send money let it be gold, as we can sell it at the rate of $22 for $1, while U.S. *money* is worth only $6 1/2 for $1.

I presume Itie will grow out of my reach if the exchange question is not settled up before the close of the war. Write often and write long. The smallest news, will interest me here. In the boxes or even in Hunts' you can send papers, magazines, books and things of that kind. . . . Don't forget the album I sent for. Should like a table knife and fork.

$$\text{◆◆}$$

Friday, Sept. 23d.
One Surgeon, Capts. [J. H.] Smith and [David B.] McKibbin[54] of the Regulars went away today on parole. The Naval officers are again put off with fair promises. Great excitement among the officers of Sherman's Army. Four Cols., 30 Capts., and 88 Lieuts., of Sherman's Army are to be exchanged at once. Preference is given to recent captures, much to the annoyance of the "old fish."[55] The 32d Ga. Regt. has been relieved from guarding us by a set of raw and rowdyish conscripts. Pumpkins are plenty and we are trying our skill at pies. I have had most excellent success.

Saturday, Sept. 24th.

The Yellow Fever is raging in the city, and may get among us. Capt. [Stephen H.] Sheldon of Richmond, has been sent here and has assumed command of the prison.[56]

Sunday, Sept. 25th.

Sherman's officers have been exchanged.

Monday, Sept. 26th.

The Naval officers have received boxes of clothing, &c., (no edibles) and money. Consequently our Mess is on its legs again after living two days on rations. I have received a letter from Capt. Burger, in which he says I shall be remembered in the next exchange. Sears has thoroughly "gone back" on the Mess by giving his spare clothing to outsiders.

Friday, Sept. 30th.

The Naval officers have gone to Richmond for exchange. They were in high glee. This gives me a pair of good blankets, and a new shirt. I wish I could now have a box from the North—or better-be exchanged!

Thursday, Oct. 6th. Columbia, S. C.

After various rumors we were started yesterday from Charleston on one hour's notice and arrived in this city this morning. Yellow fever was getting too close.[57] Several of our officers had died with it. Capt. Sheldon, the Commandant, died of the same terrible disease a few days ago. Also the Adjt.

On the trip from Charleston about 120 of our officers (1000 in all) got away. I tried my best but did not see a good chance. Many of them will be recaptured but some will get away. We are now under guard near the depot.[58]

Saturday, Oct. 8th.

Moved to a piece of woods two miles from the city.[59]

Tuesday, Oct.11th, 1864.

This is my birthday. I am 24 years old, and I hope I shall not spend more than one birthday in the "Confederacy." We are fixing up brush huts in our prison camp.

I have written to Mr. [E. P.] Williams[60] to urge my exchange for Maj. [Lamar] Fontaine who came down for Maj. [Harry] White.[61] Hope to make a raise soon if pen and ink can do it. I have two strings pulling—one at Hilton Head, and one at Charleston—perhaps one in Washington ere this.

I am now Commandant of Squad 2, in place of Maj. St. Albrands, exchanged among Sherman's Army. We have 1370 officers here. The Sanitary Commission has sent a lot of things, shirts, drawers, &c., which we have today distributed. It was a very nice lot.

Thursday, Oct. 13th[62]

This morning, much to my delight and surprise, I was notified by Capt. Semple, the Commandant, that I might get ready to go to Charleston tomorrow morning for exchange.

Friday, Oct. 14th.

Tonight I find myself in a room over the Provost Marshal's office at Charleston, and I lie down with the assurance that tomorrow is to be my last day of prison life. I am a day late, but they have telegraphed to Port Royal Ferry to delay the Flag of Truce until my arrival, so that I may go over in place of Fontaine. I am not yet fully *sure* of the result although they tell me the thing is all concluded by the two Commissioners.

Saturday, Oct. 15th.

"The best laid schemes of men and mice," &c. I find myself still a prisoner, although I am on parole and being well treated at the Hd Qrs. of the 3d S.C. Cavalry, Maj. [John A.] Jenkins commdg. When the Rebel Commissioner of Exchange reached the Ferry this afternoon, he was obliged to deliver up Maj. Fontaine as the U.S. Comm'r had no orders to receive any one else. Yet we hope that all will be well on Monday, when they meet again. Capt. N. Soulé, C.S., Commr. of Exch. tells me that my exchange for Maj. Fontaine was agreed upon by Lt. Col. [Stewart L.] Woodford for U.S.[63] and Maj. Lay for C.S. So it seems there is still hope. It was supposed that Genl. Foster would not receive me on account of fear of "yellow fever," but in that case Genl. [William J.] Hardee[64] proposed to have Fontaine paroled for 40 days longer and to allow me the limits of Charleston for 40 days, and then make the exchange. But the fact of receiving Fontaine shows that they are not fearful of Yellow Fever. During his parole Fontaine has written articles for the Charleston papers condemning his treatment while a prisoner.[65] Nothing is said about this by Foster's Commissioners, but we fear that Genl. F. has been informed of this, and considers that Maj. F. has violated his parole. In that case, my show for exchange is *slim* indeed, as they will hold onto Fontaine.

When I left Columbia I supposed that my letter to Williams had done the business, but now I can not find that Williams has done anything. Everything has been done by Col. Woodford and other Masonic friends on the other side. Woodford is now at the North on leave.[66]

Sunday, Oct. 16th.

This has been a very quiet day. I have revelled in a package of Northern papers which Capt. Soulé recd yesterday. I am still "an honored guest" at the Hd. Qrs. of Maj. Jenkins.

I find that many of these "Confed." officers openly advocate the arming of their slaves. In this case, they will give them their freedom. I really believe the Rebels will have Negro troops in less than six months.[67] The Rebs. are much interested in the Northern Election. Many of the "fire-eaters" hope that Lincoln may be elected in order that they may have a pretext for continuing the fight. The less fiery ones hope that McClellan may win, with a view to future reconstruction. I can see a general solicitude about the fate of Richmond.[68] Their brag about Hood is subsiding just now.[69]

Monday, Oct. 17th.

Thirty miles in a mule team on Saturday, and the same distance in an ambulance today, and yet no exchange. The thing is getting *"mixed."* They received one of our Surgeons today, but Lt. Col. [W. True] Bennett, Act. as Agent of Exchange for Genl. Foster[70] said that I could not be exchanged for Fontaine until they receive orders from Washington, but that they will try to get such an order. Col. Bennett proposed to Capt. Soulé that I be paroled 15 days, which was rejected. Then at my suggestion Bennett proposed that both Fontaine and myself be paroled for 15 days, until the exchange could be effected. This was agreed upon, but Soulé would not send me over today, but promised to hold me in readiness for Fontaine tomorrow at 4 p.m. So I try it once more.

Tuesday, Oct. 18th.

Thirty miles more and even the parole is exploded. The boat, which I supposed was to bear me to freedom, brought the unwelcome news that Genl. Foster had annulled the parole of Fontaine, as he had previously done with his exchange. Foster still asked for the paroling of myself which was, of course, refused by Capt. Soulé. Now I am to go back to Charleston—perhaps even to Columbia—to "chew the bitter cud of disappointment." At the suggestion of Capt. Soulé, I shall make application to Genl. Hardee for a parole of 30 days to go to Washington to effect the exchange of Fontaine.[71]

Today a young lady with a younger sister was sent across the lines. She is a native of Charleston but has been in Philadelphia for 7 years. Strange to say she has no sympathy with the South. She tells a sad story. Her father was a Northern man who came South some years ago. After his death the mother and two daughters went to the North. Since the war this young lady's brother has angrily insisted upon their coming South. The young Miss, rather than do so supported her mother, sister and herself by giving music lessons and embroidering shoulder straps until last March when her mother died. Her brother then renewed his demands for his sisters leaving the North. She finding her health failing through the exertions she had made, at last yielded to a threat of her brother to disown her, only through fear that her health would not enable her to support herself and sister longer. The interesting young lady's name is Miss S.O. Day, and she lives now at Aiken, Ga. We were not long in becoming "acquaint."

Oct. 18 1864

Mrs. Hunt,

Please request my Mother to send me $10 (gold) concealed in some manner in an old vest, which she will please [mail] by itself. I am not to be exchanged.[72]

Wednesday, Oct. 19th.

Today I returned to Charleston, and tonight I am being very well entertained by Mr. A.C. Richmond, formerly of Dubuque, Iowa, but now acting as orderly to the Provost Marshal. He was forced into the 32d Ga., but afterward sent to jail for wanting to go North.

Throughout my *trials, &c.,* Capt. Soulé has used me finely. He is a son of Pierre M. Soulé, formerly U. S. Senator from La., but now a prominent Rebel.[73] At his request the Provost Marshal has promised to allow me to remain at Charleston on parole. In that case, I shall mess with Mr. Richmond. When I found that exchange and parole were "played," I sent a line to Capt. Burger for a box by every flag of truce.

I am not discouraged yet. To pull every string, I have requested a parole of 30 days from Hardee to get Fontaine exchange[d]. I have addressed a similar communication to [Robert] Ould, Rebel Commissioner of Exchange at Richmond, requesting that he suggest any Rebel Major to be exchanged for me. Then I have written to father to go to Washington and remain there until he gets an order for Genl. Foster to exchange Fontaine for me. Besides all this I have written to Capt. Burger at Hilton Head to do all he can to get the order for my exchange from the War Dept. So among them all I will, I hope, get something.

If I have to remain here any time I shall be well supplied by the boxes from Burger. I hope that I may not be compelled to return to Columbia, where we have to endure cold and rain without any shelter except pine boughs. I am still on parole.

❧❧❧

Provost Marshall's Office
Charleston, S.C. Oct. 19th 1864
To Lt. Genl. Hardee,
Comm'd'g. South Ca., G., & Fla.
General:

Contrary to military usage I take the liberty of addressing you personally upon the subject of my exchange.

Maj. Genl. Foster, comm'd'g. U.S. Forces, has stated that he has not yet been authorized by the U.S. Govt., to exchange Maj. Lamar Fontaine for myself, as had been previously agreed upon by the U.S. and C.S. Commissioners of Exch.

I therefore have the honor to respectfully request that I may be allowed a parole of thirty (30) days for the purpose of going to Washington to secure the exchange of Maj. Fontaine for myself. If this request meet your approval I feel confident that the exchange could be easily effected.

❧❧❧

Provost Marshall's Office.
Charleston, S.C. Oct. 19, 1864
My dear Father:

I have just come very near to an exchange after most desperate exertions. I now wish you to take hold of the matter in real earnest. It had been agreed between the Union & Confederate agents of exchange that I should be exchanged for Maj. Lamar Fontaine, C. S.

Army, now a prisoner of war at Morris Island. I was carried down
to the flag of truce and just as I was about to embark for the North
a dispatch came from Genl. Foster stating that he had no authority
to exchange, but that such authority had to come from the war
Dept.[74] Now I wish you to *go to Washington in person and stay
there* until you get the War Dept. to order Genl. Foster to exchange
Maj. Fontaine (Texas Cavalry) for me. If you fail of that get some
Confederate Major paroled for 30 days to come to this city to effect
an exchange for me. Mr. White of Penn. did that for his son, Maj.
Harry White. Remember this—Genl. Hardee Commanding this Dept.,
has issued an order against *any more special* exchanges, but as my exchange was *agreed upon before* the order was issued he will [make]
my case an *exception.*[75] This then is the only chance. If you do not at
once interest yourself, and do just what I say I shall have to wait for a
general exchange, which *certainly* will not come for 6 months. I beg of
you to go to W. in person, and all will be right. I would willingly pay
the expense of two trips for this important object. Love to Mother
and all the family. I trust that you can willingly make this sacrifice
for me. Have recd mother's Baldwin letter.

Friday, Oct. 21st.

I am back at the prison camp, much to my disgust. The Prov.
Marshal, after promising to let me remain, has sent me away. I slept
in the Columbia jail last night, and this morning made my appearance in camp much to the surprise of all the prisoners, who were
foolish enough to suppose I was in the land of freedom.

In my trip on the cars I had a little talk with a Rebel Lieut. who
was wounded in a fight around Petersburg. He has a brother in one
of our prisons at the North, and I have made arrangements to furnish
him with greenbacks in return for gold to be furnished me by the
father at this place. This will be a very great advantage to both
parties. Shall have a letter from the Lt. soon.

Military Prison, Columbia, S.C.
Oct. 22d 1864.
My dear Father:

A gentleman of this vicinity who had a son in one of our Northern prisons has made arrangements to supply me with a little money, and I am to return the favor by supplying his son. So I wish you to send $100 in greenbacks to my friend George G. Kimball, clerk in Quartermaster General's office at Washington and he will receipt to you for it. From that point he can easily manage the business for me. Even if you succeed in effecting my exchange, as I pray you may do, I hope you will still send this $100 to Mr. Kimball together with a copy of this letter. I have written to him, but the letter might miscarry. In case I am exchanged I have made arrangements with one of my fellow-prisoners to get the benefit of my plan, in which case I can make myself whole upon arriving in Washington.

Now I hope you will attend to this business at once. I have already written a letter asking you to go to Washington and remain until you get an order from the Secy of War to exchange me for Maj. Lamar Fontaine, Texas Cavalry, C. S. A., now a prisoner at Morris Island. I am held in readiness for the exchange, having already been offered one, but being refused by Genl. Foster (USA) on the grounds that he needed special orders from the War Dept. Get *that special order*. You can do it very easily at *this time*. Love to all. I wrote mother a line from Flag of Truce through Mrs. Hunt of Gorham. Tell her to send the vest even if I am exchd.

[*Once again CPM wrote in small script in order to preserve space in his journal.*]

(Written with pencil and rewritten with ink from this date on.)

Oct.

A Lt. Young, of the 4th Penn. Cav. was killed two or three evenings ago, while sitting at his camp fire, by the accidental discharge of a musket in the hands of a careless sentry. He lived only three hours after the shot.[76]

Two officers of the 32d Ga. (Reb.) were killed at Charleston recently by one of Foster's shells.

Nov. 1st.

My prospect for exchange is very fair—that is, fair as compared with the prospects of others—but I have decided to take leave of this camp as soon [as] a chance of escape offers itself. I was disgusted with my trial at exchange and I am now determined to exchange myself and save "Uncle Sam" at least one Major on the cartel.

I have concluded arrangements with Dr. [Lewis] Dantzler to supply his son, who is now a prisoner at Pt. Lookout, Md.[77] Dr. D. is a Mason and will supply me with food & money here. Kimball is my agent at Washington. This is the chance obtained from the Reb. Lieut. (A. Harper) on the cars. Dr. D. has one son and three nephews to be supplied. If this plan can be perfected it will be a great blessing to me in the event of my not escaping. Dr. D. is a planter and can send me many luxuries that I could not buy here with even an abundance of money. Meanwhile I await patiently the remittances from home.

Wednesday, Nov. 2d.

This morning I learn that $30 in gold has arrived for me but I can not get it until it is converted into Rebel currency, probably at the rate of $25 for $1. Greenbacks now sell briskly at $8 but the govt. authorities pay but $7. Provisions are moderate here. Potatoes $20, Butter $10.[78]

CHAPTER SEVEN

Escape

Escape[1]
(Each entry made at sunset.)

Thursday, Nov. 3d, (4 P.M.)
Hunt, Litchfield and myself left Camp Sorghum at 3 o'clock. We saw that a large number of officers were passing in and out on parole for the purpose of getting wood.[2] We started *"instanter,"* waiting only to take a map and compass, and (picking up small sticks as if to bring large logs in with them) passed the line of sentinels with so much apparent honesty that the poor deluded fellows evidently thought us to be paroled officers in search of wood. Robbins left in a similar manner about five minutes before us. We are hiding on the banks of the Saluda River, about half a mile or less from camp, patiently waiting for darkness. The guard has just gobbled one runaway only a few rods from us. We have not seen our quondam messmate yet and perhaps may not soon.[3]

Friday, Nov. 4th.
Swam Saluda River last night just after dark—swim of 200 yds—600 yards from Reb. pickets on bridge.[4]
Travelled all night. Now hiding in wood 15 miles from Columbia. Early in the morning saw negro coming near us to cut wood. Went to him and made him promise to bring us food at night. Have suffered terribly with cold.[5]

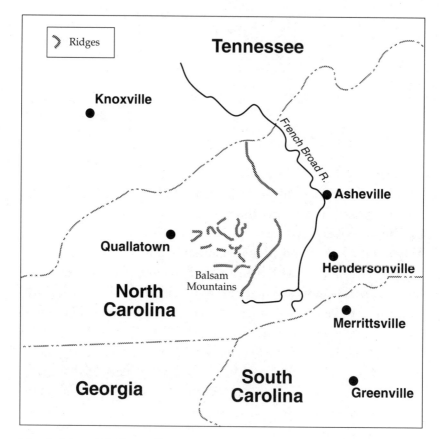

Map 2. Mattocks's Escape Route.

Saturday, Nov. 5th.

No water, nothing to eat except small piece of wet bread, wet feet & clothes until an hour after dark when the darkey came up and took us to his cabin, where we feasted on chicken, corn bread & potatoes, besides taking a supply in our haversacks. We toasted our feet by his fire and talked with the darkies until 10 o'clock, when we started again, but only made 4 or 5 miles owing to the blistered state of our feet.[6] Now hiding in a piece of wood near the Newbury [Newberry] and Columbia pike. We have 300 miles to creep along in this stealthy manner. Great prudence and good fortune may carry us through. We avoid all white men and shall communicate with darkies only while in So. Carolina. When we cross the Blue Ridge we may find some *white* Union men in N.C. who will be of great help to us in assisting us through the mountain district. We shall only appeal to the negroes even when hunger compels it. Safety is our policy.[7] Suffering and hardship shall not interfere with our success.

Sunday, Nov. 6th.

We were going along finely last night when very unexpectedly we ran upon the fire of a wagon park. We successfully flanked it however. Saw a negro and learned the distance (9 m[ile]s) to Newberry.

Monday, Nov. 7th.

This morning I "boarded" a darkey, and made him promise to bring us 4 days' provisions at dark. We are hiding in a piece of wood near a corn field where 3 or 4 negroes are working. We "take turns" in boarding these black craft, and thus far have found them as true as steel[8]. We eat but twice a day, dinner & supper—today for dinner one potato each and for supper but little more. During the P.M. yesterday a small dog came within a few feet of us and we feared he might "smell a Yankee" and set up a barking. We lay low and said nothing, which seemed to pacify the dog, as he went on about his business. We indulged in raw corn last night. It was good!!!

Tuesday, Nov. 8th.

8 miles south of Newberry S.C. while they are electing a President at home. Last night our darkey brought us a supply of sorghum & baked sweet potatoes but no bread. He promised a supply if we would "lie over." So we have voted to remain another night. Our black benefactors have visited us several times during the day. A couple of hounds came very near us in the forenoon, but as they were hunting hares instead of Yankees we escaped notice. Some one hunting fired a gun quite near us two or three times. We have cut holes in our boots for the benefit of our blistered feet. Our toes are actually raw. Swimming rivers and marching in mud with tight boots and after so long a rest from any active exercise has been rather a hard dose to take.

Wednesday, Nov. 9th.

Our darkies disappointed us not a little last night. Instead of coming "in propria persona" with two loaves of corn dodger and a peck of "taters," they sent two other negroes with a very small piece of corn bread and a "quantum sufficit" of raw sweet potatoes. Started at 10 1/2 o'clock, traveled all night and bolted through this fine little town of Newberry at 2 o'clock this morning. Newberry is 45 miles from Columbia. The negroes piloted us into the right road from our hiding place, we having made a slight mistake in our navigation. We are now spending the day in quite an exposed situation in a piece of wood near the pike. Our next point is Laurensville. Our diet is exclusively potatoes (raw) today. Hunt is a little unwell and his feet are in a horrid condition.[9]

Thursday, Nov. 10th.

Last night about six miles N. of Newberry at a sort of railroad station we overtook two more parties of "Yankees" of four men each. They started from Camp Sorghum on the 4th and were ferried across the Saluda by negroes. Seven others, who escaped about the same time, were recaptured near Newberry on Tuesday. At this R.R. Station we all provisioned for three days—a very good place. We made 13 miles last night. Now 16 miles from Newberry and 20 from Laurensville. The pike runs alongside the R.R., crossing and recrossing it every few miles. The darkies at the depot last night were delighted to see us. From them we learned that two runaways like ourselves had passed there Tuesday night. So we are sure that 13 of us have passed over this road within two days. It is getting to be quite a popular route. The road was very good last night, but toward morning—after the moon set—it was difficult to pick our way along in the dark. Hunt gave out and we halted an hour before day. My feet are very rapidly improving. A darkey, whom we "boarded" last night, treated us with apparent coolness—the first instance yet. The negroes as a whole are delighted to serve us. Even this *exceptional* darkey, however, promised not to expose us. Soon after we started last night we met a carriage with two *white* men in it. They looked at us and said nothing, and we certainly had no inclination to speak to them. In the dusk, and with our blankets wrapped about us we probably passed for 3 Rebels just arrived on the Newberry train. This morning we had a heavy shower which dampened our bed but not our ardor. Our last night's supply of corn bread invigorated us very much. We had had nothing but potatoes—mostly raw—for more than two days and were beginning to feel the effects of our vegetarianism. Now hiding in wood near pike.

Friday, Nov. 11th.

Last night's work best yet. 22 miles. Feared pursuit. Met darkey who had been possum hunting. Passed through Laurensville at 2 o'clock.[10] In passing through Clinton we saw two or three white men, who also saw but evidently did not suspect us. At the same place we saw, through the window of a sort of guard house, a solitary "Yankee" who had just been recaptured. Full of apprehensions we pulled off 4 miles in 1 hour & 15 minutes, and then, after breathing a few minutes, made 6 miles more without a rest.[11] We overtook Capt. [E.] Gordon, [81st] Ind. Regt., Capt. Nolan [Lewis Nolen], 2d Del., and Lt. [O.] Powell 42d Ills.[12] This is one of the parties we saw at the R.R. Station. We think we have now distanced both these parties. Now 7 ms. N.W. of Laurens. Today we are, as usual, hiding in a piece of wood. Game is very abundant—such as gray squirrel, woodcock, partridge, &c. Hunt is about "played" by his first attempt at *Infantry Service.* We propose to pass through Greenville tomorrow night. Have now made 82 miles and begin to be very hopeful of the future.

Saturday, Nov. 12th
Nothing new last night.[13]

Sunday, Nov. 13th[14]
1 mile N. of Greenville, 18 miles last night. Came very near being "caught." Had secreted ourselves in a piece of wood near a house to rest a little, when very suddenly the house poured forth a perfect avalanche of young damsels, who had evidently been having a sort of party. A dozen or more gents and lasses passed by us in a path not more than 30 feet distant. We lay low. If they had looked with half an eye our game would have been played. We passed through one of the principal streets of Greenville at 4 this morning, but, coming upon the camp fire of a picket or wagon park, we began a "flank movement." After going half a mile, and after the excitement was over, I was so much exhausted from marching with a lame leg that I actually fainted away in the road. After reviving and trying to go on I fainted a second time.[15] We then decided to halt in the nearest wood, where we were seen by a darkey woman in the morning. Frightened almost to death all day. Cold and frosty. Can hear the church bells plainly. In fact, we are in a sort of pasture near the outskirts of the town.

Monday, Nov. 14th.
Last night, owing to my crippled feet and *corpus* generally, we did not make more than 8 or 10 miles, and are now resting near Traveller's Rest. We were on less than half rations yesterday, and today we have breakfasted on raw corn, and have only a potato apiece for supper. A white man came very near discovering us, but

we "lighted out" and hid in the bushes as he passed by us in plain sight,—to us, but not so plain to him. We hope to get food and reach Merrittsville—10 miles—tonight. I have six blisters on one foot and am very lame in my right leg. Last night I had to limp along on my cane. My fainting and fasting has made me weak. Hunt's feet are quite sore. For the first time we built a fire last night. We lay down at first without one, but were too cold. Several negroes have passed near us this morning. Flanked a wagon park again last night. Are now on the plantation of Mr. Montgomery.

Tuesday, Nov. 15th

"*Laid over*" last night, our "good Samaritans" having failed to appear. This morning's meal consisted of half a small biscuit and a still smaller slice of venison (dried) which we obtained from an old negress last evening. Last night at 10 we visited a negro cabin where we had a nice warm supper and a fresh supply of tobacco, food, &c.[16] Even now we are starving ourselves when our pockets &c. are full of food. This we do so as to prevent calling on the negroes so often. We are told by the darkies that the "Rebs" have guards and details ahead who exercise themselves in hunting up deserters &c. These we shall have to evade "by hook or by crook." We have now become possessed of a meal bag from which I propose to make a set of haversacks.[17] We flanked another wagon park last night. At one mile North from Montgomery's are two roads running N. and N.W. We have taken the left hand (N.W.) one.

(Jany 24th 1865. Danville, Va.)

Note. By taking the left-hand instead of the right-hand road we were thrown off the Hendersonville pike and brought to Dunn's Rock across the Blue Ridge, thus leaving the Hendersonville far to our right. Had we gone to H. we should have been under the necessity of evading quite a force of Home Guards and such trash in and about H. We took the left hand road almost against our own convictions, but because we thought it would eventually unite with the main pike upon which was a wagon park fire directly before us.

I do not note the number of miles made each night, because I have made a table of miles in the end of this book [*omitted in this edition*].

Wednesday, Nov. 16th.

Marched 9 miles last night. Now resting on a very steep little mountain, near the foot of which we can see men at work, children playing, &c., & so on, to our intense satisfaction, as we are confident they can not see us. Flanked two more wagon parks last night. We heard yesterday that three escaped prisoners were carried back towards Columbia (same day), having been recaptured near the foot of the Blue Ridge. We now have rather a hard prospect ahead, but shall advance cautiously and try to flank all pickets on our path. If we get through this night successfully I shall have strong faith in our ultimate success. We hope to employ a guide in North Carolina, where they say, there are plenty of Union men who will help us along.[18] I had a very easy time of it last night, my lameness having cured itself. It seems odd for me to have sore feet and lame legs,— things which never troubled me in the army. Long imprisonment and want of exercise have rendered me unfit for active service until by trying a little moving about I harden myself. I have now nearly reached that point. We are now 131 miles from our starting point having been out 13 nights. We begin to feel the want of sleep. Although we get tired, it seems almost impossible to sleep much by day. I dream of home or of reaching our lines every night. We are in excellent spirits. We have food enough to carry us into North Carolina.

Thursday, Nov. 17th. (Blue Ridge)

Our "Rubicon" is passed and we are now on the Northern slope of the Blue Ridge, having passed through Jones' Gap last night. We started at 10 o'clock and kept up the march till 5 1/2 o'clock this morning, resting 10 minutes for every hour of marching. In this way we make 18 miles over a very rough and hilly road. In fact the road was a perfect zigzag up the mountain. By day the scenery through the

Gap must be very fine. Even by moonlight it is no mean sight. The deep ravines, the sparkling cascades and waterfalls, the mammoth southern pines growing among huge rocks, even the gloomy and deathlike solitude of the place, all had a charm for even so unsentimental beings as escaped prisoners may be supposed to be. No houses, no men, nothing living for ten miles, and yet, every rod we traveled we feared we might be unconsciously running into some watchful Rebel picket, stationed in this narrow gap to intercept the further progress of runaway negroes and Yankees. We now feel highly encouraged and think we have accomplished the most dangerous portion of our journey. Visions optimistic begin to loom up, perhaps yet to be wrested from us. We are now about 6 miles from Hendersonville, N.C. We have seen fires just ahead of us which we fear may be pickets. These we can easily flank tonight as we know their exact position. A white man passed very near our hiding place in the woods today, but did not see what game was near him although we feared he would.

After two weeks of wandering we have brought our marching down to a regular system. Start at 8 o'clock, walk an hour, rest 10 minutes, and so on until nearly daylight when we seek a good hiding place. By day and in fact most of the time by night we speak only in a whisper. We are just now upon a very small allowance of food,— for breakfast a small piece of thin corn bread, perhaps two inches square with a piece of meat of the same economical dimensions, and for supper the same in quality but a very little more in quantity. I never would have believed that a person could do so much with so little food. Perhaps one could not in another cause than going home from a Rebel prison! We must find some friendly negro tomorrow or live on raw corn until we do. For the last two days we have "patched out" our food with raw corn which actually tastes good to persons as hungry as we are. Corn bread seems to be a great delicacy. No cake ever relished better. The only regret we have is that we can not have all the corn bread we crave. Better days ahead however! Such privations as hunger, cold, wet feet, fatigue and want of sleep are as nothing when compared with the stake we are playing for. We seriously feel the want of sleep but yet our condition is improving daily. Our feet are getting harder, the blisters disappearing, &c., &c. We are now more than halfway from Columbia to Knoxville. 100 miles will bring us well into Tennessee where we shall be comparatively safe. Our friends at home are doubtless anxious because we do not write. We hope soon to explain the matter in person. We have now and then a warm day but the most of the time we suffer considerably. We have but two old blankets for three of us—no overcoats, and but little food. How different from campaigning in the army where we do our walking by day and at dark sit down to a good fire and a cup of coffee. Here we are often thankful for a drink of water on our knees from a mud-puddle in the middle of the road.

Friday, Nov. 18th.

Much to our vexation we are lost in the Mountains. Marched till three o'clock on the wrong road when we brought up in a man's barn-yard. We are now living on raw corn, having only a small piece of meat and a smaller piece of bread for supper. After much deliberating we have decided to go back and try another road tonight. There are plenty of farm houses in sight in the valleys here, but no signs of wealthy *planters* as in South Carolina. No darkies in sight. We are now on the summit of a high wooded ridge from which we have a fine view of the blue Ridge—a view which we would willingly part with as we are actually lost, although we have not lost all hopes of coming out right in the end. The weather is tolerably warm for November.

Saturday, Nov. 19th.

Started across the fields at dark towards a house where we heard negroes, but finding we should have to wade the French Broad River, we gave it up and started on the back track. I must here note down a narrow escape that Litchfield had yesterday afternoon toward sunset. We saw what we supposed to be four negroes at work in a field about half a mile from our hiding place. They were in a cornfield and "Litch" crept up slowly to reconnoitre. Finding, as he thought, that all was right, he advanced quite boldly when within a few yards of the men he discovered that one of the number was a white man. As this was not the color he was in search of, he at once dropped upon his hands and knees and crept away without having been noticed among the high corn. He came back to us and related his adventures with much excitement.

Starting on the back track last night we soon came to a house in the rear of which we could see the light of a negro cabin. But in front of the house were three large dogs which did not like our appearance. So I made a long detour and crept up to the cabin where I met a hearty welcome as soon as I declared myself an escaped Yankee prisoner. I at once repaired to Hunt and Litchfield and escorted them to an old mill where the negroes had told us to hide. Here we waited till 9 o'clock when the old negress brought us some applesauce and boiled potatoes. She could give us no "pone" for want of corn meal. After due deliberation we adjourned to the cabin where we ate our supper before a warm fire to the mutual delight of ourselves and our sable hostess. There were no male negroes about. An old negress, her daughter and some little children were all we saw. We have seldom ventured to ask food from house servants as they are not generally so Yankee-ized as the field hands. Being generally well-fed, well clothed and perhaps petted by their masters, many of them come to look up[on] slavery as an advantage to them, while their less fortunate brethren and sisters who labor in the fields from daylight till dark do not become quite so favorably impressed with the institution.

Last night through our colored entertainers, we learned that there were many Union white men in the vicinity, and by their directions after much wandering about, we were welcomed to the house of a white man—the first white man we have spoken with for more than two weeks. We are now hiding in an old corn house on his farm. This morning he brought us a fine breakfast of beef, pork, apple sauce, vegetables. I think it was the best meal I ever ate.

Sunday, Nov. 20th.

We have decided to remain here until a party of escaped Yankees can be got together, and then we shall take a guide for Tennessee. Last night at dark we went to the house, where we were regaled with a fine meat supper and a plenty of nice apple brandy.[19] At 10 o'clock we came back to our hiding place. At the door of this old house is a pile of apples and we manage to keep well filled. We are being entertained like princes of the royal blood. Several old men and young men—even young damsels—have called at our hiding place to see us, and congratulate us upon our escape from prison and our successful passage through an enemy's country. These people are the strongest for the Union question of any persons I ever saw. They are doing everything for us. We hear of several parties of our Columbia friends now hiding in this vicinity as we are. Among them are Capt. [Edward E.] Chase and Lt. [James M.] Fales, 1st R.I. Cav.[20]

Monday, Nov. 21st.

Last evening we had a repitition [repetition] of Sunday's entertainment, consisting of rye coffee with sorghum and cream, apple jack, apple butter, apple sauce, three kinds of meats, &c., &c., to our satiety. We slept on the floor before a blazing fire until 4 o'clock when with haversacks loaded, we started for the house of —— ——[21] where the party was to assemble previous to starting across the mountains. We arrived a little before daylight and found Chase, Fales, [Asa L.] Goodrich,[22] & some twelve more all ready. A thick snow storm coming up we voted to wait till tomorrow and are now enjoying a very hospitable roof and table. We have been rendering ourselves useful by shelling corn, cutting wood, paring apples, &c., for our entertainers. We shall have a party of 20 men when we get ready to start.

Tuesday, Nov. 22d.

Went with —— —— to the house of our guide[23] and started on our journey proper at 10 o'clock in the forenoon. We have made 16 miles today and are now resting at the house of —— —— where we make prodigious work among the old gentleman's apples. On *the way* we took an extra guide for 6 or 8 miles—an old man who knows every inch of the country. We have had some very queer adventures. The inhabitants here are thoroughly Union and there are many deserters and soldiers of the Rebel army, as well as a great many of the right age for conscription, who hide about in the woods and old houses, paying visits to their homes as often as safety from the details of provost guard deserter-hunters will permit.[24] When we approach a house—a thing like angels visits here—it is no uncommon sight to see two or three young men running to the cover of the woods as if for dear life. They keep a sharp lookout, and seeing us advancing, almost invariably mistake us for a party of rebels coming to conscript or arrest these sons of the mountains. When they are enticed back and find that we are genuine Yankees their joy knows no bounds, and they do all that their limited means will allow. A large tray of nice apples is at once brought forward while they gather around us to listen to our adventures. Old men and women, girls and boys, even the little children look upon us as their warm friends and perhaps their future deliverers from Rebel rule. This is a great region for "bushwhacking" and many a bloody battle has been fought between the outlyers and the provost guards sent to hunt and arrest them. Every man, even every boy above 12 years of age is thoroughly armed, and it [is] said that the long, old fashioned, but deadly, rifles have at times made sad work with the emissaries of Jefferson Davis. They are of great help to us. Tomorrow we take a new special guide for 20 or 30 miles.

Wednesday, Nov. 23d.

Started at daylight with our new guide and have made 23 miles over high hills and mountains and through deep valleys,—a dreary country. A little snow remains from Monday's flurry. A deer ran very near us this morning and our extra guide, who carries his rifle along, came very near getting a shot at him. This has been a very fatiguing tramp. We are now at the house of —— —— which we did not reach till 10 o'clock. We still enjoy these farmers' apples. We have cut up some wood and are having a very cozy time before a blazing fire. I have been reminded of what Bayard Taylor says in regard to manners and customs among many of the Northern people in Europe visited by him. This house affords a good example. Parlor, kitchen and dining-room are all combined with sleeping rooms. In fact, the house contains but one room, in which are five beds, a table, chairs, and several other articles of furniture. But more interesting yet, in one of the beds are the old man and his wife, in another his boys, in another scores, or less, of small children, a fourth stands vacant for company, while a fifth holds the precious treasure of two young ladies who, nothing abashed by the arrival of twenty Yankees, are keeping up a lively conversation with their tired but admiring guests. To our New England ideas of propriety this seems horrible, but here every night we have had similar experiences. All of the houses have but one room and the young lady with whom you were talking perhaps a moment ago, has by some miraculous legerdemain, modestly and expeditiously contrived, without your ever noticing it, to place herself upon the downy couch—vulgarly has gone to bed,—from which she surely deigns to continue the conversation with her Yankee guest. "Can such things be and not excite our special wonder," as Shakespeare or somebody else has said—who, it is hard to remember among the unliterary associations of these mountains.

Thursday, Nov. 24th.

More of the same sort! What a theme for a poet!! I was drowsing away before daylight on my bed of blankets in front of the fire when I was gently aroused from my slumbers by a gentle damsel who very naively informed me that she was hunting for her stocking which had been lost during the night. Taking pity on the fat, plump foot, which I could not fail to see peeping out from a dress not too long according to Paris styles, I at once rallied myself and tried to find the missing article. After much search, I am happy to record, it was found, much to the delight of the fair Terpsichore, who bustled around a few moments and then appeared with "nary a bare foot."

Our travels have commenced in real earnest. We have traveled from daylight till dark, over horrible mountains also through almost impassible thickets, and night finds us about 7 miles in a straight line from our starting place. To make 7 miles we have wasted about 12. We crossed Balsam mountain at noon. The ascent was hard but the descent was actually perpendicular. In many places we had to lower ourselves down from ledge to ledge by the underbrush which is abundant, and at times very troublesome to our feet. This Balsam is similar to our Northern fir and wherever it grows you find a thick undergrowth of what these mountaineers call "bone laurel." This laurel grows so thick in some places that one can walk on it without at all touching the ground. This path runs along the R.R.

Friday, Nov. 25th.

We have had a fatiguing tramp of 20 miles over a very rough tract. We are halting for the night near what the guide says is Smoky mountain, the dividing line between N.C. and Tennessee. We expect to reach houses in Tenn. by tomorrow night. We are now much reduced in the matter of haversacks. Hunt, Litchfield and myself are trying to economize our rations while some of the party have eaten up everything. We started with enough and hope to get through without suffering much from hunger. We do suffer however these cold nights. Although we build good fires and wrap up comfortably, the small hours of the night are sure to find us waking up shivering over a few embers. We have no axes or hatchets and can not get the proper wood for an all-night fire. The marching or rather, climbing up and down these mountains is the hardest labor I ever undertook. I have walked and marched and done everything with my legs which people ordinarily do in civilized life, but I find that a set of muscles have been hither neglected—a set of muscles which nothing but climbing these hills and pushing through laurel would ever have reached! This laurel, by the way, is perfectly awful! We have been lost once or twice in a growth of it, and it seemed that we never should emerge from the jungle. The growth is so thick that one can not often step upon terra firma, but must find a foothold in the branches of the detestable shrub. It is hard enough to climb the hills but all pronounce this worst of all.

Saturday, Nov. 26th.

We have been lost in the laurel all day and instead of reaching the hospitable house of some good Union man in Tennessee, we are "squatted" in an unknown region on the bank of a stream which we have waded and crossed and recrossed. Here we have shivered and fretted away and at last have succeeded in building a fire among the laurel bushes, the growth of which is so thick that we can not get room to lie down, but shall have to sleep sitting or as best we can under the deplorable circumstances. Our haversacks are empty and have been all day, our confidence in the guide is considerably shaken, and we are terribly foot sore, hungry, &c., but we are far from being demoralized. Every one hopes for the best. Besides our *chartered* guide, we have a sort of *amateur* who came with us for the sake of novelty. He pretends to no local knowledge but, being an excellent woodsman, is of as much use to us as the chief guide. The chief guide, whom we have promised $500 in "Green Backs" in case of success, has been through twice before. He did very well the first day or two, but today has seemed bewildered and not a little "mixed up." He still promises a sight of Tenn. "tomorrow." We have given away some of our rations to the hungry ones, else we might now have a plenty. We three started out most bountifully supplied. Boiled and roast pork and beef, roast chicken, corn bread, and dried venison were abundant in our haversacks when we started. If we should get lost in these mountains without food, and so far from any settlements, it is hard to say what would be our fate.

Sunday, Nov. 27th.

Worse and worse!! We have been *horribly* lost all day. For five or six hours—yes 8 hours—we waded a rapid mountain stream. (N.B. Since found to be Raving Fork.) and at the very outset I had the misfortune to tumble in and get a *sousing* even to my arm-pits. The rocks are covered with ice and it is very difficult to get along. The banks of the stream are covered with laurel so thick as to be almost impenetrable. So it was decided in the forenoon to follow the stream until we came to houses. (Note. We have since learned that it was 50 miles to any house, a distance which we certainly could not have made without food. Had we continued on the stream a worse fate than even our subsequent recapture might have awaited us.) Toward night, after due deliberation, it was decided to leave the stream & travel due N.W. by our compass, through laurel, balsam, or whatever came in our way. So on we started, and after a toilsome tramp descried what the guide declares to be Smoky Mountain, only 8 miles from Union settlements in Tenn. We have emerged from the laurel & are now on a high ridge—the leading ridge of Smoky.[25] At the first of the mountain travel I was one of the lagging ones, but now, notwithstanding the emptiness of our haversacks, I am among the foremost. Fales was very sick and came near fainting today. We have built good fires tonight, but it is very cold. We expect to dine in Tenn. by 2 o'clock tomorrow afternoon. God grant we may not be disappointed. We can not travel more than one day more without food and we can not conjecture how far we may be from human aid. Up to Saturday we had found a plenty of chestnuts, but today we have found none. We did get each a few sprigs of "crow's foot" or "crinkle root" and ivy leaves, which we devoured eagerly although we did not get enough to afford any perceptible nourishment. There has been great suffering in our little band since we left the region of houses. We are now in a very desolate region, and if we do not find houses or some sort of food in the shape of acorns or chestnuts before tomorrow night, we shall, to say the least, know what hunger is. Even now some of the party are hardly able to stand after the day's labor. Strange to say, I am actually improving on starvation. Tonight I was the first man up the mountain, next to the guides. Hunt is terribly exhausted. His feet are in a pitiful condition, being covered with painful blisters. During the last two days we have seen plenty of deer and bear tracks but "nary a bar." They say this region supports now and then a panther but we have not been honored with any indications of the presence of that gentle animal! The mountains we have climbed, the streams waded and the laurel penetrated by our weary legs have been enough without receiving any undue attention from wild animals. Campaigning in the army is often hard, but until this trip I never knew what it was to actually suffer from hunger, cold, thirst, sore feet and many other similar little delicacies! Everything was boy's play when compared with this. Yet I would endure it all over again—yes, a dozen times—rather than go back to prison and wait until Butler had concluded to exchange the prisoners now held in the cow pen at Columbia. We thought we saw a fire in the distance today, but it is very doubtful. Everybody is in good cheer over the prospect of dining in Tennessee tomorrow, a thing which our guide promises us a certainty. God grant we may not be disappointed. We have earned our liberty and are eager to have our wages.

Monday, Nov. 28th. Recapture.

Prisoners again! The promised dinner in Tenn. is a dream. We are recaptured and soon will be consigned to our miseries a second time. We started a little before day, and were on a trail leading N.W. Immediately in our front was a mountain which the guide last night declared to be Smoky Mt., but which this morning sorely puzzled his thick skull. He was doubtful and rather thought Smoky was beyond, so that perhaps it was 20 miles instead of 6 or 8 to our Union friends in Tenn. So relying upon our compass, we determined to keep on.

We had not gone more than a mile when one of the party descried what appeared to be a house about 6 miles to our left. Then ensued a long debate, some wishing to go to the house, get food and return and run the risk of recapture, while others, either believing there was no house or hoping to cross Smoky before night, wished to keep on. Fritz and one of the two others turned toward the house while the rest of us kept on. Presently, however our chief guide turned back and as might have been expected, nearly all of us followed him. [Asa L.] Goodrich, Brown, [J. E.] Lewis, and two others kept on.[26] We straggled in squads of one, two and three toward the house. Hunt being nearly exhausted, Litchfield and I went along slowly with him, stopping to pick chestnuts which we found in abundance as soon as we left the ridge and descended into the valley. We reached the house but found it deserted. So we took the old road leading from it and went on expecting to find another house,—a fatal house for us. I was walking leisurely along with two others when suddenly and unexpectedly, from a corner of the road popped up two white men and an Indian not ten feet from us and with fearful oaths and wild demonstrations of—consisting of a leap and a yell from the Aboriginee(!)—demanded our surrender. We wasted no time in useless deliberation or parley but respectfully lifted our hats to our "chivalrous" captors, who thereupon ordered us to "come out of those haversacks and blankets". We thought we were fortunate not to be killed by the blood-thirsty "Yahoos." One of our party—Lt. Helm of Penn.—who was walking alone was fired at by one of these scamps who pretended that he ordered him to halt before he fired, but the probability was that he had an eye to plunder, as he at once stripped Helm of his dress coat and overcoat, both of which were nearly new. We were now conducted a few rods over a hill to the house of one Joe Gunter, where we found the rest of our party guarded by Indians and worse than Indians—just such abortions of humanity as had captured us. The leader of this motley crew was Joe Gunter himself, who with great show of hospitality, regaled us with a dinner of corn bread and boiled cabbage. We ate as hungry men always eat. We succeeded in getting back a part of our plundered property by dint of hard pleading with Joe Gunter & Co. Now Joe was only a citizen and governed his gang purely by moral suasion,—a kind of discipline which proved ineffectual with the Indians. Their only answer was "me want it" which meant that our blankets were as good for Indians as for white men! We rested for two hours and received the tantalizing information that in the morning we were at the base of Smoky Mountain and on[ly] a mile and a half from Tennessee line, or 7 miles from a Union settlement in Tenn. So if we had marched N.W. 7 miles instead of 7 miles to Joe Gunter's, we should have been safe. We are all indignant with our chief guide. The assistant guide was recognized by Joe Gunter, but we are palming off the principal guide as a Lt. Spofford of an Ohio regiment and may succeed in getting him to Columbia and have him exchanged as a Federal officer. His real name is Gilbert Sautel—the other's Joseph Henry, an old deserter.[27] At two o'clock we started under a strong and brutal guard, for the so-called post of Quolle [Quallatown],[28] which consists of one house and one barn. Here we are in room cooking pones, inwardly cursing our luck and thinking alternately of home and Columbia. We have traveled 17 miles today and some of the party are thoroughly "played" since their recapture. Hunt did not come up to Gunter's and a man who went out to hunt for him could not find him. He must have given out on the way.[29]

On the way from Gunter's we had a very humiliating scene. Joe G's son had taken Lt. Boltsford's knife and Lt. B. reported the fact to Joe G himself. The young Gunter was enraged and seized Lt. B. by the collar, struck him, kicked him, cussed him and gave him several other assurances of Southern superiority.

Major Parker's Recruiting officer.

I had almost forgotten to record an amusing adventure which occurred on the second day after we left our lurking place in Transylvania County.[30] Our guide was leading us directly toward a small house which had been occupied by a quasi-Union man, a member of the Provost Guard, &c., but which was not supposed to be unoccupied. So we advanced boldly and had got almost to the very door before we discovered that the house was occupied and the owner and his numerous family were eating their dinner. It was too late to turn back and in order to disguise our true character, the guide made bold to ask for a drink of water for all hands and an opportunity to rest. We soon learned that our host was a recruiting officer for Maj. Parker's battalion of [Col. William H.] Thomas's Legion, a sort of home guard, provost, horse stealing organization which attempts to maintain the military dignity of J. Davis among the mountains of Western North Carolina.[31] For the purpose [of] evading a subsequent pursuit we told the zealous young recruiting officer that we had "come over" from Transylvania Co. on a sort of excursion, that we were citizens of that Co. who had been "lying out" in the bush to escape conscription, that we had found it too hard during this cold weather—in fine, that we had become penitent and decided to enlist in Maj. Parker's battalion if we could suit ourselves as to terms, but that we must see the Maj. himself first. The happy recruiting officer declared himself pleased, said we should make a great addition to the command, that Maj. Parker would be at Webster[32] "next Saterday" and we could send an agent down to see and converse with him. It seems almost incredulous that we should thus beard the lion in his den, but it was easy as our appearance did not prove us to be anything in particular. Our Clothing was part grey, part blue, and the insignia of rank had long since been done away [with]. Then we had three North Carolinians and four or five Tennesseeans who did the most of the talking while the New Englanders concealed their Yankee dialect by a judicious silence. We bade the delighted emissary of J. Davis an affectionate adieu and sent word by him to Maj. Parker that we would meet him at Webster "next Saterday." I must here say that we afterward met Maj. Parker, who complained that we did not visit him as agreed upon. We visited him subsequently not as recruits for the Rebel armies but as delegates for Rebel prisons once more,—thus reluctantly fulfilling our "manifest destiny." Suffice it to say that we did not long impose upon Maj. P. or his "sub," as they learned long before the "next Saterday" that a party of 21 Yankees answering to our description, had started on a mountain trip from Transylvania Co. under the leadership of native guides &c., &c. & so on. Maj. P. and his band hunted us one day without success having taken our trail from Scott's Creek across Balsam Mt. A few days after our capture we learned that 5 different parties started out in search of us, but none of them could have caught us if we had known where we were and continued one day longer on the N.W. trail. At any rate we should have reached Tenn. where we might possibly, but not probably, have fell into the hands of Rebel scouts.

Military Prison, Asheville, N.C.
Dec. 6th 1864
My dear Mother:

After a month's silence I have a chance to explain the interruption of our correspondence. Capt. Litchfield, Lt. Hunt and myself made our escape from Columbia on the 3d Nov. and succeeded in getting within *1 1/2 miles* of the Tennessee line, after a tiresome night tramp of 250 miles, and much suffering from hunger and cold, when much to our chagrin and disappointment, we were recaptured (28th Nov), and are now on our way back to Columbia. The gold you sent had arrived at C. but had not been delivered when we left. Continue to send it. Capt. Burger will keep you posted as to what can come through. Anything sent in his care is safe. Please go to Fernald and [get] 1 doz. large & 1 doz. small Infantry buttons & send them. Hunt and I are both well, although we have had a hard time. We were travelling over mountains, wading streams and waddling through snow nearly a week—the three last days *lost* in the mountains and entirely without food. Since being recaptured we have been kindly treated. We had hoped to spend Christmas and New Year's with [you]. We certainly tried hard enough, but fate was against us. From being within 10 miles of safety we are doomed to a new trial of prison life. I trust you will continue to send boxes and money. The same for Hunt. Butter, cans of eatables, tea, coffee, &c. A pair of heavy *good* boots, (calf) no. 9. would be acceptable—cost about $8 or 10—thick-soled, sowed. Get them ready made of [Alexis] Abbott,[33] he had my measure. Tell Mrs. Hunt to get Abbott to make Hunt a pair of same, 7 in size, 8 in length. I am entirely out of clothing. Send small bag of buck wheat flour. Anything will be acceptable. Will write from Columbia.

Sunday, Dec. 11th, 1864. Danville (Va.) Prison.
Neglecting dates and minor occurrences we find ourselves established as prisoners of war at this place among a lot of recent captures

from the Army of the Potomac who have not yet lost the idea of an immediate & general exchange. They think us demoralized when we say that there will be no general exchange *at present*. But I must record our travels from the mountains to Danville.

After resting two or three days near the scene of our recapture, and feasting our hungry stomachs on corn bread and nice fresh apples, which we bought for $6 Reb. money or 3 large buttons(!) pr. bushel[, we marched on]. While here the authorities gave us the benefit of a thorough search for the purpose of finding our compass, but "Litch" hid it in his stockings. They suspected we had it, although we assured them that Lt. Goodrich & the others, who kept on had taken the compass along with them.

From Qualles we were marched 60 miles to Asheville under an Indian guard of more numbers than the prisoners. The guard was commanded by Lt. Tirrell who for four days feasted us on apples, & all the way. We had frequent intercourse with Union men, especially in the vicinity of Scott's Creek—the very place we had passed but a few days before. Being very destitute of everything, I sold my watch for $150 in Reb. money, after much delay and deliberation. The watch was given to me by father just as I stepped on to the cars when our Regt. left the good old State of Maine. He gave it to me in place of the gold one I left at home for safe keeping, but which was afterward stolen.

At Asheville we had a very fine time, especially the Free Masons of the party—4 of us—who were visited, fed, clothed and "moneyed" to a degree by Masons of Asheville & vicinity.[34] Among the most zealous was Joe Robertson and T.C. Kilbourne, the latter a Maine man, who told us to apply to him when we got "broke." We rested at Asheville two days and then marched 60 miles to Morgantown in 3 days—quite a hard trip for many of our party who are nearly used up by their mountain travel. Hunt has had a very hard time. He rode all the way from Quallee to Asheville and has had to "take to horse" several times since. He is pretty well disgusted with his first attempt at Infantry service. From Asheville we had a militia guard commanded by a Lt. Porter, for whom we all conceived a thorough disgust. At Morgantown we took the cars and in due season arrived at Danville, where we find 336 of our fellow officers. We are, for a day or two I presume, to be the "lions of the prison."

By my table of distances I find we have marched 413 miles and ridden by cars 140 miles,—all for nothing! We hear that 500 of the Columbia officers have been exchanged.[35] From Asheville I wrote home for a box to be sent to Columbia. If 500 of the Columbia fellows have gone North the whole thing is rough for me as I was promised the first exchange by both Foster's and Hardee's commissioners.

Here we are crowded into an old tobacco storehouse—alive with lice! —instead of being exchanged or having escaped.

Monday, Dec. 13th.

We eke out a miserable existence. Money all gone. Have about half as much corn bread as we could well eat. Have tried to be sent to Columbia but it is "no go." Have written to Soulé, Long, Burger, Dantzler, Kilbourne and Burpee about exchange, boxes, &c., &c.

Sunday, Dec. 18th.

Have made a raise by selling a woolen shirt for $35—one which I wore away from home, over a year ago. This money we invest in rice at $2 pr. pound and have succeeded in getting up a second meal, instead of eating breakfast and making that do for the day.

❦

Military Prison, Danville, Va.
Dec. 18th, 1864.
My dear Mother:

Instead of spending New Year's and Christmas with you as I had hoped I am beginning a new imprisonment at a new place, and, of course, am as destitute just now as I was eight months ago. However, we trust we shall soon get the things you have sent us. Have you ever sent that vest I mentioned in Hunt's letter to his mother? If not, no

matter about it. If Captain Burger thinks boxes &c. can come to
me, send them. Always consult him, and keep him supplied with
money to be used for my benefit. I have authorized him to call on
father for more money. Your last letter (rec'd) was Sept. 27 or there-
abouts, in which you spoke of the box for me and Hunt. We shall
soon get the back letters. Before we left Columbia I had notice that
money had arrived for me, but I do not know how much.[36] I wrote
you from Ashville [Asheville], N.C. two weeks ago, and have told
Burger to write. Perhaps you do not yet know that I escaped from
C. and was recaptured near Tennessee. 400 miles on foot and here I
am. Prospect for exchange slim. Write to Miss Harriet Kilbourne,
Bridgton, that I saw her brother T.C.K. at Asheville, N.C. well, in
Confed. Commissary Dept. Write same to Thos. Rae, Mott Haven,
N.Y.

Saturday, Dec. 24th.[37]

Exchange high among the fresh fish! They think they will soon
be away. Downing, Litchfield, McGrayel and myself have had a call
from Rev. Geo. W. Dame, Master of the Lodge at this place, who
promises us some little Masonic aid. We are greatly in need of assistance being very destitute of bedding and underclothing. We have
blankets and dishes enough at Columbia, but it [is] hard to say when
we shall get them. I have sent home for boxes from home, but I
presume it will be a long time before I shall receive any tidings of
them either. Our mountain tramp has given us an *enormous* appetite, and our slim rations of corn bread, even when spliced out with
a very little rice with rebel salt for sauce, is rather slim fare. But slim
fare is the fate of every prisoner here, and I suppose we must take our
share.

The "fresh fish" here are very sanguine upon the subject of
exchange. Many of them expect to be home before February. They
think, or seem to think, that they ought to be exchanged before the
Columbia officers.

Sunday, Dec. 25th.

Anything but a "Merry Christmas" for us. Our prospects for money and clothing, &c., are very good but our present condition is most deplorable.

Friday, Dec. 30th.

We have rec'd (4 of us) about six lbs. of rice from Mr. Dame, and Litchfield has rec $300 from Mr. Luke Blackmir of Salisbury,—a lawyer there, but born in the State of New York. He got it by signing a note for $15 in gold, —without interest.

Sunday, Jany. 1st, 1865.[38] *Danville, Va.*

We begin a New Year with good prospects for everything but exchange. Sherman has captured Savannah with many valuable stores, &c. *Our* side of the war never looked so favorable.[39] Grant will have to look to his laurels or Sherman will eclipse him. The weather is cold and our quarters and clothing filthy & *lousy*—I must record facts, disagreeable though they be.

Military Prison, Danville, Va.
Jany 1st, 1865.
My dear Mother:

Upon the first day of the first week of the first month of a new year of imprisonment I send you a line wishing you all a happy new year with your good dinners and sleigh rides, pleasures which I must forgo for a time. My health continues most excellent, although I have been a prisoner long enough to have some excuse for getting sick. Many of the prisoners here have not been captured more than three or four months, far different from our old friends at Columbia.[40] I wish father to answer all of Burger's calls for money, the same by Kimball at Washington. They will from time to time have chances to supply me. Hunt is well. We have no letters from home of later date than Sept. 27th but expect the back mail from Columbia daily. We have now been here three weeks. You can imagine how much I desire to hear from you all or how much more I desire to see you. The question of exchange still puzzles us, and we have no idea of the future of that important dispute. Please request the officer Commd. 17th to send my valise to Washington to the Maine State Agent to be kept till called for. Please have one woolen shirt made, like the last, and one pair of drawers of similar goods.

Some time ago I wrote you to have Fernald make a vest from that cloak cloth. Have him do so, if he has not already, and send it with my military pants (think I left them at home) to the Maine State Agent at Washington to be kept for me, also a small necktie, old style, yours. Have Abbott make me a pair sewed calf, double soled, (best quality) boots and send them to W. with the other things. Also give McCarthy, Exchange St., an order to make me another pair of top boots, just like the first ones, but half a size larger and a little looser above the instep. Send these along in the same way. Hurry up all these things and have them sent to W. to be kept till called for. "Just like Chas." you will say. Love to all. Tell Itie I shall bring him something this time, but when?

Wednesday, Jany. 4th.
Recd a very kind letter from Dr. Dantzler with $100 enclosed, in which he says his son has been exchanged. He says nothing about repaying the $100.

Thursday, Jan'y 5th.
8 months ago today I bade farewell to liberty. Litchfield has just recd a letter from Columbia stating that he has been called for exchange twice since he escaped—also that a box has arrived and will be forwarded to this place. Mr. Dame brought us (4) in a shirt and pair of drawers each. Robbins was recaptured twice.

Friday, Jan. 6th.
Wrote to Dr. Dantzler for boxes of edibles & more money.

Military Prison, Danville, Va.

Jany. 7th, 1865

Wm. H. Savage

Merchant

Boston, Mass.

My dear Friend:

My *wandering* disposition has prevented me from receiving the longed for answer to a letter I wrote you many weeks ago. I now write on business. I wish you to put me up a large box (say 50 or even 100 lbs.) of eatables, that too *at once,* & forward it by express to Maine State Agent at Washington, directing him to send it to me immediately. Direct Maj. Chas. P. Mattocks (or order) Prisoner of War, Danville, Va. via Richmond, &c. Let no talk of exchange prevent or even delay you. Call on father for the pay or charge it to me on int. as you may see fit. Send about as follows, 10 lbs. coffee, 15 Loaf Sugar, 10 Butter, 6 cans condensed milk, 1 Ham, 5 lbs, Flour, Sardines (Large Boxes), 10 lbs. Bologna Sausage, Mince Meat, Farina, Corn Starch, Tappioca [Tapioca], Chockalate [Chocolate], All Spice, Nutmeg, Cinnamon, Ground Cloves, Peppers, Oil of Lemon, Baking Powders, Dried Fruit, Cheese, Tin Plate, Cup, Knife & Fork, Spoon, Pocket Knife, Paper, Envelopes, Pens, Ink, Pencil, Needles & thread, Towel, Soap, 1 pr. Socks, Slippers, Briar Root Pipe, 1 Box Cigars, Mustard, Club Sauce, Ketchup, Few cans of Meat, &c., Dried Prunes, Few Pickles, and almost anything your taste may suggest. Send imperishable articles. Write to Mother to send me a 25 lb. box of Preserves, Pickles, & such things as she used to send in *better days.* Tell her that we shall probably get the September box in a few days via Columbia. Still more. Please go to Ft. Warren and supply or agree to supply any Confederate prisoner (whose relatives live *handy* to this prison) with money, clothing & eatables upon condition that he order his friends to supply me with an equivalent here—1/2 in Confed. money & 1/2 in Boxes of Bacon, Flour, Molasses, Dried Fruit, Meat of any kind—cooked or raw—he to give me a dollar's (gold) worth for every dollar's (gold) worth you give him. Make the first advance at my risk. Call on father for funds. Tell the prisoner to order his folks to *express* the goods to me (or order) at this place. In my box please send pamphlet "David Copperfield," Ollendorf's German Method, Any German Newspaper or Speech, or book, also a small (white paper) Blank Book for Diary, Cheap & very small copy of Shakespeare or Tennyson. Last Nos. of "Atlantic Monthly" & U.S. Service Magazine. Excuse me for troubling you so much with the wants of Yr. Military Successor. Regard to your family—Especially the young lady who still owes me a *photo*. Dont delay the box. It will benefit somebody even if I am exchanged. Send no letter in box, except list of articles. Use old newspapers for wrapping. 1 pr Shoes long slim 9s—sewed—

Sunday, Jan'y 8th.

Wrote to Savage for 50 or 100 lbs. box eatables & through him to Mother for 25 lbs. box same. Rev. Mr. Dame preached again this afternoon. We have had no meat issued since Christmas. Our mess eats the rations for breakfast, and affords itself a soup or mess of griddle cakes for dinner. No answer yet from any of my letters except from Dr. Dantzler. $120 now in *Treasury,* and a week's supply of flour, beans, &c.

Monday, Jan'y 16th.

Litchfield has just returned from an interview with Lt. Col. [Robert C.] Smith, comm'd'g Prison. Smith gave him a drink of apple brandy and allowed him to receive the whole of Blackmer's last (Saturday's) remittance, instead of parcelling it out at $100 pr. month. The remittance is $1000 "Confed." which will put our Mess "on its legs" for some time. We have "run" through $400 in about 16 days, but we have had to expend $100 for dishes, &c. This evening we had fresh pork, potatoes and griddle cakes and invited three of our hungry friends to supper. I have today written a second

time to Mr. Kilbourne & Capt. Burger. I fear the first letters miscar-
ried.

Tues. Jan'y 24th.[41]
Recd a letter from Burger date Jan'y 12, with home letters enclosed.
One from Goodwin of Oct. 14 says Col. West is discharged for disability
and that Lt. Col. M has tendered his resignation and it has been accepted. Lt. Roberts killed. One from Burger, Oct. 2d, with $10 enclosed
by him but not recd by me. Where it is I can not say.

Thurs. 26th.
Gen. Hayes left last night. Exchd[42]

Sunday, Feb. 5th.
Three officers have escaped within two days while out for water.

Monday, Feb. 6th.
6 officers in all.

Tuesday, Feb. 7th.
Recd $500 from Luke Blackmir Salisbury at $12 for $1 in gold.
Sent note. Entertained by Lt. Col. Smith.

Wednesday, Feb. 15.
Recd box from L. Dantzler by Exp. yesterday. Chase and 9
others went to Richmond last night for exch. Gave Chase order for
two mos. pay. Papers say Genl Exch. is agreed upon, &c. Exchange
stock high. Have written to [Lt. Col. John E.] Mulford[43] about my
case. Dantzler's son is again a prisoner captd at Ft. Fisher.

Thursday, Feby. 16.
We are ordered to start for Richmond for exchange tomorrow.
Great excitement. Everybody is busy cooking.

Friday, Feby. 17th.[44]

We were called out of prison this morning but were immediately brought back on account of the train having broken down. Tonight we are ordered to go at 8 *without fail.*

Sat. Feby. 18.

Left Danville at 11 P.M. and at Libby Sunday Morning. Recd box from Kim[ball] Sunday.

Tuesday, Feby. 21.

Left Richmond 8 A.M. for exch. having signed parole yesterday.[45]

[*On February 22, 1865, Charles Mattocks sent the following telegram to Isaac Dyer.*]

Annapolis, Md.

 Arrived here from Richmond this morning.

National Hotel. Annapolis, Md.

Feby. 23d, 1865.

My dear Father:

 I have already sent a telegraphic despatch announcing my arrival here yesterday morning at 8 o'clk. The Richmond prisoners have all arrived—among them Lt. Hunt of Gorham. We expect to get leaves of absence. You may expect me in P. by Tuesday or Wednesday. I shall come as soon as I can I assure you. We are on parole and probably will not be declared exchanged for some weeks.

 I hear that West is a Brig. Genl. that I was commissioned as Lt. Col., that the commission was revoked & Hobson appointed, &c. &c. I have none of your letters of later date than Sept. 27th. You can not imagine how glad we are to be free once more.

Washington. Tuesday. Feby. 28th, 1865.

My dear Mother,

I wrote from Annapolis that you might expect me at P. by the last of this week. We have experienced great delay in obtaining our leaves of absence, and I shall not be able to reach Maine before the *last* of next week. I think I shall run down to the Army before going home, as I do not expect to be exchanged before May, and you are aware that I can not join the Army *officially* before I am declared exchanged. Until that time I am on parole and virtually belong to the Rebels—an allegiance which I shall be willing to shake off. I hope Erastus will be at home during the month of March. I am now visiting Kimball of my class and having a very good time.

I think I understand the Hobson matter now. I did not know that I had been commissioned as Lt. Col. until I reached Annapolis. I find that they waited for me as long as they could. All officers mustered in after the 18th of Feby. had to be mustered for 3 years—those before, for the unexpired time—about 6 months. So it would have compelled four officers to be mustered for 3 yrs. instead of six months, if they had waited for me. Of course I feel very badly, though not *slighted,* at losing the position. I do not propose to leave the service on account of the disappointment. After what I have seen for the past year I can not afford to deprive the Rebels of the benefit of my services, however slight, or in however humble a capacity. In case they raise any new Regiments in Maine I shall propose to father to help me make a strike. Now do not mention this to *anyone.* You may imagine how much I wish to see you all, as my last intelligence dates in September—a long time ago it seems to me. Remember me to Mrs. C's family. Tell Mrs. Perry that I shall once more give her an opportunity to "pass the pepper."

I have learned that the good people of the United States had flattered themselves that our runaway party had met with an untimely end—eaten up by the blood hounds—&c.! It seems amusing to meet old friends here and have them look upon me as if I have no business to be alive. We did[,] it is true[,] have a narrow escape from being lost in the mountains and starving to death, but I am happy to say that we are all right but one. One poor fellow of our party of 20 was left behind—unable to keep up-& has never been heard from. It is a luxury to write a *sealed* letter, and you see I am indulging with a vengeance. Hunt will probably go to Maine with me. His health is much improved since leaving Rebeldom. His mountain travels came near using him up. I am happy to say however that my wanderings actually did me good—physically—not in any other respect. I was called for exchange two days after my escape, and had I been on hand to respond, might have [been] home in Nov. and now on duty as Lt. Col. of the 17th, and if we had not been compelled to serve an additional time for escaping I could have got away in Dec. instead of February.

Love to all. Tell Itie I will bring him something this time. I have the $100 that father sent to Kimball.

American House Portland, Me.
March 17th, [1865]
My dear General [West]:[46]

Mr. Fletcher has just been in and shown me your note. I can not go to Boston, but shall be here if you come on Tuesday. I return to Annapolis by Wednesday or Thursday, and shall very much regret it if I do not see you this time. I am as yet unaware of your military status. You sent word by Moore and wrote to Mr. Fletcher that you were going out of service, and by Verrill that you were coming home on leave. So I conclude that you are now on leave. Verrill's letter says you have an outside place for me in case I do not wish to serve under Hobson's choice. I do not now, nor have I ever wished to leave my own Regt. If the powers that be wish me to leave the Regt. they must signify it in some different way. I shall not leave the service of my Uncle Samuel on account of disappointments,—at any rate not until my three years are up. If I felt guilty of deserving to be jumped I perhaps should look upon the present situation differently. To speak plainly, the view I take of the whole affair is this. If I deserved to be jumped I deserved to be court-martialed. You send me many messages about not having anything to do with Hobson's apptmt. as Lt. Col. Of course I believe you, *but* if Hobson got the place without your help and without Regimental or house influence as I am informed he did[,] it must have been by some trick. If so, he laid himself liable to military law. I have not yet heard of any *litigation* against W. H. You will excuse me for speaking *plainly.* If you have *allowed* what you did not *sanction,* I am of course to draw the inference—"out of sight, out of mind." I do not grumble, & what I have said would have remained thought but *unsaid,* had not the fact of these messages brought out my opinion. I still stick to my text of allowing every Col. to manage his own Regt., and I bow with *heroic fortitude* (!) to my unexpected fate. During my imprisonment I did not know of the appointment either of myself in Oct. or Hobson in Dec.[47] and I am thankful that I learned it no sooner.

But I anticipate. It will be better and perhaps more satisfactory to both of us to talk than to write about these things. There is something curious about the whole affair. I can not find that my commission has ever been revoked as yet. I have it in my possession and it has never been called for. Many of my friends have advised me to go to Augusta and see *His Excellency,* but I probably shall not inflict myself upon him.[48] Ten months' imprisonment has brought me the universality of the maxim "A man has no business to be captured."

Hoping to see you and with best regards to Mrs. W. I am

As ever

Your dutiful Major

CHAPTER EIGHT

Rejoining the Regiment: Petersburg

Earthworks before Petersburg, Va.[1]
Friday, March 31st.

I reached the Regt. this morning at 11 o'clock and found the boys all in good spirits.[2] It looks like a new Regiment. Many of the old officers are now dead or out of the service. Some are Captains now who were Sergeants when I left the Regt. about a year ago. Lt. Col. Hobson is in command[3] and we are in 2d Brig., Brig. Genl. Pierce, 3d Div., Brvt. Maj. Genl. Mott, 2d Corps, Maj. Genl. [Andrew Atkinson] Humphreys.[4] None of my old Generals are now in service. Birney died, Hayes was killed, and Ward mustered out in disgrace.[5] We all expect to move soon, and attack the enemy. Grant is extending his line to the left, probably with a view to outstretching the Rebels, previous to making an assault. Every one is in good spirits, and from the talk, one would suppose that the city of Richmond would very soon be ours. When Petersburg is captured Richmond must fall, for we shall have the South Side Railroad,—now the only line of supplies for the Rebel metropolis(!).

Saturday, April 1st.

Still behind our breastworks. Our casualties today amount to one spent musket ball over the colors!

Sunday, April 2d.

At 2 o'clock this morning in accordance with orders from Army Head Quarters, our forces commenced feeling the strength of the Rebel line of fortifications which was soon found and penetrated at a weak point by a successful charge of the 6th Corps. [Gen. Philip Henry] Sheridan[6] had previously pushed around the enemy's left flank, and the 5th Corps had fought them quite fiercely for a day or two previously.[7] Soon after our whole line advanced through the Rebel fortifications toward Petersburg, where the enemy made a stand until night. Several shells passed over our Regt. and one came flatteringly near me while taking out a detail of skirmishers. Two Rebel ten-pounders opened on us soon after we passed the Rebel earthworks, but our telescopic rifles soon silenced and drove them away by creeping up and getting close range.

❧✦❧

Bivouac 3 miles from Petersburg.
10 P.M. Sunday—Apr. 2d, 1865.
My dear Mother:

I say bivouac because our victory has been so easy that I can not designate this ground as a battlefield. The papers will give you the details. Our Brigade has lost a few men. Our Regt has been under Artillery fire and has Exchanged a few shots with the enemy, but we have not lost a man. One shell came very near killing me or my horse to-day—striking in front and ricocheting (bouncing) over my head. Dont mention this outside, as it is too small an affair. All things in the Regt. are lovely. Recd yours with Allie D[ana]'s letters. We expect to take Petersburg in the morning with an easy fight. We have had a running fight with the Rebs to-day. Grant has done a wonderful thing in the way of strategy. We have captured many of the enemy.

Our Regt. is in 2d Brigade (Brig. Genl. Pierce), 3d Division (Maj. Genl. Mott), 2d Corps (Maj. Genl. Humphreys.) Direct 17th Me. Inftry. 2d Army Corps, Washington, D.C.

... 6 A.M. Monday

Petersburg reported evacuated.

We are off—   C

Monday, April 3d.

This morning there is no enemy to be seen and we learn that the 9th Corps has taken possession of Petersburg. Of course, we are jubilant at the turn affairs have taken. I suppose we shall now try to follow up our success and tie up that bag which has so long been supposed to contain the Rebel Army. We have marched 20 miles today, and every one is in good spirits. It has been officially announced that the negroes have taken possession of Richmond.[8] So the pride of the Great Southern metropolis has been humbled by the black man. The Army was never in better spirits and I should judge from the number of Rebel deserters and voluntary prisoners that the hopes of the Confederacy are about exhausted. Still we expect a few more fights with some of the "last ditch" men.

Tuesday, April 4th.

Today three Regiments of our Brigade, the 17th among the number, were sent back a short distance to corduroy the roads under the command of Lt. Col. Hobson, who seemed, as Demosthenes said of Philip—"somewhat perplexed by the magnitude of his affairs." We had a great deal of sport during the day.[9]

Wednesday, April 5th.

Marched nearly all day, taking a position on the left of the 5th Corps. I called on the 20th Maine at night.

Thursday, April 6th.

This morning we started for Amelia Spring (or Sulphur Springs), and soon after passing the Springs were put in line of battle. Our Regiment was assigned to the 1st Brigade, as a support to their left Regt.—the 73d N.Y. About this time Maj. Genl. Mott was wounded, and the command of the Division fell upon Brig. Genl. De Trobriand. We advanced slowly at first, and soon found the enemy behind rifle pits and breast-works. They opened upon us with artillery and musketry. Between us and the enemy was a ridge upon which were a few buildings. I was in favor of charging at once and getting the cover of these houses from which we could return the fire with at least a moderate effect. Lt. Col. Hobson was opposed to the plan, but we finally had to start, as the Brigade was upon the point of going. We charged to the houses under a heavy fire, and when we reached them, opened fire ourselves with good effect. After firing about 6 rounds, I noticed the Rebs. beginning to give away on our left. I then urged Hobson to order a charge. He would not, so I took the Color-bearers and started on my own hook, the Regiment, or rather those who could keep up, following with a yell.[10] On we rushed over the breast works, and bagged about 100 Rebs., 10 or 12 officers, two battle flags, besides killing and wounding a great many. The artillery and one or two battleflags escaped together with about 300 Rebs. All who fought it out were killed, wounded or captured, except a very few. One Rebel caught up the colors of his Regt. and escaped by leaping upon a horse and running off under a heavy shower of *lead.* While we were hesitating behind the houses, and during this last charge, we lost quite heavily. Lt. Col. Hobson was wounded just before we charged. Lts. [Scollay G.] Usher[11] and [James] Webb[12] were struck about the same time. I had, as usual, some warm escapes, but, as usual, escaped without a scratch. We halted a short time to get our breath, as every one was nearly exhausted. The Rebel wagon train was now in sight some 3 or 4 miles ahead, and soon the whole line was ordered forward, and forward we went for 2 miles, when we found the enemy making another stand, their wagon train being about a mile beyond them. On we rushed in double-quick and reached the cover of a house about a quarter of a mile or more from the coveted train. Here we received quite a heavy fire and exchanged a few shots with the enemy. Genl. Pierce placed himself in front of the 17th, then on the right of our Brigade, and on the left of 1st division of this Corps, and ordered a charge. On we rushed with a yell and the 17th did not stop until it had charged by the wagon-train, across the stream beyond, and to the wooded ridge which the enemy precipitately abandoned. Our rush was so rapid that not more than 100 men were able to follow the colors. Nearly all of the officers succeeded in keeping along. Capt. [George P.] Dunn and Lt. [Edwin A.] Duncan[13] were wounded in this last operation. The colors were bravely carried throughout the day by Sergt. Bishop of Co. "B" and Corp. [Andrew J.] Miller of Co. "A" [K]. Lieuts. Matthews [Robert H. Mathes], [William H.] Sturgis and Paine[14] particularly distinguished themselves. Capt. Green acted as Field officer after the command fell upon me owing to the disabling of Lt. Col. H[obson].[15] I rode my horse "Charley" on the first charge but when our line opened fire he became almost unmanageable and I sent him to the rear. After we took the rifle pits I rode Hobson's horse which had just been brought up. At the wagon-train and beyond we bagged about 50 Rebs and captured one piece of Artillery. In the charge we received a heavy fire of Artillery and musketry. The Rebels, or at least many of them, did not deserve to be taken prisoners. They would crouch behind fences and other hiding-places and continue to fire upon men until with[in] ten or twenty feet, and then throw up their hats as a signal of surrender. Yet these fellows were taken and treated kindly. One of the colors captured belonged to the 21st N.C. Regt. From the wagon-train we obtained many valuable curiosities, such as Rebel officers' uniforms, books, spurs, swords, shot guns, &c. I have Lt. Genl. [James] Longstreet's[16] General Order Book, a nice English double-barrelled shot gun, a nice silver-plated bridle, &c., &c. The loss of the Regt. today is 1 officer killed, 4 wounded 4 Enlisted men killed & 23 wounded. The loss of officers is one in five, of men, one in ten. This charging is death to officers, as they have to say "come on" instead of "go on."[17]

Friday, April 7th.

We advanced again today, and overtook the enemy at 2 P.M. We built breast works under a light and to us ineffective fire of the Rebel skirmishers. One man of this Regt. was wounded by a piece of cap from his own musket, and another, who had straggled and been put into another Regt., was hit in the foot.

Saturday, April 8th.

Marched all day without rations—through the village of New Store. The enemy are in full retreat. Many of them are falling into our hands. They are sadly "demoralized" and many of them will soon find that "last ditch." The wagon train we captured on the 6th, and through which we marched yesterday was a sorry sight. The enemy left in so much haste that the horses, or many of them were still in harness, their drivers have escaped or surrendered, if they were fortunate enough to escape being hit. The wounded still remained in the ambulances, and some of these poor fellows were wounded a second time. We fought through an open country nearly all day, and it was a rich sight to see the enemy running before us all day. Our troops as a whole never were in better spirits, and of course fought with a vengeance.

Sunday, April 9th.

This day will live in history. Just as our Corps was advancing to the attack we were halted by the news of the Surrender of the Rebel Army of Northern Virginia to the U.S. Forces.

This took place near Patterson's Farm, in Appomattox County.[18] The troops are wild with excitement. Cheer after cheer went up, and speeches were made. The Army surrendered amounts to only 19000 men. We have captured about 30000 men since we left our earthworks before Petersburg. It is glorious to have served with the Army for these ten days! I am thankful that [I] got back in time for the funeral!

❦

Bivouac near Clover Hil[l]'s (Appomattox, C.H.)
Monday, April 10th, 1865.
My dear Mother:

I presume you have already heard the glorious news. The Army of Northern Virginia (Rebel) surrendered to us yesterday afternoon just as our Corps was advancing to the attack once more. Our triumphant march was suddenly checked amid the rejoicings of thousands. These last ten days have almost repaid me for ten months of misery. As you have perhaps already learned, the 17th was quite hotly engaged on the 6th. We made three distinct charges, captured about 150 prisoners, two Rebel battle flags, 12 or 14 Rebel officers, some 40 or 50 wagons, belonging to the train captured by a simultaneous charge of our 1st & 3d Divisions. I was as usual among the fortunate, escaping without a scratch. We went in with 26 officers and lost 5. One killed and one probably mortally wounded. Col. Hobson was hit in the first of the fight. The command devolved upon your young hopeful. The charges were really glorious and afforded ample chances for the ambitious to "show their hands." The Regt. lost in all 32 on the 6th, and 2 on the 7th. We have been under fire several different days, but have been very fortunate. Our loss of officers was about 1 in 5, and of men, 1 in 10. So you see the officers had their full share of the danger as well as glory.

We are now halted, and all offensive operations have ceased. I can well imagine how rejoiced you are at the North. I never saw the 17th in so good spirits. We had a running and most successful fight for 5 miles in line of battle. Our second charge was upon a line of Rebel rifle pits under a very heavy fire. The last Charge was upon the Rebel wagon train under a heavy artillery and musketry fire combined. The rebs ran like sheep, and many who would not surrender, but tried to escape, were shot down without mercy.

From the Rebel wagon train we took many curiosities—such as Genl. Lee's private baggage, orders *& c* (!) Hobson is only slightly wounded. I have not had a letter for more than a week. We hear that West is out of service, but are uncertain.

The Lt. Usher that was killed used to live in Baldwin. He received his wound in attempting to take a Rebel battle flag. We conclude that we have fought our last fight, and we are glad we had so good success in it. It seems to me that I am bullet proof—although I must confess that I did not lack much of getting hit several times. I was mounted nearly all the time. I presume every one will now regret that they were not in at the "wake." Now do you think I was foolish to hurry away? I would not have missed these ten days for all the world.

The papers will probably give you detailed accounts of all these affairs much better than I can.

Let me hear from you often. Houghton can see this letter, *but* do not let it get into the papers. The mail is expected to go in a day or two. Now get the house!

Monday, April 10th.
Resting from our labors all day in the mud and rain.

Tuesday, April 11th.
Started on the back track, and reached New Store in Buckingham Co.—13 miles.

Wednesday, April 12th.
Still marching. Halted at night near Burkesville. 15 miles.

Thursday, April 13th.
Marched nearly all day—the latter part on the railroad. Halted near Burkesville at night.

Friday, April 14th.
In statu quo! Drew some clothing.

Hd. Qrs. 17th Maine Regt.
Near Burkesville, Va.
April 14th, 1865.
My dear Mother:
We have just received a week's mail, including your letter about the joy over Richmond. I have already written you of the humble

part I have had the fortune to perform in the movements of the last ten days. I presume there are no copperheads at home now. We all feel our importance now. Our Corps was advancing to the attack when Lee gave up the contest. Two days after we started back, and are now near the railroad. We have rumors of more fighting under Sherman—that is, that we are now to turn our "victorious arms" to his benefit. We hardly credit the rumor.[19] Let me hear from you often. We have had hard work, but I am in excellent health. Tell father to look out now. A sort of natural sympathy always attaches to a wounded man, and Hobson, may steal another march on us. Father must look out for that public functionary at Augusta. We do not seem to get rid of West in a hurry. I can get a petition from the officers of the Regt. but do not wish to lay myself under obligations. The affair of the 6th was a good chance for me and you may be assured that I improved at no small risk to my precious head.

I feel ashamed that I was unable to send the money to Uncle L[uther]. Regards to all. Wish I could have seen Albert.

The mail is off. We shall remain here a day or two. Recd Lizzie's letter.

❧❧

Saturday, April 15th.
Yesterday we received the first mail since we left our works before Petersburg. I have no word from West, except by Capt. Moore, who returned last night, and says he heard that G.W. had tendered his resignation. He may stick in service if he has not got out before the recent turn of affairs. . . .

We went into the fight with 26 officers and about 235 muskets—came out with 21 officers and with 200 muskets. There are, of course, a few stragglers & skulkers. They will have a dose of discipline at the first regular halt. The most of the officers and men did their duty well. The Regiment has nobly wiped out the disgraceful conduct of the 6th of May, when the command devolved upon Capt. Perry after Col. West was wounded. The Regt. did as well as any men would do under similar circumstances. The officers and men had no confidence in the courage or ability of Capt. Perry & of course became a little demoralized. At another time they behaved badly under the leadership of Perry. Now every one feels finely over the new phase of affairs.

Genl. Pierce has not come out in orders yet, but has privately complimented the Regt. for the part we performed on the 6th. I was Division officer of the Day yesterday, and upon reporting to Genl. de Trobriand this morning he proposed to recommend me to Gov. Cony as Col. of the 17th. Although the thing is sure enough as it stands I have no objections to a *clincher*. Genl. Pierce, commdg. Brigade, will start the thing, and Genl. de T. will endorse it.

An order has come down for me to send up the Rebel flag by the man capturing it. The man, Corpl. A[sbrey]. F. Haines [Haynes], Co. H, is to have 30 days furlough and a medal of honor.

The teams came up last night and we are enjoying a change of clothing. I have been urging Lieut. Crie now Act. R.Q.M., to return to the Line, with a view to the first vacant Captaincy. I think he will concur in my views.[20]

❧❧

Head Quarters 17th Maine Infantry
Near Burkesville, Va.
April 15th, 1865.
My dear Mother:

I enclose a line to Kirke Porter and Allie Dana which you will please forward. Their letters are in my valise which is some miles away, and I have forgotten their addresses. I am cooped up in a shelter tent and have a very poor chance to write.

Since the fights of the 6th General de Trobriand, commanding Division, has himself proposed to write a communication to Gov. C. in regard to my promotion. I shall not object to this, as it will serve as a sort of *clincher*, and might be of interest to Hobson's friends if they should presume to call the Gov. to account.

I hear from a returned officer that West has tendered his resignation. . . .

P. S. I should hope you would delay that photograph of yourself no longer. Please send those photos I had taken just before I left.

Lizzie's letter is recd and shall be answered very soon. Saw Sarah [Carter] in N.Y.

❧

Sunday, April 16th.

This morning at 2 o'clock we received a dispatch that Presdt. Lincoln was assassinated at Ford's Theatre at 10:30 last night, and that Sec'y [William H.] Seward and his son Frederic, were assassinated at about the same time at their residence. The dispatch says the President can not live and that Seward is in a dangerous condition.[21] This news is sad after our recent successes.[22]

For future reference I will write down a Roster of the officers of the Regt. as it now stands. Line officers according to seniority. There are several cases of almost equal rank. Matthes and Sturgis were made 2d Lts. on the same day, and 1st Lts. on the same. Matthes was 1st Sergt. and Sturgis only Sergt. when appointed 2d Lts. So the thing is decided in favor of Matthes. Paine is Senior 2d Lt. and deserves to be promoted by his rank as well as behavior. There will soon be a chance for many of the ambitious, as Matthes, [Dexter W.] Howard,[23] [Parlin] Crawford[24] and some others desire to go into a Negro Regt. for the sake of additional rank. Capts. [Charles C.] Cole[25] and Dunn were made 1st Lts. and Capts. the same day, but Cole ranks Dunn by seniority as 2d Lt.

The Roster will soon be materially changed. I have just received a letter from West which says he tendered his resignation on the 8th of this month. . . .

Wednesday, April 19th.

This has been set apart as a day of rest and devotion, in honor of our late President. Minute guns were fired, and in our Regt. we had a religious service from the Chaplain, with music by the Band.

Today I learned that 2d Lt. Horace B. Cummings of Co. "H", was drunk in camp the other day, and was seen in state of beastly intoxication by his whole Company. I have ordered Lieut. Hobbs, commanding Co. "H", to prefer charges of "Drunkenness", "Conduct unbecoming an officer and a gentleman" and "Conduct prejudicial to good order and military discipline." The charges will, I fear, sweep him off in short metre. He probably does not imagine that I know anything about his conduct, but I fear he will soon be disabused of any erroneous impressions. Officers of the Regt. have been, but can no longer be allowed to get drunk in public. Even our wire-pulling Lieut. Col. has often appeared a little excited, so I am told by those who have been here.

Thursday, April 20th.

Lieut. Hobbs has preferred his charges, but, I fear the trial may be delayed. I have placed Lt. Cummings in arrest.

Today an order came down for Regimental Commanders to make recommendations for brevet for gallant conduct in the recent operations. Now this is by no means an easy or agreeable task. It is hard to say that one man is braver or has done his duty better than another in cases where both have done their best. However, for the credit of the Regt. I shall hope to see some few brevets awarded to us, even if it does cause some rivalry. The following is my

Recommendations for Brevets.

HeadQuarters 17th Me. Regt.
Near Burkesville, Va., April 20th, 1865.
To Lieut. C.W. Forrester, A.A.A.G.
2d Brigade, 3d Div. 2d Corps.
Lieut:-

In accordance with Circular from Superior Head Quarters calling for recommendations for brevet for such officers as may have distinguished themselves during the recent operations, I have the honor to submit the following statement in relation to this Regiment.

In the action of the 6th of April near Amelia Springs this Regt. charged three times under heavy artillery and musketry, carrying a line of rifle pits, capturing a great number of prisoners, colors, a portion of a Rebel wagon train, &c., as already reported. I consider the success of the Regt. due in a great measure to the gallantry of the following named officers:-

> Capt. Wm. H. Green, Co. G.
> 1st Lieut. Wm. H. Sturgis, Co. B.
> 1st Lieut. Robert E. Mathes, Co. A.
> 2d Lieut. Edward A. Duncan, Co. D.

Capt. Green acted as Field officer, and by his gallantry in placing himself *in front* in making these charges incited the officers and men under him to bravery.

Upon the second charge Lt. Sturgis, more than any other Line officer was instrumental in carrying the rifle pits and capturing the Rebel colors.

Lieut. Mathes was hardly less worthy in all the operations of the day. In the charge upon the wagon train he placed himself far in advance of his company and by his gallantry conduced greatly to our success.

Lieut. Duncan, after being severely wounded in the first charge, refused to leave the field, and remained with his Company and participated in the movements of the Regiment until actually forced to go to the rear from weakness and loss of blood.

As an apology for mentioning so many as four officers, I would state that the Regt. engaged the enemy with twenty-one officers and, of this number, lost one killed and four wounded,—the loss in officers being twice the loss of men in proportion to the number engaged. I mention these officers not with the expectation that brevets will be awarded to *all* of them, although I consider *each* worthy of it.

I, therefore, have the honor to recommend to your favorable consideration the following named officers as being worthy of brevets, and the following is in my opinion the relative merit of each:-

1st Capt. Wm. H. Sturgis, Co. B.
2d 1st Lt. Robt. H. Mathes, Co. A.
3d Capt. Wm. H. Green, Co. G.
4th 2d Lt. Edwin A. Duncan, Co. D.

In connection I would respectfully call attention to the fact that the three first have been in every engagement of the Regt. from Fredericksburg up to the present time. Lieut. Duncan has never been absent but twice, and then by reason of wounds and sickness.

In all these engagements these officers have conducted themselves with uniform courage and gallantry.

The above are the only recommendations for brevet of Line officers that have ever been forwarded from these Head Quarters.

> I have the honor to be, Sir,
> Very respectfully, Your Obdt. Servt.,
> Charles P. Mattocks
> Major Commanding Regt.[26]

I dare say there may be in the minds of some a very different opinion from the above, but, as far as observation went, I am about right.

Friday, April 21st.
I have written (Apr. 19) to Lt. Col. Hobson a letter urging him to recommend to the Governor Lieut. Paine and 1st Sergt. Chandler for promotion.

Paine to be 1st Lt. Co. G. vice Usher
Chandler to be 2d Lt. Co. B. vice Paine.

These are both senior in their present grades, and in every [way] deserving of promotion. I hope the appointments will be made.[27]

On the 16th I received a letter from West, stating that he tendered his resignation on the 8th of this month. As yet we have heard nothing more about it. I am terribly afraid that he may have been tempted to withdraw when he saw a prospect of no more fighting. If he resigns I feel quite sure of the commission, but if he hangs on much longer the Rolls of the Regt. will not allow the mustering of a full Colonel. We are receiving discharges every day. The Rolls today number 820 enlisted men—Total—borne on the "total enlisted, present and absent," Beside these we have 40 prisoners of war and missing in action, not accounted for in the body of the Rolls. So 860 can be used for the purpose of muster but 860 will soon become 800 at the present rate of discharges.

Today I called on Genl. de Trobriand and he told me that I have been recommended to be Brevet Col. (but I suppose he meant Brevet Lt. Col.) for gallantry(!) in the battle of Amelia Springs on the 6th of this month. He said Brevet Col. probably forgetting I had never been mustered as Lt. Col. I believe the law allows but one grade by brevet for any one fight. Even if I lose my real Colonelcy it will be some little consolation that in ten—rather six days—I obtained what Hobson has not gotten since last August—a brevet. Brevet rank brings no additional pay but I presume I shall be willing to be a "Brvt. Lt. Col." even after having had a commission as full Lt. Col. In fact, I shall actually prize the *brevet* part more than I should a regular appointment—a thing which any fool can have [through] seniority alone.

Lieut. Cummings has been notified to appear before the Court Martial at 10 o'clk in the morning. They are rushing the business just to my mind although I hope they will give the poor fellow time for preparation. I have forwarded several charges against enlisted men for straggling and misbehavior in the recent engagements.

Lieut. Howard & Lieut. [Edwin W.] Sanborn, Co. "E", have been ordered to report to Genl. [Rufus] Saxton [Jr.] with a view to an appointment in a Negro Regiment. They will leave in a day or two. 1st Sergt. Keefe[28] will go with them. I have decided to assign Lieut. Mathes to the command of Co. "E" to relieve Howard and Lieut. [William H.] Copp to Co. "C" to fill the place of Webb, wounded on the 6th. Capt. Verrill of "E" will probably remain on Staff, and this will give Mathes an assignment according to his (future) brevet rank of Capt. Sturgis is in command of "B", but when he receives his brevet I shall assign him to another Co. when Capt. Sparrow returns.

My application for the return of Quartermaster [Josiah] Remick has been return[ed] approved. He will be sent back as soon as he can close up his business. I am gradually getting in the odds and ends. Shall soon have quite a Regt. We have received nine convalescents during the past week. (No mail today).

Head Quarters 17th Maine Vols.
Near Burkesville, Va.
April 21st, 1865.
My dear Mother:

I have not time just now to answer any of your letters in a proper manner. My principal object now is to convince you and make you acknowledge that I hit the nail by hurrying back. To prove this, I will tell you that I was to-day informed by Gen. de Trobriand, our Division Commander, that I have been recommended to the President, or Vice President now, for Brevet Lieut. Col. for (supposed!) gallantry in the battle of Amelia Springs on the 6th of this month.[29] I am of course very well pleased with my first week's work. I would sooner get an appointment by my sword than by a pen, as did our worthy friend H.

Tell father to hurry up the business with the Gov. just as soon as West's resignation is accepted. The Regt. is decreasing daily from the discharge of men, and will very soon be too small to muster a Col. He may say to the Gov. that I have been recommended for a brevet, if he wishes. It can do no harm. If that does not go out I shall have to content myself with the soothing reflection that the title of Lt. Col. even by brevet, obtained in my way is worth more than its same title obtained in Hobson's way.

This however will be poor consolation for a lost *real* Colonelcy.

Remember this—Tell *no one,* outside the family, about the brevet. Time enough when its recommendation becomes an appointment—probably 2 weeks.

Friday, April 28th.[30]

Everything goes along as usual. I placed Lieut. Cummings of "H" in arrest the other day as I have already recorded. He has been tried and is now awaiting sentence.

On the 22d I issued a sort of congratulatory order to the Regt. which reads thus—

Head Quarters 17th Me. Vols.
Near Burkesville, Va., April 22d, 1865.
(General Orders No. 1)

The Major Commanding avails himself of the first opportunity to express to the officers and men of this Regt. his gratitude for their gallant conduct in the action at Amelia Springs on the 6th inst.

You advanced nearly five miles in line of battle, driving the enemy at every point. You charged him fiercely three times under heavy fire, carrying a strong line of rifle pits, capturing 150 prisoners, 2 colors, 1 piece of artillery, 40 or 50 loaded wagons, and ambulances, with a large number of horses, mules, and much valuable property.

All this was accomplished with the loss of five officers and twenty-seven men. But while we rejoice over our success, let us remember that it was gained with the loss of valuable lives.

If this is to be, as I trust it is, your last fight, all can remember it with pride and heartfelt satisfaction.

Once again I return to you my thanks for your perseverance and gallantry, to which alone your success is due.

Charles P. Mattocks,
Maj. Commdg. Regt.

We now have battalion drills in the afternoon and company drills in the forenoon. Dress Parade comes off at 5 o'clock, the Band gives us music at sunset, and our guard duty is being done very fairly. There is great improvement in everything. The Hobson rule is at an end.

Hd. Qr. 17th Maine Vols.
2 Miles from Richmond
May 5th, 1865.
My dear Mother:

As you are perhaps aware, our Corps is *en route* for Washington. To-morrow we pass through Richmond. One year ago to-day I was *gobbled*. Little more than two months ago I was marched through the streets of Richmond under a Rebel guard. To-morrow I propose to march through at the head of the 17th with band playing, colors flying, *&c. &c.*

From Richmond we expect & march to Alexandria—180 miles from our starting place—Burkesville. We have made the first 60 miles in three days. I think West's resigning is exploded. He will *probably* return, and I shall have to content myself with the kind *wishes* of Gov. Cony. Will write again soon.

Sunday, May 14th.
We have marched every day until this since we left Burkesville. Tomorrow we expect to move up, and encamp about 4 miles from Alexandria. I shall then try to polish the Regt. off.

I saw Genl. West in Richmond and he said he resigned on the 3d, and that I shall very soon get a Colonel's commission. In that case I am afraid our Rolls will get too small to muster a Col. unless it is done very soon.

Monday, May 15th. Near Alexandria, Va.
By this morning's mail I rec'd my new commission and was duly mustered as

Colonel

this afternoon, to rank from this date.[31]

Thursday, May 18th.

Big thing! I am the ranking officer in the Brig. except the Brig. Commander and, yesterday during the temporary absence of Genl. Pierce, was actually in command of the Brigade.

I have recommended Houghton for Major.

Head Quarters 17th Me.

Near Alexandria Va.

27th May, 1865.

My dear Mother:

Your letters blowing me up for not writing more and more frequently are all received. If you knew how busy we all are with making out Muster-out Rolls you would not wonder.[32] I shall soon be hope [home], I expect, and then we shall not need to confine our ideas to paper. We expect to start for home by Wednesday,—next week. Uncle Luther is making me a little visit, and we are having a very good time. I called on Kirke Porter's folks in Washington with Uncle L. the other day. We all participated in the great Review. I wish you could have seen it. It was a splendid affair. Remember me to all friends. I will try to get Uncle L. to write more at length.

[*The following was added to Charles's letter by his uncle Luther Porter:*]

Washington Tuesday Evening

May 28, 1865

Dear Martha [Porter Mattocks Dyer],

I have just come in from camp. Had a good time there. The Col. is . . . as are all the . . . Mustering out rolls &c. I think the 17th will retain its organization & some other Regt will be assigned to it to fill it up. I base my judgement upon what Gen. Pierce told me confidentially. He said the 17th was the best from Maine and therefore would be the leading star. . . . I brot the letter in from camp at Charley[']s request & added to it.

Head Quarters 17th Maine Vols.
May 29, 1865
Near Alexandria, Va.
My dear Father:

I have just time to say that we expect to start for home about Wednesday, and shall probably arrive on Friday, Saturday, or Monday.

Wednesday, May 31st.

I have received commissions for Houghton, Crie, Duncan and [Charles G.] Holyoke,[33] but they can not now be mustered as we have rec'd orders to prepare rolls for our muster out of service. The men whose term does not expire will probably be transferred to the 1st Maine Heavy Artillery. If the 1st Me. is to be regarded as Infantry Col. Shepherd's time expires and he will be mustered out, and [I] shall be held in service as I am one of those who have been mustered within the last six months of the Regiment's term of service. I have signified my willingness to remain although I am about ready to go home the more especially as we are to have a grand reception in Portland. We have about 28 officers and 233 men.

Thursday, June 1st, 1865.

We have finally completed our muster-out and transfer rolls, and shall soon be on our way rejoicing. Probably we may be able to get away by Monday. The good people of Portland are making extensive preparations to receive us, and will, I dare say do us high honors.

Sunday, June 4th.

We have been this day mustered out, and shall be paid in Portland. We expect to start tomorrow. Our men are transferred to the 1st Maine Heavy Artillery, by Special Orders, No. 140, Hd. Qrs. Army of the Potomac. We transfer 3 officers and 429 men. The order erroneously says 529 men. Capt. Faunce, 1st Lt. Paine and 2d Lt. Chandler are the "victims." I have applied to have the 6 members of our Band, who[se] term[s] do not expire, go home, but it was disapproved at Army Head Quarters. I went to Army Head Quarters today and attempted to get the thing through. When I am in reality a citizen I presume I shall think it a mean thing to deny so small a favor to men who have tried to serve their country for three long years. My love for Genl. Meade will not be intensified by his refusal of this application.

Some of the officers have proposed to take the men along and get the 1st Me. officers to call them "absent sick" or "present for duty." But I think this would be altogether too irregular and upon the whole not advisable. The men will however play us into Washington, and then return on passes.

Thursday, June 8th.

We arrived in Portland at 6 P.M. and have had the honor of a splendid reception. The 17th U.S. Inf. Band, the "Invalids," Engine Companies, and Knights Templar turned out and everything was done up in the most approved style. After being escorted through town, we went to City Hall, where an excellent repast awaited us. Speeches were made, and after sufficient feasting, we marched to Old City Hall where we are spending the night.

The 20th Maine arrived in a train before us and was in the procession with us. The 17th, however, received the most attention from the crowds of people on the sidewalks. I have never seen anything so grand and enthusiastic in P. before. We feel well over it of course.

Friday, June 9th.

This morning we marched to Camp Berry. Just before our arrival the 20th made a raid on the guard of Invalids, and raised a muss generally. After our arrival there was a gathering for a second fuss and some few of the 17th were on hand. I soon got them quiet and there was no further trouble.

Saturday, June 10th.

The enlisted men of the 17th were paid today, and many of them have started for home.

Wednesday, June 14th.

I have had my hands full of business so far, but now I expect to be more at liberty. I shall improve it.

Epilogue

It is puzzling that Charles Mattocks did not describe the Grand Review, that Washington parade in which several corps from the Army of the Potomac and from William T. Sherman's Army of the Mississippi marched before thousands of onlookers. The Grand Review marked the culmination of Mattocks's military career, as well as of those of tens of thousands of other soldiers. The young colonel must have felt especially proud, for finally, he marched at the head of his 17th Maine Regiment, the earlier command of which he had been denied because of his imprisonment. Yet, despite the probable feeling of special honor, we do not have a description or reaction from Charles. It would have been a fitting end to his story. Perhaps his imminent discharge and return home seemed to require no written record of the big event. After all, within a few days he would be able to tell his family and friends about it. However, what was his family's gain is our loss.

For a sense of the character of that day we can instead turn to Mattocks's teacher and friend Joshua Lawrence Chamberlain. The Bowdoin professor possessed the twin gifts of a facile pen and a flair for the dramatic equal to the task. During his last years, Chamberlain devoted much of his time to writing a history of the final campaign of his beloved 5th Corps. He finished this work with a stirring description of the Grand Review. The old man's memory was keen, his appreciation genuine, and his descriptive powers at their peak. The grace of his nineteenth-century prose remained undiminished by age and enhanced by a patina of unabashed sentiment. One cannot help but believe that Charles Mattocks would have admired and approved of his teacher-friend's description of the event that ended those four bloody years, and that he would have approved of giving the last word of his book not to himself, the student, but instead to Chamberlain, the mentor. And so we leave it to Chamberlain to describe the thrilling display of the Grand Review and the role played in it by the 17th Maine and its colonel:

It is the Army of the Potomac. After years of tragic history and dear-bought glories, gathering again on the banks of the river from which it took its departure and its name; . . . having kept the faith, having fought the good fight, now standing up to receive its benediction and dismissal, and bid farewell to comradeship so strangely dear.

We were encamped on Arlington Heights, opposite the capital. As yet there were but two corps up—the Second [Mattocks's] and the Fifth. . . .

Troops that had been with us and part of us in days of need and days of glory, were brought with us again: the Cavalry Corps, and the Ninth Corps, with a division of the Nineteenth. . . . Sherman's great army had lately come up, and was encamped on the river bank at no great distance below.

A mighty spectacle this: the men from far and wide, who with heroic constancy, through toils and sufferings and sacrifices that never can be told, had broken down the Rebellion, gathered to give their arms and colors and their history to the keeping of a delivered, regenerated nation. . . .

The [review's] movement was to be up Pennsylvania Avenue. The formation was in column by companies closed in mass, with shortened intervals between regiments, brigades, and division; the company fronts equalized to twenty files each, so the number of companies corresponded to the total num-

bers of the regiment, some having twelve or fifteen companies, so many had gathered now for the grand muster-out. . . .

What draws near heralded by tumult of applause, but
when well-recognized greeted with mingled murmurs of rev-
erence? It is the Old Second Corps—of Sumner and of
Hancock,—led now by one no less honored and admired,—
Humphreys, the accomplished, heroic soldier, the noble and
modest man. . . .

But now comes on with veteran pride and far-preceding
heralding of acclaim, the division which knows something of
the transmigration of souls: having lived and moved in different bodies and under different names; knowing, too, the tests
of manhood, and the fate of suffering and sacrifice, but
knowing most of all the undying spirit which holds fast its
loyalty and faces ever forward. This is the division of Mott,
himself commanding to-day, although severely wounded at
Hatcher's Run on the sixth of April last. These are all that are
left of the old commands of Hooker and Kearny, and later, of
our noble Berry, of Sickles' Third Corps. They still wear the
proud "Kearny patch"—the red diamond. Birney's Division,
too, has been consolidated with Mott's, and the brigades are
now commanded by the chivalrous De Trobriand and the
sterling soldiers, Pierce of Michigan and McAllister of New
Jersey. Their division flag now bears the mingled symbols of
the two corps, the Second and Third,—the diamond and the
trefoil.

Over them far floats the mirage-like vision of them on the
peninsula, and then at Bristow, Manassas, and Chantilly, and
again the solid substance of them at Chancellorsville, and on
the stormy front from the Plumb Run gorge to the ghastly
Peach Orchard, where the earth shone red with the bright
facings of their brave Zouaves thick-strewn amidst the blue,
as we looked down from smoking Round Top. Then in the

consolidation for the final trial bringing the prestige and spirit and loyalty of their old corps into the Second,—making this the strongest corps in the army,—adding their splendid valor to the fame of this in which they merged their name. . . .

Here passes the high-borne, steadfast-hearted 17th Maine from the seething whirlpool of the wheat-field of Gettysburg to the truce-compelling flags of Appomattox. To-day its ranks are honored and spirit strengthened by the accession of the famous old 3d Regiment,—that was Howard's. Some impress remains of firm-hearted Roberts, brave Charley Merrill, keen-edged West, and sturdy William Hobson; but Charley Mattocks is in command in these days,—a man and a soldier, with the unspoiled heart of a boy. Three of these, college mates of mine. What far dreams drift over the spirit, of the days when we questioned what life should be, and answered for ourselves what we would be! . . .

The pageant has passed. The day is over. But we linger, loath to think we shall see them no more together,—these men, these horses, these colors afield. Hastily they have swept to the front as of yore; crossing again once more the long bridge and swaying pontoons, they are on the Virginia shore, waiting, as they before had sought, the day of the great return.[1]

After the war Charles Mattocks studied law at Harvard, where he received his degree in 1867; he married Ella Robinson of Portland in 1870, had two daughters—Margaret and Mary—and practiced law in Portland. As a successful lawyer he served the people of his area in several public capacities. He was appointed attorney for Cumberland County in 1870 and was elected for the succeeding term. In 1880 he was elected to the Maine House of Representatives, where he served until 1884, and in 1900 he was appointed a judge of probate and again elected to a succeeding term. In 1893 he was appointed executive commissioner for Maine at the Columbian

Exposition in Chicago. Such were his oratorical skills that he was asked to deliver the dedicatory address in Boston at the unveiling of the statue in honor of General Joseph Hooker. Throughout all these years he kept up his interest in military matters; he worked diligently with the Maine militia, and in 1898, Mattocks volunteered for service in the U.S. Army in the war against Spain. It was testimony to his stature that Senators William P. Frye and Eugene Hale and Speaker of the House Thomas Brackett Reed all wrote letters on his behalf. On June 9, 1898, he received a commission as a brigadier general; he was posted to Camp Shipp at Anniston, Alabama, and charged with the training of troops. Also in 1899 Congress voted him the Congressional Medal of Honor for gallant service in the Battle of Sayler's Creek in 1865. On May 16, 1910, Charles Mattocks died.

The old general's funeral was memorable, and Joshua Chamberlain honored and memorialized his friend by thus describing it:

Scarcely anything like it has been seen in this city. Business seemed suspended; the streets were thronged with people moving towards St. Luke's Cathedral where the services were held. The scene in the cathedral was deeply impressive. The casket borne by old soldiers was placed in front of the chancel; nearest, four soldiers with military precision and bearing stood one at each corner; surrounding these the special bodyguard of the general's old command; in front, the color-bearers, with the colors of the 17th Maine, the old Third Corps, and the flag of the Artillery Corps; across the casket the Memorial flag of the Grand Army. . . . The out-going of the military procession was imposing in character and suggestion [as it moved toward the] cemetery, where the last committal prayer was said, the farewell volley fired, and the bugle sounded the last signal,—"Lights Out," and "Good Night,"—until the Morning![2]

Notes

INTRODUCTION

1. The reconstruction of these events is based on the Medal of Honor File for Charles Porter Mattocks in the Records of the Office of the Adjutant General Volunteer Branch, 1865 (M546-639) in the National Archives and on eyewitness accounts kept by Mattocks in his papers that are in private hands. Hereafter Charles Porter Mattocks will be referred to as CPM.
2. Wilmot Brookings Mitchell, *A Remarkable Bowdoin Decade 1820–1830* (Brunswick, Maine, 1952).
3. CPM Diary, Bowdoin College, June 2, 1860–June 4, 1861. All of CPM's prewar diaries are in private hands.
4. CPM Diary, 1860, Bowdoin College.
5. CPM to mother, May 26, 1861, Bowdoin College, Brunswick, Maine. Charles Porter Mattocks Papers, Special Collections, Bowdoin College Library. All letters and other primary documents except for the prewar diaries are in the Mattocks Papers in the Bowdoin College Library unless otherwise noted.
6. Louis C. Hatch, *The History of Bowdoin College* (Portland, Maine, 1927), 119–20.
7. Frank A. Hill to CPM, Feb. 24, 1863, Biddeford, Maine.
8. Alice Rains Trulock, *In the Hands of Providence: Joshua L. Chamberlain and the American Civil War* (Chapel Hill, N.C., 1992), 9–13.
9. After an unsuccessful attempt to recruit for Neal Dow's regiment, Charles commented in his diary: "October 2. But I think I will finish one thing before I begin another. When I finish up I shall at once take a commission and try the military" (CPM Diary, Senior Year, 1860, Bowdoin College).
10. The date of graduation is from "Commencement Program," Bowdoin College, 1862. Bowdoin College Library.
    The material on the mustering of the 17th Maine is in William E. S. Whitman and Charles H. True, *Maine in the War For The Union: A History of the*

Part Borne by Maine Troops in the Suppression of The American Rebellion (Lewiston, Maine, 1865), 446–47.

11. Mother to CPM, Jan. 26, 1863, Portland, Maine.
12. Mother to CPM, Jan. 19, 1863, Portland, Maine.
    In the Mattocks correspondence in private hands is a copy of a letter that CPM sent the governor of Maine, Abner Coburn, on July 31, 1863:

> I have been informed that I have of late been somewhat flatteringly recommended to your Excellency as a fit officer for promotion. While I feel highly complimented to be brought to the notice of the State's chief Magistrate, I must at the same time beg leave to state that I do not at present expect, desire nor deserve promotion. There are other captains who outrank me in the Regt. and to whom I am willing to resign all claims—if I have any. . . . What promotion or advantage I can not gain through a strictly military stance, I do not desire. (Copy of letter to Gov. Coburn from CPM, Conscript Camp, Mackie's Island)

Some months later, however, CPM received a letter indicating that his earlier note to the governor was probably not sincere, but rather all part of his own efforts to obtain promotion mostly through the intercession of his friends:

> Your business letter is before me. I have as yet heard nothing of any new regiments from this state. If the time comes for new ones I will act on something better for you than Maj. You have the stuff for promotion in you & if you have good health you will get it. My opinion is that if a vacancy occurs in the 17th you will fill it. Dr. Wiggin told me that he laid your claims in due form before His Excellency Abner Coburn, Gov. of Maine. Col. Roberts *knows* you desire the place and every one in the regiment knows it. I will see Col. Merrill & talk with him about the matter—*in a judicious way*—and see how the land lies. (W. H. Savage to CPM, Nov. 3, 1863)

Testimony from CPM's friends on his mother's overprotectiveness is evident throughout the correspondence. For instance, CPM's friend William Savage wrote him: "Capt. Sawyer told me you did not intend to come home at present. If you should do so your mother would have a writ of Habeus Corpus after you if you should undertake to return. If you want to prosecute your military pursuit farther you will be wise to keep out of her reach" (William H. Savage to CPM, Mar. 5, 1863). Also Mrs. Dyer was quite open about how she felt:

> I cannot feel in any way reconciled to your present position, But I am compelled to bear it. And being thus compelled, I have tried to bear it quietly. From no other cause, can you *or others* have come to the conclusion that I am more easy about you. You say you have from others that I am more easy. I am in one sense more distressed, For in all I suffered in your going away, I never began to realize that it was for so long. Now the *time* seems to me, Oh, so hopeless. So do not let this assumed cheerfulness be interpreted to mean indifference to your welfare or heedlessness of your danger. . . . Aside from all this; you nor no one else will probably ever justly estimate my disappointment that your taste, or sense of duty, or whatever it was, led you to take your place in the army. . . . I am afraid, very much afraid that we may never meet again. But trying as is the thought, how trying not many know, How much more dreadful would be the thought of not meeting beyond the grave. (Mother to CPM, Jan. 23, 1863)

13. Mother to CPM, Mar. 9, 1863, Portland, Maine.
14. Almon Goodwin to CPM, Oct. 11, 1863, Milltown, Maine.
15. Charles H. Verrill to CPM, Nov. 8, 1863, East Corinth, Maine.
    Charles seems to have had a rather different view of himself as shown in this diary entry: "Sept. 12. I have just sworn off from chasing after these 'little women' for I find it impossible to do anything in my studies or literary labors just as long as I am on a tilt for calico favors. The girls are good enough, but I can not and will not bother with them any now. I have for this very reason kept clear of the Portland girls thus far, and I hope it will be a long day ere I am troubled with a very extensive acquaintance with Portland or any other damsels. I am sorry to say that I do know a goodly number of these Brunswick *specimiens [sic]*" (CPM Diary, Senior Year, August 5, 1861, Bowdoin College).
16. The Mattocks Papers contain many letters from officers and privates in the 17th Maine. See, for instance, letters written in 1863 from William H. Savage, May 5 and 11; David M. Spaulding, July 18; James M. Brown, Nov. 1; and Charles H. Verrill, Nov. 8.
17. Edwin Emery to CPM, Oct. 9, 1863, Camp near Culpepper, Va.
18. John W. Haley, *The Rebel Yell & the Yankee Hurrah: The Civil War Journal of a Maine Volunteer*, ed. Ruth L. Silliker (Camden, Maine, 1985), 144.

19. CPM to Hon. William P. Frye, Mar. 31, 1898, Portland, Maine.
20. William B. Hesseltine, *Civil War Prisons: A Study in War Psychology* (Columbus, Ohio, 1930); Ovid L. Futch. *History of Andersonville Prison* (Gainesville, Fla., 1968).
21. Anonymous reader's report to the Univ. of Tennessee Press.
22. W. B. Hesseltine, "The Underground Railroad From Confederate Prisons to East Tennessee," *East Tennessee Historical Society's Publications* 1, no. 2 (1930): 63, 65.
23. A. J. Loftis to CPM, May 11, 1866, Brevard, Transylvania Co., N.C., in private hands.
24. For land ownership and slaves in the western North Carolina mountains see tables 1.3 and 3.1 in John C. Inscoe, *Mountain Masters, Slavery, and the Sectional Crisis in Western North Carolina* (Knoxville, Tenn., 1989); for the rejection of the initial call of a convention and the actions subsequent to Lincoln's action, see 240–57. For a recent view that contends that support for the Union was partly influenced by class divisions see Phillip S. Paludan, *Victims: A True Story of the Civil War* (Knoxville, Tenn., 1981), chap. 3.
25. For a history of this activity see E. Stanly Godbold, Jr., and Mattie U. Russell, *Confederate Colonel and Cherokee Chief: The Life of William Holland Thomas* (Knoxville, Tenn., 1990), chaps. 6–7, and for a description of the brutality of the incessant lawlessness, see chap. 3 of Paludan, *Victims*.
26. Private John W. Haley uses the word *pompous* to describe Mattocks (Haley, *The Rebel Yell & the Yankee Hurrah*, 144).
27. Joshua L. Chamberlain et al., "In Memoriam," Military Order of the Loyal Legion of the United States. Commandery of the State of Maine. Circular No. 11. Series of 1910. Number 282 (Portland, Maine, 1910).
28. Joshua Lawrence Chamberlain, *The Passing of the Armies* (1915; Dayton, Ohio, 1989), 358.
29. Mattocks, Charles P., "In Six Prisons," in Selden Connor et al., *War Papers Read Before the Commandery of the State of Maine, Military Order of the Loyal Legion of the United States* [Portland, Maine, 1898], 161–80.

CHAPTER ONE.
THE FIRST BATTLE: CHANCELLORSVILLE

1. Almon Goodwin had graduated from Bowdoin College with CPM in the class of 1862. Goodwin had been mustered into service in August of 1862 as a second lieutenant in the 19th Maine Regiment. He had soon become ill and had been discharged in November 1862 ("Bowdoin in the War," [n.p., (1867)], 28).

2. Originally named Camp Curtin, in honor of Governor Andrew Gregg Curtin of Pennsylvania, the men of the 3rd Corps renamed their home Camp Sickles in honor of Major General Daniel Edgar Sickles, their popular commander. The camp was located "near the high bridge over Potomac Creek, and within sight of the Potomac River and Belle Plain." Belle Plain was a small village about nine miles west of Fredericksburg. The "high bridge" is probably the Fredericksburg and Potomac Railroad bridge. That would place Camp Sickles somewhere on the flat plain west of Fredericksburg between the railroad and Potomac Creek.

3. Mattocks was captain of Company A. The commander of the 1st Division, of which the 17th Maine was a part, Brigadier General David G. Birney, in his report on the battle of Fredericksburg, explained that as his division crossed over the river and deployed in the rear of General George Meade's division it came under heavy enemy fire. Ordered to withdraw, Birney was asked for help by Meade and sent his men forward only to find that Meade's division was in full retreat. "The enemy now appeared in full force upon my entire front." The center of his line including the 17th Maine "under command of Brigadier-General [Hiram G.] Berry, met the brunt of the attack and poured a withering fire into their lines" (U.S. War Department, *The War of the Rebellion: A Compilation of the Official Records of the Union and Confederate Armies . . .* (128 vols. Washington, D.C., 1880–1900), ser. 1, vol. 21: 361–64). In further citations, *Official Records* will be abbreviated *OR*.

   In his own report, General Berry singled out "the Seventeenth Maine Volunteers. This was its first engagement; but very few of its members were ever before under fire. Officers and men alike nobly performed their duty; no one would have known but that they were veterans" (*OR*, ser. 1, vol. 21: 373–75).

4. General Birney was commander of the 1st Division, 3rd Corps, Army of the Potomac.

5. Captain Goldermann was captain of Company C.

6. George W. Martin resigned on April 27, 1863.

7. Major General Joseph Hooker was commander of the Center Grand Division made up of the 2nd and 3rd Corps (the 17th Maine was part of the 1st Division, 3rd Corps) of the Army of the Potomac during the Battle of Fredericksburg. President Lincoln appointed him commander of the Army of the Potomac on January 26, 1863.

8. General Birney was now commander of the 3rd Army Corps.

9. Major General Berry, a native of Maine, was commander of the 2nd Divi-

sion of the 3rd Corps. During the Battle of Fredericksburg he had been commander of the 3rd Brigade (of which the 17th Maine was a part) in General Birney's 1st Division of the 3rd Corps. General Berry "was most vociferously cheered by the men, whose affections he had won to a remarkable extent by his uniform kindness and affability, his bravery and skill, and that gentlemanly deportment which soldiers invariably appreciate and admire. When called upon for a speech, he made a few remarks to the boys of his native State . . . and in closing proposed, 'Three cheers for Joe Hooker and the next fight.' Alas! how little did any of us imagine that the next fight would be the last of our beloved and enthusiastic Berry!" (Edwin B. Houghton, *The Campaigns of the Seventeenth Maine* [1866: Gaithersburg, Md., 1987], 48–49).

10. The Reverend Hayden, who was from Raymond, Maine, was promoted on March 26, 1863. He would resign because of physical disability on August 28, 1863.

11. In his history of the 17th Maine, Edwin Houghton commented on the 1st New York that "they were all arrested, and escorted to the guard-house at division head-quarters. On the following day, the whole regiment stacked their arms and refused to obey their officers. Their arms were seized, placed in a tent, and the Seventeenth Maine was posted as a guard around their camp. Some of the instigators of the mutiny were held for trial, but the regiment, concluding that it was useless to hold out against the United States Government, returned to duty, and afterwards behaved with gallantry in the battle of Chancellorsville" (*Campaigns*, 49).

12. Prior to its defeat at the Battle of Fredericksburg on December 13, 1862, the Army of the Potomac, commanded by Ambrose E. Burnside, had endured extremely bad weather: "On the fifth of December it rained in the morning, but towards noon it commenced to snow. Snow fell during the day and evening, and on the following morning the landscape presented a decidedly northern aspect. The weather during the first two weeks of December was cold, stormy and blustering, and our cotton tents afforded but little protection from the inclemency of winter" (*Campaigns*, 16).

After the battle, the Army stayed on in the vicinity of Fredericksburg. On January 20 the 17th Maine had taken part in "Burnside's Mud March," which "words are inadequate to describe. . . . Horses, mules, wagons, and artillery were mired; and it was found utterly impossible to continue the movement. The infantry were obliged to carry their rations, slung upon rails, for miles where mules and wagons could not bring them up; twelve or sixteen horses were unable to move a single piece of artillery, and entire regiments would be detailed to haul a gun out of a mud hole from which horses and mules could not start it" (*Campaigns*, 42).

Private John Haley of Company I of the 17th heavily revised his journal after the war and personally set type for its publication. In it he commented that the January campaign was doomed, for "the weather alone was sufficient to insure failure. About midnight a most violent rain and wind set in, and by daylight the roads were in horrible condition, impassable for anything but men. . . . Burnside must have seen what was evident to us, that the situation was hopeless." After a day of misery "at night a generous dose of stimulant was served out all round and matters assumed a very lively hue" (Haley, *The Rebel Yell*, 67).

13. Maine Republican Congressman John Hovey Rice and the Honorable Charles Holden, mayor of Portland, accompanied the governor.

14. Governor Coburn was elected in 1862. John Haley described Coburn as having

> the conventional dose of "taffy" to give us. Governor Coburn is, without exception, the most wretched speechmaker that ever burnished the cushion of the governor's chair. What sin have we committed that we should be so punished, and on the eve of battle, too? He acted more like a great, blubbering school boy than like the Governor of Maine. The sum total of his remarks was the sum of all flattery, piled on so thick it fell off in great chunks. He informed us (confidentially) that "the 17th has the best record of any regiment from the state." If this wasn't the seventeenth time he said this to as many different regiments, it was only because he hasn't seen that number from our state. (Haley, *The Rebel Yell*, 76)

15. Dr. Henry L. K. Wiggin of Auburn had been commissioned a surgeon for the 17th Maine in August of 1862 but had resigned on account of physical disability in January of 1863.

16. Pettengill was in Company A.

17. Colonel Hiram Berdan commanded this regiment of skirmishers armed with Spencer rifles.

18. Barker was a private in Company A.

19. Both Bent and Private Cloudman were in Company A.

20. From Camp Convalescent "near Alexandria, Va." Cloudman wrote CPM on June 5 to "assure you that I am still in the land of the living although I am now very weak from the effects of the long march to Richmond. Rather an inglorious way to get there but so it was and I could do no better. It was very hu-

miliating to me to be marched by those dirty ragged fellows and to be nearly starved beside. The Guard treated us very well but the Citizens especially the Ladies were very insulting. After serving four days in a crowded Prison we were Paroled" (John W. Cloudman to CPM).

21. Brigadier General Ward commanded the 1st Division of the Third Corps. See entry for May 10, 1863, for a copy of General Ward's letter to Lieutenant Colonel Merrill complimenting Mattocks.

    Houghton confirmed Mattocks's version of events:

    > In the road in which the Fortieth and Seventeenth were advancing, and where the trees offered no protection to the men, the fire was disastrous and terrible. To add to the horror of the position, many of the soldiers in the left companies, excited by the shower of lead and the whistling of the bullets around them, loaded their pieces and discharged them at random in the *direction* of the enemy, but really doing more execution in the ranks of the companies in front. The companies on the right, unable to stand against such fierce and murderous volleys in their immediate front and the fire of friends in their rear, wavered and broke, pressing back in disorganized masses until company after company unable to stand firm was pressed back in disorder. It was not until eighteen companies of the twenty in column had become more or less broken that the panic was stayed. The last two companies [A and E] of the Seventeenth stood firm and the broken columns were reformed. (*Campaigns*, 57–58)

22. Houghton wrote a history of the 17th Maine shortly after the war. It is obvious from the language of some of the book that Houghton consulted with Mattocks extensively. They were friends (Houghton, *Campaigns*).

23. The sergeants were Benjamin Doe, Fayette M. Paine, Grenville F. Sparrow, and John Yeaton, Jr.

24. As might be expected, men from other corps engaged were not so understanding in their assessments. An officer in the 12th Corps saw it differently:

    > General Birney's Division [now commanded by Ward] of the Third Corps was out in front of General Williams; his men behaved badly, and after a slight resistance, fell back into our lines, losing a battery. . . . Meantime Sickles' Corps was holding its own on the right of ours, but it was rapidly getting into the same condition as the Twelfth. The rebels were driven back every time they advanced, and we were taking large numbers of prisoners

and colors. All this time while our infantry was fighting so gallantly in front, our battery of forty-six guns was firing incessantly. The rebels had used no artillery till they captured the battery from Birney, when they turned that on us, making terrible destruction in General Geary's line. (Charles F. Morse, *Letters Written During the Civil War 1861–1865* [Boston, 1898], 132–33)

25. See entry of May 7 for list of killed and wounded.
26. Whipple commanded the 3rd Division. Whipple was taken to Washington where he was promoted to major general; he died on May 7.
27. General St. Clair A. Mulholland described the scene many years later:

> The burning of the Chancellor House, during the battle, was one of the most appalling scenes of the war. The house stood between the lines, and on Sunday morning, May 3rd, five guns of Lepine's 5th Maine Battery took up a position in the orchard to the right of the house, and opened fire. General Lee happened to be in the woods, opposite, and he directed 24 guns to open on Lepine—in a moment, the plateau was a perfect hell—the Confederate shells tore up the ground around the guns, killing the men and horses. Captain Lepine and Lieutenant Kirby were both killed, and the men were blown up and torn to pieces by the exploding caissons, and bleeding limbs fell to the ground with the apple blossoms. During this terrible scene the Chancellor House caught fire, and the flames and smoke were soon pouring out of the doors and windows; some brave boys of the Second Delaware dashed into the burning buildings and began dragging out the wounded, the house was full of them, and lay bleeding forms on the grass. The rescuers stuck to the work until the house was a mass of flames. (*Philadelphia Inquirer*, Oct. 7, 1894, as quoted in Robert G. Smith, *A Brief Account of the Services Rendered by the Second Regiment Delaware Volunteers in the War of the Rebellion*, Papers of the Historical Society of Delaware [Wilmington, 1909], vol. 53: 23)

28. On May 2 General Thomas "Stonewall" Jackson had moved his 2nd Corps to the South and West of the Army of the Potomac by a road hidden from the federal army and launched a surprise attack on General Oliver Otis Howard's 11th Corps, which broke and fled. General Robert E. Lee wrote to President Jefferson Davis on May 3: "Yesterday General Jackson, with three of his divisions, penetrated to the rear of the enemy, and drove him from all

his positions from the Wilderness to within 1 mile of Chancellorsville. He [the Union army] was engaged at the same time in front by two of Longstreet's divisions. This morning the battle was renewed. He was dislodged from all his positions around Chancellorsville, and driven back toward the Rappahannock, over which he is now retreating. . . . We have again to thank Almighty God for a great victory" (*OR*, ser. 1, vol. 25, pt. 2: 768).

29. Major Hayman commanded the 1st Brigade of the 1st Division in the 3rd Corps. An 1842 graduate of the U.S. Military Academy, Hayman served in the regular army until he mustered the 37th New York Volunteers in 1861 and served as its colonel until 1862, when he mustered out of the Volunteers. He then served as major in the 10th U. S. Infantry. He remained in the regular army after the war.

30. It is a comment on how people on a battlefield see things so differently that while both Mattocks and Houghton comment on Whipple and on a sharp artillery barrage late in the afternoon, Haley wrote of that same day that "Night found our own regiment just where we had laid all day. We lost no men, nor did we fire a gun" (Haley, *The Rebel Yell*, 84).

31. Having been badly outnumbered during the entire campaign, General Robert E. Lee had requested reinforcements to take advantage of what he and General Jackson had accomplished by surprise: "General Hooker did not recross the Rappahannock after his defeat on Sunday, but retreated to a strong position in front of the United States Ford, where he is now fortifying himself. . . . I have received none of the troops ordered from south of the James River" (*OR*, ser. 1, vol. 25, pt. 2: 779). General Lee believed himself in no condition to attack the federal position.

32. Mattocks is badly mistaken as to casualties. There were, perhaps, as many as 4,457 more Union soldiers killed, wounded, and missing than there were Confederates.

33. Haley, having rewritten his journal after the war and having had the benefit of hindsight, was not as complimentary of General Hooker or his subordinates:

> Twice now we have been led as sheep to the slaughter. Twice have our plans miserably miscarried without proper cause. . . . General Hooker is not wholly to blame. . . . General Hooker allowed the 3rd Corps to stand the brunt of battle and be mutilated when he had 37,000 troops on the flank of Jackson's column who never fired a gun. This will [be] no easy matter to explain, except we consider the injury Hooker sustained at the Chancellor House. [*Hooker was rendered senseless by the concussion of*

an artillery shell that landed near him.] It is fair to infer, however, that General Hooker had communicated to *some* of his subordinates his intention to bring up this column to attack. But neither . . . [of his immediate subordinates] assumed the responsibility, and the movement was never made. (Haley, *The Rebel Yell*, 87)

Others were even more critical of the commanding general. Charles F. Morse of the 12th Corps evaluated General Hooker:

The commander of our army gained his position by merely brag and blow, and that when the time came to show himself, he was found without the qualities necessary for a general. If another battle had been fought on Monday, it would have been by the combined corps commanders, and the battle would have been won. . . . I have written in this letter a pretty full account of the operations as I have seen them, and I don't believe any one has had a better chance, for during the fighting, I was at different times at every part of our lines, and in communication with General Hooker and other generals. (*Letters*, 137–39)

34. Westcott, from Standish, Maine, was an assistant surgeon in the 17th, and Hersom, from Sanford, Maine, had just been transferred in March of 1863 from the 20th Maine to be surgeon for the 17th.
35. Major General Sigel was born in Germany and attended the German Military Academy. He commanded the 11th Corps until February 1863, when he resigned because of illness. Major General Howard, a native of Maine and a Bowdoin graduate, assumed command of the 11th Corps in April.
36. In his report on the Chancellorsville campaign General Birney wrote: "Col. S. B. Hayman . . . has been specially recommended by me for promotion for gallantry on this occasion" (*OR*, ser. 1, vol. 25, pt. 1: 410).
37. Birney was promoted to major general on May 20, 1863.
38. Lord was from Auburn, Maine; he had been hit in the legs by a shell and had one leg amputated. He was subsequently appointed to the Invalid Corps.
39. Captain Merrill of Farmington, Maine, was wounded in the arm, which had to be amputated; he was transferred to the Invalid Corps in December of 1863.
40. Battery E of the 1st Rhode Island Artillery was attached to the 1st Division of Sickles's 3rd Army Corps.
41. Major General Burnside had twice refused command of the Army of the

Potomac and then accepted the position in 1862 only on the urging of his subordinates. His catastrophic loss at Fredericksburg led to his removal; unlike many other commanders, he admitted his mistakes and accepted lesser assignments.

42. About 12,700 union troops were killed or wounded at the Battle of Fredericksburg.

Haley had his own view as to what Sedgwick had done. All the Confederate shooting of May 4 had been done to screen a Confederate counterattack on Sedgwick's Corps, which had crossed the river and taken the heights of Fredericksburg.

> Thus situated, Sedgwick could fall on the Rebel rear whenever the auspicious moment arrived. But not content with the measure he had attained, Sedgwick pushed onto the Rebel rear. Old [Jubal] Early [of Lee's army] had returned and laid on Sedgwick's rear, thus Sedgwick fell into the very trap Hooker had planned for Lee.
>
> Hooker could have saved Sedgwick if he had known of his predicament in time. But the deed was done and Sedgwick was now in for it. He could only do two things: surrender or (perhaps) hold his ground until night, then sneak out and cross the river at Bank's Ford. Sedgwick was enveloped on three sides and it was doubtful that he could get out. The Rebels closed in on him and tried hard to crush him. They didn't accomplish this, and after dark he recrossed the river.
>
> All this time Hooker was doing absolutely *nothing,* and here is a great mystery. Lee held Hooker all day with a skirmish line while he paid his respects to Sedgwick. (Haley, *The Rebel Yell,* 84)

CHAPTER TWO. GETTYSBURG

1. Twitchell was from Bethel, Maine, and attended Bowdoin College with Mattocks; he graduated with the class of 1860 and enlisted in the 5th Maine in May 1861. In December of that year he was appointed second lieutenant in the 5th Battery of the 1st Mounted Artillery. In November 1863 he raised the 7th Maine Battery, of which he was commissioned captain.

2. In his after-action report Lieutenant Greenleaf T. Stevens, commander of the 5th Maine Artillery, wrote:

> On arriving and reporting [at Chancellorsville], we were ordered into position on the northerly side of a circular field some 500 or 600

yards across. The enemy's line of infantry extended across the field and into the woods, at a distance of not more than 450 or 500 yards. As soon as our battery emerged from the woods and made its appearance upon the field, the enemy's line of infantry divided in center. . . . This movement disclosed their artillery . . . which appeared to consist of two light batteries. Our men and horses began to fall before we got into position. Their artillery was served with great vigor and remarkable precision, opening with canister, spherical case, and shell.

The ground being hard, and affording no cover, their projectiles ricocheted, causing the loss of a large number of horses, and inflicting many severe wounds upon the cannoneers and drivers. Our guns were served deliberately, so that the ammunition in the limbers might not become exhausted, and the effect of our fire might be noticed; the right half of the battery engaged the enemy's artillery, the left half holding in check a large body of infantry massing on our left. The ammunition in the limbers of the right section was expended; that in the center section, with the exception of 4 or 5 rounds, which were ignited by an exploding shell and the limber destroyed; that in the left section was expended . . . when, by the direction of General Hancock, there being but one limber which could be moved, and the remaining cannoneers completely exhausted, the prolongs were attached, and the guns moved by the infantry support to the rear. . . .

Notwithstanding the disadvantages under which we labored, our men behaved in the most gallant manner, continuing to work their pieces until their ammunition was exhausted and the enemy's skirmishers had approached within the distance of 150 yards. (*OR*, ser. 1, vol. 25, pt. 1: 285)

3. William Speer Kirkwood was, indeed, a brave and determined man. At Second Bull Run he was "severely wounded in the left leg, being twice struck." Yet when he learned of the upcoming Chancellorsville campaign "he manifested great impatience to lead his regiment, though his wounds were still open. His surgeon remonstrated with him, but he declared that he must see his command fight and be with it. So crippled was he . . . that he had to be lifted upon his horse. . . .

"Colonel Kirkwood, while conducting the fight and leading his men with unsurpassed bravery and skill, was stricken down [at Chancellorsville], receiving wounds which proved mortal" (Gilbert Adams Hays, *Under the Red Patch: Story of The Sixty Third Regiment Pennsylvania Volunteers 1861–1864* [Pittsburgh, 1908], 443–44).

4. The full report is found in *OR*, ser. 1, vol. 25, pt. 2: 428–31.

5. Anna Etheridge was from Wisconsin and had served as a nurse since First Bull Run. She would serve until Lee's surrender. She was awarded the Kearney cross for bravery by General Birney. Although only wounded (slightly) once, her clothes were riddled with bullet holes (Mark M. Boatner, III, *The Civil War Dictionary* [New York, 1959], 267).

6. Itie was CPM's seven-year-old half-brother, Isaac W. Dyer. This letter is in private hands. Mattocks's disparaging comment about the "9 months men" refers to the men who were drafted for nine months service in August of 1862 after an earlier call for volunteers had failed. The nine-months men were scheduled to be discharged in May of 1863.

7. Major General Sickles commanded the 3rd Corps.

8. General Berry was killed while leading a bayonet attack. As to Whipple, in his report on Chancellorsville, General Sickles described how on Sunday, May 3, his defensive "works were begun under an annoying fire of the enemy's sharpshooters, who were soon handsomely driven by Berdan, to whom the outposts were confided, but not until the brave and accomplished Brig. Gen. A. W. Whipple, commanding Third Division, had fallen, mortally wounded, while directing in person the construction of field-works in his front" (*OR*, ser. 1, vol. 25, pt. 1: 393).

9. The *New York Herald* of May 9, 1863, had an article on page 6 entitled "The New Campaign—the Army of the Potomac—Who Is The Man To Command It?" which stated: "It is abundantly proved that General Hooker has neither the skill, the grasp of mind, nor the steadiness or self-possession which ought to belong to the Commander of the Army of the Potomac." Later in the same article it was suggested that "we therefore call the attention of President Lincoln to General Sickles as the man for this position, for he has shown in the recent nine days' campaign on the Rappahannock the skill and coolness of a great commander."

10. Hobbs was seriously wounded in the thigh.

11. From late August through October of 1862 the 17th Maine had manned a series of forts along the Maryland shore of the Potomac River. Company A had been assigned to Fort Greble, which is 1 3/4 miles North of Alexandria, Va., and 1 1/8 miles inland from the Potomac River.

12. Spaulding had a slight wound to the cheek made by a minié ball.

13. Hatch was a private in Company B.

14. Indeed Company A had been receiving a "good press" at home in Portland. In addition to hearing from his family about all of the compliments coming

their way on how well Company A under CPM's command had done, Charles was also receiving letters from men in the regiment who had been wounded in the Battle of Chancellorsville and had been sent home to recover. An example is that from Augustus Goldermann, Captain of Company C, who wrote CPM on May 20, 1863, from Mechanic Falls, Maine: "There is no use in denying the fact Co. A is under better discipline than any other Company in the Regiment. I have always noticed them, their neatness, good drill and prompt obedience of orders. Let me thank you for your kindness in allowing two of your men to assist me off the field. But for their assistance I should have been taken prisoner." Also see letters from Jim Bluff, May 29 and 30, 1863, Portland.

15. The first use of a badge to designate a particular Corps was when General Philip Kearney had his men wear a red diamond. Later General Hooker, as commander of the Army of the Potomac, had ordered every corps to have a distinctive badge. The 3rd Corps badge was a lozenge (a four-sided planar figure with a diamondlike shape). According to Houghton, "The division was paraded to witness the presentation of the Kearney medals. These were of bronze and in the form of a Maltese cross. They were presented by parties in Philadelphia, at the suggestion of General Birney, to such enlisted men as had particularly distinguished themselves in action by bravery and gallantry" (*Campaigns*, 70).

16. In his journal, Haley gives a very different picture of the awards ceremony: "May 10th–31st. . . . Nothing of any consequence was done for several days. There was simply the usual routine of camp life and the presentation of 'Kearney medals' to those whose conduct was especially meritorious in the late fight. This was a most foolish and unjust performance. Had the thing been reversed and the medals, two to a company, been given to those who had been notoriously cowardly, it would have been just right" (Haley, *The Rebel Yell*, 87).

17. Hobson was from Saco, Maine. In 1864 he would be promoted to major and then to lieutenant colonel when he assumed command of the 17th Maine in January 1865.

18. The 37th had been popular with the Maine men. Haley commented about them on June 3:

> The New Yorkers had a great day of it, playing hurdle races, catching greased pigs, and shinning greased poles. But the chief diversion was seeing how much old rye they could put themselves outside of. Some of McClellan's admirers . . . demanded three cheers for "Little Mac," and when one of Hooker's staff demanded three for Hooker, the 37th New

York showed him they had a greater faculty for fisting than cheering. He was pummeled almost into jelly and nearly torn from his horse. It was feared he would be killed, but he finally cleared himself and galloped off. (Haley, *The Rebel Yell*, 88)

19. George W. Tucker was a private in Company A.
20. Flint was a private in Company A.
21. Bealeton Station is located on the Orange & Alexandria Railroad about five miles northeast of where the railroad crosses the North Fork of the Rappahannock River.
22. Catlett's is northeast along the Orange and Alexandria Railroad. The Third Corps would travel along this rail line to Manassas Station then directly North to Blackburn's Ford across Bull Run Creek.
23. "The weather was very hot, and the march a severe one; the roads on either side were literally lined with soldiers, who, unable to march, had fallen out of the ranks exhausted. Before night over eight thousand men of the Third Corps fell behind the column, and many died from sun-stroke. It was currently reported, and generally believed, by the soldiers, that two of our generals had made wagers upon the marching of their respective divisions, and that our rapid and cruel march was the result of a desire on the part of the commanding general to win his inhuman wager, even though at the sacrifice of the lives of his men. For the truth of the statement, the writer is not prepared to vouch" (Houghton, *Campaigns*, 73).

   Haley provided another possible reason for the terrible march: "Various rumors flew about as to the cause of the fearful rushing of the forenoon, most of them too foolish to repeat. The probable reason was a fear that the Rebels would get possession of some point in the neighborhood of Manassas essential to us, thus menacing our rear and Washington. But once we had passed a certain point there was no danger, so we were not hurried after noon" (Haley, *The Rebel Yell*, 91).
24. "The country in this vicinity was infested by guerillas, and promiscuous straggling was peremptorily forbidden. Gum Springs was a most desolate looking place, —in a state of complete decay. Some twenty old time-worn and weather-stained tumble-down buildings constituted the village" (Houghton, *Campaigns*, 75).
25. Haley had another explanation for the reports of guerillas:

   Referring to my map, I find we are near Gum Spring. Soon after rising we went on picket and were posted in a field near some farm houses in

the rear of the division. The inmates of said homes were soon made
acquainted with us and, for a trifling consideration, seemed pleased to
furnish us with all the luxuries of the season. Our visits became so
frequent and protracted that our officers resorted to several stratagems
to deter us. Among other things, they reported guerrillas in the
vicinity, and that several of our men have been found murdered.
Although these yarns were received with a grain of salt, they had the
desired effect on many, though some daredevils continue to come and
go as they please. They fear nothing so much as an empty stomach.
(Haley, *The Rebel Yell*, 93)

26. When Robert E. Lee had decided to move into Pennsylvania he had left some
    of General James Longstreet's and General A. P. Hill's forces on the
    Rappahannock to deceive General Hooker as to what the Army of Northern
    Virginia was doing. When General Hooker realized that Lee was on the
    move, he had begun his own movement up the Orange and Alexandria Rail-
    road. Both the Confederate and Union armies had cavalry covering their
    movements, and they clashed several times. Among the more tenacious of
    battles were those at Middleburg and Aldie. Actually, after the initial clash at
    Middleburg, General J. E. B. Stuart's cavalry withdrew about one-half mile
    into a defensive position that was not attacked by the Union cavalry.
27. The 1st Maine was part of General Judson Kilpatrick's 3rd Division of
    General Alfred Pleasanton's Cavalry Corps. The 1st Maine suffered twenty-
    nine casualties at Aldie.
28. The rumors about heading for Goose Creek proved to be correct, for
    Edward's Ferry is located at the confluence of Goose Creek and the Potomac
    River, six miles east of Leesburg, Va., and northeast of Gum Springs.
29. The Chesapeake and Ohio Canal runs alongside the eastern bank of the
    Potomac.
30. Bodkin had been wounded at Chancellorsville. He had written CPM: "I
    Take my Pen this morning to Pen a few lines to you and to let you no the
    Hosbutal that I am in. I am rearl smart this morning thankes be to God. I
    fear that my leg will be stiff. Well if so so I can have a heal put under my
    toe as the Irish man Said" (P. P. Bodkin to CPM, [undated], Queen Street
    Hospital, Alexandria, Va.).
31. Although many contemporaries and later historians have believed that
    General Reynolds was the most qualified, President Lincoln appointed Gen-
    eral Meade instead, partly because his foreign birth made him ineligible to
    run for president. General Hooker departed the command with grace:

In conformity with the orders of the War Department, dated June 27, 1863, I relinquish the command of the Army of the Potomac. It is transferred to Maj. Gen. George G. Meade, a brave and accomplished officer, who has nobly earned the confidence and esteem of this army on many a well-fought field.

Impressed with the belief that my usefulness as the commander of the Army of the Potomac is impaired, I part from it; yet not without the deepest emotion.

The sorrow of parting with the comrades of so many battles is relieved by the conviction that the courage and devotion of this army will never cease nor fail; that it will yield to my successor, . . . successes worthy of it and the nation. (*OR*, ser. 1, vol. 27, pt. 3: 373–74)

General Meade took command with the directness for which he was known:

By direction of the President . . . I hereby assume command of the Army of the Potomac.

As a soldier, in obeying this order—an order totally unexpected and unsolicited—I have no promises or pledges to make.

The country looks to this army to relieve it from the devastation and disgrace of a hostile invasion. Whatever fatigues and sacrifices we may be called upon to undergo, let us have in view constantly the magnitude of the interests involved, and let each man determine to do his duty. (*OR*, ser. 1, vol. 27, pt. 3: 374)

32. The news was premature. Vicksburg would not capitulate until July 4.
33. Houghton, the author of *Campaigns of the Seventeenth Maine*, served as acting assistant inspector general on Brigade and Division Staff.
34. Mattocks fails to mention one of the most important aspects of this duty:

It was the good fortune of the writer [Houghton] to accompany the brigade commander and a few invited guests through the academy buildings. . . . St. Joseph's Academy is an institution of the Sisters of Charity, and is the head-quarters of that peculiar sisterhood in the United States. It is picturesquely situated among the most delightful scenery imaginable.

The grounds are very extensive, and beautifully laid out, in grass plots, walks, lawns, gardens, and fountains and embellished with several fine statues of a religious nature. . . . It being vacation, but few of the young lady pupils were present; but those we saw were very pretty and accomplished. . . . The Seventeenth encamped upon the grounds of the seminary, and a guard was detailed by command of Colonel Merrill, —at the request of the officers of the institution. As the duty of guarding a nunnery was of a novel and delicate character Captain Mattocks was selected to take charge of the detail, his well-known asceticism rendering him peculiarly fitted for the post! (*Campaigns*, 85–88)

35. General Sickles had been under orders to stay at Emmetsburg and watch the South Mountain pass, but when he received General O. O. Howard's summons on July 1—the day the battle began—he left two brigades (among which was Colonel de Trobriand's) to guard the pass and headed for Gettysburg. His Third Corps arrived at 10 P.M. and took its place in a low-lying area between the Round Tops and Cemetery ridge. When General Meade decided to concentrate at Gettysburg and fight the Confederates there, he ordered the two brigades of the 3rd Corps that had stayed behind to guard South Mountain up to the battle line. De Trobriand and the other brigade reached the battle line at about 10 A.M. on the second.

36. The *Courier* for this period is not extant.

37. General Sickles had not been satisfied with the placement of his corps. It occupied the southern end of Cemetery Ridge, which was flat to the Round Tops and faced higher ground littered with boulders (Devil's Den) and planted areas (the wheat field and the peach orchard), and woods that gave cover to the enemy, which, he discovered, was not too far distant. Having been given ambiguous orders as to the placement of his corps, and believing that he faced the main Confederate force, Sickles ordered the corps forward to occupy the higher ground. So his 10,000 men had marched out in formation at about 3 A.M. across three-quarters of a mile of open farmland to come to rest in front of the rest of the Army of the Potomac. The movement forward had created a jagged Federal defensive line and had left a gap between Sickles's 3rd Corps and the 2nd Corps located to its right. Unfortunately for the 3rd Corps, the area that it now occupied lay in the path of General Longstreet's target for the day.

Although roundly condemned by some contemporaries and later historians for the placement of his corps, General Sickles had the satisfaction of receiving a compliment in later years from his adversary. In 1902, in a letter responding to an invitation from Sickles to the unveiling of a monument to General Slocum on the battlefield at Gettysburg, former Confederate Lieutenant General James Longstreet wrote: "I believe that it is now conceded that the advanced position at the Peach Orchard, taken by your corps and under your orders saved that battlefield to the Union cause. It was the sorest and saddest reflection of my life for many years; but, to-day, I can say, with sincerest emotion, that it was and is the best that could have come to us all, North and South; and I hope that the nation, re-united, may always enjoy the honor and glory brought to it by that grand work" (September 19, 1902, copy).

38. Charles was mistaken. General Sickles survived the war.

39. General Sickles was wounded in this, the second day's battle, and was replaced by General Birney. The Confederates used up Birney's Division, exposed as it was between Devil's Den and the Wheat Field.

40. "For distinguished bravery and good conduct on this occasion, Corporal Joseph F. Lake, who brought off both colors, after the bearers had been shot, was presented by Captain Mattocks, his company commander, with a pair of sergeant's chevrons, and promoted to sergeant on the spot" (Houghton, *Campaigns*, 93–94).

41. Blake eventually had to leave the service, causing Colonel West to comment: "Am Sorry that we have lost poor Blake for he was a Splendid Soldier" (George. W. West to CPM, Nov. 1, 1863, Camp Near Warrenton Junction, Virginia).

42. Four months later Spaulding wrote CPM:

> After so long a time I am able to write you a few lines to let you know whare I am and how I am. I have been very sick with my wound. The Dr. thought for a few days I should not get beter. The gangrene got into my wound and it has eat a plase as big as my hand or biger and I have suferd a good deale of paine but I dont have much paine know. The Dr. of the thirty sevent N Y tends on me and if he heade not . . . I should lost my lage or life.
>
> You tell Barnes how I am and give my best respects to the boys and tell them I should be glade to be with them. (Priv. David M. Spaulding to CPM, Sept. 18, 1863, McDougal Hospital, New York)

43. Sickles's Corps had withdrawn from its exposed position during and after the battle on July 2; by the morning of the third the Federal line from Cemetery Ridge to the Round Tops was aligned.

44. The losses at Gettysburg are estimated at 23,049 for the Federals and 28,063 for the Confederates.

45. Mattocks is referring to the battle immediately preceding Antietam.

46. General Couch had been appointed to head the Department of the Susquehanna after he had requested reassignment following disagreements with General Hooker after the battle of Chancellorsville. At this time his command was located in Chambersburg, Pennsylvania. General Foster commanded the Department of Virginia and North Carolina. General Dix commanded the Department of Virginia and the 7th Corps until July 15, 1863.

47. Houghton was not quite as sanguine as Mattocks at the lost opportunity: "It was palpable to all, that a deep gloom was cast over the rank and file of the army, when it was discovered that Lee had escaped. We might have successfully attacked, and routed the Army of Northern Virginia at this place; and it seemed to be the general opinion of the men, that we should have done so" (*Campaigns*, 111).

President Lincoln shared the despondency of the men in the ranks. In a letter written (but never sent) in response to a request by General Meade that he be relieved of command, Lincoln stated the case:

> You fought and beat the enemy at Gettysburg; and, of course, to say the least, his loss was as great as yours. He retreated; and you did not, as it seemed to me, pressingly pursue him; but a flood in the river detained him, till, by slow degrees, you were again upon him. You had at least twenty thousand veteran troops directly with you, and as many more raw ones within supporting distance, all in addition to those who fought with you at Gettysburg; while it was not possible that he had received a single recruit; and yet you stood and let the flood run down, bridges be built, and the enemy move away at his leisure, without attacking him. . . . Again, my dear general, I do not believe you appreciate the magnitude of the misfortune involved in Lee's escape. He was within your easy grasp, and to have closed upon him would, in connection with our other late successes, have ended the war. . . . Your golden opportunity is gone, and I am distressed immeasurably because of it. ("To Major General Meade, Washington, July 14, 1863," *The Collected Works of Abraham Lincoln*, ed. Roy P. Basler, vol. 6: 327–28)

48. General McClellan had wasted a splendid opportunity to destroy Lee's army at Antietam; President Lincoln had removed him from command after he permitted Lee's army to escape after the Union's near victory.

49. Vicksburg fell on July 4, 1863.

50. Confederate General Lafayette McLaws was turned from his effort to take

Harper's Ferry by the Federal army moving on him through Crampton's Gap in the early stages of the Antietam Campaign. McLaws succeeded in holding the Federal force long enough to permit the taking of Harper's Ferry and the saving of his own force.

51. The cook may have been Jonas Reynolds of Company A, the only Jonas on that roster.

52. "Here that gallant little soldier, SERGEANT-MAJOR BOSWORTH, fell mortally wounded by an unexploded six-pounder shell. A universal favorite among those with whom he associated, 'Fred' had in a peculiar degree won the love and esteem of the officers and men of the regiment, and his loss was severely felt" (Houghton, *Campaigns*, 116).

53. Not all men in the 17th were doing as well; on July 28 John Haley recorded: "After we went into bivouac, a portion of the division was made to stand in line for two hours, in marching order, for yelling 'Hard Tack!' at General Ward as he rode past. Although many haven't eaten for a day or two, and are nearly insane from hunger, they should realize such behavior will not help. . . . Present rations are about enough to keep a chicken in fair order. . . . We are victims of systematic robbery by the quartermasters, and knowing that our good Uncle Sam *pays* for a generous diet although we have it not makes us doubly exasperated" (Haley, *The Rebel Yell*, 116).

CHAPTER THREE. HOME AGAIN

1. The National Hotel stood at the corner of Pennsylvania Avenue and Sixth Street. It had been established in 1827, when it incorporated six three-story town houses and had since been enlarged to include three more stories. Because of its convenient location it was used by many prominent politicians, including Daniel Webster, Alexander H. Stephens, and Henry Clay, who died there in 1852 (Fremont Rider, *Rider's Washington: A Guide Book for Travelers* [New York, 1924], 4, 100).

In 1841, in his *American Notes*, Charles Dickens described the hotel like this:

> The hotel in which we lived was a long row of small houses fronting on the street and opening at the back upon a common yard, in which hangs a great triangle. Whenever a servant is wanted, somebody beats on this triangle from one stroke to seven, according to the number of the house in which his presence is required; and as all the servants are always being wanted, and none of them ever come, this enlivening engine is in full performance the whole day through. Clothes are drying in this same

yard; female slaves, white cotton handkerchiefs twisted around their heads are running to and fro on the hotel business; black waiters cross and recross with dishes in their hands; two great dogs are playing upon a mound of loose bricks in the center of the little square; a pig is turning up his stomack *[sic]* in the sun, and grunting "that's comfortable"; and neither the men, nor the women, nor the dogs, nor the pigs, nor any exalted creature takes the smallest notice of the triangle, which is tingling madly all the time. (Quoted in James M. Goode, *Capital Losses: A Cultural History of Washington's Destroyed Buildings* [Washington, D.C., 1979], 168)

2. Major Russell B. Shepherd, from Bangor, Maine, had graduated from Waterville College in 1857; he would be promoted to lieutenant colonel in September 1864.

3. When it became clear that state governors were no longer able to raise sufficient troops, Congress passed the Enrollment Act on March 3, 1863. By January 1863 Maine had been able to raise only 643 men to fill vacancies in the old regiments. The draft was poorly received among the states; the worst reaction came in New York City, where draft riots lasted from July 15 through July 17. During the month of July, Maine's Governor Abner Coburn was ordered to conscript 9,519 men. Under the terms of the Enrollment Act, veterans who volunteered for new duty received one month's pay in advance and a bounty of $402; all other recruits who were not veterans would receive one month's pay in advance and a bounty of $302 (*OR*, ser. 3, vol. 3: 3, 36, 462, 828).

   On July 16, 1863, Thomas C. J. Bailey, captain of the 17th Infantry and acting assistant provost marshal general for Maine, assured the provost marshal of the United States: "It is not apprehended that any difficulty will arise in enforcing the draft, and should such difficulty arise it will be seen, by the within report of the adjutant-general of Maine, that there is both sufficient force in the State and sufficient willingness on the part of the State authorities to put it down." The report mentioned by Bailey had remarked: "With the arms deposited in our arsenals by regiments discharged for expiration of enlistment, and ammunition in U. S. arsenal at Augusta for ordnance, smooth-bore and rifled, and for muskets and rifles, if they can be had when required (that is, before mobs can perfect their work, as in New York), Maine will guarantee to the General Government the full and entire enforcement of the draft without the aid of troops raised for the United States and mustered into its service" (*OR*, ser. 3, vol. 3: 512–13).

4. Bowdoin College is located in Brunswick, Maine.

5. According to the pamphlet "Bowdoin in the War":

> Thomas H. Green . . . was commissioned Captain and placed on the staff of Gen. Prince; . . . at the battle of Cedar Mountain, Aug. 9, 1862, rushing to the rescue of his commander, Gen. Prince, who had been taken prisoner, he was slain, as is supposed, in the attempt, for he was not seen or heard of more. He fell at the age of 20 years, a gallant officer.
>
> Willard M. Jenkins . . . was mustered in, Aug. 1862, 1st Lieut. 17th Me., and immediately left for the seat of war; was seized with bilious fever, and died at Poolsville, Md., Nov. 1862, aged 24 years.
>
> George W. Edwards . . . mustered into service, Aug. 1862 . . . was killed in action at Fredericksburg, Dec. 1862, gallantly leading his men in a bayonet charge, at the age of 23 years. ("Bowdoin in the War," 28–29)

6. After recovering from his wounds, Beecher was "promoted Captain, but his injuries compelled him to leave the service, and he was honorably discharged" ("Bowdoin in the War," 28).

7. Mackie Island is located about 1 3/4 miles north of the entrance to Portland Harbor, almost one-half mile east of Porter's Point, where the Presumpscot River flows into the sea. The island is relatively small, measuring about one-half mile long by just under one-third mile wide.

8. This could be Almon Goodwin or Sergeant Charles J. Goodwin, who accompanied Mattocks to Maine to help him recruit.

9. Aroostook is the northernmost county in Maine.

10. Perry was captain of Company F.

11. Savage had been captain of Company A of the 17th Maine but had resigned because of physical disability on December 4, 1862.

12. While a student at Bowdoin, CPM made an expedition to the Bay of Fundy in July 1861 with several friends aboard the schooner *Halcyon*. He kept a journal of his trip, which is in a collection of Mattocks materials in private hands.

13. Cony was born in Augusta, Maine, graduated from Brown University, and became a lawyer. In 1850 he was elected state treasurer of Maine, a post to which he was reelected five times. Although he had been a Douglas Democrat, after the war broke out, he supported the Republican party in Maine. He won the gubernatorial election by 18,000 votes. He would be twice reelected, choosing not to seek another term in 1866 (*The National Cyclopedia of American Biography* [New York, 1896], vol. 6: 314–15).

14. Jackson was a regular army officer who had served in the Mexican War.

He was on detached service, the 3rd New Hampshire being at Morris Island in Charleston Harbor (D. Eldredge, *The Third New Hampshire And All About It* [Boston, 1893], 930).

15. Morse was on detached service "bringing conscripts from Long Island, Boston Harbor, to the Army of the Potomac" (Morse, *Letters*, 147).

16. The City Hotel was Alexandria's premier hostelry. Located at the southwest corner of Cameron and Royal streets, the hotel was very close to the Market, the historic center of town, and had originally been known as Gadsby's Tavern, "the older or Cameron St. portion of which was built in 1750–54. Here Washington had his headquarters as colonel of the Virginia Militia when drilling his troops in 1754. Here the first celebration of the adoption of the Federal Constitution was held June 27, 1788, and from the doorway on Cameron St., April 16, 1789, George Washington, on his way to his first inauguration, responded to a farewell address made by the Mayor. . . . Here Lafayette and John Paul Jones first met, in 1777. In 1799 the hostelry was enlarged by the addition of the four-story building on the corner, known as Claggett's Tavern, and in more recent years called City Hotel" (Rider, *Rider's Washington*, 516).

17. Emery was a private in Company F of the 17th Maine. He had been in school with CPM both in Lewiston and at Bowdoin. He taught school in Gardiner, Maine, before enlisting in the 17th in 1863 as a substitute for one of his friends. He had written CPM from Sanford, Maine, in August:

> I guess there has not been a day since I saw you but that I have thought of my conversation with you, and have weighed this matter carefully. Were it not for my mother I would be with you immediately, and as it is I am almost persuaded to tell you I will go. . . . If I go, I go as a substitute for somebody, I care not who it is. Will that make any difference about my rising? . . . I am not a fighting character you know. . . . When I see how we are situated, and hear the Northern traitors talk, it makes one ashamed to remain at home, and I know, if this struggle ends, as I pray God it may, I can never feel so proud as I could, if I was in the army as a defender of that flag, which every true man is willing to protect. (Edwin Emery to CPM, Aug. 18, 1863, Sanford, Maine)

Emery was one of the few college graduates to enter the regiment as a common soldier: "You would laugh, I know, to see this '*intelligent private*,' cook his *pork* & potatoes, make his coffee, and eat like any one of the 'common kind.' It is coming down a peg or two, from what I was accustomed to do in Maine. I expect to endure hardships and will not grumble" (Emery to CPM, Oct. 9, 1863, Camp near Culpepper, Virginia).

Corporal Temple, who was from Litchfield, Maine, was also a classmate of CPM's at Bowdoin.

18. This entry marks the end of a journal.

19. Private Haley makes no mention of the replacement of Colonel Merrill, but on October 9 he does comment that "in the afternoon Colonel West joined us and, if any disturbance is to be made, we are glad to see him. Otherwise, we much prefer his absence. He is a kind of necessary evil" (Haley, *The Rebel Yell*, 122).

Houghton only mentions West's promotion (*Campaigns*, 132).

20. Perhaps the sister of Charles G. Holyoke of Yarmouth, Maine, who was sergeant-major of Company D, 17th Maine.

21. Goldermann had been captain of Company C, but after his wound he was mustered out for disability on August 19, 1863.

22. Mattocks is mistaken. Thompson would be promoted from first lieutenant of Company I to captain of Company K on February 23, 1864.

23. This was the wife of Dr. Thomas Dwight, professor of anatomy and physiology in the Medical School of Maine, which was part of Bowdoin College.

24. Sometime later Charles received this reply to his inquiry: "You wish *us* (Houghton & myself) to write you about all the gossip & quarles [sic] in the Regt. I am astonished to hear you express such a wish after the advice and example you have given us in regard to such things. . . . In regard to those vaccant [sic] 'Captainces' [sic] I dont know the first thing about them whether Col. West has or will reccomond [sic] anyone" (James M. Brown to CPM, Nov. 1, 1863, Camp near Bealeton Station, Virginia).

25. An American card game in which players may elect to pass, but if they elect to play, they must take three tricks, or they are said to have been "euchred" and the opponents gain two points.

26. Packard had been in the army a very short time, probably a nine-month enlistment, and he characterized his service as a staff officer as "not an enviable one and I was a nobody—a sort of interloper and hanger on. . . . I found myself in a word entirely out of my place and was going down hill with diarrhea and Typhus." After leaving the army, Packard studied at the Bangor Theological Seminary in Bangor, Maine, and taught school at Limerick and Biddeford, Maine (Packard to CPM, February 4 [Bangor Theological Seminary], and May 29, 1863 [Biddeford]).

27. Mattocks is referring to the trouble he had while in college with the Tutors. In one of his college journals CPM has the following entry: "June 5 In the

evening a crowd of students from all classes were enjoying a boxing exhibition given by the diminutive 'yaggers' when Tutor Snow rushed into the 'ring' and ordered them all to their rooms; of course they did not obey and there they stood, Tutor and students" (CPM Diary, 1859, Bowdoin College, in private hands).

The college records carry on the story from the faculty's point of view: "Mattocks being conspicuous in proceedings which were insulting to the officer. . . . Mattocks, having repeatedly shown in times past, a contumacious spirit & a manner & language insulting both to the Tutors, & in a marked degree on Tuesday above, the President is to see him at one as a preliminary to decisive action on Monday evening next. . . . Mattocks declares that he did not intend his insulting language should be heard, & did not suppose they were heard. The government [college faculty] were not satisfied with the declaration. . . . He also declared that he did not start the insulting song" (Bowdoin College. "Records of Executive government," 1849–1868 Misc., Bowdoin College Library).

Mattocks recorded part of the "insulting song":

> We think it no great sin, sir,
> To suck the Tutors in, sir,
> And rob them of their tin, sir,
> To drive dull care away,
> To drive &c. . . . (CPM Diary, 1859, Bowdoin College, in private hands)

Mattocks was severely reprimanded but not expelled.

28. The Bowdoin Peucenian Literary Society had originally been called the Philomathean, but since the word *Philomathean* is used to refer to any literary society, the name had been changed to make the organization more distinctive. Mattocks is here using the word generically.

29. This issue of the *Courier* is not extant.

30. Mattocks would later assert that he had remained neutral in what appears to have been a bitter rivalry between officers in the 17th, but his correspondence does not bear him out. Although CPM's letters are missing, the letters written to him during this period are extant. For instance, Colonel Merrill wrote CPM in October of 1863:

> I thank you for your plainness of speech in regard to the men who have mis-represented the right while enjoying the favors bestowed upon them.

I agree with you in the estimation of their conduct, formed and expressed by you and hope they will be punished as they deserve. But as the fiat of Gov. Coburn [of Maine], and the efforts of the bearded part, your friend Hobson, have taken from me the power to act. I shall leave the whole matter for the "powers which be."

One thing is to be said in extenuation of the conduct of these men, Sergts of Cos. H & I, they have never under their company commanders been in a condition to learn by precept or example, a soldiers duty.

Here, Colonel Merrill is especially aiming these remarks at Captain William Hobson; CPM would continue to develop an adversarial relationship with Hobson (Charles B. Merrill to CPM, Oct. 21, 1863, Catlett's Station, Virginia, in private hands).

CPM also received a letter from his friend A. B. Twitchell: "I was up this afternoon to see his Ex'y the Gov. Of his own accord he alluded to the 17th Regt. in his conversation and said that Col. West was in command of the Regt. . . . Said he had rec'd very many letters expressing satisfaction from the officers of the Regt. since he promoted Maj. West.

"He does not like Lt. Col. Merrill any to well. Said that Gen Birn[e]y . . . of the two men rather favored West" (A. B. Twitchell to CPM, Oct. 29, 1863, Augusta, Maine).

Colonel West had already begun to establish his new regime. On October 28, 1863, he had issued an order that since he "has learned with regret that the practices of Gambling, using obscene language and singing obscene songs prevail to an alarming extent in this Regiment," he was commanding that it stop immediately (Regimental Order Book, 17th Maine Volunteer Infantry, National Archives).

31. Crawford had commanded the 3rd Division of the 5th Corps at Gettysburg and had been given command of the entire 5th Corps for part of October 1863.

32. Chamberlain had left his teaching post at Bowdoin College on the pretense of going abroad to study but instead had enlisted as colonel of the 20th Maine. He had led his regiment in a brilliant defense of Little Round Top during the battle of Gettysburg, for which he was awarded the Congressional Medal of Honor. Chamberlain went on to division commands in the 5th Corps. After the war he served both as governor of Maine and president of Bowdoin College, and he wrote *The Passing of the Armies*, which was published posthumously by G. P. Putnam's Sons in 1915 and is currently available in a reprint edition (Dayton, Ohio: Morningside Bookshop, 1989). For a history of the

20th Maine see John J. Pullen, *The Twentieth Maine* (1957; Dayton, Ohio: Morningside Bookshop, 1984); for a biography of Chamberlain, see Alice Rains Trulock, *In the Hands of Providence* (Chapel Hill: Univ. of North Carolina Press, 1992).

33. Donnell was commissioned an adjutant to Chamberlain in September of 1863; he was Mattocks's classmate at Bowdoin.

34. After Gettysburg both armies returned to Virginia, where they maneuvered around one another. In October, while Mattocks had been in Maine, General Lee had tried to surprise General Meade with an attack around Bristoe Station, Va., but Meade had successfully escaped. During November General Meade decided to launch an attack of his own, which is known as the Mine Run Campaign. However, Lee quickly detected the maneuver and so entrenched his forces that Meade decided not to engage him. The Army of the Potomac then went into winter quarters around Culpepper.

35. George E. Randolph commanded the artillery for General William H. French's 3rd Army Corps.

36. Meade had been appointed commander of the Army of the Potomac on Hooker's removal after the Battle of Chancellorsville.

37. "Here we saw the benefit, as well as the beauty, of our corps badges and battle-flags. There the modest stars and stripes, of General Meade, indicating army head-quarters; the crossed cannon of the Artillery Corps; the crossed sabres of the Cavalry; the plain circular patch of the First Corps; the trefoil, or 'ace of clubs,' of the Second; the lozenge, or 'ace of diamonds,' of our own Third, the oldest decoration in the army; and the greek cross of the Sixth, were waving in the breeze at the head of each corps, division, and brigade. The beautiful maltese cross of the Fifth Corps was not in sight. Our lines moved with as much precision as though on drill, and the scene was one of grandeur and beauty" (Houghton, *Campaigns*, 137).

38. In his report of November 9, 1863, to Brigadier General John L. Hodson, adjutant general, state of Maine, Colonel Edwards wrote:

> Under cover of the night, we approached to within 25 yards of the enemy in his pits, when I gave the order to 'charge.' At this moment we received a terrific volley from the enemy's infantry, and the next our boys had sprung into the rifle-pits, sweeping everything before them. These intrenchments [sic] were occupied by more than double the men that my own front presented, but so sudden and unexpected was our movement upon them that the enemy seemed paralyzed. After disarming them, by a Rapid movement to the Right we succeeded in

capturing nearly the whole force in the pits, who were then ignorant of the fate of those on the left.

During the entire charge my regiment did not fire a gun, carrying all at the point of the bayonet, and the following are the captures made by this regiment alone; 1,200 prisoners, 1,200 small-arms, 1 caisson, and 4 stand of colors. . . .

We occupied the fortifications during the night, advancing to near Brandy Station yesterday. The affair was a complete and glorious victory. (*OR*, ser. 1, vol. 29, pt. 1: 594)

39. As usual, Private Haley's recollections differ from those of Mattocks. They agreed that Captain Sawyer "was a genial, warm-hearted, and impulsive man, liked by all under him. He died deeply lamented." Brown, however, was another matter. According to Haley:

> The other [Lieut. Brown] was exactly the reverse and was thoroughly detested. Indeed, I do believe he was so hated that he was shot by some of his own men, for he caused more fellows to be punished than all the other officers in the regiment. His whole aim seemed to be to catch the men in some trifling violation of orders and then have them punished out of all reason. At the Resurrection morning he will probably be found crawling out of some other person's grave whither he had been to see whether the rightful occupant hadn't done something punishable. . . . There should have been no fight here—we never should have been on this road. However, in view of the demise of Lieutenant Brown, I fully absolve General French for the blunder. Whoever sped the bullet did this regiment an inestimable service. (Haley, *The Rebel Yell*, 129)

In this instance, Haley's feelings may have been more widely shared than Mattocks's, for Houghton made a unique comment on this particular engagement: as an author, Houghton wrote, he had "avoided the too prevalent custom of eulogizing officers, who have fallen in action, yet he cannot refrain from paying a tribute, in this place, to the memory of Captain Sawyer, in whose death the regiment lost a splendid soldier and a gallant officer, the country a devoted patriot, and society a valued member." Not a word for Lieutenant Brown (*Campaigns*, 144).

In all fairness to Brown, it should be noted that he had made a good impression on CPM's mother, whom he had visited while recuperating from his earlier wound sustained at Chancellorsville. Mrs. Dyer wrote CPM: "We invited Lieut. Brown down to tea yesterday. He keeps himself looking very neat & is improving fast, begins to have the old fleshy look. He is quite a chap. A little rough but always talks good sense & never tedious. He is a great admirer of his Captain [CPM]. Says he always tried to do just as he told him. He don't know as he always suited him but he tried to. And Says he is just the best officer in the Regt" (Mother to CPM, June 22, 1863, Portland).

40. Lake was wounded in the back.

41. Egan was colonel of the 40th New York. He had taken command of the 3rd Brigade on November 22.

It is evident from the correspondence of CPM with his friends in Maine that Charles had been hoping for the appointment as major. It appears that CPM had tried to enlist the aid of Captain Savage, who had earlier commanded Company A and who subsequently wrote him:

> Your letter of the 4th came duly. My partner is absent and I am consequently unable to leave to go to Augusta as I would *gladly* do if it was possible to do so. I have written to a gentle man—a brother in law of the Gov. with whom at sundry times I have spoken and corresponded in deference to your claims, who will speak to the purpose mit his Excellency. I also wrote to the Gov. himself a little while since at the suggestion of said Gentleman who said he would back my words. I have just been told that Lieut. Brown & Capt. Sawyer were killed at Mine Run. I hope to hear it contradicted. In case it is true it will render unnecessary any effort to secure for you the position of Maj. The question will then arise in regard to the Lt. Colonelcy. You will have it of course. I wish I were in my old place now. But I am *here* and the honor will fall to better hands. (W. H. Savage to CPM, Dec. 9, 1863, Boston, Mass.)

42. "Chamberlain had been a sick man during the battle. A malarial fever was gnawing at him, and one night shortly afterward he made the mistake of sleeping on the ground in a snowstorm, without shelter or a fire. The disease flared up, and Chamberlain was shipped off to a hospital in Washington, lying unconscious on the floor of a cattle car" (John J. Pullen, *The Twentieth Maine: A Volunteer Regiment in the Civil War* [1957; Dayton, Ohio, 1984], 166).

43. Prince was a Bowdoin classmate of Mattocks. He would go on to serve Chamberlain as judge advocate when Chamberlain was promoted to general and given command of the 1st Division of the 5th Corps.

44. Thompson had been promoted to Captain from Co. I on November 10, 1863.
45. William H. Green was transferred from Company E.
46. Temple had written "Friend 'Matt'" on December 9:

> I am out of those infernal ambulances and may the world come to an end before it will be necessary for me to enter another. . . .
>
> This *pital* nearly as I can judge is of good repute. Still it is a *Soldiers*, consequently our rations of "*butter*" are *meagre* and *mangled*, indicating I think several attempts on the part of the procurator to get even *the* "living morsel." I suppose it is all right; for U.S. is poor, he has been defrauded of many millions and has many "incidentals" to pay so of course must economize some where, and pray tell me where better than in giving his wounded soldiers half rations of butter! . . .
>
> My wound is doing tollerably tho it is mighty troublesome. My general health convaliscent for I have gone thro' with three kinds of medicine and now my "contents" are one swallow of coffee a piece of soft bread two inches by three with butter and sauce to correspond. . . .
>
> I want a furlough from this place as soon as I can have it. If you *can* help me you must. (C. A. Temple to CPM, December 9, 1863, Grosvenor Hospital, Alexandria, Va.)

47. Haley presented a different view of Colonel West: "During a portion of the time at this camp, Colonel West, of our regiment, has been in command of the brigade. Contrary to expectations, under him we have greater freedom from arduous labors and more liberty than ever before. Several complaints have been lodged against us at his headquarters but were dismissed and the petitioners given prompt permission to withdraw" (Haley, *The Rebel Yell*, 134).
48. Woods who was from Farmington, Maine, did not accept the position. He went on to a distinguished career as a music teacher and composer in Boston. *General Catalogue of Bowdoin College and the Medical School of Maine: A Biographical Record of Alumni and Officers 1794–1950* (Brunswick, Maine, 1950), 124.
49. Faunce had been commissioned captain of Company D in 1862, then had resigned because of physical disability in January of 1863. Later he was once again commissioned as captain to serve in Company A.

CHAPTER FOUR. IN COMMAND

1. Porter was Charles's uncle who was a farmer in Danville, Vermont. He was fifty-four years old and had been listed in the 1860 census as owning $3,000 in real property and $700 in personal property.

2. Moses Porter was Charles's cousin, the son of J. S. and Sarah Porter. Moses worked on his father's farm in Danville, Vermont, and was twenty-eight years old.

3. As a company commander Mattocks had issued an order concerning tents that he periodically reissued, as he was a particularly meticulous person: "In accordance with instructions from the Medical Department Company commanders will have every tent provided with a suitable floor or corduroy upon the entire bottom. . . . No cook sinks will be dug, but barrels will be furnished each company for the deposit of slop." Even after he was captured, the order continued to be issued in his name (see Order of June 15, 1864, Regimental Order Book, 17th Maine Volunteer Infantry, National Archives).

4. Seven thousand pairs of mittens.

5. The colonel may have been Harry White of the 67th Pennsylvania, who would later be breveted a brigadier general.

6. Botts was a Virginian who had served in the U.S. Congress for all but two terms from 1839 to 1849. Botts had opposed secession, and at the beginning of the war he had retired from public life and settled on his farm near Richmond. After being imprisoned by the Confederates in 1862, he moved to Culpepper County. He would resume his political career after the war but would lose influence because of his grudging support of the Radicals.

7. The second cook could be Thomas Labaree, formerly of Company E.

8. Houghton shared Mattocks's view of Botts:

> Our encampment was upon the grounds of John Minor Botts, who owned (nominally) all the neighboring farms. We were forbidden to use wood from his place, and consequently were obliged to "tote" it nearly a mile.
>
> It appeared to be the opinion of the troops, unanimously, that J. M. B. was an "unmitigated fraud." Several complaints were made by him to General Meade, and it was finally decided to move our camps. Accordingly, on the morning of January tenth, 1864, we marched about three miles and encamped in a fine oak grove. (*Campaigns*, 152–53)

C. A. Stevens, who wrote the history of Berdan's Sharpshooters, recalled differing views of Mr. Botts:

> Mr. Botts didn't like the idea of their cutting off his timber or taking his rails, but it was done nevertheless, stealthily or otherwise. The soldiers thought that if Botts was a Union man, he should be glad to contribute so much for the cause; if a Confederate, the timber was by all the rights of war their property. But in after years, Gilman K. Crowell, of Company E, takes this considerate view of it: "John M. Botts had one of the finest places I saw while in Virginia. He would not give us any straw to make our beds; and looking at it from my present stand-point, I don't think we ought to blame him much, for the enemy had just stole all his grain and part of his stock, and if we had taken his straw he would have nothing for what little stock he had left. They had burned most all his fences, and I remember that we rebuilt some of them for him." (*Berdan's United States Sharpshooters in the Army of the Potomac 1861–1865* [St. Paul, 1892], 393)

9. Kimball was from Wells, Maine, and was serving as a lieutenant in the 10th New Hampshire Volunteers assigned to the U.S. Civil Service in Washington.

10. Wescott had been discharged December 5, 1863.

11. "The officers of the Third Corps had made arrangements for a grand ball, to which distinguished officers and numbers of ladies from Washington were invited. A spacious hall ninety-six by thirty-six feet, covered with wagon covers, and tent flies, had been erected, adjoining a once elegant mansion, and beautifully decorated with flags and evergreen. The effect was decidedly fine, as the gay couples moved in the mazes of the dance. Three bands were in attendance, and the hall was brilliantly illuminated. It was a new thing to see sentinels, with fixed bayonets, on duty in a ball room" (Houghton, *Campaigns*, 154).

12. Hyde graduated from Bowdoin in the class of 1861. He had commanded the 7th Maine through the spring of 1863, when he was appointed to several successive staff positions and finally to lieutenant colonel in December. In 1891 he was awarded the Medal of Honor for his action in the Battle of Antietam ("Bowdoin in the War," 25–26).

13. On January 28, 1864, General West had issued the following order: "Regimental Commanders will at once organize in their respective commands Military Schools for the education of their Company officers. Regulations

and the tactics will be the branches taught and two evenings of each week must be devoted to examination. Company commanders will organize similar schools for their Sergeants" (Regimental Order Book, 17th Maine Infantry Volunteers, National Archives).

In 1862 the Union Army had adopted Silas Casey, *Infantry tactics, for the instruction, exercise, and manoeuvres of a soldier, a company, line of skirmishers, battalion, brigade, or corps d'armée*, 3 vols. (New York, 1862), as an official manual. Mattocks had picked up his copy of Casey on the Gettysburg Battlefield on July 4 (Inscription in CPM's hand on the endpapers of the Casey volumes in the Mattocks Collection of Mr. James M. White, Jr.).

14. Fernald was Mattocks's tailor in Portland.

15. In a letter dated March 3, 1864, Mrs. Dyer wrote CPM: "George Rounds told Albert that a member of the 17th wrote home that Lieut. Brown was Shot by one of his own men. It cant be possible. Mr. Rounds would not give the Source of his information" (Portland, Maine, in private hands).

16. In October 1863 the 11th and 12th Corps had gone with General Hooker to Tennessee to participate in the Chattanooga Campaign.

17. "While at this point the regiment suffered the loss of the commander, Lieut.-Col. Casper Trepp, who while taking observations of the situation in front, was shot through the head, the bullet entering at the red diamond on his hat [the Corps emblem]" (Stevens, *Berdan's*, 387).

18. Major George G. Hastings.

19. "Capt. Marble was among the first who enlisted at Madison, Wis., early in September, '61, at the age of 22 years, in Company G, of the First Regiment of the Sharpshooters, and before leaving Camp Randall was elected by the company First Lieutenant. On the death of Capt. Drew, Lieut. Marble became captain" (Stevens, *Berdan's*, 536).

20. Mattocks was not exaggerating the esteem in which the 17th Maine was held by his superiors. On March 9, 1864, after an inspection of his brigade, Colonel T. W. Eagan complained of "defects in the appearance and equipment of the troops" and appealed to the "pride of the officers and men" to urge them to a higher standard. Colonel Eagan went on: "The officers and soldiers of the 17th Maine Volunteers, are excepted from this reproof. Their appearance on inspection on Sunday last went far to compensate for the chagrin caused by the lose [sic] show made by the rest of the Regiments inspected" (Regimental Order Book, 17th Maine Volunteer Infantry, National Archives).

21. In his entry for February 29, Haley gives his version of the trouble between West and Merrill:

During the afternoon Major West returned from furlough, remarking as he rode into our midst, "You can't go into a fight without me!" This statement has an element of truth in it, for we do like having him around when there is trouble. We feel he has the ability to get us safely out of a bad spot, for he has few, if any, superiors as a tactician, and would, in this respect, make an excellent commander. If a battle is imminent, we are glad he is here; otherwise we much prefer his room to his company. . . .

He is just dying for a chance to jump over Lieutenant Colonel Merrill, who has been in command since Colonel Roberts resigned previous to Gettysburg. Colonel Merrill doesn't coquette with death nor dally with danger. He believes there is danger enough when men do what they are *ordered* to do, without offering to assume the share belonging to others. He isn't ambitious enough for promotion to risk his own or other lives unnecessarily.

West is all courage and dash, but with no feeling. He only regards men as a means to accomplish an end, that end the "West end." He is intensely selfish and will use anybody as a stepping stone to gratify his ambition. He is empirious [*sic*] and overbearing. Colonel Merrill is the exact opposite, sometimes too much so for the good of the regiment. He often allows men to address him more familiarly than they would a corporal in the regular army. This is laxness of discipline which, in some cases, can only be detrimental to himself and others whose notions might be formed by observing this. Colonel Merrill is too tender-hearted for a warrior, but he perhaps has more of *true courage,* for it requires a heap of moral courage to admit a deficiency of physical courage in a place like this. A lack of moral courage, by contrast, has held many a man on a battlefield. (Haley, *The Rebel Yell*, 138)

22. Neal Dow was a temperance crusader who, in 1851, was primarily responsible for the passage of the "Maine Law," which made liquor illegal in that state. In 1861 he raised the 13th Maine Regiment of which he was made colonel. Dow had been heavily involved in abolitionism before the war, and the 13th Maine had a reputation of being a temperance and abolitionist regiment. Dow may have been against liquor and slavery, but his penchant for sending home confiscated furniture from the Gulf of Mexico region where he served upset his own soldiers. One young man serving under him wrote: "You say you would like to have me confiscate a piano. I tell you what it is, there is precious little left to confiscate after Gen. Dow leaves. He don't allow

a fellow a fair chance in that line" (Charles B. Thurston to Frank Thurston, Dec. 2, 1862, Charles B. Thurston Papers, Emory Univ. Library, Atlanta, Ga.).

Dow's theft also earned him a reprimand from none other than General Benjamin Butler, whose own reputation was not exactly squeaky clean. Butler scolded Dow: "I cannot permit the shipping of furniture or other articles North by any officer for his own use. Such taking of private property, whether belonging to rebels or others . . . is . . . denominated 'plundering'" (*OR*, ser. 1, vol. 15: 584–85). For a discussion of Dow's ongoing difficulties with Butler and Dow's attitude toward confiscation see Frank L. Byrne, *Prophet of Prohibition: Neal Dow and His Crusade* (1961; Gloucester, Mass., 1969), chap. 11; for Dow's reception in Portland at which he called his Confederate captors "semi-barbarians" see Byrne, *Prophet of Prohibition*, 104–5.

Dow was captured and exchanged in March 1864 and resigned from the service in November.

23. Neal Dow had been commissioned colonel of the 13th Maine in 1861, and apparently Mattocks's stepfather had recommended Charles to serve in that regiment, but Mattocks had decided to graduate from Bowdoin before enlisting.

24. Abraham Lincoln had appointed Ulysses Grant "General of the Armies of the United States" in March of 1864; Grant chose to stay with the Army of the Potomac.

25. The Sharpshooters had been provided with the Sharps breech-loading rifle after Colonel Berdan had provided President Lincoln with a spectacular demonstration of the efficiency and accuracy of the Sharps versus the muzzle-loading Springfields his superiors were insisting his regiment use. The Sharps was accurate up to six hundred yards and could be accurately fired at three times the rate of muzzle-loaders. The Sharps was fired by first opening the breech and inserting a paper or linen cartridge; when the breech was closed, it cut the end of the cartridge to permit firing; the hammer had to be cocked manually. Christian Sharps had patented his rifle in 1848.

26. Erastus was a neighbor of the Dyers in Baldwin. He is listed in the 1860 census as being thirty-six years old and a farmer.

27. *Itie* is a nickname for Charles's eight-year-old half-brother, Isaac W. Dyer.

28. Henry Mattocks of Company F of the 1st U.S. Sharpshooters was killed in action on May 19, 1864.

29. Hancock commanded the 2nd Corps, to which he had returned after being severely wounded at Gettysburg.

30. William Chetwood DeHart, *Observations on Military Law, and the Con-*

stitution and Practice of Courts Martial . . . (New York: D. Appleton & Co., 1861); and Stephen Vincent Benet, *A Treatise on Military Law and the Practice of Courts-Martial* (New York: D. Van Nostrand, 1862). Benet's book proved so popular that it had gone through six editions by 1868.

31. The Sharps rifle was commonly .52 caliber.

32. "On the 27th [April] camp was broken up, the troops removed to fields where they pitched their shelters, under marching orders; all surplus camp and garrison equipage being turned over to the quartermaster. For some time previous heavy drills took place, six hours a day, while inspections and reviews were frequent. The old soldiers didn't like it ever so much—thought they didn't require it—but they had to stand it, and soon became in good condition for more rough marches and hard fighting" (Stevens, *Berdan's*, 398).

33. The "match drill" was a result of General Hays's doubts about the usefulness of the sharpshooters:

> When Gen. Hays took command of the brigade, he came to us prejudiced against the Sharpshooters, whose fame had reached him, doubting their ability to meet the requirements of leading and successful marksmen, to entitle them to the name and fame acquired throughout the Army of the Potomac; and he bluntly told Gen. Birney, who was one of our backers, that "the Sharpshooters were no better shots than ordinary infantry," and he "should therefore employ them in ordinary line of battle." In other words he was one of those old officers who evidently didn't believe in the Sharpshooter service; and would soon prove to Birney and staff, and other invited guests, that "the Sharpshooters were pets, and not particularly expert with the rifle." Of course our regiments heard of this, and didn't fancy Hays very much just then, while Capt. Marble in command of the First Regiment at once selected a detail "for a particular purpose," of "ten men in light marching order," who were ordered to report to brigade headquarters, with an invitation extended to our officers to "come and witness the test shooting determined upon."
>
> Marble of course was careful to select reliable men, the least liable to become disconcerted no matter how difficult the test, as he was determined to guard against the possibility of a similar detail from some of Hays' "pets"—in other words he didn't propose to be taken at a disadvantage, but was ready to meet all comers on equal terms, in all manner of shooting and at all distances.
>
> The result was, that Gen. Hays was completely surprised, his sour

looks at us changed to "sweet smiles," in a speech acknowledging that he was "very much mistaken, and that henceforth he would be a Sharpshooter," at the same time ordering from Quartermaster Marden, a pair of green pants in token of his appreciation of our men's proficiency in the use of the rifle. (Stevens, *Berdan's,* 399)

34. There is reason to believe that the Sharpshooters were looking improved; the 17th Maine under Mattocks's leadership had become an exemplary regiment, and he was well on the way to doing the same thing to his new command. Mattocks's handling of the 17th was characterized by one commentator in this way: "Col. West being in command of the brigade the command of the regiment devolved upon Maj. C. P. Mattocks, senior officer present. The time was devoted to drills and the regiment attained a very high state of discipline and efficiency. The ranks were filled with returned convalescents and about thirty recruits, so that at the commencement of the spring campaign there were five hundred men for duty, with twenty-one commissioned and five acting officers."

    At this very review by General Grant, Mattocks's old regiment received a well earned accolade: "About the middle of April the Second Corps was reviewed by Gen. Grant, who specially complimented the regiment [the 17th Maine] on its fine appearance" (Whitman, *Maine in the War For The Union,* 452).

35. Starbird did better than Mattocks supposed. In October of 1864 he made major, and in the following November he went from lieutenant colonel to colonel. After suffering a serious injury in April 1865 he was breveted brigadier general ("Bowdoin in the War," 30).

36. Roswell Weston had a history of sickness; he had most recently been absent from duty because of sickness in March, when he was reported as suffering from "acute Rheumatism and Fever." Arrested April 15, 1864, he was "dismissed the service of the United States" on May 24, 1864. However, his service record shows that he was reinstated and subsequently resigned in that same year (Service Records, National Archives).

37. Isaac Dyer was Charles's stepfather. Dyer, aged sixty-three, had been born in Baldwin, Maine, and had lived there all of his life. He was a lumberman and was listed in the 1860 census as having $6,000 in real property and $4,000 in personal property. Apparently he had moved his family to Portland in order to be closer to his business dealings with the government.

38. The conflict between Major West and Lieutenant Colonel Merrill was obviously bitter. The muster rolls for the regiment from November 1863

through February 1864 list Merrill as being "on detached service in Maine," where he was in the "Recruiting Service at Camp Berry in Portland." The muster roll for March and April 1864 written out in the 17th Regiment's camp listed Merrill as "absent without leave," but another muster roll written out in Portland for the same months of March and April list Merrill as present in the "Draft Rendezvous Portland, Maine." A muster from Portland dated April 9, 1864, described Merrill as assuming command of draft rendezvous in Portland.

The muster roll originating from the 17th for May and June 1864 listed Merrill as being "In arrest by order of Maj. Gen. Birney." The next roll for July and August 1864 explained that he had "Relieved Major Gilbreath 20th Ind. Vols. from command of the Regt. July 10, 1864," and then that for September and October described him as "Dischgd by S.O. 337, W. Dept. Oct 7, 1864." In August General Birney had requested the provost marshal in Maine to investigate Colonel Merrill's situation. The penmanship of the request was so poor that the provost marshal had read the name as Corporal Morrill. Nevertheless, the provost marshal reported to General Birney: "I find that Corporal Morrill acted under advisement and supposed his furlough extended." The report is presently found in Colonel Merrill's file in the National Archives, so either in 1864 or in 1891, when an investigation of the entire matter was made, any possible confusion in names was cleared up. It appears that Major West, in his seeming eagerness to discredit his rival, took advantage of some confusion about Merrill's assignment to report him as absent to General Birney. Some years later Merrill sought vindication with the following results: "It has this day, June 2, 1891, been determined by this Department from records on file that the charges of absence without leave standing against him are erroneous." So for purposes of pension and back pay Merrill was considered commissioned lieutenant colonel 17th Maine Vols from August 1, 1862 (Service Files, National Archives).

On October 12, 1864, when he was at Fort Sedgwick, Va., Merrill wrote a letter to the men of the 17th Maine: "The War Department having accepted my resignation, tendered in consequence of pressing claims of a private nature, my official connection with this regiment is terminated. . . . How shall I speak of the noble sons of Maine who in the suppression of this accursed rebellion have laid down there [sic] lives upon the Alter of our Country! . . . The heroism and bravery and persistent devotion to duty of the soldiers of this Regiment need no fulsome praise. Upon our Banners they have inscribed the record of there deeds, and with there Bayonets written there own history! To one and all both officers and men I must say farewell" (Regimental Order Book, 17th Maine Volunteer Infantry, National Archives).

39. Mattocks was not exaggerating the effect of drunken officers. In his history of the 57th Massachusetts, which was in the 1st Brigade of the 1st Division of the 9th Corps, Warren Wilkinson describes the situation created by a drunken division commander during a battle in June of 1864: "The commander of the 1st Division never materialized that evening to lead his troops in the fight," and that lack of leadership created problems of communication that deprived the 57th of much-needed ammunition. "As soon as he could, young Colonel Weld, in an absolute rage at his commander's betrayal, sought out General Ledlie [the 1st Division commander] to report the disaster and to vent his spleen. He found him passed out on the ground near his field headquarters in the rear of the ravine. Ledlie's own adjutant, equally furious, went over to the general and kicked him until he woke up, and then poked the drunk commander and said, 'Colonel Weld wished to report.' Weld, barely able to control himself, then said, 'General, we have been driven back and our men are all scattered, and I don't know what to do.' In an alcoholic fog, Ledlie clumsily sat up and replied, 'Why, Colonel Weld, there are thousands of men all around here,' and he passed out again" (*Mother, May You Never See the Sights I Have Seen: The Fifty-Seventh Massachusetts Veteran Volunteers in the Army of the Potomac 1864–1865* [New York, 1990], 177, 179).

40. Chase was secretary of the treasury in Abraham Lincoln's first administration. He printed a great deal of money to finance the war.

41. At this time the 9th Corps was in Tennessee, nominally under Burnside's command but actually under the direct command of General Grant. On May 24, 1864, the 9th Corps was transferred to the Army of the Potomac. Burnside had once commanded the Army of the Potomac but had been relieved after the disaster at Fredericksburg; unlike other inept commanders who had led or would lead the army, Burnside assumed total responsibility for his fiasco and agreed to serve in subordinate positions after Fredericksburg. He commanded the 6th Corps during the Wilderness Campaign until once again relieved after mishandling troops during the Petersburg mine assault.

42. All were prior commanders of the Army of the Potomac.

CHAPTER FIVE. CAPTURE AND MACON PRISON

1. Although Joseph E. Hooker, commander of the Army of the Potomac during Chancellorsville, did have a reputation for drunkenness—he seems to have had a very low tolerance for even a small amount of alcohol—there is

little evidence that he was drunk during that battle. Indeed, some historians contend that part of his problem was that he stopped drinking when he was appointed to command the Army of the Potomac. The rumor of his drunkenness may have come from his being knocked senseless during the battle by the nearby explosion of an artillery shell.

2. This spot was also a place of sad reminiscence for the Sharpshooters: "While here, a number of articles were found formerly belonging to the regiment, among them their lost knapsacks which were mostly burned, strips only of them being left, and pieces of green clothing; also the graves of several of their former comrades. Human skulls and bones were scattered over the ground—grave reminders of the grim past. It was near the ground where the determined '80' drove back the 'Stonewall men,' where the Sharpshooters rested for the night" (Stevens, *Berdan's*, 400).

3. Commander of the 5th Corps.

4. Mott commanded the 4th Division of the 2nd Corps.

5. The 2nd U.S. Sharpshooters was assigned to General Ward's 1st Brigade of Birney's 3rd Division and was commanded by Lieutenant Colonel Homer R. Stoughton.

6. Walker commanded a brigade in General Henry Heth's division of General A. P. Hill's 3rd Corps.

   In his essay "In Six Prisons," CPM mentioned an episode that supposedly occurred at the time of his capture but that is not found either in his journals or in his letters home: "I saw what few can record, and that was Grant and Lee actively engaged in the same battle, for shortly before I went forward Grant had ridden by, and shortly after my capture I noticed a fine, soldierly-looking general officer, with less of a staff retinue than graced some of our brigadier-generals, ride by amid considerable cheering, in the rear of the Confederate lines, and upon asking who the officer might be, was informed by a Confederate sergeant that the man inquired about was known among the soldiers as 'Bobby Lee.'" It appears that in the intervening twenty-seven years CPM's memory had played tricks on him, for it is highly unlikely that he would have neglected writing something of these events shortly after his capture (*War Papers*, 162).

7. This was the second time that Lieutenant Leigh had been captured. On May 2, at the Battle of Chancellorsville, Leigh was captured during a charge of Ward's Brigade .

8. After commenting that Berdan's "sharpshooters were out as skirmishers in our front, and they kept the enemy at bay, so that we soon had a line formed," Haley went on to report: "Major Mattox, of our regiment, who

was temporarily in command of the sharpshooters, was taken prisoner. I can't think of any officer I'd sooner part with, for he was very pompous and had yards and yards of superfluous red tape about him" (Haley, *The Rebel Yell*, 144).

Houghton's recounting of the affair was more restrained, and most likely taken from conversations with Mattocks, for it followed Mattocks's account (*Campaigns*, 167–68).

Stevens, in his history of the Sharpshooters, describes the event perfunctorily: "Whereby the right of the line composed of the Swiss and Vermonters suffered considerable loss in a few moments, while the major commanding— C. P. Mattocks of 17th Maine,—was taken prisoner. It was a hot reception for the boys, but they endeavored to pay it back as earnestly." Mattocks's capture received this scant attention even though he had been in command since the end of March. Although his tenure had lasted only about five weeks, Mattocks had made them memorable by having put the regiment through some hard training, which Stevens seems to admit had been necessary. However, Stevens also indicated that the veterans in the unit had resented Mattocks's treatment. In his book, Stevens mentioned Mattocks by name only twice—the first when he took command and then Stevens used only his last name, and the second when he was captured. It appears that Mattocks had taken due pride in what he believed he had accomplished with the Sharpshooters, but that he had also been correct in believing that he had not been popular, perhaps even disliked (*Berdan's*, 401, and see note 32 in chap. 4, above).

About a month and a half later someone at Brigade headquarters wrote the Portland *Courier* explaining that Mattocks was safe and giving a peculiar version of the events of his capture:

> On the morning of the 20th ultimo after Smalls attack on our right and rear we captured many prisoners. An officer of the SharpShooters was talking with a Rebel Sergeant who jokingly remarked[:] "You have got me at last but I *gobbled* one of your Majors the other day that I used to know in Maine." When asked who it was he replied[:] "Charlie Mattocks of the 17th Maine. We were chums and schoolmates together for a long time and were quite intimate 'friends.'" He described the manner of his capture substantially as narrated above and said the Gallant Major was much chagrined at being thus "taken in."
>
> It is a very singular coincidence that the Majors own Regt should capture his captor and also that he should prove to be an old schoolmate. This singular war between brothers however is full of such incidents and it is by no means uncommon for old friends to meet on the battlefield.

There is no evidence for the truth of this story (*Inspector* to *Courier*, June 19, 1864, Hd Quarters 1st Brigade 3rd Division 2nd Corps).

9. Hays was in fact killed early in the engagement.

10. Paxton was a cavalry officer.

11. Pipkin was in Company F of the 16th Louisiana Infantry.

12. Hopper was in the 7th Virginia Infantry.

13. Bridgford was in the Mississippi Cavalry.

14. J. V. Hadley also described this incident:

> We received the attention of an interesting lame major, who bore the title of Provost Marshall. He was an exquisite gentleman. His long hair, generously lubricated with bear's-oil, rolled under at the bottom, and on his Prince Albert coat he had more gold lace than Lee and all his corps commanders. His was the painful duty of examining our pockets. We were called one by one into a small room, and while two brave guards with fixed bayonets stood over us the lame Major with superb politeness requested us to disgorge upon the table.
>
> When this was not performed to the satisfaction of his grace it was suggested that one of the guards might assist us.
>
> With the help of the guard we removed our boots and outer garments to be further inspected by the elegant Major. He claimed to take nothing but what the government furnished. In practice, his rule was to take from the enlisted man every woollen blanket and whatever other property he wanted. From the officers he wanted money and maps; the one would bribe guards, the other facilitate an escape. The ivory-handled tooth-brush of Lieutenant Brown, a heavy artilleryman, was especially pleasing to the Major, and he threw it into his curiosity collection; so also was the silver tobacco-box of Captain Mahon; it would make a nice souvenir and was therefore confiscated. (*Seven Months a Prisoner* [New York, 1898], 50–51)

15. Doe, a native of South Berwick, Maine, was a second lieutenant in Company K and was killed on May 6.

16. Hobbs, a native of Norway, Maine, was a first lieutenant in Company H and was wounded on May 5.

17. Richmond's Libby prison was an old tobacco warehouse on the James River used to imprison Union officers. By 1864 the northern press was waging a campaign against the alleged horrors of conditions in Confederate prisons, Libby being one of the most frequently mentioned. The campaign

seems to have been exaggerated, and although conditions in several Confederate prisons were poor the evidence seems not to include Libby. Fitzgerald Ross, born in England, was a captain in the Austrian Hussars. In 1863–64 he traveled to the Confederate states. Although his book tends to be oversympathetic to the Confederacy, his description of details is straightforward. When he visited Libby prison, he "found it kept scrupulously clean and well ventilated; there was not a bad smell about the place; and, to attend upon the 900 to 1000 officers confined there, forty negro servants were kept" (Fitzgerald Ross, *Cities and Camps of the Confederate States*, ed. Richard Barksdale Harwell [Urbana, Ill., 1958], 70).

Later John R. Thompson, the Richmond correspondent for the pro-Confederate London newspaper *The Index*, wrote:

> The howl of the Yankees over the alleged inhumanity practiced upon their prisoners grows louder and deeper. In company with the correspondent of the London *Times* I visited the Libby Prison and the encampment on Belle Isle a few days ago, to ascertain from personal observation what amount of truth there might be in the statements of the Northern press as to the starving condition of the prisoners. We did not see one emaciated man. Without exception, officers and men were in fine bodily health, and showed no symptoms of wasting from want of food. . . . The condition of the prisoners was far better, having reference only to the supplies furnished them in food and fuel, than that of our own armies in the field. (Ross, *Cities and Camps*, 70–71n6)

In his study of prisons William Hesseltine states that conditions in Libby were most often the result of the conditions in the city of Richmond. When meat or other foodstuff was difficult to obtain in the city so it was for the prisoners in Libby, but every effort was made to treat the prisoners well. By late 1864 conditions were adversely affected by the demise of the exchange system and the resulting overcrowding. To ease the problem of provisions and especially the difficulty of guarding the prisoners, the prison at Andersonville in Georgia was created, and prisoners began to be shipped in large numbers to that place (William Best Hesseltine, *Civil War Prisons: A Study in Civil War Psychology* [Columbus, Ohio, 1930], chap. 6).

18. Upon arriving at Lynchburg, "the officers, fourteen of us, and the men were separated—the men taken to the Fair Ground, we to the lock-up. The latter place was a miserable den in the upper story of a solid brick block,

with its north end facing the street. It had been fitted and used since the war to confine not only criminals against the State, but deserters from the army, and at this time we found in it every manner of men. They lodged us in an apartment 20 by 35 feet, with but two small single-sashed barred windows in the south end, that overlooked the sinks and back-yards of the street. To make the room as dark and dismal as possible, they had made a temporary board partition across the north end, thus cutting off a little room and shutting out the light and air from that direction. There were in the same room (in addition to our number) sixteen others, of a mongrel tribe of criminals, some of whom probably had not had a bath or clean clothes or a lungful of fresh air for twelve months. As a matter of course, they were all covered with vermin—so was the room. These wretches were never taken out for any purpose. Everything they received was brought in to them, and a row of halves of whiskey-barrels was set along the blind end of the room, to breed death among them. . . . There was no light or ventilation save what little came through the narrow windows on the south, no stool or bench, and the floor was so covered with leakage from the barrels that we could neither lie not sit down without getting befouled. To lie in the filth was most revolting to us, and we kept astir until our legs became swollen. As we took the polluted, fetid atmosphere into our lungs, it seemed like breathing the very shafts of death. We would crowd around the little apertures in the south end for fresh air, but upon the approach of a rancid criminal, disperse as if he were a scorpion. They kept us three days in this place" (Hadley, *Seven Months*, 53–54).

19. By this time the indecisive Battle of the Wilderness was over and the Union and Confederate armies had maneuvered themselves into another engagement at Spotsylvania Court House, which would last from May 7 to May 20, 1864. For the Army of the Potomac the important difference between these and previous battles was General Grant's decision after the stalemate of the Battle of the Wilderness not to retreat but instead to maneuver the army to pursue and once more engage the enemy. That persistence marked a radical departure in the history of the Army of the Potomac and in the fighting of the war in the East.

Averell reported on his raid: "Arriving near Wytheville on the afternoon of the 10th, I attacked a force stated by rebel newspapers to have numbered 5,000, under Generals Morgan and W. E. Jones, on their way eastward. This force was mostly infantry, with three pieces of artillery, and posted in an admirable position for defense or attack, impossible to turn with cavalry. . . . The enemy pressed upon both flanks and advanced in three lines sheltered by fences in front. The field was maintained four hours, the vigor of the enemy gradually decreasing. At dark there was some prospect of our being able to drive him, but after dark he retired, and I marched to Dublin" (*OR*, ser. 1, vol. 37, pt. 1: 41–42).

Averell went on to destroy some of the railroad depots and shops near Christianburg. In September of 1864 General Philip Sheridan removed Averell from command for his lack of aggressiveness in the Shenandoah Campaign.

20. There was irony in Shaler's capture, since he had once commanded the military prison at Johnson's Island in Ohio.

21. On May 15, 1864, Mattocks's friend Edwin R. Houghton wrote Charles's mother the following letter:

> Appreciating the feelings and anxious soliciture of friends at home on these "trying times," and thinking that no one has written to you I take the liberty of addressing you a hurried line to inform you that although the "Major" is reported a prisoner it gives me great pleasure to say that he was captured without being wounded and is undoubtedly safe. Although it may be some time before you receive a letter from him I assure you, you need have no fears on his account. The large number of the enemies's prisoners we have captured and hold, will compel the Rebels to treat our own with consideration and kindness. I saw him but a few moments before the fight and he was in most excellent health and spirits. His bravery and coolness is attested by the whole command, and while we regret the circumstances that will temporarily deprive us of his example, services[,] and companionship[,] [we] rejoice that he is spared from a worse fate.
>
> I do not know that words of mine can serve to ease your mind or render the sad news more agreeable, but feeling that under similar circumstances I should be grateful to any friend who would write to my mother I have written to you.
>
> Be assured that if I can serve you in any manner or give you any information of any description I shall be delighted to do so and beg that you will have no hesitation in calling upon me. The 17th has suffered severely both in officers and men as also the whole division. In that assault of the enemies works on the 12th I had my horse shot and received a slight flesh wound in my arm which, however, did not keep me from duty.
>
> I must beg your indulgence for this hasty and incomplete communication.

22. A sharpshooter killed Sedgwick while he directed the placement of his artillery. The information about Warren was erroneous.

23. Stuart was wounded at Yellow Tavern and died the following day, May 12, 1864.

24. Averell had been in Blacksburg and had destroyed the railroad through to four miles east of Christianburg, which is about seventy-five miles just south and west of Lynchburg. Sometime between May 12 and May 15 he had moved to Union, West Virginia.

25. Seymour had fought in Florida in the Seminole War of 1855–58.

26. Johnson would escape from Columbia, S.C., on November 20, 1864. After the war Johnson wrote a book about his experiences entitled *The Sword of Honor: A Story of the Civil War* (Hallowell, Maine, 1906).

27. The phrase referred to depression, or more specifically to "delirium tremens," which was characterized by tremors and hallucinations resulting from withdrawal from alcohol dependence.

28. Andersonville Prison, which had been in use since February of 1864, was located northeast of Americus, Ga.

29. Exchanging prisoners had been difficult at the beginning of the war because Union officials, especially President Lincoln, refused to recognize the formal existence of the Confederacy. To exchange prisoners with it might appear tantamount to recognition. However, in 1862 exchanges were made, but then the two belligerents disagreed as to the disposition of African-American troops. Confederates refused to exchange black troops; instead they treated them as escaped slaves to be returned to their purported masters. The recruitment of African-American troops was crucial to the Northern war effort, and Union officials were determined that black soldiers be treated like white soldiers. In December 1862, as a retaliatory measure, Secretary of War Edwin Stanton halted the exchange of officers. After General Grant became overall commander, the exchange of prisoners took place only in rare cases.

    In a letter to General Benjamin Butler on August 18, 1864, General Grant made his position on prisoner exchange clear: "It is hard on our men held in Southern prisons not to exchange them, but it is humanity to those left in the ranks to fight our battles. Every man we hold, when released on parole or otherwise, becomes an active soldier against us at once either directly or indirectly. If we commence a system of exchange which liberates all prisoners taken, we will have to fight on until the whole South is exterminated. If we hold those caught they amount to no more than dead men" (*OR*, ser. 2, vol. 7: 606–7).

30. Charles A. Humphreys, a chaplain in the Union army, was also a prisoner at Lynchburg. In his memoir, published in 1918, he wrote of his efforts to relieve the condition of the sick and wounded at Lynchburg:

Their first necessity was fitting food but there was not hope of getting that. I thought, however, that I might get a few simple medicines and proper bandages; and so I wrote a note describing the pitiable condition of the wounded, and I was permitted by one of the guards to send it by the hand of a friendly negro to the chief steward of College Hospital, where, a few rods away from our prison, the Confederate wounded and sick were treated. The only answer I received was this verbal message—"You shall have nothing. We must get *rid* of the Yankees in one way or another." All we could then do was to take for bandages pieces of worn-out clothing that the negroes smuggled in for us, and to keep the wounds as clean as we could by frequent washings in water. But without sufficient food and with no stimulants, the mortality was frightful, and the dead-cart trundled heavily with its daily holocaust of victims on the altar of Confederate cruelty. No words can adequately describe the horrors of that prison life. There seemed to be a studied effort to annoy us by withholding the thousand little comforts and conveniences that could easily have been given, and there was evident a deliberate plant to undermine our health by close confinement and insufficient food. (*Field, Camp, Hospital and Prison in the Civil War, 1863–1865* [1918; Freeport, N.Y., 1971], 116–17)

31. Mattocks's reactions to his imprisonment at Lynchburg were mild compared to those of some of his fellow prisoners:

> Full daylight did not perceptibly relieve the gloom of our dungeon; only enough rays crept in to make the darkness visible; but the Southern sun shot its *heat* rays freely through the roof, and made the steaming air more noxious and repulsive. A few pieces of sour bread and rotten pork were passed in on a tray, but we could not eat. Headache and lassitude and the prisoners' scourge—diarrhoea—so reduced our vitality that all appetite was gone, and the stomach revolted from food. The second night—with the added number of prisoners—there was not room for all of us to stretch upon the floor to sleep, and I spent all night sitting with my back to the wall and hugging my knees. . . . and the cheerful summons came to start for Georgia. Anything was better than that living death, under whose tortures flesh and heart must soon have failed. I do not believe we could have lived there a week. (*Field, Camp, Hospital,* 122–23)

32. As part of the solution to the overcrowding of the prisons in Richmond, in

early 1864 the Confederate government built Andersonville for enlisted men and enlarged the prison at Macon for officers.

33. Chaplain Humphreys, who may have had a tendency to exaggerate, was more graphic in his description of the trip:

> We were packed in box cars, fifty or more in each, and each man was given a ration of three pieces of hard bread which had to last us till we reached Danville at three o'clock the next morning. In the car in which I was placed, we were so crowded that we could not all lie down at once, and it was arranged that we should take turns at stretching out on the floor; but when it came my turn to lie down, I had not the heart to awaken my messmates, and I stood all night clinging to the iron rod that served as a brace at the end of the car. But this sleepless vigil was ten times more endurable than the guard-house in Lynchburg. (*Field, Camp, Hospital*, 123)

Hadley, like Mattocks, was also pleased with Danville:

> Danville was our next point. This was a pleasant country-town of three thousand inhabitants, and had the signs of opulence. Three large cotton factories stood within a hundred yards of each other, and the massive piles of brick, as residences, told of a better past than present for Danville. We kindled no curiosity by our entry into the place. The cotton-factories had been prison-pens ever since the war began. Disarmed Yankees were common, and as we marched up-town in the middle of the street, five hundred of us, not a man turned to look at us curiously. We were locked up in one of the factories and fed. (*Seven Months*, 55)

34. Confederates captured Chaplain Henry S. White on May 5, 1864, near New Berne, North Carolina, and sent him to Macon; he described his arrival in mid May:

> It was late in the afternoon when we reached Macon. A group of small boys surrounded us as under guard we were marched to our prison. Macon is a fine town, situated on a somewhat elevated position, and has several good buildings. Several schools, and some government works of importance are here; an arsenal and some gun works in which have been placed the machinery taken from Harper's Ferry. The depot and repair shops are fine buildings. Our place of confinement was the Fair Ground, a mile or so from the town. Since

the war these grounds have been used for military purposes; sometimes as a camp for their own troops, and then for a prison for United States soldiers. The grounds were originally surrounded by a picket fence, but the fortunes of war have made sad gaps in it, as almost everything you see in the South. On the 20th of April, some fifteen days before our capture, Plymouth, N.C. after a desperate fight of several days, surrendered to the enemy. Some two thousand of the men were at Andersonville; one hundred and thirty of their officers were at Macon. We were placed among them. A few days before the rebels had performed on them that peculiar and characteristic operation denominated "going through them"; that is, they come upon them with speed and enthusiasm, and, with several suggestive and, peculiar, epithets, pick from pockets, head or foot whatever they may chance to desire. The Union officers thought it would be a good joke to come down on us, and so in mock earnestness they surrounded us, and for a time I thought we were to be stripped, sure enough.

The camp at that time was in an open field, and guards were placed about to keep our men together. When we were seen coming, the cry was raised, "Fresh fish, fresh fish," and the whole camp at once turned out, and came down to the point where we were to be turned in. I shall never forget the pain I felt as the mock raid was made upon us. "Come out of that hat"; "Come out of those good boots"; "Here, give us your money"; "Tom, go take that man's blanket"; "Come out of those pants." In a few moments we discovered the thing was all a joke, and intended as a burlesque of the Confederate officers and soldiers. It seemed a little rough at first; but we soon saw through it all, and joined in the laugh. (*Prison Life Among the Rebels: The Recollections of a Union Chaplain*, ed. Edward D. Jervey [Kent, Ohio, 1990], 50–51)

35. "The prison at Macon was as comfortable as any I was in. It was situated south of the city, on a sandy inclined plain which had formerly been used as a county-fair ground and a small stream of water ran through the west end. There were probably three acres inclosed, and in the centre stood a large one-story frame building, formerly the floral hall of the fair, but now the bedroom of two hundred men. We had shelter for the most part here, and some boards were given us for bunks. The water we never complained of, nor the wood, for they were reasonably good.

"Our rations were claimed by the Confederates to be the same as those issued to their soldiers in the field, but if they were it is hard to understand how their army was sustained by them" (Hadley, *Seven Months*, 67–68).

36. The number of prisoners at Andersonville was growing out of all reason. The prison was originally designed to hold 6,000 prisoners. In March there were 7,500; in April there were 10,000; and in May there were 15,000 prisoners, of whom 708 died (Hesseltine, *Civil War Prisons*, 146, 152).

As Mattocks indicates, the situation at Andersonville, the worst of Confederate prisons, was growing more fearsome every day. According to what Eliza Andrews, a young woman who lived nearby, heard from persons who had been in the prison during the summer of 1864,

> the wretched prisoners burrowed in the ground like moles to protect themselves from the sun. It was not safe to give them material to build shanties as they might use it for clubs to overcome the guard. These underground huts, he said, were alive with vermin and stank like charnel houses. Many of the prisoners were stark naked, having not so much as a shirt to their backs. . . . Father Hamilton [a Roman Catholic priest from Macon who worked in the prisons] said that . . . he saw some of them die on the ground without a rag to lie on or a garment to cover them. Dysentery was the most fatal disease, and as they lay on the ground in their own excrements, the smell was so horrible that the good father says he was often obliged to rush from their presence to get a breath of pure air. It is dreadful. My heart aches for the poor wretches, Yankees though they are, and I am afraid God will suffer some terrible retribution to fall upon us for letting such things happen. If the Yankees ever should come to southwest Georgia and go to Anderson and see the graves there, God have mercy on the land! (Eliza Frances Andrews, *The War-Time Journal of a Georgia Girl 1864–1865*, ed. Spencer Bidwell King, Jr. [1908; Atlanta, Ga., 1976], 77–79)

37. Captain Tabb had taken command of the prison at Macon on May 18, 1864. He was thoroughly despised: "These rations consisted of two ounces of bacon, half a pint of rice, a pint of corn meal, and a teaspoonful of salt a day per man; but when Capt. W. Kemp Tabb took command of the prison camp he at once cut these down one-third. . . . Tabb was a cowardly rascal, who seemed to delight in nothing so much as in adding to our discomfort and annoyance.

"He did not hesitate to plunder or rob the prisoners under his charge, and if any one reposed confidence enough in him, to let him have anything of value to sell for them, they were just out that amount" (A. Cooper, *In and Out of Rebel Prisons* [Oswego, N.Y., 1888], 58–61).

38. William Chambers, *Chambers's Information for the People*, ed. William and Robert Chambers, 2 vols. (Philadelphia, 1860).

39. There are five men listed here from the 16th Maine who were captured at Gettysburg; all were captured on the first day of the battle, July 1, 1863. The 16th's historian explains:

> When the whole [Union] force was falling back, General Robinson, in order to save as much of the division as possible, personally ordered Colonel Tilden to again advance the Sixteenth, and hold the hill at any cost. The regiment advanced, took position behind the stonewall, and broke the right wing to the right parallel with the Mummasburgh road, the color company holding the apex. . . . (They held the position bravely against fearful odds, but the Sixteenth Maine was the last regiment that left the extreme front, July 1st, if four officers and thirty-eight men can be called a regiment). The intrepid color bearers . . . waved defiance to the foe, as they closed around the regiment. Although conspicuous marks, they gallantly held aloft the loved emblems until capture was inevitable, and then by advice and consent of the colonel and other officers, broke the staff and tore in shreds the silk banners, the pride of the regiment, and divided the pieces. (A. R. Small, *The Sixteenth Maine Regiment in the War of the Rebellion 1861–1865* [Portland, Maine, 1886], 118)

40. Joseph N. Whitney was in the Bowdoin class of 1864. Born in Raymond, Maine, Whitney left Bowdoin to enlist in the Rhode Island Cavalry and was captured while serving in Louisiana. He served a total of twenty-two months in Confederate prison camps ("Bowdoin in the War," 34).

41. A cotton factory in Salisbury was turned into a prison in 1861, and conditions were good until early 1864, when the prison's capacity was reached. Prisoners then began living in makeshift tents, dug shelters underground, and built mud huts.

42. William Smyth was a member of Bowdoin's class of 1856. Born in Brunswick, Maine, he had gone west after his graduation and had enlisted in a Kansas regiment. While serving in the Army of the Cumberland he was taken prisoner at Chickamauga, served fifteen months in prison and was breveted major "for meritorious services at Chickamauga" ("Bowdoin in the War," 15). Professor William Smyth entered Bowdoin as a student in 1820.

"There he pursued his course under the greatest difficulties. The firelight studies had injured his sight, and during his two years at college his lessons were read to him by his roommate, Smyth occasionally raising the green shade which he wore over his eyes to take a look at a Greek or Latin phrase, or a mathematical figure." Although he returned to Bowdoin in 1824 as an instructor in Greek, he was soon teaching Mathematics. "General Mattocks has recalled how, during a recitation, he would, in his earnestness and enthusiasm, cover himself with chalk from his chin down." Obviously, Smyth became a legend in his own time; he promoted the cause of public education and "was a vigorous supporter of the temperance and anti-slavery movements, and his home was a station on the 'underground railroad' for forwarding escaping slaves to Canada" (Louis C. Hatch, *The History of Bowdoin College* [Portland, Maine, 1927], 53–57).

43. Cochrane joined the army when he was a junior at Bowdoin and was commissioned a captain in the 16th U.S. Infantry. He was taken prisoner at Chickamauga and served seventeen months in Confederate prisons, having escaped and been recaptured twice. He rejoined his regiment in March of 1865 ("Bowdoin in the War," 28).

44. See chap. 6, note 66, of this text, which contains a letter from W. L. M. Burger explaining to Mrs. Mattocks that her letters were not reaching Charles because they exceeded the one-page limit imposed on mail to and from prisoners of war by both belligerents.

45. To be released on parole was to give either verbal or written assurance to your captors that you would not again take up arms against them unless you were exchanged.

46. Fessenden graduated from Bowdoin College and was a senator from Maine, having been elected on an antislavery platform. From June 1864 to March 1865 he would serve in Lincoln's cabinet as the secretary of the treasury.

47. Indeed, West was wounded on May 6, 1864. The medical report dated May 6 stated that the "effects of a bullet wound through the middle third of the right thigh" made it impossible for him to carry on his duties. West would be discharged for disability in October 1864 and then be reinstated by the War Department (Service Record, National Archives).

48. Baking soda.

49. Chaplain F. F. Kiner was also a prisoner at Macon. He arrived there May 4, 1862. Unlike Mattocks's description, Kiner, in his narrative written after the war, described conditions favorably, perhaps because he was contrasting them with what he endured later:

For the first two months we did not seem to fare so badly, and the food we got was reasonably good. The ration during the month of May was one pound of flour or meal per day; three quarters of a pound of pork; some rice, sugar, molasses, rye for coffee, a small portion of hard soap, &c. So we got along pretty well and began to feel as though we had made a very lucky change. Another advantage was that we had a good chance to exercise, such as walking, playing ball and moving around in various ways, which was very beneficial to our health, and gave relief to our minds by drawing them away from our condition as prisoners, and from the anxious hearts at home. (F. F. Kiner, *One Year's Soldiering* . . . [Lancaster, 1863] as quoted in *The War They Fought*, ed. Richard B. Harwell [New York, 1960], 126–27)

50. Sherman had succeeded Grant as commander of the Military Division of the Mississippi when Grant had gone east to take charge of all the armies. Under Grant's campaign plan Sherman was to pursue General Joseph E. Johnston's Army of the Tennessee, which was in the Chattanooga area, and destroy it. General Grant had just endured the bloody defeat at Cold Harbor on June 3, 1864 (he would eventually lay siege to Petersburg instead of Richmond), and General Sherman was beginning his maneuver toward Kennesaw Mountain about eighteen miles from Atlanta as he tried to trick General Joseph P. Johnston into a pitched battle.

51. On May 25 Colonel G. C. Gibbs was assigned to replace Tabb as commander of the prison at Macon (*OR*, ser. 2, vol. 7: 372n).

In August Captain Tabb was captured on his way to Richmond: "Before leaving Charleston, S.C., we were informed that Capt. W. Kemp Tabb, C.S. Army, had been captured and that he is now a prisoner in our hands, supposed to have been taken south of Richmond, Va., in a train of cars, perhaps in North Carolina. The prisoners of war very generally desire that steps be taken to visit upon Captain Tabb some of those indignities that he heaped upon them while in his hands. I am sure that a captain of our service was bucked [lain across a log as punishment] and gagged by his order and in his presence at Macon, Ga., while I was confined there" (T. Seymour to Col. W. Hoffman, August 11, 1864, *OR*, ser. 2, vol. 7: 582).

52. To his Swedish captives, Peter the Great offered military posts in which they would never be expected to serve against their own king; those who refused were "dispersed as internees into all corners of Russia. . . . As the years passed, these Swedish officers, scattered through all the provinces of the Russian empire, often lived in want, as they had not money. . . . Of the 2,000 officers,

only 200 received money from their families; the rest were obliged to learn a trade in order to feed themselves. In time, these former warriors, hitherto knowledgeable only in the art of soldiering, developed an astonishing number of talents. In Siberia alone, a thousand Swedish officers turned themselves into painters, goldsmiths, silversmiths, turners, joiners, tailors, shoemakers, makers of playing cards, snuffboxes and excellent gold and silver brocade. Others became musicians, innkeepers and one a traveling puppeteer. Some who were unable to learn a trade became woodsmen. Still others set up schools, teaching the children of their fellow prisoners (some had summoned their wives from Sweden to join them; others had married Russian women). These children were better educated than most in Russia. . . . Soon, Russians in the neighborhood were sending their own children to the foreign schoolmasters" (Robert K. Massie, *Peter the Great: His Life and World* [New York, 1981], 523–24).

53. "We attempted to obtain boxes from the North, but could receive none. The prisoners of the 'Hotel de Libby,' at Richmond [who had been recently transferred to Macon] found themselves vastly worse off, so far as help from home was concerned, at Macon than at Richmond. When there they received a few of the many boxes sent them, and what they did get was all clear gain. Flour, butter, sugar, corn, starch, rice, hams, dried beef, canned fruits and meats, dried fruits, clothing, stationery, etc., in small quantities did reach them. Of course they [the Confederates] stole nine tenths, but then one tenth was an inestimable boost to men that by it were kept from starvation. But here not a thing could reach us. Even the letters sent by our friends, a few of which were given us, had the half of the sheet not written on torn off. A box was prepared for the reception of letters, and we were informed that we might write to our friends. Many at once joyfully prepared letters for home. We were ordered to write plainly, on one side of a half sheet, and interlined, and concerning personal and family affairs only. The letters were to be left open for examination. Of course we understood that only those who spoke well of our treatment and our prison keepers, could hope to have his letter go through. All wrote most encouraging and cheerful letters. But even then they did not send them as they agreed to do, but kept them in the prison office for weeks and months till large bundles accumulated" (Jervey, *Prison Life*, 60).

54. Mattocks was mistaken. Confederates permitted prisoners captured with small amounts of money to keep it, although, if they had in their possession a large amount, that would be confiscated and kept for the use of the prisoner by the camp commandant. "In general the rules of the Confederate authorities in regard to the money belonging to the prisoners were simple. Gold

was permitted to the prisoners—to be administered through General Winder—but Federal paper was not recognized as a legal currency by the Confederacy. However, this might be sold at the prisoner's option at the prevailing rates of exchange, then the Confederate money received might be given the prisoners or retained for their use" (Hesseltine, *Civil War*, 126).

55. A game in which rings of rope or flattened metal are thrown at an upright peg, the object of which is to encircle the peg or come as close as possible, a version of which is also known as "ringers."

56. The Cold Harbor battlefield is about seven miles from Richmond.

57. The Confederates were angry at the constant bombardment of Charleston, S.C., which had been under siege since July 1863. Confederate General Samuel Jones succeeded General Beauregard in the command of the Department of South Carolina, Georgia, and Florida in May 1864. On June 1 he wrote General Braxton Bragg, military adviser to President Jefferson Davis: "The enemy continue their bombardment of the city with increased vigor, damaging private property and endangering the lives of women and children. I can take care of a party, say fifty Yankee prisoners. Can you not send me that number, including a general? Seymour [a prisoner at Macon] would do, and other officers of high rank, to be confined in parts of the city still occupied by citizens, under the enemy's fire" (*OR*, ser. 2, vol. 7: 185).

On June 9 the authorities in Richmond wrote General Howell Cobb at Macon: "General S. Jones, at Charleston, asks for fifty officers of rank, Federal prisoners, to be sent to him at Charleston for special use in Charleston during the siege. The President approves the application, and you are desired to select [from] among them as far as practicable such as have served near Charleston and send the number without delay to General Jones" (*OR*, ser. 2, vol. 7: 216–17).

Union commanders in charge of the siege became aware of the Confederate plan by June 15, and the commanding general, J. G. Foster, wrote General Henry Halleck, chief of staff of the Armies of the U.S.: "I think the cruel determination of the rebels to place our officers in Charleston under our fire is an evidence of their vindictive weakness and of the destruction that the city is sustaining from our fire. This last is not so much from actual demolition as from the depopulation and desolation. Private letters speak of this and of the grass growing in the streets. I hope the President will decide to retaliate in the manner proposed" (*OR*, ser. 2, vol. 7: 371).

58. Wessells had been forced to surrender his troops at Plymouth, N.C., in April of 1864. Scammon had been captured in West Virginia and had been

imprisoned first at Libby in Richmond. Heckman was captured at Drewry's Bluff, Va., in May 1864. All of the brigadiers except Scammon ended up under the siege guns at Charleston.

59. This incident involving Lieutenant O. Gerson, 45th New York Volunteers, made a great impression on the prisoners. Several men who testified before the special committee of the House of Representatives formed in 1867 to look into "the treatment of prisoners of war and Union citizens held by the confederate authorities during the recent rebellion" told the story. For examples, see *Report on the Treatment of Prisoners of War, by the Rebel Authorities During the War of the Rebellion . . .*, House of Representatives, 40th Congress, 3rd Session, Report No. 45 [Washington: Gov. Printing Office, 1869], 1084, 1088.

> One night, just as dusk was coming on, I heard the report of a musket down in the direction of the brook in the west end of the stockade at Macon. Like a flash it was told through the camp that another officer was shot. I ran out to see, and Lieut. O. Gerson, of New York was lying amid some men who gathered about him. The ball passed in at the right shoulder just over the shoulder-blade, down through into his vitals, and about midnight he died. He conversed some time, and then fell asleep. He must have been standing with his back partly toward the guard. I went down and examined the place next morning, and the pool of blood on the ground were [sic] he fell showed that he was from ten to fifteen feet from the dead line, with face from it, when the guard shot him. I went to the hospital just outside, and held service at his funeral. (Jervey, *Prison Life*, 68)

Another officer's version confirmed the basic facts:

> We always found that our treatment was fair whenever we were guarded by old soldiers who had seen service at the front; but when the *new issue*, who were a cowardly lot of home guards, were placed over us, there was no extremity of cruelty and meanness that they would not resort to, to render our condition more miserable and unbearable, even to shooting an officer who was quietly attending to his own business. A case of this kind occurred on the 11th of June, when Lieut. Gerson of the 45th New York Volunteers, who was returning from the sink about 8 o'clock in the evening, was shot and killed by one of the guards named Belger, of the 27th Georgia Battalion (Co. E). This was a *BRUTAL AND DELIBERATE MURDER*, as the officer was not within ten feet

of the dead line and was coming from it towards his quarters, besides the full moon was shining brightly, and the sentry could not have thought he was trying to escape. The truth is, he had told his girl when he left home, that he would shoot a Yankee before he returned, and was too cowardly to attempt to kill one who was armed. (A. Cooper, *In and Out of Rebel Prisons* [Oswego, N.Y., 1888], 63)

On June 16 Captain Gibbs wrote Richmond:

On assuming command of these prisons, June 2, 1864, I had the honor to state:

It is plain that any officer who is expected to command this military prison, the most important in the Confederacy, as being composed of officers only, must be of rank to command at least the officers of the guard furnished him. . . . In the event of attempted outbreak or other trouble I respectfully ask who commands the prison guard?

The latter contingency has occurred, resulting in the death of one officer, a prisoner. Timely notice saved, doubtless, the lives of 1,000 prisoners, and perhaps a few of us. Most of these officers are known to be intelligent, some fearless, many desperate, and all are of more or less notoriety—I had almost said distinction. The question is still unsettled, and again I respectfully ask who commands the prison guard, myself or the lieutenant-colonel of "reserves" or "militia?" Having had some military experience as colonel of a regiment in the field, I hope I may be excused for expressing strongly my disinclination to serve under such officers. (*OR*, ser. 2, vol. 7: 372–73)

By June 26 Gibbs had not heard anything, and he once more complained of his situation:

Again has the question which twice before I have had the honor to ask arisen, viz, who, in the event of revolt among the prisoners here, commands the force to quell it, myself or the officer commanding that part of the Georgia Reserves from which my guard is drawn? . . . There is more danger to the railroads, wires, and bridges in this section of country, particularly in the direction of Atlanta, in the 1,400 prisoners (officers) here than in 20,000 enlisted men in Andersonville, especially when it is remembered that my guard is supplied by a regiment not 400 strong, imperfectly armed, and almost entirely without discipline or drill. While I again express my extreme disinclination to serve under the orders of inexperienced officers of that corps, I will be thankful if the question is in some way settled.

To settle the question Captain Gibbs was promoted to colonel (*OR*, ser. 2, vol. 7: 418, 419).

60. "I wished to know for myself how this could come out, and so kept my eye upon the matter. After a day or two the boy, whose name was Belger, and who was about fifteen years of age, disappeared. About a month afterward I said to one of the subordinate officers, 'What did they do with young Belger that shot Gerson?' At first he did not seem to wish to tell me, but as we were on good terms, and as I urged him, he told me they made him a sergeant, and gave him a furlough for twenty days. The guards were encouraged to shoot us. There was no sorrow when we were shot at or when we died. The impression among us was that they were glad we were out of the way" (Jervey, *Prison Life*, 68–69).

61. Paul Belloni Du Chaillu, *Explorations and Adventures in Equatorial Africa . . .* (New York: Harper & brothers, 1861). Du Chaillu was born in France and educated by Jesuit missionaries in West Africa. In 1852 he came to the United States and secured sponsorship by the Philadelphia Academy of Natural Sciences for a trip to central Africa in 1856. That trip lasted almost four years and resulted in the publication of *Explorations and Adventures*. Du Chaillu's observations about the origins of several African rivers and his discovery of the Fan tribe of cannibals created a minor scientific furor, during which he was ridiculed by a major portion of America's scientific community. During the next few months, however, further reports by others vindicated much of what Du Chaillu had maintained. In 1863 he returned to Africa determined to corroborate his findings with scientific observations, which he subsequently published and which established for him a firm reputation. He lived in New York City and earned a living by writing and lecturing. He later did a book on the Scandinavian countries, and some thirty years afterward, while preparing a similar work on Russia, he died in St. Petersburg.

Bayard Taylor, *Hannah Thurston: A Story of American Life* (New York: G. P. Putnam, 1863). Taylor was born on January 11, 1825, in Pennsylvania. After becoming acquainted with numerous authors and editors, Taylor traveled to England in 1844 and began a career in which he wrote numerous travel books. He also lectured widely, but he aspired to a great literary career writing poetry and fiction. He remained known primarily for his travel literature. In 1862 he began a diplomatic career with an appointment to St. Petersburg, and in 1878 he was appointed minister to Germany.

62. According to F. F. Kiner, as early as 1862 the food had deteriorated:

> Our flour was now changed to corn or rice meal. The corn meal was
> of the coarsest kind, having often pieces of cob in it, and whole grains
> of corn, and this unsifted. This meal we had to bake as best we could,
> there being but few skillets or ovens. Many, yes very many, had to
> gather up any old piece of tin or sheet iron, or any piece of flat iron
> they could find, and make plates and pans. We would stir the meal up
> in any old thing we could get to hold it. Sometimes we could buy a
> little saleratus at two dollars and a half per pound, and scarce at
> that. As for salt, they issued us about a tablespoonful to the man for
> seven days; sometimes we bought it at the rate of ten cents per
> spoonful. At these rates our cakes had often neither salt nor soda,
> and baked in every kind of shape. . . . The meal was brought in
> barrels, or old sugar hogsheads; the meat was thrown out upon the
> ground and literally crawled with maggots. They put guards around
> these rations till they were issued, and we often told them it was
> necessary to guard it to keep it from crawling off. Some of these
> hams and sides of meat were so badly spoiled that we could push a
> finger through and through them, as if they were mince meat. In fact,
> that was what was the matter with it, the worms had minced it too
> much. It had spoiled mostly from want of salt, for the grease we got
> from it was not salt enough to use for gravy. Of this rotten stuff, we
> got one half pound to the man per day. (Harwell, *The War They
> Fought,* 128–29)

The lack of cooking utensils was sorely felt by many of the prisoners at
Macon, although Mattocks does not mention it:

> So far as the ration of pork was concerned, I never could eat it, but
> found it useful in greasing the pan in which I cooked the corn cake.
> Our mess-pan—which was more precious to us than gold, and which I
> carried with me nine hundred miles through the Confederacy—was the
> iron part of a broken shovel which I had picked up in Virginia. It was
> very convenient to hold over the fire while the cake was baking. I will
> confess here for the encouragement of young housekeepers that with
> all the care I could give I burned several cakes, but I trust they will not
> have to suffer for it as I did and go hungry until the next rations were
> issued. (Humphreys, *Field, Camp, Hospital,* 128–29)

63. Gillmore had been in command of the Department of the South until May

1864, when he had gone to Virginia to command the 10th Corps. Mattocks was unaware that Gillmore had been replaced by Major General John Gray Foster, who commanded the Department of the South from May 1864 to February 1865.

64. At this time Butler was commanding the Army and Department of the James. An influential politician from Massachusetts, Butler was an incompetent general whom President Lincoln would allow General Grant to remove after the 1864 elections. The excuse for Grant came from Butler's failures in the campaign against Petersburg and his unsuccessful attempt to capture Fort Fisher in North Carolina.

65. Stanton was an Ohio politician who had succeeded Simon Cameron as secretary of war in 1862. Stanton was generally unpopular, for he was known as a competent administrator but an irascible man.

66. Indeed, the privates at Andersonville were suffering far more than their officers at Macon. After receiving reports of terrible conditions in Georgia prisons, President Davis decided to appoint a senior commander for Andersonville, and he chose General John H. Winder, who in November would become commander of all prisons. Winder left for Andersonville and arrived on June 17. He endorsed a report dated June 21, 1864, made by one of his staff to General Bragg in Richmond:

> I proceeded on receipt of your telegram of 15th instant to inspect prison depot at Andersonville. Number of prisoners at depot on 20th instant was 23,951. The guard . . . consist of four regiments State reserves, a detachment from Fifty-fifth Georgia Volunteers, and Dyke's Florida battery, the aggregate effective strength being 1,588. The reserve troops are poorly instructed and without discipline. The prison camp is surrounded by a stockade seventeen feet high, and covers an area of sixteen acres and a half, only twelve acres of which can be occupied. It is crowded, filthy, and insecure. An addition now being made will give ample room. Rations issued to prisoners the same in quality and quantity as those issued to the guard. Average rate of mortality during present month has been thirty-six per diem. The guard should be strengthened by the addition of at least 1,500 men. Additional surgeons and 150 hospital tents are immediately needed. (*OR*, ser. 2, vol. 7: 392–93)

In his biography of Winder, Arch Blakey describes Andersonville:

Over 2,200 Federals had died, and thirteen surgeons ministered to some 2,000 current patients, assisted by uncaring prisoners on parole. The hospital latrines had polluted the water supply, and the stockade was a frightful scene. The constant movement of men using the sinks on the creek banks had created a putrid swamp covering three and one-half acres in the center of the prison, and the swamp then became the latrine. Fecal matter from thousands of men suffering from dysentery polluted the entire area; maggots bred in the slime to a depth of fifteen inches; a small scratch might become a raging infection overnight with gangrene sure to follow. The command was truly a hell on earth, and the horror mounted with the passage of each day. (*General John H. Winder C.S.A.* [Gainesville, Fla., 1990], 184)

Blakey lays the responsibility for this disaster ultimately on the abandonment of the exchange cartel by both the Confederate and Union administrations. Although he sees Lincoln as the primary mover, Blakey acknowledges the probable necessity for the decision in order to shorten the war. Generally, Blakey exonerates Winder, blaming conditions on a lack of supplies, support, and understanding in Richmond (*General John H. Winder C.S.A.*, 214–15).

67. The Union prisoners were not the only persons who were angry and horrified by conditions. On June 23, 1864, a private in the First Regiment, Georgia Reserves, named James E. Anderson wrote Jefferson Davis:

Being but a private in the ranks at this place [Camp Sumter, the original name for Andersonville], consequently if I see anything to condemn (as I do) I have no power to correct it. Yet as a humane being and one that believes that we should "do as we would be done by," I proceed to inform you of some things that I know you are ignorant of, and in the first place I will say I have no cause to love the Yankees (they having driven myself and family from our home in New Orleans to seek our living amongst strangers), yet I think that prisoners should have some showing. Inside our prison walls all around there is a space about twelve feet wide, called the "dead-line." If a prisoner crosses that line the sentinels are ordered to shoot him. Now, we have many thoughtless boys here who think the killing of a Yankee will make them great men. As a consequence, every day or two there are prisoners shot. When the officer of the guard goes to the sentry stand, there is a dead or badly wounded man invariably within their own lines. The sentry, of course, says he was across the dead-line when he shot him. He is told he did exactly right and is a good sentry. Last Sabbath there were two shot in their tents at one shot. The boy said that he shot at one across the dead-line. Night before last there was one shot near me (I being on guard). The sentry said that the Yankee made one step across the line to avoid a mud hole. He shot him through the bowels, and when the officer of the guard got there he was lying inside their own lines. He (the sentry) as usual told him that he stepped across, but fell back inside. The officer told him it was exactly right. Now, my dear sir, I know you are opposed to such measures, and I make this statement to you knowing you to be a soldier, statesman, and Christian, that if possible you may correct such things, together with many others that exist here. And yet if you send an agent here he will of course go amongst the officers, tell his business, and be told that all is well, but let a good man come here as a private citizen and mix with the privates and stay one week, and if he don't find out things revolting to humanity then I am deceived. I shall put my name to this, believing that you will not let the officers over me see it, otherwise I would suffer, most probably.

On July 23 the letter was "Respectfully referred, by direction of the President, to the Honorable Secretary of War" and then endorsed by the assistant secretary of war, J. A. Campbell, as follows: "Refer to Brigadier-General Winder" (*OR*, ser. 2, vol. 7: 403–4).

68. The details of exchange over which both sides bickered were largely pretexts by which the Union could avoid exchanges. By November of 1864 the situation in Confederate prisons would become so critical that Confederate authorities decided to send Union prisoners home without insisting on man-for-man exchanges.

In 1863 General Grant had decided to parole the approximately 20,000 Confederate prisoners he had captured at the fall of Vicksburg, for he had not wished to become encumbered with the necessity of transporting and providing for them. In addition, about 50 percent of the prisoners were sick and unfit for service. Grant had been enraged during the battle of Chattanooga in the fall of 1863 to find among Confederate prisoners taken during that battle unexchanged Vicksburg veterans whom he had earlier paroled.

69. Charles O. Hunt was born in Gorham, Maine. He enlisted in the 5th Maine battery and had been wounded at Gettysburg; he was captured on June 18, 1864 ("Bowdoin in the War," 25).

70. Emery had been wounded twice at the Battle of Spotsylvania on May 12 and had been promoted to the rank of second lieutenant on June 28, 1864.

71. Morrell was killed in the Battle of Spotsylvania.

72. West had indeed been wounded in the thigh. Also, since Mattocks's capture, much had happened among the leadership of the 17th: "On the sixteenth [of May] Lieut. Col. Merrill returned from detached service and relieved Maj. Moore of the Ninety-ninth Pennsylvania Volunteers, who had commanded the regiment from the seventh. . . . On the fifth [of June, 1864] one hundred and twenty-nine men from the Third regiment were transferred to the Seventeenth, augmenting the strength of the regiment to over two hundred guns." On June 17, B. C. Pennell, "at the time in command of the regiment, . . . was instantly killed by a shot from a sharpshooter" (Whitman, *Maine in the War For The Union,* 544–55).

73. The celebration was well remembered by the prisoners, and long after the war they told variously elaborate versions in their reminiscences:

> On the Fourth of July, after the regular morning count, we repaired to the big central building and held an informal celebration. One officer had brought into captivity, concealed on his person, a little silk national flag, which was carried up into the cross-beams of the building, and the sight of it created the wildest enthusiasm. We cheered the flag and applauded the patriotic speeches until a detachment of the guard succeeded in putting a stop to our proceedings. They tried to capture the flag, but in this they were not successful. We were informed that cannon were planted commanding the camp, and would be opened on us if we renewed our demonstrations. (W. H. Shelton, "A Hard Road to Travel Out of Dixie," *Famous Adventures and Prison Escapes of the Civil War* [New York, 1917], 250)

> The Fourth of July was by no means forgotten by the prisoners. Captain Todd, of the Eighth New Jersey, had managed somehow to smuggle into prison a little six-by-ten Union flag.
>
> Immediately after roll-call, the "magic little rag" was unfurled to the breeze and hoisted on a staff. In an instant the prison was in an uproar; shouts for the Union and cheers for the Red, White, and Blue broke forth from every quarter. The excitement was wonderful. Two or three hundred men formed in columns of fours and followed the little flag about the prison, making the walls reverberate the echoes of the inspiring song of "Rally Round the Flag, Boys." Then they marched into

the floral hall for speaking. A rough structure by one of the pillars of the building, called a table, was used as a rostrum, from which short speeches were made till late in the afternoon. They were of the most patriotic and radical order, interspersed always with some national air, sung by the entire audience.

The Confederates were a little troubled over this, and twice sent in a corporal's guard and demanded the flag; but these were only laughed at, and sent away empty. A third time the officer of the day came in with a squad of men and bore orders from the commandant of the prison that the flag must be surrendered, peaceably or forcibly. Colonel Thorp, First New York Cavalry, was speaking at the time, and, turning to the officer, said: "Lieutenant, be pleased to say to Captain Gibbs that the flag we are rejoicing under is the property of the prisoners, and that it will not be surrendered peaceably, and that if he attempts force, twenty minutes afterward we will be burning and sacking the city of Macon." (Cries of "That's it!" "We'll do it!" "Now's the time!")

The guards stood amazed only a moment, for when they heard such ejaculations from the crowd as "Kill the d——d rebels!" "Take their guns from them!" "Rally to the gate!" they left the prison in a hurry, and it was the last time they ever demanded our flag, though its display was an every-day occurrence afterward. (Hadley, *Seven Months*, 73–75)

74. Litchfield was from Rockland, Maine.

Born in Union, Maine, Robbins enlisted as a private in the 4th Maine and was taken prisoner at Gettysburg. Robbins was a prisoner in eleven different southern prisons over a twenty-month period; he escaped frequently and was always recaptured ("Bowdoin in the War," 16).

75. President Davis had placed General Joseph E. Johnston in command of the Army of the Tennessee in December 1863, and Johnston had retreated skillfully in the face of Sherman's overwhelming strength. The two had engaged in a battle of maneuver throughout the Atlanta campaign. Many people in the Confederacy disliked Johnston, for they believed that he wasted his forces in unproductive retreats. In this particular campaign, however, it seems obvious that trying to goad Sherman into attacking him was the only possible way to injure Sherman's forces. Sherman had been trying unsuccessfully to catch Johnston in a weak defensive position or in a weak position on the march. At the end of June Sherman decided to assault Johnston's troops entrenched at Kennesaw Mountain, and he was severely repulsed. Johnston then withdrew to the Chattahoochee River, where he made a stand on July 4–9; Sherman turned his flank, and Johnston once

again moved his troops, this time to Peach Tree Creek. Before another battle could be fought, President Davis relieved Johnston of his command for lack of aggressiveness and replaced him with General John Bell Hood, who was brave but foolish.

76. The rumor was untrue. From Standish, Maine, Sturgis was surgeon in the 2nd U.S. Sharpshooters until that regiment was mustered out; he then returned to the 17th as assistant surgeon. He was mustered out with the 17th in June 1865.

77. The report was false. Rilliet was discharged in August, and Merriman in September of 1864.

78. Confederate authorities were concerned over the probable threat to the security of the prisons at Macon and Andersonville posed by Sherman's imminent capture of Atlanta. General Winder had made repeated requests for more troops to guard the prisoners, and it appears that by the end of July he had decided that he could not maintain the prison at Macon. Major General Samuel Jones, Confederate commander of the Department of South Carolina, Georgia, and Florida, wrote Richmond authorities: "I have just received [26 July] telegram from General Winder saying that by your authority he will send to Charleston on Thursday 600 Federal officers, prisoners of war, and continue to send until all the officers, prisoners, are sent. The presence of so many prisoners in Charleston will complicate negotiations for exchange of those now there. If the prisoners must be sent from Macon allow me to exercise some discretion as to where they shall be confined, and, if possible, give me a few additional troops" (*OR*, ser. 2, vol. 7: 502).

Indeed, Sherman and his troops were eager to get to Andersonville and Macon, for they were well aware of conditions there. In his memoirs General Sherman described the Union attempt to free the prisoners:

> On the 26th [July] I received from General [George] Stoneman a note asking permission (after having accomplished his orders to break up the railroad at Jonesboro') to go on to Macon to rescue our prisoners of war known to be held there, and then to push on to Andersonville, where was the great depot of Union prisoners, in which were penned at one time as many as twenty-three thousand of our men, badly fed and harshly treated. I wrote him an answer consenting substantially to his proposition. . . . [In early August] rumors came that General Stoneman was down about Macon, on the east bank of the Ocmulgee. On the 4th of August Colonel Adams got to Marietta with his small brigade of nine hundred men belonging to Stoneman's cavalry,

reporting, as usual, all the rest lost, and this was partially confirmed by a report which came to me all the way round by General Grant's headquarters before Richmond. A few days afterward Colonel Capron also got in, with another small brigade perfectly demoralized, and confirmed the report that General Stoneman had covered the escape of these two small brigades, himself standing with a reserve of seven hundred men, with which he surrendered to a Colonel Iverson. Thus another of my cavalry divisions was badly damaged. . . . Stoneman had not obeyed his orders to attack the railroad *first* before going to Macon and Andersonville, but had crossed the Ocmulgee River high up near Covington, and had gone down that river on the east bank. He reached Clinton . . . then went on and burned the bridge across the Oconee, and reunited the division before Macon. Stoneman shelled the town across the river, but could not cross over by the bridge, and returned to Clinton, where he found his retreat obstructed, as he supposed, by a superior force. There he became bewildered, and sacrificed himself for the safety of his command. He occupied the attention of his enemy by a small force of seven hundred men, giving Colonels Adams and Capron leave, with their brigades, to cut their way back to me at Atlanta. The former reached us entire, but the latter was struck and scattered at some place farther north, and came in by detachments. (William Tecumseh Sherman, *Memoirs of General W. T. Sherman*, ed. Charles Royster [New York, 1990], 561, 571–72)

79. There may have been some shelling of Atlanta about this time, but the effort was random. General Sherman had not yet begun his planned bombardment of the city. On August 7 he telegraphed Washington: "I do not deem it prudent to extend any more to the right, but will push forward daily by parallels, and make the inside of Atlanta too hot to be endured. I have sent back to Chattanooga for two thirty-pound Parrotts, with which we can pick out almost any house in town. I am too impatient for a siege, and don't know but this is as good a place to fight it out on, as farther inland. One thing is certain, whether we get inside of Atlanta or not, it will be a used-up community when we are done with it" (Sherman, *Memoirs*, 575).

80. McPherson was killed on June 24.

81. General Early had been causing havoc and had levied some $220,000 in Maryland. He was not effectively challenged until after August 7, when General Grant gave General Philip Sheridan command of Union forces in the Shenandoah Valley and sent him after Early.

82. Davis had been an assistant to General Winder. After his capture at Gettysburg, Davis had escaped from a federal hospital.

83. The officers were constantly trying to escape, and many succeeded, although just as many were caught. "One day a young officer from Massachusetts attempted to escape by passing himself off as one of the guards, and going out as others were going in; he obtained a pair of dirty grey pants, made, I think, of an old meal sack, that somehow was 'obtained'; he got an old slouch hat and a coarse cotton shirt; he passed the guard and got out of prison, and was going along when a rebel called out to him to stop, and on coming up said, 'You can't come that game on me, for your shirt is too clean. I know you are not a rebel.' Poor fellow! He came back quite reluctantly, A dirty shirt would have passed him out" (Jervey, *Prison Life*, 72).

84. Hadley describes the incident of the first tunnel:

> Tunnelling was a big business at Macon. There were three tunnels under way at one time, and all came near being successful. One was ready to be opened up the last of June, but to accommodate the managers of the other two it was delayed until the night of the 3d of July, when the others would be ready. The three had capacity to let every prisoner out by midnight, and thus afford an interesting time in Georgia on the Fourth of July. But the treachery of an Illinois Captain revealed the whole scheme, and our guards came in on the morning of the 3d without a guide and deliberately took possession of the holes. It is said that the Captain was promised a special exchange, and he probably got it, for, after the fact was learned by us through a negro, the traitor was taken outside and never appeared among us any more. (*Seven Months*, 70–71)

85. Mattocks is referring to article 77 of "Instructions for the government of armies of the United States in the field": "A prisoner of war who escapes may be shot or otherwise killed in his flight; but neither death nor any other punishment shall be inflicted upon him simply for his attempt to escape which the law of war does not consider a crime. Stricter means of security shall be used after an unsuccessful attempt at escape. If, however, a conspiracy is discovered the purpose of which is a united or general escape the conspirators may be rigorously punished even with death; and capital punishment may also be inflicted upon prisoners of war discovered to have plotted rebellion against the authorities of the captors whether in union with fellow-prisoners or other persons" (*OR*, ser. 2, vol. 5: 676).

Francis Lieber was born in 1798 in Berlin in Prussia, where he acquired in his youth a fervent liberalism. In the 1820s he immigrated to the United States. Although he hated slavery, he had a high regard for the Constitution and the Union, which led him to try to mitigate antagonisms between the North and South. As a professor at the University of South Carolina, he established his reputation as an expert in the law, a staunch defender of the Union, and an avowed opponent of secession. After the trustees of the university failed to elect him to its presidency in 1855, he resigned and moved North. Since 1853 he had seemed to consider conflict between the two sections inevitable, and with his move to the North he became a fervent and open critic of the South. Lieber's writings on international law and on the laws of military conflict were well known to General Henry Halleck, who himself had written a book on military tactics. Given the complexity of determining what was proper conduct in Civil War, the appointment of General Halleck as chief of staff was fortuitous for Lieber. Halleck asked the professor to "propose amendments or changes in the Rules and Articles of War and a code of regulations for the government of Armies in the field as authorized by the laws and usages of War." Lieber's efforts appeared in May 1863 as General Orders No. 100, entitled "Instructions for the Government of Armies of the United States in the Field" (Frank Freidel, *Francis Lieber: Nineteenth-Century Liberal* [Baton Rouge, La., 1947], 332–34).

CHAPTER SIX.
CHARLESTON AND COLUMBIA PRISONS

1. Among the fifty officers released was Major W. S. Baker, who wrote Mattocks's stepfather, Isaac Dyer, from Hilton Head, S.C., on August 4, 1864, and signed his letter "Late Prisoner of War": "Maj. Mattocks, 17th Me. now a prisoner in Charleston requests me to write you that 'he is well and in good spirits.' He did not request it but I would advise you to send him a small amount of gold, worth in Charleston from sixteen to twenty per dol. in confederate. I am sure he will receive anything sent to the care of Maj. Genl. Foster, Hilton Head, S.C. I left Charleston yesterday."

2. Sears was from Providence, R.I., and a paymaster in the U.S. Navy. He had been captured on February 1, 1864, at New Berne, N.C. After being exchanged on October 18, he wrote Secretary of the Navy Gideon Welles on October 27, 1864: "While confined in Charleston S.C. I was informed by a prominent *Union* citizen that all the signals made by our Fleet are understood by the Rebels on shore, and consequently they could prepare for any change . . . that might be

made. The above statement can be relied on, as I am well acquainted with the gentleman making the statement and know him to be a loyal citizen and staunch supporter of the present Administration" (Reports from Officers & Seamen of the U. S. Navy who Were Prisoners of War in the South . . . Nov. 1862 to July 1865, Navy Department. National Archives).

3. Lares and Penates were Roman gods who watched over the household or community; Penates were more specifically two gods of the storeroom.

Chaplain Humphreys gave the following description of the workhouse:

> There were four stories to the building, and as an awful reminder of our dangerous exposure there was a gaping chasm down through the roof and every floor, marking the track along which a shot from one of our batteries had forced its way to the cellar. The Swamp Angel battery was full five miles away, and yet every fifteen minutes of my three weeks' stay in this prison, a 200-pound shell from its belching jaws burst over our heads. About every fourth shell was loaded with Greek fire, and at night by its lighted fuse we could see it rise like a star from the horizon and ascend almost to mid-heaven, then gracefully curve downwards and burst and drip its liquid flame upon the roofs of the city. Then in a few moments we would hear the bells of the fire-brigade rush past our bars to try to stay the conflagration that almost inevitably ensued. The fate that awaited us if our prison caught fire was too horrible to imagine, and yet the danger was constantly before our eyes. At first the mere sound of the bursting shells—Gil[l]more's reports, as they were called—made us give a startled jump; but soon we got used to it, and their terrific explosion passed almost unnoticed in the daytime, and at night scarcely disturbed our dreams. (*Field, Camp, Hospital*, 134–35)

4. The fifty Union officers exchanged earnestly sought retribution for what they considered injurious treatment at the hands of the Confederates. They wanted the United States to handle Confederate prisoners exactly as they had been treated by the Confederates. One of the exchanged officers, Brigadier General Seymour, in a letter to the commissary-general of prisoners suggested that a commission

> draw up a code or rules, founded strictly upon their personal experience while prisoners of war, for the government of those Confederates while in U.S. custody.
>
> The subject of treatment of such prisoners has, of course, often

and fully presented itself for your consideration, but to us who have practically and personally experienced the attentions of Southern jailers, the subject is one of bitter remembrance, only to be referred to with vindictive and retaliatory spirit.

The Southern authorities claim that they give to prisoners precisely what their soldiers are allowed in the field. It is probably true of the ration, but of nothing else. The Southern soldier, even in his most prosperous days, lived simply upon the handful of corn and bit of bacon upon which he now is supported. Few Northern men, except in an almshouse—and I know of none that ever fed so scantily—were ever reduced to the common rule of diet of the Southern race. But beyond their ration the prisoner enjoys none of those essentials to cleanliness, and consequently to health, that are so strictly indispensable. Fresh air, water in abundance for washing and bathing, and opportunity for exercise have been rigidly ignored or forbidden. The most gross lack of administration has characterized their prisons. But, as already referred to, air and water have, although the cheapest luxuries in the Confederacy, been studiously refused, and this more particularly at Andersonville and at Macon, the most recently established of the depots for our captured soldiers. Why should not rebel prisoners be treated exactly like our own? . . .

The Southern authorities are exceedingly desirous of immediate exchange of all prisoners. . . . Their urgency is unbounded, but we [Seymour and Gen. Wessells] asserted that it was the poorest possible policy for our Government to deliver to them 40,000 prisoners, better fed and clothed than ever before in their lives and perfectly equipped for the field by Northern generosity, while the United States received in return an equal number of unfortunate men worn out with privation and neglect, barely able to walk, often drawing the last breath, and utterly unfit to take the field as soldiers.

But this anxiety on the part of the rebels is one of the strongest possible proofs of the failing strength of their cause. Between Lee's and Hood's armies the country is a waste, redeemed only by the labor of the females, the very young and very old male and the slave. Their last men have gone to the field of battle, and rather than re-enforce their armies as an exchange would do, it was urged that it would be much wiser, although hard upon our poor fellows, to let them stay yet longer where they now are. The South can be compelled to treat them well. Give Confederate prisoners the same measure of humanity that they mete out to us and there will soon be no dread or apprehension respecting the prisoner's life. And the fact that a set of rules openly and plainly declared to the world, over the signatures of officers who have themselves tasted of Southern prison fare, as the basis of future treatment, would in my judgment be a quick method of bringing Southern authorities to a just view of their obligations in this matter. (*OR*, ser. 2, vol. 7: 571–72)

5. Johnson had commanded T. J. Jackson's old division at Gettysburg and had been captured at Spotsylvania's "bloody angle." After the exchange he would once again be captured during the battle of Nashville.
6. Louis Napoleon was emperor of France; although he was a popular ruler, he is believed by many historians to have had the control of a modern dictator.
7. On August 18, 1864, Private Prescott Tracy was exchanged at Port Royal Ferry "to make up a small deficiency due at the last exchange at Charleston Harbor." Private Tracy had a petition written with the consent of the Confederate authorities by the prisoners at Andersonville to the United States government which he had brought to Charleston with him. Three privates had been elected to carry the petition to Washington. Tracy also carried a letter addressed to Abraham Lincoln given him by General George Stoneman for delivery to Union authorities. As Tracy explained:

> The petition enclosed was suggested by some of the rebel sergeants who call the role; they asked why we did not get up a petition to our Government. The authorities gave us the paper, and it was agreed, if we would tell nothing but the truth, it would be forwarded . . . to endeavor to effect a parole. I was one of the committee. I desire to be permitted to go to Washington, together with the three men, Bates, Higginson, and Noirot, and personally represent the case to the President. The statement was got up so as to pass the rebel authorities; it does not tell a tithe, no, not a thousandth part of our miseries.
>
> The letter from General Stoneman . . . was handed to me by General S. on the night before we started [for the exchange], when in Charleston prison. I hid it in my stock; my stock was taken away and thrown away by the rebels; I took it up again and brought it through, and did not take the letter out until I gave it to Colonel Hall, provost-marshal-general. I did not know its contents.
>
> The letter was dated August 14, 1864, and was signed by two colonels and General Stoneman, the ranking Union prisoner at Charleston. It read in part:

The condition of the enlisted men belonging to the Federal armies now prisoners to the Confederate rebel forces is such that it becomes our duty, and the duty of every commissioned officer, to make known the facts in the case to the Government of the United States and to use every honorable effort to secure a general exchange of prisoners, thereby relieving thousands of our comrades from the horrors now surrounding them. For some time past there has been a concentration of prisoners from all parts of the rebel territory to the State of Georgia. . . . Recent movements of the Federal armies by General Sherman have compelled the removal of the prisoners to other points, and it is now understood they will be removed to Savannah, Ga., and Columbia and Charleston, S.C., but no change of this kind holds out any prospect of relief to our poor men. . . . [*There follows a description of the trials of the prisoners.*]

Such statements as the following made by Sergeant Hindman, Ninety-eighth Ohio Infantry, speak eloquent testimony. Said the sergeant: "Of twelve of us who were captured, six died, four are in the hospital—I never expect to see them again—there are but two of us left." . . .

Few of them have been captured except in the front of battle in the deadly encounter, and only when overpowered by numbers; they constitute as gallant a portion of our armies as carry our banner anywhere. If released they would soon return to again do vigorous battle for our cause. We are told that the only obstacle in the way of exchange is the status of enlisted negroes captured from our armies; the United States claiming that the cartel covers all who serve under its flag and the Confederate States refusing to consider the negro soldiers, heretofore slaves, as prisoners of war. We beg leave to suggest some facts bearing upon the question of exchange which we would urge upon this consideration.

Is it not consistent with the national honor, without waiving the claim that the negro soldiers shall be treated as prisoners of war, yet to effect an exchange of the white soldiers? The two classes are treated differently by the enemy, the white is confined in such prisons as Libby and Andersonville, starved and treated with a barbarism unknown to civilized nations, the black, on the contrary, is seldom imprisoned; they are distributed among the citizens or employed upon Government works. Under these circumstances they receive enough to eat and are worked no harder than accustomed to; they are neither starved nor killed off by the pestilence in the dungeons of Richmond and Charleston.

It is true they are again made slaves, but their slavery is freedom and happiness compared with the cruel existence imposed upon our gallant men. They are not bereft of hope, as are the Union soldiers dying by inches. Their chances of escape are tenfold greater than those of the white soldiers, and their condition, viewed in all its lights, is tolerable in comparison with that of the prisoners of war now languishing in the dens and pens of 'Secession.'

While, therefore, believing the claims of our Government in matters of exchange to be just, we yet are profoundly impressed with the conviction that the circumstances of the classes of soldiers are so widely different that the Government can honorably consent to an exchange, waiting for a time to establish the principle justly claimed to be applicable in the case.

Let 35,000 suffering, starving, and dying enlisted men aid this appeal to the Chief Magistrate of the Republic for prompt and decisive action in their behalf; 35,000 heroes will be made happy. For the 1,800 commissioned officers, now prisoners, we urge nothing. Although desirous of returning to our duty, we can bear imprisonment with more fortitude if the enlisted men, whose sufferings we know to be intolerable, were restored to liberty and life. (OR, ser. 2, vol. 7: 615–22)

On August 21, General Grant wrote the following to Secretary of War Edwin Stanton: "Please inform General Foster that under no circumstances will he be authorized to make exchange of prisoners of war. Exchanges simply re-enforce the enemy at once, whilst we do not get the benefit of those received for two or three months and lose the majority entirely. I telegraph this from just hearing that some 500 or 600 more prisoners had been sent to General Foster" (OR, ser. 2, vol. 7: 662).

On September 6 President Lincoln penned the following to General Ethan A. Hitchcock, commissioner for the exchange of war prisoners: "Will Gen. Hitchcock please see private H.C. Higginson, who comes from our prisoners at Camp Sumpter[sic] Ga[.]" Hitchcock was one of the three privates released to carry the sergeants' petition (Basler, Works 7: 538).

8. Edward Bulwer-Lytton (Lord Lytton), "My Novel," or, Varieties in English Life (London, 1857). Bulwer-Lytton was an English politician and "dandy" who wrote many novels in addition to plays and poetry. He published historical novels, some novels of fancy, and a series of realistic novels among which My Novel is considered one of the finest. Bulwer-Lytton is described as "a writer whose restless and versatile talent took color from some fashions and helped to shape others. An opportunist alike in his parliamentary and

literary career, and driven on by need of money, he wrote too much and too fast in too many genres of literature" (Albert C. Baugh, ed., *A Literary History of England* [New York, 1948], 1364–65).

9. Sherman was from Connecticut and had served in the Army of the Cumberland. He was captured in May 1864 and would be paroled in October and would return to fight at Franklin and Nashville.

10. Modeled after the British Sanitary Commission created during the Crimean War, this organization was a result of the coming together of several women's organizations to improve the health of the military camps, to care for the wounded, to provide better food, and to augment the diet of prisoners of war as well as compiling accurate lists of the sick and wounded in the various camps.

11. Mattocks is probably referring to a combination of Mr. Micawber in Charles Dickens's *The Personal History of David Copperfield*, first published in book form in 1850, and to that same author's *Great Expectations*, which had been published in 1861. Although it appears that Mattocks had not yet read *David Copperfield* (see letter to his mother, September 2, 1864), the novel had made such a dramatic impact on popular culture that a college graduate would likely have been aware of Micawber's eccentricities.

12. Although it seems strange that Charles would have remained unaware of the one-page policy on letters for this long, it appears from his letter to his mother dated September 2, 1864, that he believed the restriction applied only to letters he wrote and not to letters he received.

13. Although the city was under bombardment, the original "Swamp Angel" was not involved. The "Swamp Angel" had been a two-hundred-pound eight-inch Parrott gun that the Federals had used to bombard the city in 1863. The gun used incendiary shells that could reach a distance of 7,900 yards; it caused a few fires but was unreliable and blew up on firing its thirty-sixth round. The Swamp Angel had been located on Morris Island at the southern part of the mouth of Charleston Harbor.

14. J. V. Hadley had his own explanation for the lack of Union casualties:

> The thousand Federal officers now in the town were scattered about through the city, "as exigencies of the service required." I must say, to the credit of General Foster, the Federal commander on Morris Island, that he seemed excellently well informed of the various changes of our localities. The Charleston papers complained bitterly of the police and city guards, because they could make no explanation of the mysterious rockets that could be seen almost nightly in different parts of the city, and more especially immediately after the removal of a party of Yan-

kees. General Foster perhaps could have given a better explanation than any policeman or guard in the city, for if a party of prisoners were removed into a locality directly under the scourge, perchance not another shell would come near; while a few hours afterward they would open up with terrible effect on the very place they had left. One example: Eighty-six of us were taken from the jail-yard to the private residence of Colonel O'Connor, on Broad Street, and while there, nearly two weeks, not a shell struck nearer than an eighth of a mile. A party of Confederate officers, for convenience and safety, took quarters within a hundred yards of us. We were removed about noon, the Confederates remaining, and that night a two-hundred-pound shell from Foster's guns came crashing through the house, killing the provost marshall and a captain instantly, and badly wounding a lieutenant. During our confinement of about a month, the only casualty among us was one man slightly wounded in the hand. (*Seven Months*, 83–84)

15. With the bombardment of Charleston by Union batteries, the Confederates first transferred prisoners of war to the city to attempt to stop what they considered the inhumane treatment of women and children and the unnecessary destruction of private property. By August, however, they were transferring prisoners to Charleston because they had nowhere else to put them. Union officials were incensed that Confederate authorities were deliberately placing Union officers in danger and, although exchanges had largely ceased in all theaters of the war, Union officials made exceptions for prisoners in Charleston partly in order to get them out from under the bombardment. In August Union authorities decided that more direct measures should be taken to protect their officers who were prisoners from bombardment, and on August 8 General Halleck informed General Foster: "The Secretary of War has directed that 600 rebel officers, prisoners of war, be sent to you, to be confined, exposed to fire, and treated in the same manner as our officers, prisoners of war, are treated in Charleston" (*OR*, ser. 2, vol. 7: 567).

General Foster had written General Samuel Jones, commander of Confederate forces in South Carolina, Georgia, and Florida on August 15:

I have received information from deserters and also from prisoners of war that were exchanged for your prisoners on the 3d instant, that a large number of officers of the U.S. Army, reported at about 600, are exposed to our fire in Charleston.

I am surprised at this repeated violation of the usages of humane and civilized warfare, as I had hoped that the exchange of our prisoners formerly exposed would have ended the cruel treatment on your part. I have, therefore, again to protest against it and to inform you that unless the prisoners are removed from Charleston and from under our fire an equal number of your prisoners of war now in our hands will be exposed to your fire. (*OR*, ser. 2, vol. 7: 598)

General Jones replied on August 20:

You are mistaken if you suppose those prisoners have been sent here for the purpose of being placed in positions where they may be reached by your shot. They are placed here by the Government simply because it is found more convenient at present to confine them here than elsewhere. When proper arrangements are made for their accommodation elsewhere they may be removed, but their removal will not be hurried or retarded by your threat to place an equal number of C.S. officers, prisoners of war, under our fire. . . . You will permit me to add that the only treatment received by the prisoners of war now in our possession that is in disregard of the usages of civilized warfare they receive at the hands of their own Government. They are certainly as prisoners of war justly entitled to fair and honorable exchange, and that their Government denies them.

I am ready at any time to send you every prisoner of war now in this department if you will give me in exchange an equal number of C.S. prisoners, man for man, rank for rank, or their equivalents. (*OR*, ser. 2, vol. 7: 625)

All Confederate prisons were filled beyond capacity, and a new stockade being built at Millen, Ga., was not yet ready. The Confederate authorities were now in the condition President Lincoln and General Grant had predicted and wanted. In spite of the bombardment and on the general matter of exchange, what President Lincoln referred to as "an old and painful subject," General Hitchcock summed up the feelings of the Union authorities: "The only sure remedy for the abominations practiced in the South by the enemy is to defeat his armies." And so it went, day in and day out (*OR*, ser. 2, vol. 7: 575).

16. Henry H. Hunt was born in Gorham, Maine, and after graduating from Bowdoin enlisted in the 5th Maine Battery. At this time he was serving in the Army of the Potomac, having been part of its campaign from the Rapidan to the James, and presently was in the Shenandoah Valley under Sheridan ("Bowdoin in the War," 29).

17. Vickars was in the 4th New Jersey Infantry.

18. Burger had enlisted at age twenty-eight as a lieutenant in the 1st New York Engineers on October 10, 1861. He is listed as an adjutant by December 31, 1861. He went to work on the Georgia Sea Islands for General Gillmore in March 1862 and remained in that vicinity for the duration of the war (Combined Service Records. National Archives).

19. Lieutenant H. A. Johnson, also a prisoner in Charleston, remembered the shelling as entertainment: "Gen. Foster paid not the slightest attention to the demand to cease firing upon the city on account of our exposed position, but, if anything, increased the severity of the siege. As the casualties among the prisoners from this artillery duel were very small, (being so well sheltered in these buildings,) we rather enjoyed this change in our prison life. We liked to watch the effect of these hundred pound shells from guns four miles away, to hear them come tearing into the city, see them strike buildings, watch them crumble and after a while be destroyed by these terrible engines of war" (Johnson, *Sword of Honor*, 21).

20. As Mattocks insinuates, the prisoners were grasping at straws: "Mobile, August 30—A flag of truce boat arrived today bringing letters and papers from New Orleans. From prisoners captured in Mobile Bay, we learn that the Confederate Surgeons, prisoners, are to be sent over by the first boat to Pascagoula.

    "The Federal and Confederate Agents of Exchange have come to a perfect understanding. The prisoners on either side are to be exchanged shortly. Six vessels are off Dog river bar this evening" (*Charleston Daily Courier*, Aug. 31, 1864).

21. Morris Island fronts the Atlantic and forms the southern part of the entrance to Charleston Harbor. At this time part of the island was occupied by Federal troops.

22. Woodford was lieutenant colonel of the 127th New York; in March of 1865 he would be colonel of the 103d U.S. Colored Infantry and would serve as the Military Governor of Charleston.

23. A similar experience was recounted by Daniel Avery Langworthy:

    One of our number, who was a major in the regular army, started a secret society [while we were imprisoned in Macon], which I joined, and which soon grew to hundreds. The object of the organization was for mutual help. It was organized as a regiment, with companies, etc. The major was the colonel.

    One day in July a detail was ordered to be ready to move at a certain hour the next morning. They were ready, but waited for an hour or more. The major and many of our new order were in the detail, including myself. While waiting, several of our organization exchanged places and thereby got in so that when we marched out our society was well represented. We were put on board a train of box cars and started east, arriving at Savannah about nightfall. We were unloaded and were there in the yards an hour or two. While waiting, the major said to us, "I have learned that we are going North, I think to Charleston. When we get about so far from here we will be only about twelve miles from our men at such a place on the coast. I will be sure to get in the front car and will detail officers to be in command of each of the other cars. They will detail men to look after the guard in their cars. At the proper time I will swing a lantern out of the side door of the front car and swing it around as a signal for you to overcome the guards in your cars. Take their guns and care for them and when the train stops jump out and overcome the guards on the top of the cars, in the rear car and then march for the little station on the coast."

There were four or five guards in each car and about the same number on the top and one group commanding the rear car. We all sat on the floor, including the guards. I was in command of one of the cars and watched very sharply for the light, but it did not show up. The major had learned that there was suspicion of something being done and did not think it best to take the risk. We all knew apparently when we approached where we should see the light, and as it did not show up the men soon began to tumble out of the side doors. Upwards of one hundred of them got out of the cars in a comparatively short time. The guards on top fired at them. I do not know whether any of our boys were hit or not, but within a few days after our arrival at Charleston all of them, except four or five, were with us, showing the efficiency of the organization for the recapture of escaped prisoners." (*Reminiscences of A Prisoner of War and His Escape* [Minneapolis, 1915], 27–29)

24. Rice was a first lieutenant in the 75th Ohio Regiment; he escaped from Columbia on December 13.

25. Alexander William Kinglake, *The Invasion of the Crimea; its origin, and an account of its progress down to the death of Lord Raglan* (New York, 1863–88). The first two volumes of Kinglake's *Crimea* were published in 1863. Kinglake was a British historian and barrister who was born in 1809 and died in 1891. He visited the Crimea at the time of the war and met Lord Raglan.

In 1856 Lady Raglan asked Kinglake to undertake a history of the war, which he did with extraordinary research and a felicitous style.

26. The Republican-Union party had met in convention in Baltimore in June and nominated Abraham Lincoln for president and Andrew Johnson for vice-president. The Democratic party had met in late August in Chicago and had nominated George McClellan, the one-time commander of the Army of the Potomac, for president, and George H. Pendleton from Ohio for vice-president.

27. Mattocks, like most Union sympathizers, either chose to overlook, or was unaware of, prison conditions in some places in the North. The issue of the treatment of prisoners of war was emotional and easily subject to exaggeration and propaganda. Also few people, South and North, comprehended the magnitude of the needs and demands created by this war. The immediacy and magnitude of the issues surrounding prisoners seemed to exacerbate all the other problems of both governments, and captured men both in the North and in the South suffered.

Among the many descriptions of poor prison conditions in the North is that by the Confederate, Anthony M. Keiley, who was captured in early 1864 and spent five months at two Yankee prisons, Point Lookout and Elmira. Here is part of his description of life in Point Lookout:

> The routine of prison-life at Point Lookout was as follows: Between dawn and sunrise a "reveille" horn summoned us into line . . . and here the roll was called. . . . About 8 o'clock the breakfasting begins. This operation consists in the forming of the companies again into line, and introducing them under lead of the Sergeants, into the mess-rooms, where a slice of bread and a piece of pork or beef—lean in the former and fat in the latter being contraband of war—are placed at intervals of about twenty inches apart. The meat is usually about four or five ounces in weight. These we seized upon, no one being allowed to touch a piece, however, until the whole company entered, and each man was in position opposite his ration. . . . The men then busy themselves . . . until dinner time, when they are again carried to the mess-houses, where another slice of bread, and rather over a half pint of a watery slop, courtesy called "soup," greets the eyes of such ostrich-stomached animals, as can find comfort in that substitute for nourishment. . . . For my part, I never saw any one get enough of any thing to eat at Point Lookout, except the soup, and a tea spoonful of that was *too much* for ordinary digestion.
>
> These digestive discomforts are greatly enhanced by the villainous

character of the water, which is so impregnated with some mineral as
to offend every nose, and induce diarrhoea in almost every alimentary
canal. It colors every thing black in which it is allowed to rest, and a
scum rises on the top of a vessel if it is left standing during the night,
which reflects the prismatic colors as distinctly as the surface of a
stagnant pool. . . .

Another local inconvenience is, the exposed location of the post.
Situated on a low tongue of land jutting out into the bay, and, as I
have before remarked, but a few inches above ordinary high tide, it is
visited in winter by blasts whose severity has caused the death of
several of the well-clad sentinels, even, altho' during the severest
portion of the winter of 1863–4, they were relieved every thirty
minutes—two hours being the usual time of guard duty. And when a
strong easterly gale prevails for many hours in winter, a large potion
of the camp is flooded by the sea, which finds convenient access by
means of ditches constructed for the drainage of camp. When this
calamity befalls the men, their case is pitiable indeed. The supply of
wood issued to the prisoners during the winter was not enough to keep
up the most moderate fires for two hours out of the twenty-four, and
the only possible way of avoiding freezing, was by unremitting
devotion to the blankets. This, however, became impossible when
everything was afloat. (Harwell, *The War They Fought*, 321–24)

28. General Hood abandoned Atlanta on September 1, and Sherman's troops
entered the city the following day. In his *Memoirs*, General Sherman remembered that

orders had been sent back to him [General Slocum] to feel forward
occasionally toward Atlanta, to observe the effect when we had reached
the railroad. That night I was so restless and impatient that I could not
sleep, and about midnight there arose toward Atlanta sounds of shells
exploding, and other sounds like that of musketry. I walked to the house
of a farmer close by my bivouac, called him out to listen to the rever-
berations which came from the direction of Atlanta (twenty miles to the
north of us), and inquired of him if he had resided there long. He said he
had, and that these sounds were just like those of a battle. An interval of
quiet then ensued, when again, about 4 A.M., arose other similar
explosions, but I still remained in doubt whether the enemy was engaged
in blowing up his own magazines, or whether General Slocum had not
felt forward, and become engaged in a real battle.

> The next morning General Hardee [whose Confederate forces had opposed us] was gone, and we all pushed forward along the railroad south, in close pursuit. . . . While bringing forward troops and feeling the new position of our adversary, rumors came from the rear that the enemy had evacuated Atlanta, and that General Slocum was in the city. Later in the day I received a note in Slocum's own handwriting, stating that he had heard during the night the very sounds that I have referred to; that he had moved rapidly up from the bridge about daylight, and had entered Atlanta unopposed. His letter was dated inside the city, so there was no doubt of the fact. (Sherman, 581–82)

29. President Lincoln had despaired of being reelected, but the capture of Atlanta gave the Union the major victory Lincoln's campaign needed. On September 3 Lincoln issued this order: "The national thanks are herewith tendered by the President to Major General William T. Sherman, and the gallant officers and soldiers of his command before Atlanta, for the distinguished ability, courage, and perseverance displayed in the campaign in Georgia, which, under Divine favor, has resulted in the capture of the City of Atlanta. The marches, battles, sieges, and other military operations that have signalized this campaign must render it famous in the annals of war, and have entitled those who have participated therein to the applause and thanks of the nation" (Basler, *Works* 7: 533).

30. Confederate officers in Charleston were adamantly opposed to the movement of more prisoners into the city. On September 5 General Samuel Jones wrote Confederate Secretary of War James A. Seddon: "Brigadier-General Gardner informs me that a large number of prisoners have been ordered from Andersonville to this place. Please have the order revoked or send me additional troops. It is with great difficulty that these now here can be guarded; no others can be at present" (*OR*, ser. 2, vol. 7: 773).

31. Jones replaced General Beauregard as commander of the Department of South Carolina, Georgia, and Florida in March of 1864.

32. Luther Porter was Charles's mother's brother.

33. Alexandre Dumas's *The Three Musketeers* first appeared in the United States as *The Three Guardsmen* (Baltimore, 1846); it was published along with its sequel *Twenty Years After or The Three Mousquestaires. A Sequel to the Three Guardsmen* (Baltimore, 1846).

34. It appears that prisoners paid varying amounts for supplies provided by the citizens of the city. At this same time Colonel John Fraser of the 140th Pennsylvania was paying up to three dollars a quart for milk (John Fraser, *A Peti-*

tion Regarding the Condition in the C.S.M. Prison at Columbia, S.C. Addressed to the Confederate Authorities, ed. George L. Anderson [Lawrence, Kans., 1962], 15).

35. Fort Warren is located in Boston Harbor. At this time Federal officials were preparing to transfer all Confederate naval officers who were prisoners at Johnson's Island in Ohio to Fort Warren. No mention is made of an alderman in the *OR*.

36. In his introduction to Colonel John Fraser's *Petition*, George L. Anderson states, after reviewing much of the literature created by the ex-prisoners of war:

> There are extremely few references in the statements made by the prisoners to instances of individual philanthrophy *[sic]* on the part of southern residents. If some credence can be placed in the testimony provided by those who shared Fraser's experiences, the people in the cities and towns resented the presence of the prisoners and considered that whatever was given to them was too much and too good. A gift from a fellow member of the Masonic lodge; the consistent, but small scale efforts of the Sisters of Charity in Charleston; and an occasional crust of bread or cup of water from a by-stander, seem to have been the only exceptions to the general attitude of hostility and indifference. The prisoners had to depend for their survival upon the official rations supplemented by what they could buy with their own funds.
>
> These seem to reflect Mattocks's experiences and his reflections on them (*Petition*, 16–17).

37. One of the first men imprisoned at the "race course" left this description of the conditions on the first day:

> We were placed in the centre of the Fair Ground, with no shade or habitations, except such as we might construct from our garments or ragged blankets; but there was a cool breeze from the ocean, and the sound of bells and the rattle over pavements came pleasantly to the ear. The sight of green foliage refreshed the gaze of miserable men, for a long time unused to pleasant sights and sounds. . . .
>
> On the morning following, the people of Charleston came in flocks to see the Yankees. A majority of these were women. Some few came with food to sell, but were not allowed to trade over the guard line with prisoners. Others, actuated by pity, watched for chances, and, when the rigor of the guard was relaxed, threw cakes, potatoes, or some like luxuries, over the guard line among the wretched creatures who gathered

waiting for luck to favor them in some manner. (Warren Lee Goss, *The Soldier's Story of His Captivity at Andersonville, Belle Isle, and Other Rebel Prisons* [Boston, 1868], 190–92)

An officer who had a direct experience with one of the Sisters left this vivid anecdote:

> The general in command of the Confederate forces at Charleston was a Roman Catholic, hence his church people, and especially the Sisters of Charity, had free access to the hospitals, prisons, etc., and did much good work.
>
> A few days later I noticed some sisters in our building. I went to one of them and said: "Sister, have you been out to the race course?" "Yes," she said, "We have just come from there." "How are they?" I asked. "Very, very bad," she replied. . . . "You poor men have suffered enough, but not what they have; they are very bad." "Sister," I continued, "there are some of my men there whom I have not seen since they went to Andersonville prison last April. I would like to learn all I can about them." "They are very bad," she said, "that is about all. We tried to minister to one poor fellow this morning. In giving him a bath we scraped quantities of maggots from under his arms and other parts of his body. They are very, very bad." "Sister," I persisted, "if they had some money would it be of any help to them?" "Yes, it would. They could not get with it what you would think they should, but they could get something and that would be a help to them." "Will you be going there again soon?" I asked. "Yes, we will go there every few days," she replied. "Could I ask you to take some money to one of my men?" "I would be pleased to do so," she said. "Is he a non-commissioned officer?" "Yes, a sergeant," I replied. "I will be here awhile longer," she said. . . . I went and did as she told me to do and gave her the letter [with the money]. A few days later I saw some sisters in the building, and going to them saw her to whom I had given my letter a few days before, and spoke to her. "Yes, captain," she said, "I was going to look you up. We just came from the race course. I feel quite sure I found your man and gave him your letter. . . . Well, when we got there inside the race course, they all came around us, hoping we would do something for them," she said. "I asked for Mr. Jones. Nearly all the men there were named Jones. I did not tell them any more, but began asking questions. A few less were George Jones, a few less George Washington Jones, a few less were sergeants and in Company 'E,' and in the Eighty-fifth New York,

etc., until I got down to one man and am quite sure he was the right one." I thanked her and told her how greatly I was obliged to her, and said: "Sister, I certainly have no reason to doubt what you say, but cannot understand it." "How so?" she asked. "I know those men thoroughly," I said, "and know them not only to be good soldiers, but truly honest, truthful, upright, manly men." "That's right, captain," she said, "but as I told you before, you have not suffered and passed through what they have. I believe that if you or I had been through with what they have we would not be one whit different from what they are and in my heart I cannot blame them." (Langworthy, *Reminiscences*, 32–35)

38. "The yellow fever broke out among us at Charleston. This is the king of terrors to the Southern people, and as he took hold on us with determined fatality, our guards became much alarmed. It was among us five days in the city, and it was reported that out of thirty cases among the prisoners, not one recovered. In this calamity we were visited by the Sisters of Charity. Every day after the fever broke out, and occasionally before, these pale-faced, devout, veiled creatures made their rounds of the prison, with their baskets of medicine and food for distribution among the sick. It was touching to see them moving about the prison in pairs, heeding none but the suffering, and ministering to them with that pious dignity and tenderness characteristic of their order. The personal sacrifices of these women was surprising. Whether it was fanaticism, or rational devotion to Christian duty, is not for me to say, but theirs was the only faith strong enough to reach us; and in the day of final account it is not apt to go unrequited by the dispenser of just judgments" (Hadley, *Seven Months*, 84–85).

Another prisoner was even more graphic about the conditions in which the Sisters were willing to work:

A sutler was appointed for the camp, who was not allowed to ask of prisoners higher prices than asked in the city. This was a convenience to those who had money, but the great majority had none. The sutler's store of goods contained by few varieties—black pepper, unground, turnips, sweet potatoes, and baker's bread. Ten dollars in Confederate money for one in greenbacks was the general rate of exchange; and this was obtained through the Sisters of Charity, who visited us, doing acts of kindness to the suffering, bringing clothes and food, carrying messages to our officers, prisoners in the city, and bringing the reply. To people so clean we must have been objects of disgust. The vermin, visible upon all prisoners, could not have been pleasant to refined persons, unaccustomed to such misery. Our dirt-begrimed, half-naked persons must have been revolting, yet no word or look from these kindly Sisters showed shrinking or disgust. I have seen them bending in prayer or in offices of mercy over almost naked creatures, whom disease and filth had rendered indescribably loathsome, never, by word or look, showing other feeling than pity, and never making the object of their care feel humiliation or shame. (Goss, *The Soldier's Story*, 195–96)

39. Winder had been too old for battlefield command and was put in charge of prisons in Richmond. In June 1864 he was assigned to command Andersonville, and in July he assumed charge of all prisoners in Alabama and Georgia. At Andersonville, on June 30, 1864, Winder issued General Order No. 57: "A gang of evil-disposed persons among the prisoners of war at this post having banded themselves together for the purpose of assaulting, murdering, and robbing their fellow-prisoners and having already committed all these deeds, it becomes necessary to adopt measures to protect the lives and property of the prisoners against the acts of these men, and, in order that this may be accomplished, the well-disposed prisoners may and they are authorized to establish a court among themselves for the trial and punishment of all such offenders" (*OR*, ser. 2, vol. 7: 426).

40. General Winder was not removed. He died on February 6, 1865, while continuing to try to better prison conditions.

41. Mattocks's mother wrote him on September 15:

Last night your Father sent me your letter to him, dated Aug. 26. I hope he complied at once with your request in sending what you need. He has opposed me about sending any thing. In my last letter but one I enclosed by way of experiment a gold dollar. He has opposed my sending the box. I am uneasy about it, but I am up here [in Baldwin] and all my things are in town. And you know how it is. And he constantly answers me with "I think he will be at home this week." To me it is all hope deferred. But I have no great confidence that you will get any of my letters and only live in hopes that what every body says must be true "That you will soon be exchanged." (Mother to CPM, Sept. 14 and 15, 1864, Baldwin, Maine)

42. On October 2, 1863, Secretary of the Navy Gideon Welles opened a correspondence with Confederate officials concerning the possibility of the general exchange of naval prisoners. By some mistake Welles's proposal did not reach the Confederate Navy Department. In July 1864 Confederate Secretary

of the Navy Stephen Mallory learned of the proposal, and on August 20 he accepted the terms of the exchange. However, on October 5 President Lincoln sent the following note to General Grant:

> I inclose you a copy of a correspondence in regard to a contemplated exchange of naval prisoners through your lines, and not very distant from your headquarters. It only came to the knowledge of the War Department and of myself yesterday and it gives us some uneasiness. I therefore send it to you with the statement that as the numbers to be exchanged under it are small, and so much has already been done to effect the exchange, I hope you may find it consistent to let it go forward under the general supervision of General Butler, and particularly in reference to the points he holds vital in exchanges. Still, you are at liberty to arrest the whole operation if, in your judgment, the public good requires it. (*OR*, ser. 2, vol. 7: 924)

General Grant agreed, but the question of the exchange of the captured crew of the Confederate raider *Alabama*, which had been sunk by the U.S. *Kearsage*, complicated the matter for a time. The exchange finally took place at City Point, Va., on November 16 (*OR*, ser. 2, vol. 7: 661–62, 924–25, 961, 1132–33, 1158–59).

43. On September 4 General Foster informed General Jones: "I this day learn from recently released prisoners that our Union officers are still kept by you under the fire of our guns. I have therefore to inform you that your officers, now in my hands, will be placed by me under your fire, as an act of retaliation" (*OR*, ser. 2, vol. 7: 763).

44. There seems to have been no foundation for the rumor.

45. Mattocks and his fellow prisoners faced being moved inland but not for the reason he gives. For several weeks General Jones had been trying to persuade the officials in Richmond that he had to reduce the number of prisoners in Charleston in the face of a probable attack: "An advance in such force as was made in July last would compel me to withdraw all guards from the prisoners and trust to the railroad authorities to remove them without guards other than such as the companies could furnish. I respectfully urge that the prisoners be sent away from Charleston and Savannah. Small as my force is I would rather detach a part of it to guard prisoners at some point in the interior rather than be embarrassed by their presence at two such important and exposed points" (*OR*, ser. 2, vol. 7: 789).

46. The entry in H. A. Johnson's diary reads: "Sept. 17. Shells from our guns

caused a large fire last night, destroying twenty-nine buildings, several shells striking our prison, not doing much injury" (*Sword of Honor*, 22).

47. Foot, who was in the 92nd New York Infantry, would escape from Columbia on December 12.

48. Lieutenant Commander Pendergrast, who was from Yarmouth, Maine, had been captured in Ossabaw Sound, Ga., on June 3, 1864. In a letter dated June 8, 1864 he wrote General Sam Jones, CSA, from "Charleston Jail":

> that we have always expected to be treated as such [prisoners of war], this treatment has not been accorded us, in any of the many prisons in which we have been confined, and we are, at this moment occupying a prison designed for the safe keeping of Criminals and felons, a part of whom are let loose upon us every day. For the last two days, rations of such a kind have been issued to us, which are better calculated to increase starvation than support life, and even if the rations of your government, had been issued to us the want of proper cooking utensils would have rendered it impossible to have eaten them.
>
> The dirt and piles of filth which surround us on all sides in such a confined place without any system of police, and with only the scanty shelter afforded us after being exposed to rain and the almost tropical rays of the sun for 50 hours, even before this slight shelter was given us will necessarily generate disease and soon commence the work which the conduct of your government evidently indicates, and secretly desire but, are restrained from doing, by the fact that such an act must, sooner or later, become public to the world. . . .
>
> I need not remind you that the officers and crew of the *Atlanta* and other of your navy who have been unfortunate enough to fall into our hands have met with far different treatment than we have experienced at the hands of confederate states officers.
>
> Hoping this communication will meet your early consideration and induce you to remove us from the vile associations connected with this building.

In a letter to Gideon Welles dated October 24, 1864, Pendergrast explains that to the above "I received no answer" (Reports from Officers & Seamen of the U. S. Navy who Were Prisoners of War in the South . . . Nov. 1862 to July 1865, Navy Department. National Archives).

49. Mattocks's mother wrote him on September 24: "You must not allow

yourself to think us Stupid and dilatory because we have not sent Money to Capt. Burger. It is only because we think you will not get it. Every thing appears so uncertain. One of the Express Men Said he should consider it no more probable than if we tossed a feather in the air. A favorable wind might waft it to you. . . . You need have no fear that because you give considerable attention to boxes, we shall think you are unmindful of us. I am glad to have you make yourself comfortable if you can. And will do all I am allowed to do for you" (Mother to CPM, Sept. 24, 1864, Portland).

50. Governor Cony, who proved to be both able and popular, was handily re-elected.

51. Major General Benjamin Butler sent his "justification of the action of this Government" on the matter of prisoner exchange to the *New York Times* on September 5 because the Confederate Commissioner on Exchange had printed his offer for an agreement on exchange in the public press before Butler had had a chance to reply. Mattocks and his fellow prisoners probably read Butler's "justification" in the *Times* (*OR*, ser. 2, vol. 7: 768–69).

When Benjamin Butler had been named commissioner for exchange, Confederate officials were infuriated. Because of actions he had taken while he had presided over the occupation of New Orleans—he had issued the infamous "Woman Order" in which he ordered any woman on the streets of the city who was disrespectful of Union soldiers to be treated "as a woman of the town plying her avocation," and he had ordered hanged a man who had pulled down from a public building the flag of the United States—Butler had made himself the very symbol of Yankee contempt for the Confederacy. In a deliberate attempt to be insolent, Confederate officials in charge of exchange corresponded on the issue with Butler's subordinates rather than have anything to do with the general. A firm supporter of the use of African Americans as soldiers, Butler was determined to protect the rights of captured black Union troops. In August of 1864 he wrote Robert Ould, the Confederate Commissioner of Exchange, the following:

> Your note to Major Mulford, assistant agent of exchange, under date of 10th of August, has been referred to me.
>
> You therein state that Major Mulford has several times proposed to exchange prisoners respectively held by the two belligerents, officer for officer, and man for man . . . ; that you now consent to the above proposition, and agree to deliver to you (Major Mulford) the prisoners held in captivity by the Confederate authorities, provided you agree to deliver an equal number of officers and men. As equal numbers are delivered from time to time they will be declared exchanged. This

proposal is made with the understanding that the officers and men on both sides who have been longest in captivity will be first delivered, where it is practicable.

From a slight ambiguity in your phraseology, but more, perhaps, from the antecedent action of your authorities, and because of your acceptance of it, I am in doubt whether you have stated the proposition with entire accuracy. . . .

In May last I forwarded to you a note desiring to know whether the Confederate authorities intended to treat colored soldiers of the U.S. Army as prisoners of war. To that inquiry no answer has yet been made. To avoid all possible misapprehension or mistake hereafter as to your offer now, will you say now whether you mean by "prisoners held in captivity" colored men, duly enrolled and mustered into the service of the United States, who have been captured by the Confederate forces, and if your authorities are willing to exchange all soldiers so mustered into the U.S. Army, whether colored or otherwise, and the officers commanding them, man for man, officer for officer?

At an interview which was held between yourself and the agent of exchange on the part of the United States, at Fort Monroe, in March last, you will do me the favor to remember the principal discussion turned upon this very point, you, on behalf of the Confederate Government, claiming the right to hold all negroes who had heretofore been slaves and not emancipated by their masters, enrolled and mustered into the service of the United States, when captured by your forces, not as prisoners of war, but, upon capture, to be turned over to their supposed masters or claimants, whoever they might be, to be held by them as slaves.

By the advertisements in your newspapers, calling upon masters to come forward and claim these men so captured, I suppose that your authorities still adhere to that claim; that is to say, that whenever a colored soldier of the United States is captured by you, upon whom any claim can be made by any person residing within the States now in insurrection, such soldier is not to be treated as a prisoner of war, but is to be turned over to his supposed owner or claimant, and put at such labor or service as that owner or claimant may choose; and the officers in command of such soldiers, in the language of a supposed act of the Confederate States, are to be turned over to the Governors of States, upon requisitions, for the purpose of being punished by the laws of such States for acts done in war in the armies of the United States.

You must be aware that there is still a proclamation by Jefferson

Davis, claiming to be Chief Executive of the Confederate States, declaring in substance that all officers of colored troops mustered into the service of the United States were not to be treated as prisoners of war, but were to be turned over for punishment to the Governors of States. . . .

If . . . you are so willing to exchange these colored men claimed as slaves, and you will so officially inform the Government of the United States, then, as I am instructed, a principal difficulty in effecting exchanges will be removed. . . .

The wrongs, indignities, and privations suffered by our soldiers would move me to consent to anything to procure their exchange, except to barter away the honor and faith of the Government of the United States, which has been so solemnly pledged to the colored soldiers in its ranks.

Consistently with national faith and justice we cannot relinquish this position. With your authorities it is a question of property merely. It seems to address itself to you in this form: Will you suffer your soldier, captured in fighting your battles, to be in confinement for months rather than release him by giving for him that which you call a piece of property, and which we are willing to accept as a man?

You certainly appear to place less value upon your soldier than you do upon your negro. I assure you, much as we of the North are accused of loving property, our citizens would have no difficulty in yielding up any piece of property they have in exchange for one of their brothers or sons languishing in your prisons. Certainly there could be no doubt that they would do so were that piece of property less in value than $5,000 in Confederate money, which is believed to be the price of an able-bodied negro in the insurrectionary States. (*OR*, ser. 2, vol. 7: 687–91)

Ever watchful of the rights of those he was sworn to protect and keenly aware of the trickery of which men in public life were capable, he himself being adept at political manipulation, Butler continued careful negotiations on these issues, making sure to personally review all correspondence on the matter. Ever vigilant for the political or legal trap, on September 18 General Butler wrote Secretary of War Stanton concerning the discussions over the exchange of prisoners who had been convicted of a crime

before some competent tribunal of offenses known to municipal law, the laws of nations or of war. . . . It will be seen that Mr. Ould is willing to make exception of those convicted or held under charges of breaches of municipal law, but not of the laws of war or of nations, and that he expressly puts into his exception whether the breaches of municipal law occurred before or after the capture of the prisoners of war. In that sentence of Mr. Ould there is ground for very careful reflection, because the Confederate States hold that the freeing of slaves is a breach of their municipal law and they may claim to hold any one of our prisoners of war as excepted from the proposition, because of some supposed breach of their laws in regard to slaves.

Indeed, that is the very ground of Davis' proclamation in regard to turning over officers of the United States to the Governors of the several rebel States for punishment, and I think that before we should agree to the proposition finally this matter should be very carefully scanned and critically examined. (*OR*, ser. 2, vol. 7: 839)

52. Charles had always taken pride in his physical condition. In 1860 he wrote his mother: "Our new Gymnasium wears well. We shall give a *public exhibition* in about a week when a few of the best will perform. I am one of the '*Deacons*' on Gymnastics, *sure*. My *muscle* is quite a sight to behold, and still it is growing daily" (CPM to Mother, Nov. 11, 1860, Topsham, Maine).

In his next letter Charles explained that he missed the college gymnasium, "But I am not to be cheated out of cultivating my *muscle* and accordingly I have constructed a private *Gym*. . . . I am in just the best health (as far as I can see) that a mortal can be. . . . I am very *tough*" (CPM to Mother, Dec. 18, 1860).

53. Mattocks's feelings about Charlestonians were shared by other Yankee prisoners. One of the first to be brought to the city described the behavior of its people on initially seeing Yankee prisoners: "The shell and shot from Gilmore's [*sic*] batteries had a civilizing influence over its people, for in no place were we so kindly treated by citizens and soldiers as in Charleston. Women and children looked pityingly upon us, and such expressions as 'Poor fellows!' 'Too bad!' &c., showed pity and sympathy for our condition, which we had never before experienced in the Confederacy" (Goss, *The Rebel's Story*, 187).

54. Smith was in the 16th Iowa, and McKibbin was in the 14th U.S. Cavalry. They both lost their paroles, for they were among the prisoners at Camp Sorghum in Columbia in early November. Smith escaped from Columbia on November 12.

55. Generals Hood and Sherman had carried on an "angry" correspondence concerning the possibility of exchanging prisoners since the fall of Atlanta. The exchange Mattocks mentions was reported to Washington in a letter of October 1 (*OR*, ser. 2, vol. 7: 907–8).

56. Sheldon belonged to the 15th South Carolina Infantry.

57. General Jones wrote Richmond officials from Charleston on September 29: "I have sent an officer to Columbia to endeavor to procure a place of confinement for Federal officers, prisoners, and will send all prisoners from here as soon as possible; the enlisted men all to Florence. The prevalence of yellow fever as an epidemic makes this necessary precaution. I recommend that a few acclimated troops be sent here for duty in the city" (*OR*, ser. 2, vol. 7: 894).

58. The Union prisoners remained at the depot because the Confederates had not prepared for this movement:

> Commandant Jones, on October 4th, succeeded in getting some cars, and away we went to Columbia, S.C., without letter or despatch, and fell upon that high place of treason like a thunderbolt; and had we been all armed, and commanded by Sheridan, we could hardly have surprised them more. The provost marshal, who seemed to be a pretty clever kind of an enemy, fretted and complained a good deal, insisting that it was an imposition so suddenly to send fifteen hundred prisoners to him, without even a chicken-coop, or a dozen men at his command. He at first refused a receipt to Cooper, the Charlestonian, for the prisoners, but after some altercation and compromise the matter was fixed up in such a way that Cooper could stay with his men and take charge of us until other arrangements could be made. (Hadley, *Seven Months*, 85)

Other prisoners were not as reticent as Mattocks about their reception: "Placed in an open field and kept in the burning sun all day without shelter of any kind; no rations of any sort given us for the past twenty-four hours. Toward night it commenced raining and continued throughout [*sic*] the night, and we prisoners, without any protection, without blankets or coats, passed a sleepless and most miserable night" (Johnson, *Sword of Honor*, 23).

South Carolina officials had opposed the construction of a prisoner-of-war camp close to Columbia. The controversy further delayed the construction of a proper prison camp, and prisoners were arriving to an open field with no provisions for their incarceration. Having first written the war department on October 6 with his protest, South Carolina's governor, M. L. Bonham, received the following reply, dated October 12: "I will consent to locating the prison at any safe and convenient point in the State upon which you and he [the engineer in charge of construction] may agree, making it a condition that you will render him every assistance . . . to accomplish a speedy completion of the work. This is necessary, because a removal will delay proceedings and there exists now the greatest need of the establishment" (*OR*, ser. 2, vol. 7: 975).

Not satisfied with his negotiations, on October 29 Bonham wrote directly to President Jefferson Davis: "I feel it my duty to call upon you to stop the proposed construction of the prison camp within four miles of the capital. . . . It seems to me that there should be no prison camp within twenty or thirty miles of the capital of a State. It increases the temptation to raids, and can, of course, add nothing to the defenses of the place. . . . The place selected is not healthy, as I learn from Dr. Gibbes, surgeon-general, a physician of long standing in this community, and has nothing which should have induced its selection in preference to many others at a distance from this place" (*OR*, ser. 2, vol. 7: 1062).

On 12 November the issue was finally settled as J. A. Seddon, secretary of war, wrote Governor Bonham: "Instructions have been given, in deference to your views, to discontinue construction of prison at Columbia." The governor had won, but the prisoners being held at Columbia had lost, for the decision meant that a proper prison would not be made available, but the prisoners would remain (*OR*, ser. 2, vol. 7: 1151).

59. Lieutenant Charles O. Hunt, a member of Mattocks's mess, later described the arrival in this way:

> Arriving in Columbia the next day, we were "yarded" like so many cattle, in a small enclosure near the station. It was large enough for us all to lie down, but not much more. There were about fifteen hundred of us. During the afternoon there was a heavy shower, which soaked everything we had on, as well as our blankets, and rendered the ground a quagmire; and in this condition we were obliged to worry away the night, sleep being out of the question. . . . The next day we took up our line of march for our new quarters. We were taken out of the city, and across the river Congaree by the covered bridge, which was burned the next spring when Sherman made his appearance on the other bank, opposite Columbia. After marching two or three miles, we were turned off from the road a short distance into an old field partly covered with scrub pines, where we were halted and a line of guards thrown round us, and we were informed that this was our destination. They made promises that plenty of tents would soon be furnished us, but like most of the rebel promises to prisoners, they were not intended to be kept, but only to keep us quiet. The tents were never given us, and all the time we were there, we had to take the weather as it came, with only such shelter as could be made out of pine boughs, or by sacrificing blankets which were needed for bedding. Our mess was rather better off in the way of supplies than most; for when in Charleston we had with us two naval officers, who were exchanged, and left to the rest of us their supply of

blankets, and a small mattress that one of them had obtained in some way. So, with two blankets put up for a tent, and one end closed with brush, we managed to be partly sheltered during the rains. But many of the men had no blankets, and must have suffered very much, especially late in the season. (Charles O. Hunt, "Our Escape From Camp Sorghum," *War Papers Read Before the Commandery of the State of Maine . . .* [Portland, 1898], 85–86)

Another officer also gave a description of the camp:

Late in September, by another transfer, we found ourselves [the officers from Macon, Savannah and Charleston] together again at Columbia. We had no form of shelter, and there was no stockade around the camp, only a guard and a dead-line. During two hours each morning an extra line of guards was stationed around an adjoining piece of pine woods, into which we were allowed to go and cut wood and timber to construct for ourselves huts for the approaching winter. Our ration at this time consisted of raw corn-meal and sorghum molasses, without salt or any provision of utensils for cooking. The camp took its name from our principal article of diet, and was by common consent known as "Camp Sorghum." A stream of clear water was accessible during the day by an extension of the guards, but at night the lines were so contracted as to leave the path leading to the water outside the guard. (Shelton, "A Hard Road," 251)

60. Lieutenant Commander Williams, U.S.N., a prisoner in Charleston, was allowed to go north to try to effect his exchange in September. Having failed to do so before his parole was up, he remained in the North, believing that he would automatically be included among the next group to be generally paroled. He was omitted by mistake but subsequently exchanged (OR, ser. 2, vol. 7: 873–74, 1158–59).

61. Fontaine wrote a good deal about his Civil War adventures in the years after the war. He was especially fond of telling of the attempts to exchange him. While he was a prisoner on Morris Island, a Union officer came to see him, and "he then asked if I had any influence with Hardee. I asked what kind of influence he meant. He then replied that they were very anxious to obtain the exchange of some Rebel Major for a Major Harry White of Pennsylvania. I replied that there was not a Yankee in Charleston that General Hardee would not give for me. He arose and said: 'Then you are the man we are hunting for.'"

Then Fontaine was allowed to read the letter Harry White had sent to the Confederates asking to be exchanged: "The contents of that letter were of such a cringing, fawning, snivelling, sycophantic, mean and base, beggarly tone, that I could hardly read it." Fontaine then sent a verbatim copy to General Foster and asked General Hardee if he could send a copy to his Cousin Dick Meade with an explanation attached; General Hardee agreed, and Fontaine sent the letter with the following appended: "Dear Dick, this is a copy of a letter written by a Yankee officer, for whom I have been sent from the Stockade on Morris Island to be exchanged for. I positively, and emphatically, refuse to be exchanged for such a —— —— —— ——. I will rot in prison first, and he may do the same."

In his letter White had written that he would never in any capacity again serve the United States government. Fontaine considered that cowardice, and faced with Fontaine's ire, Hardee suggested that Fontaine go to the prison where Federal officers were being held and select a major for whom he would wish to be exchanged. So Fontaine ended up at Roper Hospital, where he said to the Yankee prisoners: "Now, I want a Yankee gentleman to swap places with me. . . . Now, I want a Yankee Major, understand, who, when he gets back into his own lines, will fight me to a finish, do his duty, and give me a chance to kill him, or he to kill me. And I want one who, when he gets home, will not lie, but tell the truth, about how he was treated while he was a prisoner in our hands. Now, gentlemen, from a casual glance, I cannot select this Major, but I leave you to choose him" (Lamar Fontaine, *The Prison Life of Major Lamar Fontaine* [Clarksdale, Miss., 1910], 29–35).

62. As eager as Charles was for news from the 17th, especially, one suspects, news concerning the ongoing drama over leadership of the regiment, he would have been keenly interested in what happened in the regiment on the previous day: "On the twelfth of this month [October 1864] Lieut. Col. Merrill received an honorable discharge from the service, he having previously resigned his commission, and Maj. Mattocks, who was still a prisoner, was promoted to his place. On the same day Col. West, having partially recovered from the effects of his wound, returned and took command of the regiment." (Whitman, *Maine in the War For The Union*, 456).

63. Gen. Foster had appointed Woodford as "Agent of Exchanges for Department of the South," a title that Foster created in order to permit Woodford to take over the duties of arranging for all special exchanges and seeing to the delivery of all packages and money sent to Union servicemen who were prisoners of war. Later, Foster was ordered to abolish the title and the duties associated with this task (*OR*, ser. 2, vol. 7: 1119).

64. Lieutenant General Hardee had been named commander of the Department

of South Carolina, Georgia, and Florida in September of 1864, and had the impossible task of stopping General Sherman's March to the Sea.

65. Fontaine had been angered at the conditions of his imprisonment. In his book *The Prison Life of Major Lamar Fontaine*, the major described his capture and treatment: "On the 12th day of May, 1864 . . . in the fearful charge to recover our breastworks, in the 'Bloody Angle,' at Spotsylvania Court House, in Virginia, I was shot down, and left upon the field, and, with the other wounded Confederate soldiers, removed to the hospital tents, under our own surgeons. Our army moved forward, and left many of our wounded behind, I, among the rest. A few days afterwards the Yankees appeared and took us all prisoners." (7).

Fontaine was transported to Morris Island, where "by will-power alone I followed my companions into our stockade, a pen about three hundred feet square. Here, [we were] surrounded by the 54th Massachusetts negro regiment, nominally under the command of Col. C. D. Shaw. . . . This stockade was a few hundred feet, just in front of Battery Wagener. . . .

"We had to dig holes in the sand, and drink the siep water, which was of a stale, brackish taste. We had old Sibly 'A' tents, put up in streets, with four men assigned to each tent, out on the hot sand bar, in the blazing September sun, with a hundred brutal negro soldiers watching you day and night" (Fontaine, *Prison Life*, 7–26).

66. On this date Captain Burger wrote Mattocks's mother the following letter, in which he points out that Charles was responsible for his own frustration over the lack of mail because of the constant advice to his mother to write long letters:

> I have the extreme pleasure of informing you, that the box sent by you to my care for your son Maj. Mattocks, was received by me this day, and will be sent to the Major by the First Flag of Truce. I was obliged to open the box and take out your letter, for fear that the rebel authorities would reject the box on account of it, as it was much over one page in length. In looking for the letter I discovered a little spare room in the box and filled it up with some coffee, tea and condensed milk; as I am assured that such articles can be sent to special friends I have written to the Major informing him of what I have done, and also giving him all the points of your letter, that I could squeeze on one page, and have retained the original with the other one both subject to your order or the Major's. If I can possibly get these originals across the lines I will most certainly do so. I notice that you complain very much to the Major because your letters do not reach him; but if you will confine yourself to one page of letter paper there

will be no trouble. Thousands of letters are received for every Flag of Truce, and all have to be read twice, once by the reviewing officer on this side of the line and again by the reviewing officer on the other side. Consequently the rule of one page has been established on each side of the lines. When a letter is opened and found to be over one page it is immediately put into the waste basket without being read. Fortunately I have not this duty to perform, for I should dislike very much to destroy a letter, written under such circumstances, simply because they are too long. Letters to your son, if enclosed to me will be examined by myself, and will always go by the next Flag of Truce. I having but a few sent to me in this way. The reviewing officer has so many to pursue that almost every flag he is obliged to let some remain over for want of time to examine them. Letters that I mark go immediately in the mail bag and are not examined again until received by the rebel authorities; they are more particular than ourselves. I have requested the Major to send his letters to you, enclosed to my address, in which case they are not examined on this side of the line (coming from a Union officer) and I can always forward them to you at once.

67. Mattocks was right on the mark. Although the question of freeing and arming the slaves had arisen earlier, by September 1864 the issue was being openly debated by the members of Congress in Richmond and in the Confederate press. Feelings on both sides ran high, and for the rest of 1864 the issue was debated theoretically. It was not until March 1865, with defeat imminent and with the expressed approval and urging of General Robert E. Lee, that the Confederate Congress passed a bill allowing the arming of slaves; even this act, however, left the question of freedom for those slaves ambiguous: "Nothing in this act shall be construed to authorize a change in the relation which the said slaves shall bear toward their owners" (Emory M. Thomas, *The Confederate Nation: 1861–1865* [New York, 1979], 292–96).

68. Grant's army was at this time laying siege to Petersburg. Grant had no plans for capturing Richmond except as a by-product of the entrapment and destruction of Lee's army in the confines of Petersburg.

69. At this time General Sherman was pursuing General Hood north of Atlanta and, by the end of the month, would decide to cease the fruitless chase and send General Thomas to destroy Hood while he took the cream of his army through Georgia to the sea.

70. Foster had chosen Bennett to replace Woodford while Woodford was on leave.

71. After the war Fontaine and Mattocks carried on a correspondence, which Fontaine tells about in his book. He quotes a letter from Mattocks dated

February 21, 1890, in which Mattocks refers to the letter Harry White had written that had so insulted the Confederate major:

> This letter, instead of going to Richmond got into our lines and was opened, and the matter was brought to the attention of our government [that White had said he would never serve again] and orders were immediately issued that this Major was not to be exchanged for you, and that nobody else would be taken except myself. I was suddenly hurried to Pocataligo, S.C., expecting to be exchanged for your own good self. After going to our lines three days in succession in the hope of being exchanged, I was informed by Secretary of War Stanton that special exchanges had been stopped in that section, which I thought was either on account of the yellow fever or Stanton's peculiar views on the negro question. (Fontaine, *Prison Life*, 36)

Fontaine was freed on December 15, 1864.

In his book Fontaine went on to explain that in 1898, when Mattocks was serving as a brigadier general and encamped at Chickamauga, he had invited the ex-Confederate to visit him and his troops, among whom were some Mississippians. Fontaine made that trip. Finally, the raconteur, who became somewhat of a controversial celebrity, says of Mattocks: "When the roll is called in the last grand encampment beyond the Mystic river, I will feel no hesitancy to grasp the hand of Charles P. Mattocks, Soldier, Statesman and Patriot, of Portland, Maine, and answer 'HERE,' in his presence. There was but few like him in that great army that poured down upon the beautiful land of Dixie in those dark, bloody days, that are now echoing far away in the dim and misty past" (Fontaine, *Prison Life*, 38–39). For an article that claims that Fontaine was a genuine hero, see James H. Stone, "Lamar Fontaine's Civil War Tales," *Tennessee Folklore Society Bulletin* 39, no. 4 (1973): 107–10.

72. Captain Burger forwarded this note to Mrs. Hunt; in his own letter explaining the circumstances to her, Burger showed some irritation at CPM's situation: "Cannot some of the Majors *Male* friends or relatives endeavor to use a little influence at Washington, and get him exchanged for a *Major Lamar Fontaine of the 2d Alabama,* (Rebel). He is now at Hilton Head and the exchange could be made here" (W. L. M. Burger to Mrs. Hunt, 21 October 1864, Hilton Head, S.C.).

73. Pierre Soulé was born in France but escaped from that country after being jailed for opposing the government in 1825. Soulé was admitted to the Louisiana bar and served as senator from that state from 1847 to 1853. He was

named minister to Spain in 1853 but was expelled in 1855 for plotting against the government. He lived in New Orleans during the early part of the Civil War and was arrested by order of General Benjamin Butler, who explained to Secretary Stanton:

> Having been fully convinced by strong proof collected since this city has been occupied by my command that Mr. Pierre Soulé ... has been and still is engaged in plotting treason against the United States Government I ordered him to be arrested ... [and] transferred ... as a political prisoner. ... The charges against him and the evidence of his guilt elicited are as follows: Charge 1.—That Pierre Soulé is a member and the leader of a secret society known as the Southern Independence Association, of which each member is solemnly sworn to "allegiance to the Southern Confederacy and to oppose forever the reconstruction of the old Union at the peril of his life if necessary, whatever be the fate of the war and to whatever extremities and disasters treachery or incapacity may reduce the country," and "each and every member further pledges himself to assist to the utmost of his power in carrying out all laws of the Confederate Congress and all laws of the respective States composing the Southern Confederacy which have for their object resistance to the United States by armed force or otherwise, the retaliation of injuries, the confiscation of property and the detection and dispersion or punishment of spies and enemies in our midst."
> ... Mr. Soulé's influence and position, social and political, here render him in my judgment so dangerous, his treason so flagrant, the overt acts so plain, that I send him forward to the Government at Washington. Had he been actually in arms I should have tried him by military commission and executed the sentence, and will do so now if so directed by the Department. (*OR*, ser. 2, vol. 3: 612)

Soulé once again escaped and went to Charleston to assist General Beauregard; as part of rendering services to the Confederacy, Soulé went to Europe and tried to recruit a foreign legion. After the war he returned to New Orleans, where he resumed his law practice.

74. General Foster had been liberal in his exchange policies, but early in October he had received from General Halleck the following, dated October 5: "The Secretary of War is not pleased that you should, without authority, send paroled officers to New York to negotiate personal exchanges through the War Department. Hereafter when prisoners of war come into your lines under parole for special exchange their cases will be reported for the action of the War Department; but until notified of that action you will not allow

them to leave your department, except to return on the expiration of their paroles" (*OR*, ser. 2, vol. 7: 925).

75. The order here referred to by Mattocks appears to be missing. Indeed, on October 13 General Hardee forwarded the following to General Foster:

> You were informed in a communication addressed to you by Major-General Jones, then in command of this department, that the Federal prisoners of war at that time in Charleston might be removed to other localities.
>
> It is proper to say that as these prisoners were not sent to Charleston to be placed under the fire of your batteries they have all been removed from the city. It is hoped the communication of this fact will cause the removal of the Confederate prisoners of war from Morris Island to a place of greater security.
>
> I propose in the interest of humanity, to make an exchange of all prisoners of war in your possession, man for man, officer for officer, or their equivalents; or, if this be too general, to exchange the men and officers captured in our respective departments, as has been recently done by Generals Hood and Sherman. (*OR*, ser. 2, vol. 7: 981–82)

Hardee appears to have been eager to continue the exchanges. Perhaps Mattocks confused the names and meant to write General Foster, who had on October 17 responded to General Hardee's communication of the thirteenth in the following way: "In the matter of exchange, I would state that I have at present no authority to make exchanges, either special or general, but will forward your communication in reference thereto to the U.S. authorities at Washington" (*OR*, ser. 2, vol. 7: 1007).

76. A fellow prisoner gives another version of this event: "One night a sentinel fired at a prisoner who was inside the dead-line and where he had a right to be, but the guard asserted that he thought the prisoner was intending to run the guard. The man aimed at escaped unharmed, but another prisoner, quietly sitting on the ground, received the bullet in his breast and died in a few hours" (James E. Fales, *Prison Life of Lieut. James M. Fales*, ed. by George N. Bliss [Providence, 1882], 49–50).

77. "If you will have through your influence North My Son—F. W. Dantzler, My Nephew E. L. Dantzler, and their two cousins C. H. Hart and F. C. Hart furnished with a blanket, pair of shoes, and such under and outer clothes as they need, I will guarantee to you upon the *square* and *words* of a *Master Mason* to furnish *you* or your *friend* its equivalent in Confederate money or such provisions as you may *elect* if within the reach of my

cabletow; you being allowed to receive it, and taking *Gold* as the basis"
(Lewis Dantzler to CPM, Oct. 25, 1864, Vance's Ferry P.O., S.C).

78. At this time Colonel John Fraser of the 140th Pennsylvania Infantry, a
former college professor of mathematics, was preparing a petition from the
officers incarcerated in Camp Sorghum addressed to Confederate Lieutenant General Hardee protesting conditions in the prison camp. The petition
is contained in a notebook that Fraser kept while in prison; in that notebook Fraser included the names of officers imprisoned in the camp, among
which is the name of Charles P. Mattocks of the 17th Maine Infantry. According to the editor of Fraser's petition, it was probably finished sometime
after November 11, that is after Mattocks had escaped. This editor also
believes after examining the statements of Fraser's fellow prisoners that the
petition was "moderate and restrained." The petition read in part:

> As union prisoners of war we have had heretofore almost uniformly
> good reasons to complain of rations short in quantity & very inferior in
> quality, of an extremely inadequate supply of cooking utensils, & of
> very long detention of letters, monies & boxes from home, but never
> before we were placed in this prison have we had reason to complain
> that the confederate authorities had aggravated these standing grievances
> ten fold by exposing us as they have done here to the inclemency of the
> weather in a camp in which not a structure of the humblest kind had
> been erected for our accommodation. . . .
>
> During the first fortnight of our imprisonment here, there were
> only eight very unserviceable axes among 1400 officers, six of which
> were private property. Subsequently twelve new axes were issued to us
> by the commandant of the prison. With these twenty axes, & with 14
> spades which were also issued for our use, we have erected such
> shelters as were practicable under the inevitable embarrassments
> caused by the restrictions of prison discipline. At present most of us
> have only very rudimentary shelters of pine branches. . . . Our great
> want of adequate shelter makes us all feel the more keenly the other
> hardships of our prison life. Many officers weak & sickly from long
> confinement & insufficiently supplied with clothing, blankets & shoes
> have suffered severely from cold & rain. The want of shelter makes us
> especially feel the want of proper rations. No meat or lard has been
> issued to us for the past forty days.
>
> In conclusion we can affirm with truth that we have not exagger-
> ated any thing or set down aught in malice. The gravity of our case has

made us very careful that an action in the premises should not be impaired by exaggeration or abuse. (*Petition*, 27–30)

CHAPTER SEVEN. ESCAPE

1. There is irony in a letter Capt. Burger sent to CPM's mother on November 13, before Burger learned of the escape: "I am very glad indeed that you did not mention to your son the fact of the endeavors now being made by Mr. Dyer to effect his exchange, as in case of a failure, the disappointment would have been most severe" (W. L. M. Burger to Mrs. Isaac Dyer, Nov. 13, 1864).

   On the other hand, it appears from a letter from Burger written a month later, that Isaac Dyer never went to Washington. Dyer's "endeavors" were restricted to the mails: "Mr. Dyer, in my opinion, could accomplish more in one day by going to Washington than he could in a month by writing provided he has any acquaintance with any of the officials" (Burger to Dyer, Dec. 11, 1864).

   Burger finally learned of CPM's escape in mid-December and wrote Mrs. Dyer: "I was also informed that about one week after the Major succeeded in making his escape an order for his exchange was received" (Burger to Dyer, Dec. 15, 1864).

2. "About the first of November, there was a storm which left the ground covered with about six inches of snow. This caused fearful suffering, and we held a mass meeting and sent a committee, composed of generals and colonels, to see the major commanding the prison. This committee told the major that we must have wood for fires, or we should break through the guard at any cost of life, as we thought death by bullets better than freezing to death. The major said he had no men to cut wood for us, but that he would allow one or two squads of twenty to go out of the prison to cut wood for the others, if the prisoners thus going out would give their parole not to escape" (Fales, *Prison Life*, 50–51).

   Lieutenant Charles O. Hunt had been with Mattocks since Macon. Hunt escaped from Camp Sorghum with Mattocks, and after the war he wrote an account of the escape and read it on December 3, 1890, before the Maine Chapter of the Military Order of the Loyal Legion of the United States. This was the same group before which Mattocks read his own paper entitled "In Six Prisons." The collected papers of this chapter of the Loyal Legion were published in 1898 as volume 1 of *War Papers*. . . .

   In his paper Hunt described how the "mess" came to decide on their method of escape:

Every few days a wood party was made up. Its members signed a parole not to escape, and they were allowed to go to the woods without a guard, and cut and bring to camp as much wood as they could. One would have supposed that the rebels would have been sharp enough to compel the party to go out and come in, in a body. But instead of that, they allowed them to go and come as they chose, making several trips, generally two or three together in order to carry the heavier logs. I do no[t] think any of the men violated their parole, strong as the temptation must have been when they found themselves alone in the woods. But it was soon discovered by the prisoners that it was possible for some who had not given their parole to pass out with the rest when making their second trip, without being detected. As our little apology for a tent was on the front line of the camp, near where the parties went out, we soon caught on to this little dodge, and determined to seize the first opportunity to make a strike for freedom. (Hunt, "Our Escape," 89)

3. There was an unusual reason for caution:

Others had gone out with the wood parties, as we were planning to do. But we also knew that, almost without exception, they had been caught and brought back. It was not so difficult to get out of the prison camp, but the real difficulty was in traveling so far through their country to reach a point held by our troops. At that period of the war almost every able-bodied man was in the army, and the mere appearance of two or three men in the country, even if disguised by citizen's clothes, was sure to excite suspicion. . . .

As it was cold and rainy, a blanket could be worn over the shoulders without being noticed, for this was a common practice. Litchfield and Mattocks did this, but I, fearing lest it might excite suspicion to see so many blankets going out, decided to put on an extra flannel shirt instead.

Almost directly opposite our little tent was the camp of the guard, with the officers' tents nearest the prison enclosure. Still farther away was a road running easterly and westerly, the same by which we came out from the city of Columbia. The wood party went out this road toward the west for some distance and turned to the right into the woods.

When the right time seemed to have come, we started boldly toward the guard line, bearing off to the left, so as to strike the line some distance from the camp of the guard. As we approached the line,

to our disappointment, the sentinel halted us. One of the party
explained that we were going out for the rest of our wood. His reply
was that we could not get out there. I remarked as carelessly as
possible, "Never mind, boys, we can get out at post No. 1," which
was the one directly in front of the officers' quarters. The guard only
said, "He may let you out if he chooses, but you can't get out here."
So we sauntered along the line to post No. 1. Just before we reached
the post, Mattocks, who was in advance called out, "Come, hurry up,
boys, or those other fellows will steal all the wood we have cut," and
following we marched past the guard without being challenged. As we
passed through the camp of the guard we held our breath, and with a
good deal of effort restrained our impulse to hurry. The road was soon
reached, and walking as rapidly as we dared, we soon came to the
woods. (Hunt, "Our Escape," 89–91)

Among the many others who had similar experiences was Hadley:

We had not long to wait. A party of eight or nine men were approaching. I set out alone, aiming to reach the dead-line from the inside about
the same time and place they would reach it from the outside. As we
met I communicated my design in a low tone. They favored me, threw
down their wood and gathered together while I glanced to the right
and left to see that no guard was looking in my direction. In a moment
I was in the party; and seizing a handspike from the hands of one of
them, laid it across my shoulder, and we all started for the woods. My
blanket was spread over my haversack and shoulders, but this created
no suspicion, for the day was so bad that every man who had a
blanket had it on. There were two other blankets in the party I joined,
and I walked out through the guard-line within ten feet of two
Confederate muskets, and within easy range of fifty, without any
guard being the wiser. (*Seven Months*, 100–101)

4. Hunt explained:

Our [prison] camp was on the west side of the river Congaree,
opposite Columbia. We saw, by our map, that the Saluda River made a
junction with the Broad, forming the Congaree, near Columbia, but on
account of its small size we could not tell whether the junction was above
or below the bridge by which we crossed the city. . . . It was about three
P.M., when we left Camp Sorghum, and we lay here till about 5.30 P.M. It
was then quite dark, but there was light enough to see the compass and

get our direction. We had not gone far before we found ourselves on the bank of a wide, deep river. Here, then, was the Saluda, above us instead of below, as we hoped. . . . The river at this point must have been from one hundred and fifty to two hundred yards wide. Mattocks was a good swimmer, Litchfield was only fair, but I was a poor one. In hunting along the bank, we found two small pieces of plank, partly water soaked. They could not have been more than six or eight feet long, for I remember that in swimming with our feet, unless we were careful, we kicked each other. We all wore high boots. . . . Whatever the reason, we went into the water with all our clothes on [including our boots]. The bank was steep with deep water close up, and it was some time before we found a place where we could get a footing on the edge of the stream, preparatory to our final plunge. The blankets were folded and put on the two ends of the planks. Mattocks had a watch which he put into his hat. Litchfield had the right, Mattocks, the left, and I the center. All things ready, we stepped off into deep water, with our hands on the plank and swimming with our feet.

The water was very cold, our blood was thin, and the chill of that plunge is still very vividly remembered. In the darkness we could not very well estimate the width of the river. Our progress was slow, and after long effort, I looked back over my shoulder and said despondently, "Mattocks, the shore we have left looks much nearer now than the other side." I shall never forget Mattocks' reply. It was characteristic of the man. "Don't look back. Look ahead and kick out." He was always plucky and never despondent under the most discouraging circumstances. Then came another long struggle in silence. Finally Litchfield broke out in despairing tones, "My God, Mattocks! we never can get across." Again Mattocks' cheery reply was, "Yes, we can. Look ahead and kick out." I must confess visions of our dead bodies floating down the river came up before me very vividly. But still we struggled on, till at last, when it seemed as if all our powers were exhausted, we reached the other shore. (Hunt, "Our Escape," 90–93)

5. Hadley attests to the unusually bad weather:

The 4th of November, 1864, was a very bad day. It had been raining almost incessantly for thirty-six hours, with a brisk, cold, east wind blowing, and in the afternoon there was some snow driving through the rain. Probably not a dry thread could be found on all the 1,500 prisoners. Grouped together here and there around a little, smoky, green pine-wood fire, they sat wrapped in whatever clothing they might have—wet, cold, hungry, and disconsolate. It was one of the gloomiest times we saw in prison. With nothing to eat but meal and molasses, the meal wet and sour, winter approaching and no shelter, nor hope of exchange, everybody was blue and cross, and quarrels and blows were so frequent that they ceased to attract attention. (*Seven Months*, 97)

6. Hunt explains more clearly the problem with their feet: "We soon realized that we had made a mistake in not taking off our boots and stockings before swimming the river. For, with these wet, we had not walked far before our feet were blistered in many places. This was the cause of much suffering for a long time" ("Our Escape," 94).

7. The apprehension Mattocks and his companions felt was shared by all the officers imprisoned at Columbia, for although many escaped, most were soon returned. On November 7, H. A. Johnson recorded in his diary: "Thirteen officers who had some days before succeeded in getting by the guard at night, were recaptured; every white man in the country is hunting rebel deserters or escaping Yankee prisoners" (*Sword of Honor*, 24).

8. "At this time, as in all subsequent cases, when we wanted help from a negro, we always told him plainly that we were Yankee officers who had escaped from prison, and needed his help. We never met one who showed any disposition to betray us to the whites. Most of them showed great willingness to help us all they could. Some seemed inclined to get an equivalent for the food they gave us, and I remember one surly fellow who would have nothing to do with us, and would not so much as talk with us, but even he promised that he would not inform his master of our being in the neighborhood" (Hunt, "Our Escape," 95).

Escapees were amazed at the help they received from slaves and free blacks. No matter in what direction the fleeing Yankees headed, African Americans were willing to risk much to help them escape. When H. A. Johnson escaped from Camp Sorghum, he was protected for days at a time by slaves and passed from one black guide to another as he tried to make his way: "Remained in a corn house during the day, the blacks bringing us plenty of food. At night our guide informed us that he could not take the road with us until the following night, so we are obliged to wait one day longer; but it may be as well, for the negroes report that Sherman is nearing Augusta. If so we may attempt to strike his army rather than continue our long tramp to Knoxville, Tenn.

"Nov. 27. Still at Ford's plantation, where we are kept secreted during the day, but at night go to the negro cabins where we are plentifully fed."

Johnson knew what this help could mean for the slaves: "Every mile we advanced toward our journey's end, Tennessee, the stronger was our regard for the poor blacks; for the feeding or assisting an escaping Federal Soldier was the promise of 100 lashes, well laid on. And knowing this would certainly follow, they never failed to meet us with full hands and willing hearts, and even after their hard day's work, they were never too weary to guide us on our journey to places of safety." (*Sword of Honor*, 28, 32–33).

Escapees who headed for the coast encountered the same friendly aid. Morris Foote escaped from Camp Sorghum on November 29, hoping to make his way down the Congaree and Santee rivers to the coast, where he might be able to hail a gunboat:

> At dark we ventured out and went up to the Negro cabins. We were soon surrounded by a wondering crowd of two or three dozen men, women and children. We confided in them fully, told them who and what we were and said we wanted some kind of a boat and provisions to enable us to go down the river and escape to a free land. After some consultation, they decided that it was too late to attempt anything that night. Boats of any kind were scarce and they would have to hunt one up. It would be better for us to hide until the next night when they would try to have some kind of a boat ready and would start us off, as we were then near the river.
>
> It was not thought safe for us to stay in their cabins, so we were put in an old corn barn where we made a comfortable bed among the bundles of cornstalks and had a good rest and sleep which we were much in need of. We remained concealed in the barn all the next day, keeping a lookout through the chinks. We watched the overseer of the plantation, heard him swear at the Negroes, and once he rode so near the old barn that we were afraid he would discover us. (Morris C. Foote, "Narrative of an Escape from a Rebel Prison Camp," *American Heritage* 11, no. 4 [June 1960]: 68)

Hadley's experience was similar:

> We depended mostly upon the negroes for direction and food, and applied for their assistance nearly every night. About ten o'clock, when everything was quiet, we would approach their quarters, all going up within two hundred yards, when two would stop, a third go within one hundred yards, and the commander go alone to the huts. The negroes were remarkably familiar with each other and the country for a radius of ten or fifteen miles. They seemed to be acquainted with every peculiar tree, or stone, or cow-path, within that distance. If we were among a lot

of negroes at night, before leaving we would ask them to give us the
names of one or two of the oldest and most reliable negro acquaintances,
ten, twelve, or fifteen miles ahead, or as far as we aimed to go that night.
They were always able to give us the name, Joe, Jim, or Jerry, and to tell us
precisely where to find them. Their descriptions were very minute, and
would generally give the number of the cabin in the row, the position in
relation to the cotton-gin, pig-pen, or massa's house, just the safest way to
approach, whether there were any dogs, and if so, how many and how fierce.

There was not an instance on the whole journey where we were
misled by a negro's description. (*Seven Months*, 113–14)

South Carolina slaveholders worried about the complicity of their chat-
tels, but in most cases their efforts to prevent slaves from helping escaping
Yankees were fruitless. Emily Harris of the western South Carolina district of
Spartanburg was in charge of the family farm and ten slaves while her husband was serving in the Confederate army on James Island. In her husband's
absence she worried much about her ability to control their slaves; in December 1864 she wrote in the family journal: "I have learned through negroes
that three Yankee prisoners have been living for several days in our gin house
and been fed by our negroes. The neighbors are now watching for them with
their guns. . . . The search for Yankee prisoners on our premises ended without
success or information except the unmistakable evidence that some one or
more had been lodged and fed in and about our gin for some days. We tried to
get the negroes to tell something about it, but in vain. We could hear of their
telling each other all about it but they would tell us nothing" (Philip N. Racine,
ed., *The Journals of David Golightly Harris 1855–1870* [Knoxville, Tenn.,
1990], 353, 354).

9. Hunt was well aware of his condition: "This was one of my hardest nights,
and the following day was a blue one, as I began to fear lest I was the weak
one of the party and would have to fall out and give myself up so as not to
detain the others" ("Our Escape," 100).

10. It appears as if Laurens posed a similar challenge to many Yankee escapees:

It was two o'clock in the morning, and everything in silence and
slumber, when we crawled on hands and knees over the bridge and into
the edge of the town. Now, thought we, it will be just as perilous to go
round the town as to go directly through it; besides, if we go directly
through we can keep our road, which we may have much trouble to find
if we leave it. Off we started, one after the other, reaching out for dear
life, in the middle of a street covered with loose sand, making no more

noise than four cats. A lamp was burning at each street-corner and in many of the business-houses. These lights were vexatious, but the most embarrassing feature was the short legs of Lieutenant Goode, which were ill adapted to pedestrian matches, and unfortunately held the position of number two in the march. He was as willing as could be desired, and his steps as frequent, but his measures were vastly inadequate to the occasion. Number one rapidly extended his interval, and numbers three and four closed theirs, and were then unkind if not cruel enough to take advantage of their longer legs and transpose the vigorous Irishman to the rear.

But we got through the town of four thousand inhabitants without any serious difficulty. (Hadley, *Seven Months*, 134–35)

11. "As soon as we had got a safe distance we broke into a run, and for the next six miles we ran almost all the way, expecting every minute to hear dogs and men in pursuit. When we could get no further, we dropped down under a tree by the roadside to rest. To our delight we found that the tree was a persimmon and the ground was well covered with the ripe, delicious fruit. It was a great treat to us who had had nothing in the shape of fruit for months" (Hunt, "Our Escape," 101).

12. Nolen, Powell, and Gordon escaped together from Columbia on November 11 and made their way to Knoxville, where they arrived on December 1.

13. Unlike Mattocks, who failed to mention it, Hunt reported an interesting conversation with an African-American family that fed the escapees:

It was our custom to talk with these people about the war and its bearings upon their future condition (not entirely disinterested perhaps). It was a surprise to us to find how thoroughly they realized what the results were to be, and how well informed they were of the course of events. These people here seemed specially intelligent. They told us how their masters talked to them about the Yankees; told them they had horns, and that they would carry them off to a more horrible slavery than anything they had experienced. They said they pretended to believe all that was told them, "But Lor', Mars', we know better." (Hunt, "Our Escape," 102)

14. On this date Captain Burger wrote Mattocks's mother the following:

Your very kind letter, to me, of the 1st inst. enclosing several to your son Maj. Mattocks reached me by the last steamer. I will send the letters by the first Flag, as you request, as their is nothing 'contraband' in any of them. I am very sorry to be obliged to inform you that Maj. Genl. Foster has received by the last steamer, from the Secy. of War, through Maj. Genl. Halleck, instructions to send no more money or supplies to our prisoners of war, now held by the Confederate authorities, over our lines. In consequence of this I shall not be able to send Maj. Mattocks any more money. I sent him two hundred and ninety-five dollars in Confederate money on the 24th of last month which will probably keep him supplied for some little time; besides this, I sent, about the same time, the box received from you, and a much larger box containing eatables. I was preparing to send him another box when this order arrived from Washington. I am very glad to hear that efforts are being made to have the Major exchanged. I have moved every stone and have exerted myself to the extent of my powers to secure for him a parole, but, so far, to no purpose, still I have not given it up yet, and am now working as hard as ever. I will not give it up until I am satisfied that the thing is impossible. If Mr. Dyer is now using his influence to procure the Major's exchange probably the suggestion of a name would not be out of place in me to give. Maj. Lamar Fontaine, 4th Alabama Regt. captured at Ringold Ga., Nov. 27th, 1863, the Rebel authorities are very anxious to have this officer exchanged, and it may be of some service to Mr. Dyer who could suggest the exchange of this officer for Maj. Mattocks. Maj. Fontaine is not confined at this place. I request, as a personal favor, that my name may not be used as giving the name of Maj. Fontaine. Maj. Genl. J.G. Foster, the Commanding officer of this Department, on whose staff I have the honor to be serving, is perfectly powerless to exchange or parole any prisoners of war now held by him, otherwise I could have satisfied your wishes long ago and had the Major exchanged. I wish I could say what I thought of the whole matter, but my shoulder straps prevent me from expressing my thoughts. I am very glad indeed that you did not mention to your son, the fact of the endeavors now being made by Mr. Dyer, to effect his exchange, as, in case of failure, the disappointment would have been most severe. You say the Major has not intimated anything in regard to his exchange to you: on the contrary, in his letters to me, he has given me some of the very strongest kind of hints, it is impossible to construe them in any other way than intended. The prisoners were removed from Charleston to Columbia in consequence of the prevalence of yellow fever at the former city. We have just as frequent intercourse between them as before, but it takes longer for a letter to reach. Letters will be forwarded to our prisoners of war as heretofore. No restrictions having been put upon them.

In regard to the freight on the box you sent, I do not know anything about it, I have not been charged with it that I am aware of. In regard to the request sent to Mrs. Hunt to have $10 in gold secreted in a vest, I have to make the following explanation. Your son was promised a parole by the rebels, and came down with a flag of truce, expecting to come over the lines; but the rebels, making a request, that could not be complied with by Maj. Genl. Foster, took him back to Columbia. Expecting to come over the lines he received a small scrap of paper from Lt. Hunt, on finding that he could not be allowed to come over, he hurriedly [wrote] on this scrap of paper and secretly gave it to Lt. Col. Bennett, our flag of truce officer with a request for him to hand it to me, for me to forward to Mrs. Hunt which I did. I have written to Lt. Hunt offering to assist him in any way possible, but have as yet received no reply. Now that the late restrictions have been put on money and packages going over the lines at this point, I am afraid I shall have little opportunity of being of much service to him. I shall try however to effect either his exchange or parole as soon as I can, without interfering with the prospects of the Major. In writing you may cover one page of letter or Cap paper. Anything longer will not be delivered by the Rebel authorities. Although I have not heard of the reception of the boxes sent to Maj. Mattocks, I have no doubt whatever but that he will receive them all right.

You ask me to excuse the long letter to me, as you think it will be a draft upon my time. There is no need at all for this request. I myself have a dear mother living who takes as much interest in my welfare as you do in your son, consequently I can appreciate your earnestness and am only too happy to give you any information that lies in my power that you may wish.

I, myself, am a young man like your son (I presume he must be a young man although I have never had the pleasure of meeting him) and should certainly appreciate the endeavors of any one in my behalf, if I should ever be so unfortunate as to be situated in the same manner.

I congratulate the Major on his promotion to be Lt. Col. and hope soon to hear that he will have an opportunity of assuming the duties of his new office. I hope when he is exchanged that it may be at this point, as I am extremely anxious to take him by the hand & making his personal acquaintance.

15. Hunt remembered the incident in greater detail:

On this night, when we were at this distance from Greenville, it was still early, and the question came up whether we should make a camp or push on. Mattocks was in favor of stopping lest Hunt should give out before we had gone a safe distance beyond Greenville. There had been times when I had found it hard to keep pace with the rest, but on this night I was feeling remarkably well, the marching was easy, and I assured him he need have no fear of me. Litchfield was impatient and anxious to push on. Still Mattocks showed a great deal of solicitude in regard to my powers of endurance, and several times urged the necessity of stopping. But we would not listen to it. Evidently we were not marching so well as the night we went through Laurens, for it was four o'clock before we reached Greenville. We found it a very much larger place than Newberry or Laurens, but we planned to go straight through as we had the other places. Everything went well till we reached the outskirts on the westerly side, when we found a fire in the road before us which compelled us to take a cross street running to the north. We had hardly got outside the houses of the town when Mattocks said, "Boys, I don't feel very well," and down he dropped in a dead faint. We opened his shirt collar, and to our relief he soon revived, and we got him on his feet, but he had hardly taken a step before he went down again. We let him lie longer this time, and then carefully assisted him over the fence out of the road. It was getting dangerously near daylight by this time, and after resting as long as we dared, we started for some woods not far away. Mattocks put his arms over our shoulders and we half carried him. He was ready to admit now that his anxiety to stop the other side of Greenville was for his own sake rather than for Hunt's. ("Our Escape," 103)

16. "As we came out of the woods by a farm road we passed a small log cabin standing by itself, a long distance away from the other negro quarters, which was occupied by an old negro woman who lived there by herself. Quite late in the evening, when we had become quite discouraged and cold and hungry, we went back to this house to see what we could do with the old woman. We had hard work to make any impression upon her. She sniffed and snorted and said we had better go about our business, and that she hadn't anything for us. Litchfield with great earnestness argued the case with her, endeavoring to show why the negroes should feel gratitude to the Yankee soldiers, that through them freedom was surely coming, etc., etc. It came out, at last, that she thought we were rebel soldiers, but when she was finally convinced, she treated us handsomely, cooking a good hot supper for us" (Hunt, "Our Escape," 105).

17. "During the day Mattocks made from the meal bag three very serviceable haversacks which did us good service during all the rest of our prison life" (Hunt, "Our Escape," 106).

18. The rumors of strong support for the Union among the people of western North Carolina were widespread:

> We longed much for the loyal whites of North Carolina, of whom we had heard so much all along the way, and we were now very near their border. We felt that as soon as we placed South Carolina at our backs our work would be almost done—that we would be nearly home. The night that we expected to pass the border we walked with perhaps more spirit than on any other occasion. We pushed right on, through branches, over the foot-hills, up the side of the Saluda Mountains, until about midnight, when we came upon a pillar of hewn limestone, standing four feet out of the ground, upon the summit, on the south face of which was inscribed "S.C., 1849," and on the north face, "N.C., 1849."
>
> The nearer we approached North Carolina the more we had been assured of the loyalty of the people of the mountains, and that we would be safe when we got out of South Carolina. We merrily shook hands all around at the boundary stone, rested a few minutes, then skipped off down the mountainside into North Carolina with hearts as light as homeward-bound school-boys. (Hadley, *Seven Months*, 148–49)

19. After the war the man who owned this house, Mr. A. J. Loftis, wrote CPM asking about how his "Yankey friends" had fared after they left him. Loftis ended his letter by writing: "If you hav forgot me and my name remember the house you cam to in the nite and got the Bradey out of the Barrell in the ground" (A. J. Loftis to CPM, Mar. 16, 1866, Brevard, N.C., in private hands).

Lieutenant Hunt appreciated the special type of hospitality shown by Mr. Loftis:

> Instead of taking us in at the back door as we expected, he went on by the house a little distance, only saying, "Come this way, boys." Here was an old pair of cart wheels, such as may be seen in any farmer's back yard. Getting down on his knees under the axle he began to scrape away the dead leaves and grass. Then apparently he lifted up a short piece of board. Next came a short round piece of wood about three inches in diameter and one inch thick. Then, from the grass near one of the wheels, he drew out a long stick which looked like a reed pipe stem, and, apparently thrusting this into the bowels of the earth

said, "There, boys, suck away at that. It will do you good." As I have already said that old man made apple-jack; further explanation is unnecessary. We were certainly in prime condition for a good supper and a pleasant evening. . . . By the time we were well under way the apple-jack began to put in its perfect work. I remember how Litchfield waxed eloquent as he discussed the questions of the war and his excessive politeness to the ladies. His plate and his cup, in their frequent trips to our hostess for new supplies, were always accompanied by, "If you please, Mrs. Loftis." Mattocks as regularly made apology for his phenomenal appetite by saying, "Fact is, Mrs. Loftis, we've been living on raw corn for three days." Of what the other member of the party said and did there is no record. ("Our Escape," 112–13)

20. Both Chase and Fales were captured during a battle at Middleburg, Va., on June 17, 1863 (Fales, *Prison Life*, 5–9).

21. Apparently Mattocks did not include the name in case he was captured and his diary confiscated. Hunt, however, writing many years after the events, named the man: "We went up to the house at night, as before, and while there word came that all the Yankees in that neighborhood were to rendez-vous the next day at the house of a Mr. Hamilton, about ten miles from where we were, to make arrangements to go over the mountains. This Mr. Hamilton was deputy-sheriff of the county, but was a true Union man not-withstanding" ("Our Escape," 113).

22. Goodrich was a captain in the 8th New York Cavalry who also had es-caped from Camp Sorghum.

23. Gilbert Semple, a deserter from the Confederate army, was the guide (Hunt, "Our Escape," 115).

24. H. A. Johnson also described these Union sympathizers in his entry for De-cember 16:

This morning the Outliers began to come into our camp, having heard we were there. Now we have twenty men well armed, who will go through to our lines with us, or die in the attempt. The wives of these men came to see us today, and say they are willing their hus-bands and sons should go with us as they are certain to be caught and shot by the rangers before long, if they remain here. Went at night to the house of two Union women. It is a relief to talk with people who are loyal to the Union; for it has been all secesh for many months.

Dec. 17. The women came to our camp before daylight this morning to see their husbands. They are intelligent, these rough mountaineers, and true as steel. Can fire a rifle and bring down a deer as well as a man. At dark went with two Outliers to their homes up the mountains ten miles away; slept in a feather bed for the first time for three years, but with my clothing on all ready to jump and take to the woods if we are surprised by the rangers. (*Sword of Honor,* 37)

25. "After four days of this travelling, the guide said that, owing to the snow altering the appearance of his land-marks, he had lost his way, and got too far to the south. In trying to find our way, we got into a swamp, where the balsam trees, horse briars and high laurel made such a tangled mass that the clothing was nearly all torn off of us. . . . Just at night we came to a brook running through the swamp, and getting into it, waded down the stream. The water was icy cold, the rocks covered with ice, and we found frequent falls of ten or twelve feet, which made our travel very difficult. When it was too dark to go further, we were still in the swamp, and, leaving the water, we cleared away a little place on the bank for a camp. We were wet nearly all over with the ice-cold water; it rained all night, and we could not make any fire, although we tried to start one for two hours, but everything was too wet to burn. We had nothing left to wear, and had been at least twenty-four hours without food. It was a night of intense suffering; I thought I should freeze to death" (Fales, *Prison Life,* 60–61).

26. Lewis, who was an adjutant with the 11th Connecticut Volunteer Infantry, and Goodrich, who was in the 8th New York Cavalry, both had escaped from Columbia and made their way to Knoxville.

Hunt remembered the number who left the party differently:

The next morning we pulled in our belts a little tighter, and started again. About noon we got out of the thicket, and ascended a ridge, which gave us an outlook over the country. We also struck a well marked trail leading in the direction we wished to go. Far away down in the valley, some six or eight miles distant, we saw a solitary house. A halt was called for consultation. Many of the party were showing signs of weakness, and we had been obliged to make frequent stops to allow those in the rear to close up. The question was put in this way. We have here a good trail leading in the right direction. Shall we follow it? We have been already three days without food. The guide acknowledges that he is lost and has no idea how long we will have to travel before we can reach a settlement. With another day of this hard traveling, some of the party are going to give out and perish in the wilderness, and perhaps all will. On the other hand, if we go down to this house we see, the

chances are even that we will find it occupied by a Union man. And
even if he is a rebel, he could not capture such a party as this, each
one armed with a good hickory stick. It seemed wiser to the majority
to go for food, and all so decided except young Loftis and two
others, who said they would starve in the woods rather than take
one step backward. They went on and before night they found help,
and soon were safe in Knoxville. We turned back. ("Our Escape,"
118–19)

27. In a letter written after the war to CPM, A. J. Loftis, one of the Union men
who helped the escapees, explained:

> I was truley sorry to heare of your Suffring so from hungrey. My wife
> sais that She would be glad to hav this Brut that you speak of Joe
> Gunter to deal with a while upon a hungry Stumick[.] She thinks she
> could make him remember the Starved yankes that he carried of[f] to
> prison[.] I well [k]now whare you was captured[.] It is about 75 miles
> from my house[.] You had got two fare to the west and fell into
> Qualley Town among the Luftey Indians and thare was some of as
> mean Rebels thare as ever the Lord let liv upon this green Earth[.] You
> wanted to [k]now what had went with those guides[.] Sentel was
> hancuffed in the prison in Ashville [Asheville] and handed over to Som
> Skouts and after they had draged him over 2 or 3 counteys tha Shot
> his Brains out and left him l[y]ing in the Publick road with the Irons
> upon him. The other one Henrey knocked down the gard at the prison
> in Asheville and maid good his retret among a Shower of Shot and I
> dont [k]now whare he has gon to. The old darkey that gav you the
> tobaco has gon to House keping for hur self and is well. The Sheriff
> and famley is all well and sendes his best respects to you. The old
> Laidey that you Speak of Brining the chickens to you is well and hur
> name is Rebeca Havil. The girls is genereley well[.] A good meney of
> them married since the close of the war[.] The little grand child is well
> and tha[y] nemed it for Litchfiel[.] (A. J. Loftis to CPM, May 11,
> 1866, Brevard, N.C., in private hands)

28. Quallatown, presently known as Bryson City, is located forty-three miles
west and just south of Asheville on the Oconatufee River in extreme western North Carolina.

29. Hunt was having his own unfortunate adventure:

Up to this last day I had endured the hard marching over the mountains as well as the average of the company. Although not always able to keep up with the head of the column, I was, by no means, in the rear. But I had the misfortune to get seriously lamed the previous day in our march down the bed of the stream. The constant pounding, caused by jumping from rock to rock with wet boots, developed a large blood blister the full size of one of my heels. I did not feel it so very much all the time, but the following day I found it hard to keep up, as I was obliged to walk altogether on the toes of the disabled foot. When we decided to go down the valley to the house we saw in the distance, I told them not to wait for me, as I could not well miss the way, and I would take my own time.

They were soon out of sight, and I hobbled my way slowly and painfully down the valley alone. When I was still some distance from the house I was looking for, I heard one or two rifle shots ahead. Although entirely in the dark as to what they might signify, there was nothing for me to do but push on as well as I could. When at last I reached the little clearing, and the house I had seen, I found, to my disappointment that it was not a dwelling-house, but a little mill. . . . There was no sign of the rest of our party. I supposed they had pushed on still farther down the valley to find an inhabited house.

But I was pretty thoroughly played out by this time, and it was nearly night and I felt unable to go any farther. In looking over the building I found that the attic was filled with corn fodder. . . . I thought that if I could get in among that fodder I would have a comfortable bed for the night. . . . With considerable difficulty, I proceeded to bore my way into it, and had got my body in, when I was startled by a voice below saying, "Here, you Yank, come down out of that or I'll shoot." . . . My disappointment was bitter, but there was no help for it, and I was obliged to accept the situation with as much philosophy as I could muster. What to do with me was the next question. It was getting late and they could see for themselves that I was in no condition to march to Qualla. They said that if I would be "reasonable" they would take me to one of their houses, which was not far away, for the night, and would get a horse for me to ride the next day. ("Our Escape," 119–21)

30. Transylvania County, which includes Hendersonville, is in western North Carolina on the South Carolina border directly north of Greenville, S.C.
31. The name Parker appears to be incorrect. Perhaps Mattocks was referring

to Colonel John B. Palmer. Colonel William H. Thomas, a chief of the Cherokee nation who was as comfortable in the world of white entrepreneurship as he was among his own people, had raised several companies in the mountains of North Carolina in 1862 and had served in eastern Tennessee until 1863, when he and his mountaineers were ordered to western North Carolina to investigate the terrorist activities of "organized bands of armed men." Thomas's companies included two companies of Cherokee Indians (John G. Barrett, *The Civil War in North Carolina* [Chapel Hill, N.C., 1963], 196–97; and E. Stanly Godbold, Jr., and Mattie U. Russell, *Confederate Colonel and Cherokee Chief: The Life of William Holland Thomas* [Knoxville, Tenn., 1990]).

32. Webster is almost 40 miles west and south of Asheville and about 8.5 miles southeast of Quallatown.

33. Abbott was a bootmaker whose business was located on Congress Street in Portland.

34. Lieutenant Fales was somewhat piqued at the special treatment: "There were four members of the masonic fraternity among our number, who were furnished with a complete outfit of new clothing and all the food they needed, by their brethren in Asheville, who frequently took them out of the prison to dine with them at their homes. Not being one of the fortunate ones I received no such aid and comfort" (*Prison Life*, 65–66).

35. Confederate authorities had heard of the conditions at Columbia, and they had sent General Winder to investigate. When Governor Bonham wrote General Winder, the commander of all Confederate prisons, about "the escape of Yankee prisoners, and that they are thronging the country to the great annoyance of" South Carolina's citizens, Winder replied: "My own observation . . . satisfied me that as much vigilance and care has been used as the circumstances and facilities for guard would permit. There has been no place heretofore to confine them, no stockade, no entrenchments, not even a fence around them. . . . It must be manifest to all that it is vain to guard a large, or even small, body of reserves in an open plain. . . . again assuring you that at the earliest moment the prisoners will be removed entirely from this vicinity" (*OR*, ser. 2, vol. 7: 1184).

Three days later in his report to Adjutant General Cooper in Richmond, General Winder remarked that he had found the prison "entirely unfit for the purpose, nothing but an open field, guarded by raw troops (reserves); the consequence is that 373 have escaped." Winder asked for permission to buy land fourteen miles closer to Charlotte on which to build a new prison (*OR*, ser. 2, vol. 7: 1196–97).

There seems to be nothing in the *Official Records* indicating that five hundred federal prisoners at Columbia had been exchanged.

36. On December 7, before Captain Burger learned of CPM's escape, he wrote Isaac Dyer the following: "I have not heard from the Maj. in some time and feel a little anxious as I have not received a letter from him since I sent him two hundred & ninety five dollars ($295) in Confed. money. I am fearful he may not have received it, yet think it barely possible, as I was promised faithfully that it should be delivered" (W. L. M. Burger to Isaac Dyer, Dec. 7, 1864, Hilton Head, S.C.).

37. On December 21, 1864, George G. Kimball, in the quartermaster general's office, wrote Mattocks's stepfather, Isaac Dyer:

> I received a letter from Charlie . . . with power of Attorney enclosed to draw two months pay for him, with instructions for the disposal of it. I have done as he requested, but owing to his not describing in the Atty, his servants, I could not draw pay and allowances for them, only his pay proper as Major, being ($90) ninety dollars less than he supposed himself entitled to. He can however draw it himself when discharged. I should say exchanged, or by sending me the proper description in his next letter. I have written to him and stated the case, so that he can attend to it in his next letter. I am in hopes, however, he may be speedily exchanged. Two hundred officers came up yesterday morning just from Columbia! I shall hunt some of them up tonight to learn something of Charlie. I am longing to see him. I have just received an envelope from yourself which I find contains a hundred dollars for which I enclose my receipt. Also copy of his letter to yourself.
>
> Having known him for the past seven years, four of which as classmates we passed in closest intimacy at college and loving him as a brother, I need not assure you that all that lies in my power to be done for him shall be done. He speaks of our getting an order from the Secy. of war for his exchange. I think if it can be procured I can get it, as Mr. Gooch, Rep. from Mass., a connection of my family is on the War Committee, author of report on conduct of the war, and he has great influence at the War Dept. I will see him this evening and see what he can do, and if you come to Washington [I] should be happy to cooperate with you to procure the same end.

38. Far from Mattocks's mind at the moment was the politics that seemed to

dominate command of the 17th Maine and that had for a long time so interested Charles. The events that would once again so interest him were continuing however: "The regiment at that date [Dec. 31, 1864] numbered about three hundred men for duty and was commanded by Maj. William Hobson. Lieut. Col. C. P. Mattocks was still held by the enemy as prisoner of war. Col. West received the appointment, by brevet, of Brigadier General Volunteers, 'for gallant conduct in the battle of the Wilderness.' He was at that time absent on account of his wound" (Whitman, *Maine in the War For The Union*, 457).

39. Sherman's troops entered Savannah on December 21, 1864. On December 22 General Sherman had wired President Lincoln: "I beg to present you as a Christmas gift the city of Savannah, with one hundred and fifty heavy guns and plenty of ammunition, also about twenty-five thousand bales of cotton" (*Memoirs*, 711).

President Lincoln had mirrored the feelings of the Union armies when he had responded: "Many, Many thanks for your Christmas gift, the capture of Savannah. . . . And taking the work of General Thomas into the count, as it should be taken, it is indeed a great success. Not only does it afford the obvious and immediate military advantages, but, in showing to the world that your army could be divided, putting the stronger part to an important new service, and yet leaving enough to vanquish the old opposing force of the whole—Hood's army—it brings those who sat in darkness to see a great light" (*OR*, ser. 1, vol. 44: 809).

40. "I had often seen men suffering for want of food, but here, for the first time, I saw a strong man cry with hunger. He was an infantry captain, six feet high and of powerful form; he had been a prisoner only about four weeks, and had not, like his fellow-sufferers, become hardened by calamity. It was about three o'clock in the afternoon, he had eaten all the food given him for twenty-four hours and could expect nothing more until the next morning, and sitting down on the floor, he cried like a baby. No one taunted the sufferer" (Fales, *Prison Life*, 67).

41. Mattocks had been busy trying to make arrangements to better the condition of his mess, just as he had done while imprisoned at Columbia. He had written Mrs. L. R. Jones of Harrisonburg, Va., on January 21, and he received this reply: "My husband being so fortunate as to have a great many friends in the North has been and is still supplied with Every thing necessary for his comfort. . . . I wish very much I could alleviate your situation, but I expect to start upon a long and expensive journey in a few days and will need all the money I can command." She gave CPM the address of another Confederate

general's wife who she thought might be willing to strike an arrangement (Mrs. L. R. Jones to CPM, Jan. 28, 1865, Harrisonburg, Va.).

42. General Hayes, a native of the state of Maine, had been imprisoned in Libby Prison. According to General Orders No. 299, dated December 7, 1864: "Brig. Gen. Joseph Hayes, U.S. Volunteers, and Col Stephen M. Weld, jr., Fifty-sixth Massachusetts Volunteers, prisoners of war, are selected by the Government of the United States as the officers to be placed on parole, agreeable to the arrangement entered into by Lieutenant-General Grant and Commissioner Ould to receive and distribute to the U. S. prisoners of war such articles of clothing and other necessaries herein mentioned as may be issued by the Government or contributed from other sources" (*OR*, ser. 2, vol. 7: 1198).

43. Mulford was U.S. assistant agent for exchange. He worked for General Butler.

44. On February 17 Captain Burger once again wrote Mattocks's mother from Hilton Head:

> I have the honor to acknowledge the receipt of your letter of Jan. 23rd, for Adams Express, enclosing one hundred dollars. From the amount I have paid Dunbars and Franz thirty-nine dollars and seventy-cents ($39.70) the cost of one box only, they positively refused to be paid for the other box sent to Maj. Mattocks. I received some time since from a friend of the Majors fifty dollars, which about covers my expenses. I have therefore, now in my possession sixty dollars and thirty cents ($60.30) which, with your permission, I shall retain for a short time for the following reasons, viz:
>
> We have been ordered by the war department to exchange all prisoners of war now in our hands, and I shall endeavor to have the Major exchanged with the rest, provided they will consent to send him here from Danville: If the Major is exchanged here, he will want a little money and I shall therefore retain what I now have, unless you wish otherwise, for him when he gets home.
>
> I desire that you will have the goodness to send me by return mail the place and state of the capture of the Major, also Lieut. Hunt, or any other officer you may feel interested in, and I will do all in my power to have them exchanged.
>
> The exchange will take place in about a month, and the Major's can be effected, provided we can get him here from Danville.
>
> The Rebels may object to exchange an officer who is so far away from this point.

45. Mattocks was paroled at Aikens Landing on the James River, Va., on February 21, 1865, and reported to Union authorities on February 22, 1865; he was "granted leave of absence on 26 February 1865 for 30 ds to report to Regt." Of course, Mattocks could not serve until officially exchanged (Service Record, National Archives).

46. West had been wounded in the Battle of the Wilderness and been discharged from the service, but was restored by the War Department. He was appointed brevet brigadier general. He would resign from the service on April 17, 1865.

47. Mattocks was promoted from major to lieutenant colonel on October 20, 1864. He was not "mustered on account of being a prisoner in the hands of the enemy. Commission revoked." Hobson was promoted from captain to major on October 20, 1864, but was "not mustered, as no vacancy occurred." He was then promoted to lieutenant colonel on January 13, 1865 (Houghton, *Campaigns*, 293–94).

48. Augusta is the capital of Maine, and Mattocks is referring to the governor.

CHAPTER EIGHT.
REJOINING THE REGIMENT: PETERSBURG

1. Mattocks was exchanged on March 22, 1865. On March 17, 1865, Charles wrote to E. D. Townsend, A.A.G., requesting an extension of his leave. He explained that when he escaped from Columbia: "I succeeded in reaching a point only a mile and a half distant from the Tennesee [*sic*] and N. Carolina line, when I had the misfortune to be recaptured by a party of Indians and Bushwackers, after having been lost for five days, the last three entirely without food among the laurel thickets of the Smoky Mountains. . . . Although my health does not warrant an extended or sick leave I am convinced that my condition would be benefitted by more rest after so long an imprisonment." The extension was not approved (Office Commissary General of Prisoners. Miscellaneous Prisoner Records of Federal Prisoners of War. RG 249 Entry 31. National Archives). Mattocks's Combined Service Record file erroneously records him as having "Reported to Regt direct from home Apr 10/65."

General Grant had been laying siege to Petersburg since June 18,1864. During that time Union forces had extended their lines southward and had attempted several times to turn Lee's right flank or to breach Southern defenses by frontal attacks. All had failed. However, by April 1865, Lee's condition was critical, as he had been forced to weaken his defenses to reinforce General Pickett, who protected the vital railroad located on the Confederates' right flank that supplied Lee's army. On April 1 Pickett was badly mauled by General Sheridan at the Battle of Five Forks. Learning from deserters that Lee had removed troops all along his Petersburg defenses in order to reinforce Pickett, General Grant ordered an attack at dawn on April 2. Early that morning General Lee informed President Davis that Petersburg and Richmond would have to be evacuated.

2. Haley was not as happy to see Charles: "At night Major Mattox, who was captured in the Wilderness, returned to us. If anybody went into raptures over his return, I didn't see them. Too much bandbox and red tape never enthused me worth a cent." In an earlier entry in his diary (July 23) Haley revealed at least part of the reason he disliked Mattocks: "Our camp is quiet enough to suit anybody. To break the monotony an inspection is held occasionally, but as long as Colonel Merrill has command, we have not fear of needless drill exercise. Colonel Merrill has great sympathy for the men; in fact, he is as tender-hearted as a woman. This would not be the case if Major West, or Mattox, were in command" (Haley, *Rebel Yell*, 183, 256).

   Edwin Houghton had a more lighthearted response: "Major Mattocks, who had been a prisoner in the hands of the enemy since the battle of the Wilderness, rejoined the regiment, and reported for duty at this place, 'just in time for Lannigan's Ball.'" (*Campaigns*, 264).

3. Hobson was promoted from major on January 13, 1865.

4. Humphreys was a topographical and civil engineer who had written an important book on the physics of the Mississippi River which would form the basis for future flood control; he had served on the staffs of both Generals McClellan and Meade and had commanded a division at Antietam and Chancellorsville and a corps at Gettysburg. He assumed command of the 11th Corps in November 1864.

5. General Birney died of malaria in October 1864. General Hays was killed in action during the Battle of the Wilderness in May 1864. As to General Ward: "Up until the battle of the Wilderness in May, 1864, Ward had been almost universally eulogized by his superiors for bravery and ability. Thus, it was a distinct shock to many of his associates when he was relieved from command on May 12, 1864, 'for misbehavior and intoxication in the presence of the enemy during the Battle of the Wilderness'" (Ezra J. Warner, *Generals in Blue: Lives of the Union Commanders* [Baton Rouge, La., 1964], 538).

   Charles A. Dana, assistant secretary of war, in his report to Secretary Stanton, was more direct: "General Hobart Ward is under arrest for running away in the Wilderness battle" (*OR*, ser. 1, vol. 36, pt. 1: 65 [also quoted in Warner]).

   Ward was never tried on charges but instead was honorably mustered out of service. Warner reports that several prominent people wanted Ward tried so that his guilt or innocence could be ascertained, but Secretary Stanton was adamant about the dismissal.

6. At age thirty-three Philip Sheridan had already conducted one of the great cavalry raids of the war when he devastated the Confederate army in the Shenandoah Valley between August of 1864 and March of 1865; he then returned to Petersburg and, at Five Forks, defeated the Confederates defending the southern end of the only rail line supplying Lee's army. He would go on to block Lee's attempt to escape from Appomattox Courthouse.

7. The 5th Corps had played a major role in the Battle of Five Forks, yet in his splendid *The Passing of the Armies,* a history of the 5th Corps during its final campaign, Joshua Chamberlain explains that too much credit for the events of the following few days have been given Sheridan and the 5th Corps. Chamberlain seeks to set the record straight by giving due credit instead to General Humphreys, the commander of the 2nd Corps, and especially to General Miles of the 1st Division of that Corps. Since Chamberlain was an astute observer and student, it is only proper that due consideration should be given to his critique of General Grant's version of these events given in his *Memoirs* in which, according to Chamberlain, Grant credits Sheridan for too much.

8. The first Union soldiers to enter the capital were African-American cavalrymen and infantry. General Godfrey Weitzel accepted the formal surrender of the city at 8:15 A.M. on April 3. [Virginius Dabney, *Richmond: The Story of a City* (New York, 1976), 192–93; Alfred Hoyt Bill, *The Beleaguered City: Richmond, 1861–1865* (New York, 1946), 276.]

9. "The roads are very bad. Colonel Hobson's horse stepped into a hole and broke his leg, and had to be shot. It was concluded that some road must be corduroyed if we are to make much progress. Large bodies were detailed for this purpose. We cut and laid timber nearly all day, getting over many bad places" (Haley, *Rebel Yell,* 260–61).

10. "Major Mattocks, with the colors, and as many of the regiment as could keep up, charged with a yell, rushed over the breastworks, and captured about one hundred men, ten or twelve officers, and one battle flag, . . . besides killing and wounding a large number of the enemy" (Houghton, *Campaigns,* 267).

It was for this action that Charles Mattocks was awarded the Congressional Medal of Honor on March 29, 1899. The citation read: "Displayed extraordinary gallantry in leading a charge of his regiment which resulted in the capture of a large number of prisoners and a stand of colors" ([John F. Kane], *The Medal of Honor of the United States Army* [Washington, 1948], 200).

11. Usher was from Saco, Maine. Haley made special mention of Usher: "Lieu-

tenant Usher, to whom I am much indebted for favors and for my only promotion, was mortally wounded" (Haley, *Rebel Yell*, 25–26).

12. Webb, originally from Westbrook, Maine, was wounded in the leg, which
    was amputated. He mustered out with the regiment in June 1865.

13. Dunn, from Poland, Maine, was captain of Company K. Duncan was from
    Kittery, Maine, and was promoted to first lieutenant for gallant and meri-
    torious service during this battle.

14. Mathes was from Durham, New Hampshire. Lieutenant Sturgis was from
    Standish, Maine, and was a member of Company B. Fayette M. Paine had
    been promoted from sergeant in Company A to second lieutenant in Com-
    pany B in October of 1864.

15. Captain William H. Green had first been promoted from lieutenant in
    Company E and then transferred to Company G, where he was serving at
    this time. He would later be appointed brevet major for his "gallant and
    meritorious conduct" at Amelia Springs.

    Lieutenant Colonel William Hobson had been promoted from major
    in January of 1865 and, at Amelia Springs, "was wounded by a musket-
    ball in the leg" (Houghton, *Campaigns*, 268).

    Haley commented that Hobson "was wounded in the thigh and sus-
    tained a heavy loss of blood" (Haley, *Rebel Yell*, 260).

16. General Longstreet had made himself famous as commander of the 1st Corps
    of the Army of Northern Virginia under Robert E. Lee; in May 1864 he was
    wounded by his own men and did not return to duty until October, when he
    was placed in charge of troops at Bermuda Hundred and north of the James.

17. Mattocks was awarded the Congressional Medal of Honor in 1899 for his
    actions in this battle. Justice Charles C. Cole of the Supreme Court, who
    had been Captain of Company I in the 17th Maine, submitted this affidavit
    as to Mattocks's actions on the 6th:

    > The part of the line in which our regiment [was located] was met
    > with stubborn resistance on several occasions. On one occasion our
    > advance was checked for some time, and our Regiment was in an
    > exposed position, compounded by a strong line of the enemy
    > entrenched in rifle pits and supported by artillery, and we were losing
    > a man in killed or wounded every few minutes. Major Mattocks, then
    > in command, placed himself in front of the Regiment opposite the
    > colors and said to the color bearers that he would order and lead a
    > charge and carry one of the colors himself. They objected to his taking
    > either of the colors and said they would go as far as he would. He then
    > ordered the Regiment to follow him on a charge and led it in advance

of the colors all the way to the enemy's line, capturing 200 armed men, a number quite equal to our own and two pieces of artillery. We lost but few, if any, men in the charge; if any, fewer by far than we would to have remained in our exposed position many minutes longer. . . . He was warmly commended and congratulated on the field by Gen. Pierce, commanding the brigade. (Adjutant General's Office. Office of the Adjutant General Volunteer Branch, 1865 [M546–639]. National Archives)

In a deposition given May 4, 1899, Manual Thomas, who had been a private in Company H of the 17th at Little Sayler's Creek, reported on Mattocks's conduct during that battle at the end of which he stated: "At the National Encampment of the Gr[and]. A[rmy]. [of the] R[epublic]. held in Portland, Maine in about 1884 said [Lt. Col. William] Hobson said to me that he was properly in command of said regiment but that said Mattocks took the command away from him, but that if he himself had not been wounded he would have had said Mattocks court-martialed" (letter in private hands).

18. Actually the surrender took place in the home of Wilmer McLean in the hamlet of Appomattox Courthouse.
19. Although Union plans had originally called for the joining of Grant's and Sherman's armies, that was hardly necessary now. At this time General Johnston was preparing to surrender to General Sherman, which he officially did on April 17. General Sherman's terms were more generous than were General Grant's, and President Johnson refused them, insisting that Johnston surrender according to the same terms as had been accepted by General Lee. Johnston did so.
20. Indeed, Crie, who had been a first lieutenant in Company C, was promoted to captain of Company H in May of 1865.
21. President Abraham Lincoln was shot in the head by John Wilkes Booth shortly after 10:00 P.M. on April 14; he died without regaining consciousness at 7:22 A.M., April 15. William Henry Seward, secretary of state in the Lincoln administration, was severely wounded by an accomplice of Booth's, but he survived. Seward's son was not hurt.
22. Haley told an amusing story that illustrates the feelings of the soldiers: "One individual who expressed satisfaction at the murder was hurried down to a nearby frog pond and treated to a little hydropathic practice—to so much of it, in fact, that he was taken from the water more dead than alive, coated with green slime and frog spawn. In this miserable plight he presented himself to his colonel to complain about the assault. When the colonel heard the

facts of the matter he replied, 'they served you right, only it is a d——d shame they didn't drown you!'" (Haley, *Rebel Yell,* 269).

23. Howard was from Leeds, Maine, and was a first lieutenant in Company E. He did succeed in transferring to the United States Colored Troops.

24. Crawford was from Gardiner, Maine, and a first lieutenant in Comapny F; he did not get a commission in the United States Colored Troops.

25. Cole was from Hiram, Maine, and had been promoted captain of Company I in January of 1865.

26. All four men recommended for brevets by Mattocks received them.

27. The appointments were made.

28. The only Keef [the named is spelled without the last e on the company roll] in the 17th Maine was George Keef of Company G.

29. Mattocks is referring to what would come to be known as the Battle of Sayler's Creek.

30. In his diary entry of April 23, Haley recorded the following: "Sunday. Major Mattox was seized with an overwhelming curiosity to know what was in our knapsacks and ordered an inspection. If this is the way he's going to carry on, I am not obliged to the Johnnies for releasing him. Dress parade at five ended the day" (*Rebel Yell,* 270).

31. Actually, Mattocks's service record shows him having been promoted to colonel on May 5, 1865 (Service Record, National Archives).

32. Since his last journal entry Charles had received the following telegram:

U.S. Military Telegraph
Alexandria, Va. May 22, 1865
By Telegraph from Portland. May 21, 1865.
To Col. Mattocks:—
    All the recruits assigned to 17th Maine Vols. are mustered out.
    sd/H. Rollins (Company Order Books, 17th Maine Volunteer Infantry,
                                                        National Archives)

33. Holyoke was from Yarmouth, Maine. He was promoted to sergeant-major on May 24, 1865, but was not mustered.

EPILOGUE

1. Chamberlain, *Passing of the Armies,* 327–59.
2. Chamberlain, "In Memoriam."

Works Cited

MANUSCRIPTS

Bowdoin College. Miscellaneous Records of Executive Government. 1849–1868. Special Collections. Bowdoin College Library.

Mattocks, Charles Porter. Charles P. Mattocks Papers 1840–1910. Special Collections. Bowdoin College Library.

Mattocks, Charles Porter. "In Six Prisons." Charles P. Mattocks Papers. Special Collections. Bowdoin College Library.

Peucinian Society Records, 1842–58. volume 5. Special Collections. Bowdoin College Library.

GOVERNMENT DOCUMENTS
Published

[Kane, John F.]. *The Medal of Honor of the United States Army*. Washington, D.C.: Government Printing Office, 1948.

Report on the Treatment of prisoners of War, by the Rebel Authorities During the War of the Rebellion . . . In 40th Congress 3d Session Report No. 45. Washington: Gov. Printing Office, 1869.

U.S. War Department. *The War of the Rebellion: A Compilation of the Official Records of the Union and Confederate Armies. . . .* 128 vols. Washington, D.C.: Government Printing Office, 1880–1900.

Unpublished

National Archives. Complete Military Record. Records of Adjutant General's Office. Washington, D.C.

———. Medal of Honor File. Records of Adjutant General's Office. Washington, D.C.

———. Miscellaneous Prisoner Records of Federal Prisoners of War. Office of the Commissary General of Prisoners (RG 249 Entry 31). Washington, D.C.

———. Record Group 94, Entry 13. Order Books of Volunteer Organizations. Civil War. Records of the Adjutant General's Office. Washington, D.C.

———. Record Group 109, No. 29. List of Federal Prisoners of War Received at Confederate Prisons. Records of the Office of the Commissary General of Prisoners. Washington, D.C.

———. Record Group 109. No. 31. Register of Federal Prisoners of War Who Escaped From Confederate Authorities. Records of the Office of the Commissary General of Prisoners.

———. Record Group 109. No. 31. Sutler's Records, Nov. 1, 1864–Feb. 16, 1865. Records of the Office of the Commissary General of Prisoners. Washington, D.C.

———. Record Group 109. No. 32. Rolls and Reports of Federal Prisoners of War Who Escaped From Confederate Prisons ("Escape Rolls"). Records of the Office of the Commissary General of Prisoners. Washington, D.C.

———. Reports from Officers & Seamen of the U.S. Navy who Were Prisoners of War in the South . . . . Nov. 1862 to July 1865, Navy Department.

———. "Volunteer Organizations, Civil War." Regimental Papers. Maine. 17th Infantry. Co. A (Box no. 1557). Office of the Adjutant General. Washington, D.C.

NEWSPAPERS

New York Herald, May 11, 1863.

Portland, Maine, *Evening Courier,* June 19, 1864.

BOOKS AND ARTICLES

Bill, Alfred Hoyt. *The Beleaguered City: Richmond, 1861–1865.* New York: Alfred A. Knopf, 1946.

Blakey, Arch Fredric. *General John H. Winder C.S.A.* Gainesville, Fla.: Univ. Presses of Florida, 1990.

Boatner, Mark M., III. *The Civil War Dictionary.* New York: David McKay Co., 1959.

Byrne, Frank L. *Prophet of Prohibition: Neal Dow and His Crusade.* 1961; Gloucester, Mass.: Peter Smith, 1969.

Callahan, Edward. *List of Officers of the Navy of the United States . . . .* New York: Haskell House, 1969.

Chamberlain, Joshua Lawrence. *The Passing of the Armies.* 1905. Rpt. Dayton, Ohio: Morningside Bookshop, 1989.

Clark, Charles E. *Maine: A Bicentennial History.* New York: W. W. Norton, 1977.

Cooper, A. *In and Out of Rebel Prisons.* Oswego, N.Y.: B. J. Oliphant, 1888.

Dabney, Virginius. *Richmond: The Story of a City.* New York: Doubleday, 1976.

Dantzler, D. D. *A Genealogical Record of the Dantzler Family From 1739 to the Present Time.* Orangeburg, S.C.: R. Lewis Berry, 1899.

Eldredge, D. *The Third New Hampshire and All About It.* Boston: E. B. Stillings, 1893.

Escott, Paul D. *After Secession: Jefferson Davis and the Failure of Confederate Nationalism.* Baton Rouge: Louisiana State Univ. Press, 1978.

———. *Many Excellent People: Power and Privilege in North Carolina, 1850–1900.* The Fred W. Morrison Series in Southern Studies. Chapel Hill: Univ. of North Carolina Press, 1985.

Fales, James M. *Prison Life of Lieut. James M. Fales.* Ed. by George N. Bliss. Providence, R.I.: N. Bangs Williams, 1882.

Fontaine, Lamar. *The Prison Life of Major Lamar Fontaine . . . .* Clarksdale, Miss.: Daily Register Print, 1910.

Foote, Morris C. "Narrative of an Escape from a Rebel Prison Camp." *American Heritage* 11 (June 1960): 63–75.

Fraser, Col. John. *A Petition Regarding the Conditions in the C.S.M. Prison at Columbia, S.C. Addressed to the Confederate Authorities.* Ed. George L. Anderson. Univ. of Kansas Publications, Library Series 14. Lawrence: Univ. of Kansas Libraries, 1962.

Godbold, E. Stanly, and Mattie U. Russell. *Confederate Colonel and Cherokee Chief: The Life of William Holland Thomas.* Knoxville: Univ. of Tennessee Press, 1990.

Goss, Warren Lee. *The Soldier's Story of His Captivity at Andersonville, Belle Isle, and Other Rebel Prisons.* Boston: Lee and Shepard, 1868.

Hadley, J. V. *Seven Months a Prisoner.* New York: Charles Scribner's Sons, 1898.

[Haley, John West]. *The Rebel Yell & the Yankee Hurrah: The Civil War Journal of a Maine Volunteer.* Ed. Ruth L. Silliker. Camden, Maine: Down East Books, 1985.

Harwell, Richard B., ed. *The War They Fought.* New York: Longmans, Green and Co., 1960.

Hatch, Louis C. *The History of Bowdoin College.* Portland, Maine: Loring, Short & Harmon, 1927.

Hesseltine, William Best. *Civil War Prisons: A Study in War Psychology.* Columbus: Ohio State Univ. Press, 1930.

[Hodsdon, John L.]. "Bowdoin in the War." n.p., 1867.

Houghton, Edwin B. *The Campaigns of the Seventeenth Maine.* 1866. Rpt. Gaithersburg, Md.: Butternut Press, 1987.

Humphreys, Charles A. *Field, Camp, Hospital and Prison in the Civil War, 1863–1865.* Boston: Geo. H. Ellis, 1918.

Hunt, Charles O. "Our Escape from Camp Sorghum." *War Papers Read Before the Commandery of the State of Maine . . . ,* 85–128. Portland, Maine: Thurston Print, 1898.

Inscoe, John C. *Mountain Masters, Slavery, and the Sectional Crisis in Western North Carolina.* Knoxville: Univ. of Tennessee Press, 1989.

Johnson, H. A. *The Sword of Honor: A Story of the Civil War.* Hallowell, Maine: Register Printing House, 1906.

Langworthy, Daniel Avery. *Reminiscences of A Prisoner of War and His Escape.* Minneapolis: Byron Printing Co., 1915.

Lincoln, Abraham. *The Collected Works of Abraham Lincoln.* Ed. Roy P. Basler. New Brunswick, N.J.: Rutgers Univ. Press, 1953.

Massie, Robert K. *Peter The Great: His Life and World.* New York: Alfred A. Knopf, 1981.

Mattocks, Charles P. "In Six Prisons." Selden Connor et al., *War Papers Read Before the Commandery of the State of Maine, Military Order of the Loyal Legion of the United States.* Portland, Maine, 1898.

Mitchell, Wilmot Brookings. "A Remarkable Bowdoin Decade 1820–1830." Brunswick, Maine: Bowdoin College, 1952.

Morse, Charles F. *Letters Written During the Civil War 1861–1865.* Boston: privately printed [T. R. Marvin], 1898.

The National Cyclopaedia of American Biography. New York: James T. White, 1896.

Paludan, Phillip Shaw. *Victims: A True Story of the Civil War.* Knoxville: Univ. of Tennessee Press, 1981.

Petty, A. Milburn. "History of the 37th Regiment, New York Volunteers." *The Journal of the American Irish Historical Society* 31 (1937): 101–37.

Pullen, John J. *The Twentieth Maine.* 1957; Dayton, Ohio: Morningside Bookshop, 1984.

Ross, Fitzgerald. *Cities and Camps of the Confederate States.* Ed. Richard Barksdale Harwell. Urbana: Univ. of Illinois Press, 1958.

Shelton, W. H. "A Hard Road to Travel Out of Dixie." *Famous Adventures and Escapes of the Civil War*, 243–97. New York: The Century Co., 1917.

Sherman, George R. *Assault on Fort Gilmer and Reminiscences of Prison Life.* Personal Narratives of Events in the War of the Rebellion . . . . Providence: Rhode Island Soldiers and Sailors Historical Society, 1897.

Sherman, William Tecumseh. *Memoirs of General W. T. Sherman.* Ed. Charles Royster. The Library of America. New York: Literary Classics of the United States, 1990.

Smith, Robert G. *Papers of the Historcal Society of Delaware.* Vol 53. *A Brief Account of the Services Rendered by the Second Delaware Volunteers in the War of the Rebellion.* Wilmington: Historical Society of Delaware, 1909.

Stevens, C. A. *Berdan's United States Sharpshooters in the Army of the Potomac 1861–1865.* St. Paul, Minnesota: Price-McGill, 1892.

Stone, J. H. "Lamar Fontaine's Civil War Tales." *Tennessee Folklore Society Bulletin* 39, no. 4 (1973): 107–10.

Trulock, Alice Rains. *In the Hands of Providence: Joshua L. Chamberlain and the American Civil War.* Chapel Hill: Univ. of North Carolina Press, 1992.

Turner, George H. *Record of Service of Michigan Volunteers in the Civil War 1861–1865.* Kalamazoo, Mich.: Michigan Legislature.

Volz, Robert L. *Governor Bowdoin & His Family: A Guide to an Exhibition and a Catalogue.* Brunswick, Maine: Bowdoin College, 1969.

Warner, Ezra J. *Generals in Blue: Lives of the Union Commanders.* Baton Rouge: Louisiana State Univ. Press, 1964.

White, Henry S. *Prison Life Among the Rebels.* Ed. Edward D. Jervey. Kent, Ohio: Kent State Univ. Press, 1990.

Wilkinson, Warren. *Mother, May You Never See the Sights I Have Seen: The Fifty-Seventh Massachusetts Veteran Volunteers in the Army of the Potomac 1864–1865.* New York: Harper & Row, 1990.

Index